RITA WILL

RITA WILL

*Memoir of a
Literary
Rabble-Rouser*

*Rita Mae
Brown*

BANTAM BOOKS
New York Toronto London Sydney Auckland

RITA WILL
A Bantam Book / November 1997

All rights reserved.
Copyright © 1997 by American Artists, Inc.

BOOK DESIGN BY LAURIE JEWELL

Library of Congress Cataloging-in-Publication Data

Brown, Rita Mae.
    Rita will : memoir of a literary rabble-rouser / Rita Mae Brown.
        p.   cm.
    ISBN 0-553-09973-6
    1. Brown. Rita Mae—Biography.   2. Southern States—Social life and customs—20th cen-
tury.   3. Women novelists, American—20th century—Biography.   4. Lesbians—United
States—Biography.   I. Title.
PS3552.R698Z468 1997
813'.54—dc21
[b]   97-30829
                                                                                                CIP

Published simultaneously in the United States and Canada

Bantam Books are published by Bantam Books, a division of Bantam Doubleday Dell Publishing Group, Inc. Its trademark, consisting of the words "Bantam Books" and the portrayal of a rooster, is Registered in U.S. Patent and Trademark Office and in other countries. Marca Registrada, Bantam Books, 1540 Broadway, New York, New York 10036.

Printed in the United States of America
BVG   10 9 8 7 6 5 4 3 2 1

M*ust be a recess in heaven,*

St. Peter's letting the angels out.

To my literary angel this book is dedicated:

WENDY WEIL

To the Reader;

Enjoy your body.

After all, others have.

Introduction

THE HUMAN ANIMAL MEASURES TIME. OTHER ANIMALS SEEM FAR LESS concerned about it, but then again they are far less vain.

The smarter humans and animals do learn from time. The dumb ones check out early or are untimely ripped, as Shakespeare once wrote. Then, too, if enough time passes you see the good brought down, the evil raised up, the superficial hailed as profound and the profound ignored completely. It's absurd. I expect human society has always been this way; it's just that each generation must discover it with a bump and a thump.

This autobiography is about my time. I couldn't cram my entire life into here even if I had twenty-two volumes. Neither could you. In one year's time you and I meet more people than our grandparents met in a lifetime. The speed of our lives is astonishing but the time of our lives is invariable.

We have no more time than our grandparents or great-great-grandparents did. Medicine may be able to tack a few years onto the end of our lives but generally the quality suffers. The human animal begins to unwind in its eighties. For some this happens earlier. No matter how bright we are, no matter how truthful or good, we can't alter that internal clock, that original timepiece, the heart. Sooner or later, it stops.

At this precise moment I am in the time of my life. This is the best time I've ever had and I know it can't last but so long. If I'm extremely lucky and those strong genes I inherited stand me in good stead, I might even nudge up to and beyond a hundred. But will it be the best time? Won't know until I get there.

My publisher, Bantam Books, and my editor, Beverly Lewis, laughingly told me to write my autobiography before I forget everything. Well, I'm not that old but I'm not that young. I took their point.

Time again. I am celebrating my twentieth year with Bantam. Twenty years of highs and lows. I learned about publishing by doing. The writing was a gift. I had to discipline it but I can't take too much credit otherwise. But learning about publishing was and remains an adventure. It's a window on the world just as someone working for an automobile manufacturer will view the world from that special hilltop.

Time binds me to people and to institutions. You hold my book in your hands. I see the hands it passed through to reach yours: my editor, the publisher himself, the promotion and publicity departments, the art department, those phenomenal Bantam sales representatives and the equally blue-chip telecommunication sales department. The book has passed through readers, one ferocious copy editor, the designer, the printer, the proofreader, more galleys and more proofreading, and finally it's bound and in the hands of the shipping department. From there it sometimes goes to holding pens just like cattle and other times directly to the bookstore, where yet another set of hands unpacks it, sets it up, until lastly your hands pick it up.

Year after year this chain of hands has brought me to you and then, by post, brought you to me since so many of you write letters of thought, complaint or praise.

The hands that have held me up even longer than those people at Bantam belong to my agent, Wendy Weil. Time forged a friendship as well as a refined business relationship. Wendy and her husband, Michael Trossman, are such a part of my life that I can't imagine living without them.

This is also true of Stuart Robinson, my film agent. I can't imagine life without him. He owns a Thoroughbred and will probably own more as time goes by. This, for me, is superglue: horses and time together.

Try to write your autobiography. You'll surprise yourself. The trick is not to take yourself too seriously. Granted this is the only life you have but still—take it with a grain of salt.

You may discover what I have discovered and that is that the times we've lived through become defining, as defining perhaps as talent and character. You are bound by that time to everyone who lived through it even if you can't stand them.

What you will also discover, should you publish your life story, is that libel laws are so strict that there's a great deal you can't say even if you witnessed it.

It's a strange time to be a writer because a writer is the one person in every culture, in every epoch, married to the truth. No one knows the whole truth. But each of us knows a shredded tatter of it. The writer must convey that to you or the culture begins to fray. In order for any society, culture or civilization to breathe and grow it must breathe freely. That's my job and the job of every one of us who attempts to write. Notice I didn't say that we were glorious or even good. Many of us haven't a scrap of common sense and others of us are pompous asswipes. Nonetheless, we are committed to telling the truth as best we know it and as best we remember it.

Time plays tricks on your memory and the law is playing tricks with the truth.

Despite those handicaps, I have done the best I could.

And I've done the best I could given my temperament, my talent, the pressures of daily life. I don't think any of us can do more than that and there's always someone who will do it better. Still, you soldier on.

If in my past, in my present and in my future I have been able to make you laugh and make you think, I count myself a lucky and successful writer.

The laughter worries me. I'm beginning to think that those of us with a sense of humor are an endangered species. The times, again.

I regret I cannot name many people in my life, friend and foe. I regret the repressive climate in which we currently labor, and I deeply regret the homophobia that has kept so many people I know and even have loved frightened, embittered, shattered regardless of external fame, wealth and success.

Bad as it is, it isn't as bad as being pinned down on Missionary Ridge, being herded into a Gulag or being forced to watch daytime TV nonstop.

These times, too, will change. They always do. Laughter and lightness will make a comeback. If not, I'd settle for a return of good manners for a start.

Onward.

RITA WILL

Look Out Below

MY MOTHER WAS MUCKING STALLS AT HANOVER SHOE FARM outside of Hanover, Pennsylvania, within a shout of the Mason-Dixon line, when her water broke. Had the hospital not been nearby, I would have been born in a manger. Perhaps I came into the world knowing Jesus had already done that, and since he suffered for all of us I saw no reason to be redundant.

So I was properly delivered in a hospital. God cupped his hands to his mouth and shouted, "Look out below!" I arrived at 3:45 A.M. war time, which was double daylight saving time, on November 28, 1944. Truthfully, I'd have rather been with the horses.

My natural mother conceived me without benefit of marriage. At eighteen she was in no position to care for an infant, although the family had resources. Good blood. Good money. The goodness ran out at the socially embarrassing prospect of raising an illegitimate child. Surely there must be an ASPCL—for ladies. My poor young mother, in a maternal fit, snuck away in the middle of the night from the hospital, absconding with her own baby. My natural father, inconveniently married, drove the getaway car.

No one knew where she was or I was. The Young family, for all their commitment to corpulent emptiness and propriety, had the decency to worry.

Two weeks later, give or take a day, Juliann Young came home by weeping cross, a southern expression meaning you've been hurt and humbled. She appeared at Julia Ellen Brown's kitchen door. Before my birth, Juliann had promised Julia and Ralph Brown that since they couldn't have children of their own, they could have me—kind of like a zygotic door prize. As it was, Juts (Julia Ellen's nickname) and Juliann were related. In fact, the whole family was mixed up worse than a dog's breakfast. Juts and Juliann were cousins, or rather half cousins, with twenty-two years between them. Their mothers were half sisters.

Juts had been pitching a fit and falling in it ever since Juliann disappeared, because she wanted the baby. Although suffering at the time from pneumonia, she was formidable in her rage. Juliann confessed that she had dumped me in an orphanage in Pittsburgh, Pennsylvania.

Ralph Brown and Juts's sister Mimi lost no time rounding up ration coupons. Gas, critical in war, was controlled for civilian use by Uncle Sam, who rationed plenty else as well. The Browns and Dundores had good friends. They gathered enough coupon books to reach Pittsburgh and return, a long trip on wretched roads.

Ralph Brown put Juliann in the car. He needed her with him to release me. Twelve hours later Dad, Mimi and Juliann arrived at the Catholic orphanage—I don't know its correct name—in the Steel City. The administration was only too happy to give me the boot. I'd been there for two weeks, I hadn't gained a pound, and since I'd weighed only five pounds at birth I resembled a tiny skeleton. One of the nuns advised Dad not to take me. I would die. Dad said, "This baby will live"—a line my aunt Mimi, "Sis" to Juts, loved to quote.

So many children were born out of wedlock during the war years that the orphanages and children's homes threatened to burst at the seams. Nobody wanted us. The churches provided what succor they could, but we'll never know how many infants and young children died for lack of proper nutrition or, truthfully, for lack of love. Not all the casualties of a war are on the battlefield.

On the trip back to the Browns' home in York, Pennsylvania, a snowstorm struck, ferocious and bitter. Dad put chains on the tires, then fought to keep the car on the road. Aunt Mimi, the mother of two daughters, had brought some of their old baby clothes and blankets; she never threw anything out. She held me, wrapped like a mummy, close to her chest. Juliann Young refused to hold me. Every time they spied a light at a gas station or a farmhouse, Dad rolled off the road to ask people if they could spare some milk and heat it for the baby.

I owe my life to people I will never meet. Like Blanche DuBois, I relied upon the kindness of strangers. This wartime odyssey, with friends and strangers sacrificing some of their comforts for an infant, drives my life. I may have been born into difficulty, but I was kept alive by generosity and love. People may not always be consistently good, but they can be occasionally good, gentle and giving. I don't think we can ask more of one another.

Once home Dad immediately drove to old Dr. Horning's. The doctor told Dad and Sis that I'd never make it. His glasses halfway down his nose, Dr. Horning warned Dad not to place me in Juts's arms. She wouldn't be able to stand losing the baby. Worse, I was so emaciated, he feared I'd contract her pneumonia.

Ralph Clifford Brown, called Butch, was at thirty-nine a big, blond, handsome man, movie-star handsome really. He was not given to loudness or excessive emotional display. Of course, with Juts around there was rarely an opportunity, since she had to be the star. Dad possessed a quiet strength, which occasionally surfaced, surprising people who took him for a pushover.

My dad asked, "What do I have to do to keep this baby alive?"

The tone of his voice must have scared Dr. Horning, because he outlined an exhausting program of feedings every three hours for the next four months. Since Juts was languishing abed, that meant Daddy had to do it. Sis fed me during the day while Dad worked, then he got up during the night for the month it took Mom (Juts is always Mom) to recover. After that, they shared the burden.

Sometimes in the ensuing months Dad woke up when Mom did, so they'd feed me together. Their marriage careened into a few potholes over the years, what marriage doesn't, but I think those nights were some of the happiest times they spent together.

Not only did I live, I flourished. They fed me so much I resembled a sumo wrestler. Well coordinated, I crawled everywhere, got into everything. Mickey, the long-haired tiger cat who slept in my crib, fascinated me. I crawled after him morning, noon and night. I spoke early, too, and as luck would have it, the first word out of my mouth was "Dada." "Mama" surely followed soon after, or Mother would have burst a blood vessel through jealousy. The next grand pronunciation was "kiddle cat."

As to my natural mother, Juliann, she disappeared again. A pretty young woman, she knew she had to get out of Dodge because even if everyone forgave her, no one would forget, least of all her own father, Jack Young. He wasn't too thrilled about me, either. Then again, neither were Daddy's parents, Caroline and Reuben Brown. In fact, Caroline was positively poisonous.

Merrily crawling, cooing and cuddling with Mickey, I hadn't a clue as to the controversy I'd caused.

Juts told the tale of my beginnings many times. Aunt Mimi assisted. Surely there are other sides to this story, but I know only theirs.

I arrived by the back door, but I arrived.

You've met the irrepressible Juts if you've read *Six of One* or *Bingo*.

You've also met Mimi, who is called Louise in those volumes. I called her Little Mimi or Aunt Mimi since her mother, a glorious, radiant woman, was Big Mimi. Big Mimi Buckingham was as wide as she was tall. In the novels she's Cora.

In case you haven't read them, here's Mom: five foot two, with a trim, feminine figure, which she exploited to the fullest, dove gray eyes, curly light brown hair and a tongue that could rust a cannon. Mimi Dundore, four years older, possibly more since there was an awful lot of age fudging going on, could have been her twin. Mom was born in 1905. Let's give Aunt Mimi the benefit of the doubt and say she was born in 1901, christened Monza Alverta Buckingham after a popular stage comedienne of the turn of the century. She hated being labeled Monzie and as soon as she was legally able she changed her name to Mary. Not that the older generation paid her a bit of mind on that. She finally wore them down until even Big Mimi called her Mary.

Aunt Mimi, burdened as a child with the responsibility of "watching over" Juts, was a real bossyboots. Naturally Juts defied her, sabotaged her and goaded her at every available opportunity. Those occasions when they behaved maturely in each other's presence were rare. Generally it was like living between Scylla and Charybdis: watch out. Even their husbands ducked.

The gods gave both sisters a fabulous sense of humor. More times than not, that sense of humor freed them from yet another scrape. In a way they were the character Lucille Ball modeled Lucy on. Back then I think women weren't as earnestly good as they seem to have become, or perhaps the gray pleasures of psychology hadn't seeped in to steal away people's primary colors. One thing was certain—they were funny, wonderful and often mean as snake shit. You couldn't take your eyes off them.

Their family, the Buckinghams, were blue bloods. The first Buckingham arrived in Boston in 1620. Thomas Buckingham, perhaps driven mad by those Boston accents, headed south as soon as he could. A talent for making money never evidenced itself in the Buckinghams. Whatever they made, they spent. Mother's motto was "Tomorrow can take care of itself."

Both sisters—indeed, most people of their generation—had witnessed the deaths of brothers and sisters, close friends, or parents. Life was fleeting. Mom and Aunt Mimi had lost their older brother, John, to meningitis, and a beautiful, truly beautiful sister, Maizie, to diphtheria. They nearly died of it themselves. The youngest Buckingham, George, a handsome man—the Buckinghams are fine-looking people—lived only into his thirties.

Witnessing death at a young age terrifies some children, silences others.

In Mom and Aunt Mimi's case they wanted to sing, dance, taste the world—*carpe diem*. This lasted until Aunt Mimi was sent to McSherrystown Academy, a Catholic boarding school of some rigor. Charles Buckingham, their charming, alcoholic father, had abandoned them. They hadn't a penny. As Aunt Mimi showed musical talent, a relative who worked at the academy took her in so she was fed and properly educated. With all the passion of a grade-schooler, Mimi embraced the One True Faith and determined that the rest of us would embrace it with her.

Mom was farmed out to Sadie Huff Young, her mother's half sister. George, called Bucky, still an infant, remained with his mother. Juts once told me, and Aunt Mimi confirmed it, that before their mother found homes for them they would go down to the pretzel factory to beg for scraps. Big Mimi's vegetable garden spelled the difference between survival and disaster.

Big Mimi suffered at breaking up her family, but it was the only way to keep them alive. Mother was close to six, so Aunt Mimi had to be nine or ten.

The good thing about Juts's being placed with Sadie was that she remained close by. Big Mimi and Sadie had the same mother but different fathers. Over time Juts felt that Sadie was her mother and Big Mimi was her aunt. The two half sisters cooperated all through their lives, so Juts came out on top.

Sometimes I think my life has been framed by these two pairs of sisters, Mom and Aunt Mimi, Big Mimi and Sadie. Or perhaps *framed* is the wrong word. I've been shadowed.

Back to 1911. Big Mimi did what most women have to do in painful circumstances. She worked at any job she could find, kept up her small farm and looked for another man, a reliable one. This was before she got big as a house, so attracting men was no problem.

George "PopPop" Harmon fell in love with her. A merry creature no matter how cruel her fate, Big Mimi drew people like a magnet. People were important to her. She let them know it and she made them laugh. Hearing her tinkling laugh made *you* laugh.

I never knew how Big Mimi and PopPop met, but they both admired good hounds. I wonder if they first saw one another at a hound meet.

After they got married Big Mimi wanted her girls back. However, my aunt Mimi, popular and bright, was flourishing at McSherrystown Academy. Her schoolmates couldn't bear to see her leave. She stayed, and it's a testimony to my aunt that she remained friends with those schoolmates throughout her life.

Mother adored being at the center of life in Hanover instead of out on the farm. Hanover, a small town, might not seem like a hot spot to today's casual visitor, but to a child as impressionable and sociable as Juts, it was the center of the universe. Knowing Mother, I suspect she rather enjoyed the drama of being separated from her mother. It made her special.

Juts continued to stay with Sadie and Jack Young until tenth grade, when the boredom of Hanover High School propelled her to leave. Not getting your high-school diploma wasn't a big deal then. Since she danced the night away, was the life of every party—in fact, she was the party—both her mother and Sadie realized the futility of trying to keep her in school.

She had adventures and she even married one of them, a big secret she kept all her life. Being divorced carried a tremendous social stigma, and Mom was a divorcee by her early twenties. Somehow she managed to overcome it. Everybody knew, of course. The secret was really for the next generation and the one after that (mine). By that time divorce wasn't so awful.

Sadie Huff, as Mother has always called her, had a great effect on my mother's life and on mine. Mother wanted to be the refined lady that Sadie was and loved her aunt until Sadie's dying day.

Sadie's slow death from pneumonia allowed her to keep her wits to the end. She asked Mother to take care of her youngest daughter, Juliann. Sadie's other daughter, Betts, a few years older than Juliann, was in good shape, or at least Sadie thought she was. But Juliann at fourteen needed a strong hand.

So when Sadie died Mother took in her cousin, helping to raise her. That half cousin is my natural mother.

Like I said, we're all mixed up worse than a dog's breakfast.

Mother honored Sadie's wish just as Sadie had honored her sister's need. Really, there were three sets of sisters if you count Juliann and Betts. The debts of generations were paid off by my person.

The individual who seemed most sensitive to this was not Juts, really, but her sister Mimi. The sordid romance of my beginnings reverberated somewhere in my aunt's mind. Perhaps it was because I was a daughter. Aunt Mimi preferred daughters to sons. Juts, of course, would have preferred sons to daughters.

When I came along I was a clean sheet upon which to write Aunt Mimi's religious longings. Mother, a Lutheran, viewed this prospect with horror. Besides, she had her own plans for me. The true path of Our Dear Lord, as Aunt Mimi would say, was also the true path of gargantuan family blowouts. Aunt Mimi wanted me to rectify whatever mistakes she felt she had made with her own two girls, i.e., they hadn't become Dominican nuns. Mother wanted me to become a movie star. She'd argue with Aunt Mimi, "Look, she can play a nun, she doesn't have to be one. Think of Loretta Young."

These theological matters meant nothing to me as an infant, although I did perform admirably at my baptism. Daddy held me and I didn't cry when the holy water was dabbed on my head.

This incident was recalled to me many times in my youth as a counterweight to my occasional pranks in church. If nothing else, I was determined to find out if God had a sense of humor.

In 1940s America, especially out in the country, your church affected your business and social affiliations. We worshipped at Christ Lutheran Church on George Street. Tombstones in the small graveyard in the quad go back to the seventeenth century. It is the oldest church west of the Susquehanna River. As an old family, we had a pew near the front, the fifth row.

This was never spelled out, of course. But no one sat in your pew. The location of our pew, so prominent, meant I had an audience for my capers.

One of the first of these occurred before I could walk under my own power. The glorious choir enthralled me. Because of the stupendous Bach—one of the great things about being a Lutheran is that you listen to Bach all the time—I was inspired to sing and sing. No amount of bouncing deterred me from my mission.

Mom said that I turned around, beheld the congregation beholding me and really belted out my "hymn."

A red-faced Dad carried me out, to general relief. I, however, was displeased. It was summer, the windows were open and my bellowing carried from the courtyard. Finally, Daddy walked around the block with me.

When Mother shook Pastor Neely's hand, as is the custom at the end of the service, he said, "Well, Julia, I believe the baby will live."

I have no memory of this, obviously, but I do remember the patterns on the rug, Mom's cat, Mickey, purring, and Mom's shoes. I was still crawling, and as I grew I used to ask Mother to verify my memories, those from the time before I could talk—really talk. She was astonished at what I remembered.

I think we each remember a lot from that early time. After all, we're seeing the world for the first time. Impressions swirl in our brains. We can't tell anyone because we can't speak.

These impressions are far more vivid than, say, something you did in your thirties—or at least I think they are.

Cats and horses. Those are my earliest impressions. Daddy's deep baritone, almost bass, voice. His big hands. He could hold me in his palm. Mother's perfume, Chanel No. 5, and her laugh. But mostly I recall Mickey and the Percheron horses in the next pasture as well as the stunning Standardbreds of Hanover Shoe Farm—still there and still breeding the best.

I also remember everyone laughing at me. Big Mimi used to clap and I would "dance." In fact, I just remember laughter. The Buckingham clan—all the Dundores, the Zepps, the Haffners, the Finsters, the Weigels, the Bowerses, the Beans and even some of the Youngs—what people. They loved life.

The Browns were quite a different story.

2

Butter Wouldn't Melt in Her Mouth

WHEN CAROLINE BROWN SAID "JUMP," SHE EXPECTED HER three surviving sons to say "How high?" Daddy, the eldest, looked exactly like his father, Reuben Brown, a dramatically handsome man.

Earl, the dark middle son, didn't resemble anybody. We never knew where he came from, and he didn't act like a Brown. He acted like a banty rooster.

Claude, the youngest, another handsome blond fellow, radiated goodwill and happiness. He and Daddy were alike except that it's always easier to be the baby of the family than to be the eldest.

Dad was not the firstborn. Carrie (Caroline's nickname) bore a son, John, before my dad's birth. The death of a child is deeply painful, but in those days people knew better than to believe all their children would live to adulthood.

Carrie bore it in stride. She was a strong woman. The hopes of the Brown line now transferred to Ralph, a sunny, jovial, sweet-natured man who was willing to work hard and did. However, he was not a man to carry the burden of the world on his shoulders or even the burden of the Browns.

You see, Carrie nursed ambitions. In that respect she was a bit like Aunt Mimi. These women were going to get ahead. If they couldn't push you, they'd pull you. Failing that, they'd put a stick of dynamite under your ass.

Fortunately, Reuben possessed vision. The Browns had sprung out of the Pennsylvania soil. They'd been here since the earth was cooling. Graveyards throughout York County are filled with their ancestors. Bold, they pushed over to the west bank of the Susquehanna River—when most white folks clung to the Atlantic shoreline.

Unlike Mother's family, the Browns were tradesmen. They were greengrocers and butchers for generation after generation, with a merchant's keen eye for value. They believed in service, not just customer service but community service. Between Reuben and the three sons, they must have lent their support to every worthy cause in the town of York, Pennsylvania, to say nothing of joining organizations like the Rotary Club. They were doers, people who worked with other people, whereas the Buckinghams were people who worked with animals. It wasn't that the Buckinghams didn't get along with people; they were exceedingly popular and fun-loving. It's just that their view of life contrasted sharply with that of the Browns. The Buckinghams displayed all the characteristics of impoverished English dukes, barons or squires.

The Browns displayed the characteristics of organized, fanatically clean Swabians, the inhabitants of the German state from which they originally emigrated before the Revolutionary War. And like the Swabians to this day, the Browns were tight with a buck.

The Buckinghams belonged to the "consider the lilies of the field" philosophy of finance. They didn't give a rat's ass what you thought of them. A Buckingham liked you, or didn't like you, based on you, your character. Money couldn't sway them.

The Browns preferred that you be swaddled in the clothes of bourgeois abundance. The Victorian age was their highest point. All that overstuffed furniture, doilies, drapes, all that propriety and careful grooming of image suited them perfectly.

The Buckinghams could be happy in a bloody palace or in a simple Quaker farmhouse with a few chairs and beds. Mother and Aunt Mimi deviated from this simplicity in that both adored color.

The dominant possession of Reuben and Carrie Brown was an imposing black clock from the 1840s that ticked away on a big mantelpiece. It now ticks away on mine, and if Carrie Brown could come back from the dead and see that I have her clock, she'd pitch a hissy.

Mamaw Brown did not like me. Papaw accepted me but he wasn't a man to spend much time with children. Neither one had an ounce of affection for me. I don't remember ever being hugged or kissed by them. Perhaps they did but I can't remember, which says something right there.

How could Ralph Brown, their golden boy, the beautiful, strapping son whom everyone adored, lower himself, first to marry that wild rat, Julia Ellen Buckingham, and then fifteen years later, when they both were old enough to know better, adopt Juliann Young's illegitimate baby? No bastard could carry the unsullied Brown name.

Of course, the Buckingham name was far grander than the Brown

name, if you wanted to be picky about it, and if you weighted English
aristocracy over Swabian merchants. Mother ignored her in-laws' sense of
superiority. Aunt Mimi didn't. She'd sniff, lower her voice and say, "Carrie Brown, who does she think she is?"

Carrie and Reuben turned their backs on Dad when he married my
mother, a worldly woman. As members of the Church of the Brethren,
their views of what constituted worldliness were quaint. Mother smoked,
drank, danced all night and, horrors, worked in a silk mill.

What good were exalted bloodlines when you worked next to common
folk?

Dad rebelled and married her. It was the smartest thing he ever did.
They were made for each other.

Carrie Brown all but huffed and puffed and blew the house down.
However, the Depression roared into everyone's life shortly after Mom and
Dad married. They lived in a tree house on Long Level on the Susquehanna River. They worked like mad and saved as much as they could—
never easy around Mother, since money burned a hole in her pocket.

Had Dad chosen a suitable wife, they would have been invited to live
for free on the third floor over the store, Browns' Meat Market, on a
corner on Market Street in West York, Pennsylvania.

Earl and Claude received favors and goodies from their mother and
father. Mom and Dad got a fat nothing, but they had each other. That was
enough.

I should add that both Earl and Claude married women who passed
Carrie's test. All the Brown men had emotional sense when it came to
women. They had the sense to know what they needed in a partner. All
three marriages endured and grew, as did Reuben and Carrie's marriage,
for they too were a good team.

The Depression forced Papaw to lay off workers at the store. He called
back his oldest boy. Mother, usually a font of information, clammed up on
the details.

What I think happened, though I can't prove it, is that Reuben promised the three sons the store and probably finalized his will even though he
was in the prime of life. He may well have done this over Carrie's objec-
tions. The Browns enjoyed robust health. Built like Warmblood horses,
they had solid, heavy bones and big muscles, yet a cleanness, even refinement of facial features.

So Dad came back to the store. He and Mom moved into the third
floor of the building after all, and if Carrie wasn't welcoming to Juts, she at
least tolerated her.

Mother didn't give a fig.

However, by the time I appeared Mom and Dad lived in a small, adorable house on a hill in south York very close to the Maryland line.

Carrie couldn't abide what her son had done. She froze him out again. Mother never could understand how a grown person could be so cruel to an infant. Carrie wouldn't let me in the house.

So Dad and Mom didn't go over. Dad dutifully appeared at work. The tension probably resonated in Browns' Meat Market.

Then one evening Daddy showed up at a huge party at his parents' house with me in his arms. He strode through the door, and I expect everyone there was struck dumb, a truly amazing occurrence given that gathering. He held me up over his head in one big hand and called out, "I have the most beautiful baby in the world right here. Who will bid on this beautiful baby?"

No one knew what to do.

They tell me Uncle Jim, Carrie's brother, made a bid. Soon everyone was into the spirit of it. Carrie stood in the kitchen surrounded by "bidders."

Finally Dad yelled, "You can't have her. A million dollars won't buy this baby. She's mine!" At that everyone cheered and Uncle Claude came up asking to hold me. Dad told him he could in a minute and then, with me still over his head (the man was strong beyond belief, but I guess you get that way lifting three-hundred-pound sides of beef), pushed his way through the crowd.

Carrie, to her credit, didn't turn her back or run to another room and shut the door in a huff. She waited. Daddy placed me in her arms and said, "Mother, this is your granddaughter and she's beautiful."

Even Carrie, in all her hatefulness, couldn't resist me at that moment. Why, I don't know. By now, thanks to Mom and Dad's feeding me around the clock, I'd gained enough weight to pass for a pink cannonball.

Pretty soon everyone was cooing and aahing, and Carrie was bouncing me around and telling Dad how a baby must be treated.

Wonderful though that moment must have been, Carrie Brown couldn't truly warm to me. I know she loved Dad. The distance of years has taught me many things, one being that Caroline Brown may have been cold to me but she was fundamentally a good woman and she loved her boys.

The problem was she couldn't leave anyone alone. She lived her children's lives for them until the day she died, and Dad, number-one son, deeply disappointed her twice.

My earliest memories of her are how peachy, creamy and rich her skin was, like Devon cream. She had the skin of an angel. I also remember the smell of fresh-baked bread and her flourishing little garden along the fence line between her house and a neighbor's.

One sunny June I toddled after her—I couldn't have been more than three—bubbling as I walked. I was a happy cherub, singing, chirping and laughing. For whatever reason, I was with Mamaw alone. We both loved flowers, a step in the right direction. Mom, a crack gardener, had given me a set of baby tools. At the ripe old age of three I considered myself an expert and I prattled off the names of irises and cabbage roses.

The vibrant flowers swayed in rows like soldiers. Even Carrie's flowers were incredibly orderly.

Nestled under a drooping magnificent white peony was a pile of dog excrement. I had not yet developed a sense of what was proper to note and what should be left unremarked. I commented on this gift from a neighboring dog, and then with a sense of discovery and excitement, I said, "Look, Mamaw, it's got peanuts in it!"

I didn't know that dogs ate peanuts. Well, I didn't know a lot of things, but I knew at that moment that Carrie felt such an observation was not in keeping with a young lady's deportment. I was hustled out of the garden into the nook by Papaw's desk. A *National Geographic* rested on a window seat. She told me to look at the pictures, so I did.

Each time I visited Mamaw, once a week like clockwork, I admired her garden, kept my mouth shut and poured over those yellow-bound copies of *National Geographic* while she cooked another of her delicious meals.

I felt to my bones that Mamaw didn't like me. There was nothing I could do to change that.

Claude and Jeun, his wife, treated me with kindness. Even Earl, a cold fish, never gave me a harsh word. His wife, Helen, often went out of her way to give me something to eat.

I don't remember Carrie or Reuben Brown ever buying me a Co'Cola, a book or anything else spontaneously. They gave me a birthday present and a Christmas present each year. It was always something practical, which was fine. Even as a child I liked practical things, especially tools. The presents were beautifully wrapped.

Mother bit her tongue. On the subject of her mother-in-law she tried very hard not to explode in fury. She didn't need to, since Aunt Mimi usually did it for her. Aunt Mimi would sometimes be so disgusted with Carrie that she could hardly say hello to her.

Aunt Mimi had taken in a homeless girl, Etta, also not on the social register, and raised her with her two daughters, Virginia and Julia Ellen (named after Mom), so she thought Carrie's selfishness, as she put it, contemptible. Both Buckingham girls would help a child or an animal in need. The number of kittens, puppies, bunnies, birds and squirrels they doctored is beyond counting.

Dad didn't like his mother's attitude any more than the Buckinghams did, but she was his mother. He loved her and he too refused to speak against her, but she hurt him. I don't know if she ever realized how much she hurt him. He wanted her to love the people he loved, his two girls, Mom and me. She couldn't or wouldn't do it.

When I was in first grade, one Sunday Carrie attended her worship service and emerged a shaken woman. What I remember best about this occasion is that Mom, Dad, Aunt Mimi and her husband, Uncle Mearl, were befuddled with amazement.

The pastor of her church had preached a passionate sermon on loving all God's children. He and his wife had just adopted an orphan and he beseeched his congregation not to visit the sins of the father on the child.

Afterward Mamaw and Papaw met with Dad. I don't know what they said or even if tears were shed, but they admitted they were wrong and they would try to set things to rights.

After that Mamaw smiled at me more and Papaw answered my torrent of questions. I truly believe they tried, but the damage was done. I never loved them.

I behaved correctly. Mother would have killed me if I hadn't.

From Carrie I learned that piety is like garlic, a little goes a long way. Whenever I see someone utterly secure in the rightness of their restrictive beliefs I think, "Ah yes, this one's kin to Mamaw," and I pop into reverse and get the hell out of there.

I also remember that the only spot in heaven promised to anyone by Christ was that given to the thief who died on the cross with him. I often wonder if these strident Christians, I'm-better-than-you folks, read the same Bible I do.

For Carrie's sake I hope she got to heaven. She died in 1960. However, if our Eastern sisters and brothers are right and there is karma, I expect that Caroline Brown is right back here on earth learning more lessons. For myself, I hope she's come back as a dog that eats peanuts.

3

What a Friend I Have in Jesus

OH, HOW BIG IS THE WORLD! EVERY CHILD THINKS THIS. CHAIRS are unclimbable. You see the hems of skirts sway. A tulip stares at you eye-level and wasps are big as B-52s.

Mom's cat, a giant, really was bigger than I was for a while. Mickey's purring thrilled me. I tried to purr. He'd roll over and display his major tummy; I'd roll over and display mine. He'd jump. I'd jump. He'd climb up a tree and taunt me, but he always crawled into my crib at night and I'd wake up with Mickey staring at me, purring like thunder.

One warm May day the lilacs bloomed. I must have been two. Yellow swallowtails, black swallowtails, lovely blue butterflies and viceroys fluttered over the delectable blooms. I remember the colors, I remember the slight brush of air as the butterflies flew next to my cheek. I remember Mother pointing them out and giving me their names, which was a switch since I was usually the pointer. I'd wobble around, point and say, "Deeze." In fact, "deeze" was my favorite verb, noun, adjective and adverb. Until the day her parts finally wore out, Mom would look at me and say, "Deeze," or I'd say it to her, and we always knew exactly what the other was talking about.

Mother, a dedicated gardener, planted lavender lilacs in the yard, with white ones closer to the house. Mother would drop into one of the Adirondack chairs and inhale the fragrance.

Mickey lurked under the biggest lilac bush. I flopped down on my stomach to see him. I think that was the first time I realized that butterflies are different from cats, but I didn't know I was different from a cat.

On that day Mother picked me up so I could see more butterflies. Aunt Mimi drove up, and our neighbor, Peggy Cook, called Cookie, was there, too.

Mom and Dad were the hub of a wheel of friendship whose spokes radiated in every direction. I don't remember one day under their roof that someone didn't drop by for a cup of coffee, a lemonade, a Co'Cola or stronger spirits in the evening. No one said "a drink." That was "common."

Laughter. I lived in a world of their cascading laughter.

Mickey and I would sit side by side on the floor and look up at the adults, who occasionally looked down at us. We thought we were the center of attention because someone would scratch Mickey or kiss me. He'd get handed a sandwich scrap and I'd get puffed rice, which doesn't sound like much, but I loved dry puffed rice right out of the box, and still do.

Mom and Dad's friends ranged from my age to the nineties. Great-Grandpa Huff was pushing one hundred. He'd fought in the War Between the States as a child; at the end, the South would take anyone who could hoist a gun. He was so old his skin was translucent. Like all the Huffs, his mind raced along. No Huff ever went crazy, although they could drive you nuts.

Great–Grandpa Huff would put me in his lap and tell me about the war. I don't remember one thing he said. I just knew it was important and the wrong side won.

It was because my mother's people had fought for the South that Juts, born in Maryland, still thought of herself as southern. But if she hadn't been southern-born, she'd have come up with some other way to be different.

Aunt Mimi kept her own salon. The two sisters competed in everything. Aunt Mimi, more Catholic than the Pope, busied herself with moral uplift more than Mom and Dad did.

Daddy's brothers and their wives often stopped by. The Brown men had deep voices. His mother and dad visited infrequently. When they did, it was a state occasion. Mother would be down on her hands and knees scrubbing the floor. Aunt Mimi would be right there with her. The Buckingham girls fussed but they stuck together and worked together.

On those rare instances when I thought I might not be the center of attention, I would sway and clap my hands, my version of dancing. Then the adults would clap their hands and Mom would say, "Dance!"

Reports are that I fell down more than I danced, but I was happy. I do remember people saying, "Fall down, go boom!" But everyone says that to a rug rat.

By some miracle on Mother's part I had learned that I was not the center of attention in church. Jesus was.

The problem was I never saw Jesus. I saw a gorgeous painting of him behind the altar. The Ascension.

Christ Lutheran Church is a stunning example of early Georgian architecture. The restraint and chaste beauty of this structure might even make a believer out of an atheist. I was generally quiet, so my parents took me to services. Matins, the big eleven o'clock service, or vespers, my favorite.

However much I loved the airiness of the church, the throaty organ and Pastor Neely, truly a man of God, I wanted to see Jesus. I began to search for him behind the curtains at home. I'd bend down and peek under the stairs, where Mickey hid. Seemed like a good place to me. I'd wiggle free from Mom and Dad after the service—I knew better than to even move a muscle during the service—and I'd look for Jesus.

Once I stood in the vestibule and warbled "Holy, Holy, Holy." I didn't know any words to the hymn other than the "holy" part but I thought maybe if I sang pretty, Jesus would show up. He didn't.

Then I wondered, what if he had shaved off his beard? A friend of Dad's once shaved off his mustache and when I saw him for the first time afterward I cried. Maybe Jesus was right in front of my face but he had shaved off his mustache and beard. That troubled me.

I'd ask Mom and Dad, "Where's Jesus?"

First they tried the usual explanation. "He's in heaven."

I'd point up to the sky and say, "Where?" I wanted to see him. He could peek through a cloud. Jesus could do anything.

I evidenced some curiosity about the Blessed Virgin Mother too, but not nearly as much as about Jesus. For one thing, she wore powder blue robes, and Jesus usually wore a red cloak over his white robe. I loved red. And no one told me that the BVM, as Mom called her to torment Aunt Mimi, loved children. I figured she was fixated on Jesus.

Aunt Mimi's explanation of why I couldn't see Jesus was so complicated that I don't recall a word of it. It was wonderful that she could remember her catechism, but as a toddler, I wasn't impressed.

Frustrated, Mother finally told me, "Jesus is in our hearts."

I wailed, "But I can't see him there and it means he's tiny. I want him to be big."

Inconsolable, I cried myself to sleep. Poor Mickey wore himself out licking my tears away.

The next Sunday, Daddy took me to Pastor Neely's private chambers after the service. Pastor Neely was in full regalia: he wore the green surplice for the season of Trinity. He had a voice that could roll back the tide. He must have been in his late thirties then. Children can't judge age but I remember a man of great warmth and energy. He smiled and laughed and shook people's hands as though he was glad to touch them.

Whatever he told me satisfied me. I stopped crying when I couldn't find Jesus. That doesn't mean I didn't still want to see him. I did. I just stopped bothering the adults about it.

Looking back, isn't it amazing that a busy man, running a huge church like Christ Lutheran, would sit down with a very small parishioner and treat her question as though it was worth his attention?

One time I asked Pastor Neely if cats, dogs and horses went to heaven when they died, because if not, I didn't want to go to heaven either, even if Jesus *was* there. Mother nearly passed out. When Aunt Mimi got wind of what I'd said, I heard the word *blasphemer* for the first time.

I do remember Pastor Neely's answer: "God loves all his creatures. All souls are dear to him." He reassured me that if Mickey died first, I'd see him when my time came.

It may not be correct Lutheran dogma, but Pastor Neely eased my heart.

Aunt Mimi began a campaign of subversion. She and Mom battled over religion daily. It added spice to both their lives. Whenever Mother was busy Aunt Mimi would tell me her version—the Church of Rome's. She'd drag me to mass, where I adored the candles. St. Rose of Lima burned more candles than Christ Lutheran.

However much Aunt Mimi wished to guide me to the One True Faith, her ardor cooled on a memorable Good Friday.

By now I was three and a half. My vocabulary had exploded. I had begun to read easy stuff like newspaper headlines. It scared Mom so, she took me to Dr. Horning. He told her to give me every book she could find. Mother was terrified that I wasn't normal. In those days normal children didn't read until the first grade. Dr. Horning told her normal children grew up to be boring adults—"Give her books." Bless that man. Mother, a rebellious soul herself, worried that I wouldn't fit in. Of course I wouldn't fit in. Everyone on either side of the Mason-Dixon line knew I was illegitimate. Well, maybe that's why she didn't want me to call attention to myself.

However, she did get me books and I roared through them. Daddy read me newspaper editorials. He said there were two sides to every story, so in the morning he'd read me the Democratic point of view from the *York Gazette,* and at night he'd read the editorial from the Republican paper, the *York Dispatch*. He would simplify the issues, but he was determined that I learn to think for myself and to gather information.

Back to Good Friday, when I distinguished myself by upstaging my invisible friend, Jesus.

The difference between a Catholic, an Episcopalian and a Lutheran is the difference between tired knees and happy knees. Theologians can froth at the mouth about church doctrine, married and unmarried clergy, priestly intercessions and other items worth hundreds of years of bitching and moaning. For me it's how many times you want to kneel.

Mother and Aunt Mimi vied for the greater show of devoutness. Aunt Mimi won, since Mother's sense of humor and fun sidetracked her from perfect Christian purity. But she didn't break Lent and rarely missed a Sunday or an important feast day. On Good Friday, a very holy day, Mom's butt was bound to be warming the fifth pew.

Of course, Aunt Mimi would attend the first mass of the day, usually at 6 A.M., then return for the special afternoon service, since Christ is reported to have died at 3 P.M.

Both Christ Lutheran and St. Rose of Lima, as well as every other church in town, swarmed with people dressed somberly. It wasn't until Easter Sunday that the big hats broke out like measles.

Since I usually behaved in church, Mother had no reason to believe this Good Friday would be any different. Perhaps she forgot that I had slept through the other Good Friday services of my life, all two of them. I was big enough now to stay awake.

I'd seen Aunt Mimi and her daughters that morning as they returned from mass. Every day Mother and Aunt Mimi either called each other on the phone at 6:30 A.M. or stopped by for coffee. Except at their places of worship, they were inseparable. Mother showed them my outfit for the Good Friday service. She also showed them my Easter outfit, pale yellow with ribbons interwoven on the bodice, a beautiful straw hat with a black grosgrain ribbon, little anklets with pink roses embroidered at the top, and a tiny pair of black patent leather Mary Janes. The praise turned my head. I wanted to wear the Easter ensemble to the Good Friday service. It took all four of them to explain that just wasn't done.

I bet I heard that phrase a million times: "That's just not done." Or else it was the more pointed "Our people don't do that." I finally calmed down, agreeing to be dressed like a sorrowful sparrow for that day only.

When we walked down the aisle to our pew I noticed that everything was shrouded in black velvet: the two-story windows, the altar, lectern and pulpit. Pastor Neely's vestments were black velvet as well. And there were no flowers.

At three o'clock, just as Pastor Neely's sermon ended, the curtains were

drawn and the candles on the altar were extinguished. The organ burst
into the most dolorous sounds and rumbled beneath my seat.

"Jesus is dead!" I bellowed at the top of my not inconsiderable lungs,
and burst into sobs. Mother surely made an effort to stem the tide of my
grief, but then I shrieked, "Mommy, turn the lights back on."

No amount of cajoling or threatening promises could stop my crying or
my commentary. Finally, Mother picked me up and carried me out into
the sunshine. Glad though I was to see the light, I was afraid I'd never hear
of Jesus again.

She explained that he'd be back on Sunday. I didn't want him back on
Sunday, I wanted him right then. When she told me the angel would roll
away the stone from the tomb, I howled.

Finally, she hopped on the bus in York Square. I made myself exceedingly popular by announcing that Jesus had been crucified and then crying
all the way home. Even the promise of an ice cream sundae couldn't quiet
me. Poor Mom, worn out from apologizing to the bus passengers, was
bedraggled by the time she pushed open the back screen door of our
house.

I knew you died only once. We lived out in the country. I'd seen
chickens die, and no dead chicken ever got up and walked. How could
Jesus do it?

Mother implored me to stop crying. Sunday morning I would rejoice,
she promised, for Christ would rise from the dead.

The phone lines hummed in Hanover, Littlestown and York. My Good
Friday performance aroused the natives. Mother bore criticism for taking
such a little child to a frightening service. She should have known better.
Of course, there would follow an exhaustive discussion of Julia Ellen
Buckingham Brown, the original flapper.

Others felt that I was a sensitive child.

A few felt I must have been touched at an early age by a religious
calling. Aunt Mimi secretly hoped I'd find the One True Faith, natch, and
become a nun. Not just any nun, mind you, but a Dominican. Aunt Mimi
had a thing for Dominicans.

Mother Brown was, of course, appalled.

Dad worried that I cried so much I'd make myself sick.

I couldn't have known it at the time, but this incident showed me how
people respond differently to an event. People look out the same window
but do not see the same tree.

Well, the big day came. I attended the Easter service in my finery. I had
been instructed by Mother, Aunt Mimi and even Big Mimi about my
deportment.

I was perfect. Everyone made a point of speaking to Mother and to me after the service, which was a riot of color, rejoicing and flower arrangements as big as hippopotami. This was my first taste of conscious celebrity. I didn't much mind it.

However, I wanted to know when I would rise from the dead. Poor Mom!

Hambone

IG MIMI LOVED TO HAMBONE. SHE'D SIT ON HER PORCH, TAP HER foot, slap her knees, then slap her arms, then clap and slap her arms again. All the Buckinghams were musical, and although Big Mimi was a Rill— she had only married a Buckingham—she was musical, too.

Poor as a church mouse, she couldn't afford a piano. She never complained. Far from it. My grandmother was the happiest woman I've ever known. She'd seen three of her five children grow to maturity, marry and have healthy families. Her children materially improved their lives and bought her whatever she needed. In her late fifties, when I was small, she said she didn't need anything.

She sang to me, taught me dance steps, taught me the difference between a Black-and-Tan Coonhound, a Bluetick Coonhound and a Walker Foxhound and said the best horses were to be found at Hanover Shoe Farm. I loved horses, cats and dogs beyond reason. I couldn't learn enough about them. When Mom took us down into Hanover, Big Mimi would walk me around the main barns at Hanover Shoe Farm. Mother had a fine eye for horseflesh, too. It was the wagering part of racing that attracted her. This gambling urge of Mother's would prove especially interesting later.

We greeted friends, looked at stallions and mares, falling in love with every frolicsome foal. I didn't know it, but everyone on the great estate knew exactly who I was. Every now and then I'd overhear a comment such as "She has her mother's eyes. Other than that she doesn't look like a Young at all." Or the more cloying "Why, she looks like you, Juts." I didn't look at all like Juts, the five-foot-two fireball with a figure men admired openly. I didn't even know I was supposed to look like Mom or Dad. They were Mom and Dad, that was all I knew.

Big Mimi, unlike Mother Brown, suffered these hints and raised eyebrows with her usual blend of sweetness and good humor. She protected me as best she could and taught me as much as she could in the short time we were to be together.

She died without warning of a heart attack in the spring of 1947.

When Mother heard the news she ran up to my bedroom under the eaves. I was playing with Mickey.

She said, "Big Mimi is an angel now," tears rolling down her cheeks. She threw open the window and shouted to the meadows, "My mother is dead." Scared the hell out of me.

The funeral brought folks from as far away as Baltimore and Harrisburg. Many roads weren't paved, being winding two-lane affairs. The fact that so many people took the trouble said something about Mimi Buckingham's effect on them.

The open casket was raised, and flowers were massed everywhere. I tried to crawl into the casket because I wanted to kiss her. When Dad prevented me from pulling down the flowers, I then danced because I knew that would have made Big Mimi laugh. This proved too much for many of the mourners, and everyone burst into sobs. Dad, crying too, walked me outside.

Since Big Mimi was with Jesus, I expected everyone to be happy. I knew she was dead and yet I didn't exactly get it. She was Big Mimi. She was a fountain of light, laughter and uncommon good sense. Other creatures and people might die, but couldn't Jesus send her back? We needed her.

"It doesn't work that way, honey."

I was figuring out that the Resurrection applied to only one of us.

I still miss her. In our short time together she gave me many gifts, chief of which is "hound sense." So in addition to my "catitude" I could now communicate with dogs.

I can make friends, animal or human, anywhere. But the best friends come on four feet.

5

Death to Crinolines

I
F YOU'VE NEVER WORN CRINOLINES ON A HOT, HUMID DAY, YOU'VE missed out on a torture that separates the goats from the sheep or the trash from the ladies.

Mother and Aunt Mimi devoured *Harper's Bazaar* and *Vogue* as well as those journals of deep intellect, *Silver Screen* and *Movie Stars*. Born at the turn of the century, they were galvanized by clothes and movies. In Mother's youth, which actually never ended (even in her seventh decade, she flashed about like a silent-film star), she carried a parasol and wore hats large enough for an eagle to nest in, long white dresses with high collars, and a ribbon with a cameo around the collar.

Aunt Mimi, a look-alike for Mabel Normand, the greatest film comedienne of all time, flounced around in darker clothes than Mom, with a pinched-in waist to show off her beautiful figure.

By the time I waltzed onto this earth, the girls adored Bette Davis, Greer Garson, Katharine Hepburn, Joan Crawford and Jean Arthur. Shoulder pads filled out everything from short-sleeved camp shirts to flowing winter coats. Shoes, hat, gloves and bag were dyed to match except in hot, sticky summer, when Mom dashed about in gathered skirts, a crisp blouse and espadrilles.

I was tarted up and paraded around. Not only was Juts fanatical about my attire, so was Aunt Mimi. By the age of four I'd probably tried on more clothes than Linda Evangelista.

What I wanted was a pair of jeans and cowboy boots or high-top sneakers. Aunt Mimi had a fit of the vapors when I mentioned this. Mother, always of broader mind than her sister, nixed it with a breezy "Field hands wear jeans."

"Never forget that you're a lady," Mimi toned, "of quality."

"I want jeans."

One Friday we passed the dry-goods store just off the square. Friday was market and shopping day. Mother allowed me to zip in and she followed. Aunt Mimi prowled on the sidewalk and then, with a great show of displeasure, trudged in.

I snatched a pair of Levi's off the counter. Mother and I discussed this fully. She told me to keep my voice down.

To shut me up, she asked the clerk the cost of the jeans.

"Three dollars."

"Robbery!" Aunt Mimi's voice could have cracked glass.

The clerk considered that, then said he must have made a mistake because I'd be wearing children's size. The price dropped.

"You aren't going to give in to her, Juts? It will never end. Give a child an inch and they'll take a mile."

Actually, Mother wouldn't have bought me those jeans if her beloved older sister hadn't felt compelled to behave like an older sister. She smacked those jeans on the counter and paid up.

I was ecstatic.

Sis chewed Mother's ear the whole way home.

In a small town sound travels faster than light. By the time we got home, Mother Brown called and announced I would not be wearing jeans in her house, thank you.

Mother kept her temper but when she put the receiver back in the cradle she said, "Lardass." She lit her ever-present Chesterfield and dropped into her thinking chair. I used to believe the chair really thought.

"Mom, can I put on my jeans?"

"Yes, and be quick about it."

I reappeared, Mom rolled up the pants legs, and whoosh, we trotted out of the house. Mother marched me to the downtown market, Central Market, where we both smiled at spiteful comments about the Browns' little boy.

On the way home I said, "I thought you didn't want me to wear jeans."

A long pause followed. Mother excelled at meaningful silences, followed by an exhalation of smoke and a burst of chat. "I changed my mind."

"Oh."

When we disembarked from the bus at the top of Queen Street Hill and walked down what is now called Hillcrest Road, she grabbed my hand, swinging it back and forth as we walked.

"I can't stand some jackass telling me what to do."

"You mean Mamaw?"

"I mean the whole goddamn world. I'm doing what I want to do, when I want to do it." Profanity peppered Mother's conversations, although she usually denied swearing.

"You gonna wear jeans, Momma?"

"I most certainly am not, but if you want to wear them, go to it, kiddo."

That pair of jeans taught me that nobody can live your life for you. Do what you want. But I was also told again and again, "Don't be selfish." Being selfish and being a Yankee were bad—and synonymous. (Mother reveled in having been born in Carroll County, Maryland.) Since children are naturally selfish, I had this lesson banged into my head every hour on the hour, but at the same time Mother granted me a healthy dose of skepticism about received wisdom.

It pained her, however, that I was not a carbon copy of herself. I hated crinolines. I hated smocked dresses. I hated dainty shoes. She naively thought I would like everything that she liked. I failed dismally. She could take apart a clock and put it back together, making it run. Her incredible mechanical sense extended to cars, even tractors. I listened and watched. I copied her but I didn't love the things she loved.

Social gatherings were Mother's metier. I preferred solitude or being with animals, although I got along with other children quite well.

She loved popular music. The only music I liked as a child was the music I heard in church, especially the Bach played on the stupendous organ at Christ Lutheran. I first heard a Gregorian chant with Aunt Mimi. Somehow I knew that was my music.

Later, both Mom and I liked Patsy Cline. We both liked hot-fudge sundaes. She liked Airedales and Chow Chows. I liked gun dogs and hounds. We both loved, to the point of silliness, cats.

But the older I grew, the sharper the differences were between us. I could only be myself. Mother's instinctual rebelliousness helped her accept somewhat that I was profoundly different from her, but underneath she feared I would never be her child; I would always be Juliann's baby. Why she did not brood as much about my natural father, I don't know. She never mentioned him. It was my natural mother she feared.

Aunt Mimi, during their worst fights, would taunt Mom by telling her, "You'll never be a true mother because you didn't give birth. I knew my children in the womb. That's why we're so close."

Close, hell. Aunt Mimi kept them on a tight leash and a choke collar.

But this hurt Mother, and in turn she often hurt me either by lashing out at whatever I did wrong, like spilling a glass of milk, or in other ways, those quiet withdrawals that children feel acutely but are unable to address.

The older I got, the more Mother pulled away from me. I expect this is natural. All animals push away their young, but by the time I was in kindergarten I knew in a nonverbal way, though I couldn't explain it, that I was on my own where she was concerned.

We always shared a love of color, a vibrant sense of humor and a true passion for horses.

I was the horse of a different color.

Devil Weed

I T'S FASHIONABLE TO DECRY THE HORRORS OF TOBACCO. I SAY, thank God for nicotine. Mother was so highly strung that without her measured doses of the drug, she'd probably have killed me.

But it couldn't be just any cigarette, only a Chesterfield. Not Lucky Strike or Camel or Viceroy or even Pall Mall. Not those expensive Dunhill brands or Gauloises in light blue packs. Old Gold with the dancing cigarette pack and little matchbook was nixed by Juts the Judge of All Things Tobacco.

The red tip of her Virginia leaf cigarette would glow as she inhaled, then exhaled with a sigh of gratification. When she worked, the cigarette hung out of the corner of her mouth like a gun moll's. When the 6:30 A.M. call or visit from Aunt Mimi came, the cigarette proved as indispensable as the gossip. Aunt Mimi didn't smoke, but then her engine didn't run as hot as Mom's. Mother would stride through Hanover Square or trot under the Bromo-Seltzer tower in Baltimore, pointing out the sights with her lit cigarette. No lady of the past could have used her fan as slyly as Mom used her cigarette. It was her prize, her prop and her one-woman party.

She started smoking at twelve because she wanted to seem mature. She continued smoking but I don't think she was ever fully mature.

And the damnedest thing is her lungs held out; she never coughed, and she got her teeth cleaned frequently, so they didn't yellow. Her fingers evidenced signs of nicotine use, but that was about it. To picture Mother you have to picture that regular-size, unfiltered Chesterfield held in whichever hand was supplying the emphasis to her uncharitable and screamingly funny conversation. She referred to the Pope as His Assholiness. She mocked her sister's intermittently sincere attacks of Catholicism by dubbing her Divergent Mary. She had another friend, Mary Baer, a lovely lady who daily fought the battle of the bulge and lost; she was Mary of the Straining Girdle. These nicknames and descriptions would enliven her chat like cayenne. You had to laugh, even when you didn't want to; even when you were the butt of her observations, you had to laugh.

Being less than perfect myself—a sin as far as Mother was concerned, since I was here to reflect her glory—I might hear myself called "the Ill" for illegitimate. If a tender maternal chord twanged, I was "kid." Since I flew around with as much energy as Mom, she called me "Bumblebee," which became "Bee," which became "To Be" by her more erudite friends, and finally "Buzzer."

When Mickey and I appeared, in tandem as usual, she'd say, "The Mick and the Buzzer are gracing us with their unclean presence." Usually I'd torn my shirt, scuffed a knee or decorated myself in the freshest dirt of the day. By age five I'd driven the woman half nuts because if an object could be crawled under or climbed up to the tippy-top, I did it. One day when I jumped onto the roof from the maple tree next to the house, Mother heard the thump and came outside, Aunt Mimi in tow, the kitchen radio playing "Those dear hearts and gentle people who live and love in my hometown."

Aunt Mimi, never one to miss a dramatic moment, cried, "She'll break her neck." She listed the other breakage possibilities as well.

Mother pointed her cigarette at me, the tiny orange glow pulsating. "Even the cat has sense enough to stay in the tree."

He did, too.

A lengthy discussion erupted between the two sisters as to the cost of medical attention should I break any bones. Mother, however, shrugged and headed back for the kitchen.

I was perched at the edge of the roof, glad to be out of her reach but worried about getting down.

"Juts, aren't you going to do something?"

"Let her think about it." Mother returned to her red-painted kitchen for yet another cup of coffee.

I did think about it. I couldn't jump back to the tree because the tree limb had bounced back up after I dropped onto the roof. Mickey stared at me with eyes as big as eight balls. Fat lot of help he was.

I was stuck and the day glistened with heat. I was really on that roof because my cousin died that year.

Although only five, I would enter first grade that fall. Since I would turn six just before the first of the year, they'd let me slide in. My cousin was a year older than I was but he seemed younger because he was small. I don't recall him being in school. Maybe he was always sick.

The adults shielded all of us kids as best they could, but muscular dystrophy resists being tidied up. I wasn't close to him. He was my true cousin, being born to my natural mother's sister, Betts, but I'd seen him only a few times and when I did he was weak. Now don't for a minute think that I cared that he was sickly. If a kid couldn't play with me, I got bored and left. But when he died I looked at his small casket. It was just my size. I'd never seen adults so distraught. Like a seeping leak in a cracked mug, the enormity of death was leaking all over my pea brain. I wasn't safe. Whatever this was, it was so awful that some of the relatives couldn't walk. They sat, head in hands, and sobbed.

Not only was I not the center of the universe that day, I could do little to make anyone happy. And I had done nothing to delight my cousin. The only reason I prayed for him when I went to bed at night was because Mother made me include him. At the funeral a sliver of light, a click in the mind, a new and disturbing idea seized me. Dying young, bad as that was, wasn't as awful as knowing I'd been irresponsible and selfish.

People underestimate children. They can understand moral principles early. I understood that I had not tried in even the smallest fashion to alleviate his suffering or to include him in my games. I hated myself.

I hated Jesus, too. He had brought Lazarus back from the dead. Why didn't he help us now?

Given my natural ebullience, this flash of guilt and self-hate lasted maybe ten minutes, but it was the first time I'd felt those squeamish emotions. I didn't much like them. I didn't want to feel that way again.

My daredevil acts increased, as did my sitting at the top of trees as I stared at the clouds. I don't know if I thought I'd see an angel or Zeus—I knew the Olympians because Mother read me the stories that were too advanced for my reading ability—but I was searching for something. Jumping onto the roof was another part of the search. I liked the feeling of dropping through the air. I liked the safe sound when my feet hit the shingles. I survived.

In retrospect I know I was struggling with issues of death and my duties to others. My vocabulary hadn't caught up with my concerns. Mother, for all her self-centeredness, could be sensitive. She knew Big Mimi's death and now my cousin's had affected me. Neither of us could have known that soon we'd be clobbered with another death of someone we loved, and that one would be true agony. But she never coddled me, nor did she direct my thoughts by telling me, "This is what good girls do."

Aunt Mimi, the font of Christian teaching, directed me every time Mother's back was turned.

Dad told me that we can't question God's will. We must surrender.

To this day the word *surrender* offends me, but Dad was right.

My anger wouldn't bring anyone back, any more than pasting some snot-nosed kid who called me a bastard could change the fact that I was.

I expect my July morning spent on the roof sprang from these issues. What I didn't expect was Mother's response.

She waltzed back out after what seemed an eternity. Aunt Mimi had a glass of lemonade in her hand to taunt me.

"Hot?"

"Yes."

"How's that?"

"Yes, ma'am."

Mother smiled up at me. She had such a feminine, coy smile.

"Want me to get the ladder?" Aunt Mimi held the glass to her forehead.

"No."

"Well, Juts, you can't leave her up there any longer. It's hotter than Tophet."

"Kid, have you thought of a way down?"

"No."

"You could shimmy down the drainspout."

I'd thought of that but I feared that if I swung my leg over the lip of the drainspout, I'd tear the whole thing off with me and then I'd really get a hiding. Or I'd land in Mother's hydrangeas.

"I don't think I can."

"You could jump."

"I'm afraid."

"Julia, she'll break a leg," Aunt Mimi chided her sister.

"Jump and I'll catch you." Mother stubbed out her cigarette and held up her arms.

"Julia, Julia, she's too heavy. She'll hurt your insides."

"Sis, let me handle this." She held her hand to shade her eyes. "I'll catch you. Even if I don't do such a hot job, I'll break your fall, and then we'll both roll around in the grass."

Mickey backed down the tree and headed for the kitchen, too afraid to look, I guess.

I had the presence of mind not to leap off, but I crouched backward, grabbed the edge of the gutter, oh it was hot, and let myself hang and then let go.

Mother caught me right under my armpits. "You got to trust someone in this life, kid."

"Yes, ma'am."

That was a lesson worth learning. It was also worth remembering not to jump onto roofs without a ladder.

7

Violet Hill

MOTHER WALKED ME THROUGH THE MEADOWS FULL OF GOLD-enrod and down the country lane to Violet Hill Elementary School, a brick building squat in the middle of the pasture surrounded by a moat of macadam.

Other mothers walked their kids to school. Some whiners were bawling. I skipped the whole way. When I said goodbye to Mother to join my first-grade class of thirteen children, it was Mother who burst into tears, not me. She wasn't the only mother crying.

Mother cried, then laughed at herself. She told Eileen Shellenberger that she felt old. I wasn't hers anymore. As Eileen, a pretty, dark-haired woman, had four children, she didn't share Mother's moment of nostalgia.

I was grown-up. First grade. Books. A ruler. Pencils and a big pink eraser. Other kids. Some even rode bicycles to school. Two Belgian draft horses munched in the adjoining meadow. That was even better than having other kids to play with. This was heaven.

And it was. School is every child's passport to the world outside their home. Our textbooks were frayed at the edges. We had no audiovisual aids. We had no athletic facilities. What games we played, we played on the mowed grass. But what we had were good teachers. They stamped my passport. I was ready to travel.

The Golden Hound

IF YOU EVER TRY TO WRITE YOUR AUTOBIOGRAPHY, YOU'LL FIND that experiences jump into your mind fresh, forcing you to feel those original emotions again. You'll be overwhelmed at what you can remember, and if you're like me, you'll stumble on time sequences.

The reason is that when we're tiny we have little sense of time. If you are five years old, then one year represents twenty percent of your life experience. When you're fifty, one year represents two percent of your experiences.

Those early memories are primary colors, pure and intense. They're also a jumble. School eventually imposes an order on you and on time.

That fall of 1950 meant going to school for the first time. It also meant hunting.

PopPop Harmon, Juts's stepfather, kept hounds, as did some of Dad's relatives. Night hunters, these old fellows (most of them born in the 1870s and 1880s) would take out four or five couple of hounds and let them rip. These hunts would be liberally fueled by white lightning or store-bought liquor.

Arguments over which was the better hound—coonhounds, foxhounds, Beagles, Plott Hounds, Walker Hounds—kept these veterans of the Spanish-American War and World War I fighting all over again. Who needed Kaiser Bill to fight when tiny Verduns existed in your own backyard?

PopPop believed no hound could beat a Walker for drive and nose. You couldn't beat them for stubbornness, either. Much as he admired them he liked American Foxhounds best.

His rheumy eyes would light up and his small frame would gain energy as he recounted the wonders of his most recent hunt and the glories of Belle, his best bitch.

Naturally, I begged to be taken along. Finally, Mother relented as long as Dad accompanied me, so that if I became a pest I wouldn't spoil a good night's hunting for "the boys."

"The boys" gathered on a high meadow between Spring Grove and Hanover that first weekend of school. Some walked, their obedient hounds trailing behind them. Others chugged down country roads in pickup trucks built in the 1930s. Everyone operated on the principle "If it ain't broke, don't fix it." Also, if something still worked, you didn't replace it with a new one. People were far more practical then. The paint jobs on those vehicles displayed the relentless passage of time, as did the faces of the hunters. Few bothered to shave unless their wives fussed at them. Everyone wore suspenders, chewed tobacco and smelled like 'shine and chocolate. I loved them.

PopPop introduced me as Juts's girl. Everyone knew Juts, so they embraced me as the novitiate that I was. PopPop had explained to me the ways of red foxes. I knew catching the quarry wasn't likely. I also understood that I was there to listen to the "music."

PopPop had a stud hound, Toby, that ran silent. I asked him why he kept such a hound, since hearing them is half of the fun. He said he'd tell me later, but he always forgot to tell me. He also warned me not to talk about Toby's peculiarity. That was our secret.

Belle's prowess, greatly appreciated on both sides of the Mason-Dixon line, drew admirers seeking to upgrade their hounds. A burly fellow named Harve, his shirt slightly open above his pants, offered PopPop fifty dollars for Belle. That was a fortune then, especially for PopPop, who didn't have two nickels to rub together, the result of drink more than laziness. He'd stay off the sauce for a good stretch and then that devil alcohol would seize him again. It was a pity because he was a good man.

Dad nearly passed out when PopPop refused. Then the man tried to borrow her for twenty dollars to get a litter out of her. PopPop said he wouldn't do that either but he'd let the man know when he bred her. He wanted to control the bloodlines. Harve again pushed to buy her outright for fifty dollars, thinking repetition would wear down PopPop.

Pushing never worked with anyone in our family. PopPop shook his head. Belle, a sleek Black-and-Tan with a white throat, sat next to Beulah, a good hound although not as good as Belle. They had no interest in the financial discussion.

A skinny man got up on the back of his truck and said, "Let 'em go," and go they did. Dad put me on his shoulders so I could watch the various hounds put their noses to the ground, tails or sterns up. A little wiggle meant "This is interesting." A feathering meant "I'm about ready to roll," and when a hound bayed or gave tongue, that meant "Ready, set, go!" The first time I heard that sound the hair stood up on the back of my neck, my heart raced and I wanted to run after the hounds. Still takes me that way.

Belle's voice, midrange, carried. You knew where she was even if far away. A good hound can cover forty or fifty miles and return ready to play with you. I heard deep voices, light voices, yippy voices and Belle's distinctive bel canto.

I was worried that the hounds would kill a fox, even though PopPop told me that hardly ever happened. Dad said foxes were smarter than hounds and lots smarter than we were. Truer words were never spoken.

Dad, as I said, liked gun dogs. If he was going to hunt, he wanted to eat the quarry. Pheasant, grouse and wild turkey, fixed by Mom and Aunt Mimi, sent you back to the table for more. Since you can't eat a fox or a raccoon, Dad shied off from night hunting. He knew good hound work when he saw it, though.

A slight chill rolled up even though it had been a hot day. Those early September days can fry you. The nights will surprise you with cold. Dad handed me my jacket. The hounds cried far away, then the sound came closer.

PopPop, his grin about as big as his small face, said, "Hear my girl?"

We could. No one sounded like her.

Harve was fit to be tied. He had to own that hound.

Night magnifies sounds. The stars seemed so low I thought I could pluck one out of the dark sky.

Belle worked in a copse near us, the other hounds with her, and the sound carried to heaven. Then Belle shut up. She shot over the meadow, the other hounds behind her, and she ran right up to PopPop, dropping an umbrella at his feet.

Harve laughed so hard he nearly fell off his truck. If he'd had another swig, I think he would have plopped face first in the cut-over hay.

"Harmon, I wouldn't give you five cents for that hound now."

The men laughed. In those days no gentleman would swear in front of a lady, so even though they might have thought "damn" or "shit" or worse, they'd die before they'd say it.

PopPop took the umbrella from Belle, patted her. Beulah was next to her, so he patted her too.

"Good girls. Good girls."

Meanwhile Harve was whooping it up, carrying on like sin.

PopPop smelled the umbrella. "Sniff, Buzzer."

I sniffed, stepped back, wrinkled my nose. My eyes watered.

"What's it smell like?" he inquired in his soft voice.

"A skunk."

"Sniff again."

I did. "Kinda like a skunk and kinda like something else."

Dad tested the umbrella's scent, too. He blinked his eyes.

"That's a fox. Like a sweet skunk." PopPop patted the hounds again and then patted my back as though I were one of the hounds. He strolled over to Harve, handing him the umbrella.

"Expecting rain, Harmon?" Oh, he laughed and hollered.

"Your nose still working, Harve?"

"Sure is." Harve inhaled over the umbrella. "Uh . . ."

"Let me have that," another younger man said. He took a whiff. Then he handed it to the man next to him. The umbrella made the rounds.

A moment of silence followed, since "the boys" knew a fox when they smelled it.

PopPop took me by the hand, Belle and Beulah at his heels, to walk back home.

Harve, shamed now, grew sullen. He yelled at PopPop, "How'd that umbrella get out here?"

PopPop stopped and replied, "When I walk on water, I'll let you know."

The War of the
Candy Apples

T HAT FIRST WEEK OF ELEMENTARY SCHOOL WAS ONE OF THE BIG-
gest weeks of my life. Not only did I start school and go to a hunt, it was
the week of the York Fair.

Each year since 1765 York has hosted a huge fair. Farmers bring pump-
kins and produce, women bring their pies and canned goods, the harness
racers fly around the beautiful track, and the midway entices you with
rides, games of chance and candy apples.

Mom had taken me to the fair before, but those visits were hazy. This
fair, in 1950, I remember with crystal clarity.

For one thing, I could go in the back entrance free. Browns' Meat
Market was only about a block away and the market contributed to the
fair, so they knew everyone working the fair, the gatekeepers, the police,
the administration.

Not only could I get in free, but if I brought my cousins, Kenny and
Wadie, and my best friend, Cheryl Shellenberger, we could all get in free.
The guard would wave us by.

The fair was attended by the children of the entire county because we
got one day off school to go, different days for different schools. That
didn't work for us because Kenny, two years older, and Wadie, my age,
attended the Catholic school. We stuck together.

Mother and Eileen Shellenberger escorted us. The mothers played
bingo, hauled us through the agricultural exhibits (the other kids were
bored, but I adored it, especially the cattle) and best of all, bought us white
straw cowboy hats with our names drawn on the front in grease pencil.
Sounds tacky but it looked great.

Kenny and Wadie wanted to see the serpent girl at the freak show. I
didn't. We all rode the whip and the Ferris wheel. We watched a man and

a woman who didn't speak English walk a low tightrope, ride a bicycle on it and even sit in a chair on it. I was shocked. I didn't know there were other languages and I'd never heard anything as peculiar.

I'd heard Mamaw use German phrases in the Swabian dialect. Not that I knew it was a Swabian dialect, but I did know it wasn't exactly English, except I'd heard *"Gott im Himmel"* so many times it seemed like English.

I was so fascinated by hearing them talk to one another. I wanted to see the show twice, but Mom said that was selfish, other people wanted to see other things.

We won an Indian-print blanket playing bingo. I still have it.

We went to the booth where you throw baseballs at stuffed cats. I spent a quarter trying to win a huge blue stuffed horse. I was fixing to cry when I couldn't win it but Mom told me I couldn't cry in public and it wasn't a hot idea to cry at home either. Weaklings cried. So I gulped and left but I babbled on about that horse. I wanted a real horse, but Mother adamantly refused, for reasons that would reveal themselves in time.

Mom promised that I could go to the fair every day after school.

As this was our day off from school, we kids made the most of it. Cheryl and I ransacked the exhibition hall. We were given samples of Taylor ham, a delicious ham with a lingering aftertaste, as well as key chains with miniature Taylor hams. Smithfield hams, the pride of Virginia, are full hams. These Taylor hams were rolls covered in white canvas.

The boys were at another booth and when they saw our key chains they wanted some, too. The Taylor ham booth was in the back corner of the exhibition hall, which was under the grandstand. The fellow at the booth gave everyone more ham samples and the boys received their key chains.

Happy with our freebies, we blasted back out onto the midway. Cheryl wanted a kewpie doll. Cheryl was a pretty little girl with honey brown hair, a sweet smile and a cute nose. All the Shellenbergers were fine-looking people, and boys and men melted at the sight of Cheryl.

Kenny—Mr. Big, because he was in third grade—said he'd win her a kewpie. You had to swing a hammer, which would send a plug up a scale. The higher the plug rose, the more prizes you received.

Kenny, who was actually no bigger than a minute, meant to impress Cheryl. I was disgusted. He could hardly lift the hammer, but he hit the pad. The plug rose pitifully, then slid right back down. No prize, just a smartass comment from the carny telling him to eat his Wheaties.

Crestfallen, Kenny stood there, his big eyes imploring. A teenage boy had been watching. He walked over, paid his money, picked up the hammer as though it were a toothpick and knocked the pad so hard the plug hit the top with a ring.

The mothers admired him. We kids stared agape. He grabbed a kewpie and a box with a chameleon in it tethered by a chain. He handed them both to Cheryl, gave the carny a dirty look and told Kenny, "Keep trying."

Then he walked off.

We all learned that help shows up in the most surprising, delightful ways or, as Aunt Mimi often said, "The Lord moves in mysterious ways, his wonders to perform."

I asked Mother if I could return to the cattle judging. She said that was fine, and I told the group I'd meet them at the tractor exhibition.

No one worried about a five-year-old going off alone. Also, people knew you.

The Herefords drew me. So many people raised Angus, but I liked Herefords. I liked the polled Herefords also, but the large chestnut animals with the long horns fascinated me. I sat and watched the cleaned and primped behemoths being led into the ring. The judge watched them move, checked out front, rear, left and right. Then he'd make his decision. Most of the judges were officials in the various cattle-breed associations and some were professors at Penn State, which boasts a fine agricultural department.

Dad would buy flesh on the hoof for his market. He would show up at the various judging exhibitions and then buy the animals that appealed to him based on what he felt the quality of the meat would be. Dad couldn't slaughter the animals. He'd slaughtered one bull when he was a young man and swore he would never do that again. But he would dress the carcasses.

I hoped he'd show up for the Herefords but he didn't, so after the judging I skipped back to the tractors. Mom had given me fifty cents (oh the wealth), so I stopped to buy a candy apple.

I found my cousin Kenny sitting on a big John Deere row-crop tractor. Mom, Cheryl and Eileen were looking at other tractors. I started to climb up, which wasn't easy, but Kenny put his foot on my head.

"Girls can't drive tractors."

"You're soft as a grape."

Wade agreed with me. He and I usually agreed on most things anyway. He said it didn't matter about being a girl.

Kenny, lording it over us, grew belligerent.

I vaulted up by stepping on the PTO, the rotating part that sticks out of the back of the tractor, and Kenny swung around in the seat to swat me down. I crowned him with my candy apple. Those things are hard.

Kenny saw stars; then he saw red, sticky red in his hair.

We fought over the seat. Mother heard the commotion but so did Violet, a leading light in the 4-H Club and a two-ton Tessie if ever there was one. She waddled over to reprove me just as Kenny kicked me off the seat. I landed on the hind back wheel.

Wade crawled up on the other side of the tractor. One fight is as good as another. It was king of the hill played out on a spanking-new green and yellow John Deere, the Rolls-Royce of tractors.

Violet pulled me off the hind wheel.

"That's no way for a lady to behave."

"None of your business," I saucily replied.

"You're Jack Young all over again." She pointed her finger at me.

Jack Young was my natural maternal grandfather, a power in the Republican Party and a county commissioner to boot. He was not universally admired, but then, what politician is?

"You're a sow all over again." I whacked at her with my candy apple, besmirching her floral-print dress.

Mother arrived, grabbed the candy apple and smacked my butt hard. "Apologize!"

"But I'm not sorry."

"You'll be good and sorry in a skinny minute." She raised her hand to me.

"I'm sorry."

Mother wanted to give Violet money to clean her dress, but she refused it. She felt compelled to inform Mother as to the future I could expect if I stayed a "rowdy hoyden," then she flounced off.

Mother, embarrassed, punished me. "You can't go with Aunt Mimi to the grandstand tonight."

A shot to the heart. "He started it!"

"Did not."

"Did too."

Kenny prudently remained in the driver's seat, fearing another sock if he climbed down.

"She hit me on the head with her candy apple." He bent over so the red goo could be seen in his white-blond hair.

"What's the matter with you?" Mother sternly reproached me.

"He said girls can't drive tractors."

"Why do you listen to that stuff? You can drive a tractor when you're big enough."

She was right. I'd seen farm women drive tractors.

"He made me mad."

"Then it's your fault for letting him get under your skin."

Cheryl, not a speck of dirt on her dress, watched silently. I was in jeans, of course. I glared at her, wondering how she could be so perfect and how it was I was always landing in hot water.

"Yes, ma'am. Am I really not going to the grandstand show?"

"Correct."

Kenny swelled with satisfaction, waiting for the tears to fall. They didn't.

"And why did you hit Violet?"

"She pulled Reets off the tractor wheel," Wade said.

"And she said I was Jack Young all over again."

"That bitch!" Mother forgot herself. "I'd wring her fat neck except I can't get my hands around it."

I giggled. I knew who my natural mother was. It wasn't a big deal. I couldn't remember when I'd been told who she was. I didn't have a clue about my natural father except that the summer before, Mom had taken me to see Richmond, Mount Vernon, Montpelier and Monticello. I remember only three things from this tour, which as I recall was to take a break from Mother Brown, who was on the warpath about something. I remember mule-drawn carts at the C&O station at Charlottesville, Dolley Madison's pretty grave and Mother's commenting, "Your father's people are from here. One of your relatives founded Hampden-Sydney College."

I don't remember another thing. And I knew not to ask about my natural father. Somehow I just knew.

Well, Violet's jab about Jack Young didn't bother me as much as it bothered Mother. Neither one of us much liked Juliann's father. As to Juliann, she rarely returned to visit her father, and if he treated her the way he treated me, small wonder.

Mother fumed at Violet's barb. Eileen laughed because Mother's bursts of temper, so long as they weren't directed at you, were funny.

Seeing my chance, I said, "I am sorry, Mom, but she was wrong."

"You bet she was." More expletives followed.

"Will you forgive me and let me go to the grandstand with Aunt Mimi?"

"No. You're too clever by half. You had no business climbing up on this tractor and picking a fight. If I have to, kid, I will beat good manners into your skin."

Being denied the big show was both punishment and incentive. I would develop self-control if it killed me.

That night Dad woke me up. He must have heard the whole story but he didn't say anything. He put the big blue stuffed horse next to me in bed.

Silks and Sons
of Bitches

ALTHOUGH BANNED FROM ATTENDING THE GRANDSTAND SHOW, I was allowed to spend all day Saturday at the fair so long as I stuck with Mother.

While I had seen the backstretch before, foxhunts before, Christmas pageants before, I was now able to put them in the order of seasons. I could also recall other people clearly.

I knew I had a past, that there had been life before I arrived, and that life was being played out around me. I wanted to know everything. Language came so easily to me that I could speak and read beyond my years.

I was learning from other people. This was a good thing because Mom put me to work.

The York Fair's track brought in horsemen from Pennsylvania, Maryland, West Virginia, even a few other states. Harness racing was big in those days.

The last generation born before the automobile took over was at this time gliding toward late middle age. The real old-timers harked back to the 1870s, when your carriage, cart or wagon displayed your place in society. They remembered when the arrival of a coach in four meant someone violently rich was about to cross their threshold. A light, graceful phaeton meant summer elegance, and the horses who pulled these works of art were works of art themselves. Harness racing grew out of the day when one swell drove up next to another and said, "Bet my trotter is faster than yours."

Harness racing, like steeplechasing, springs from the country as naturally as alfalfa and red-bud clover.

Hanover Shoe Farm bred the best Standardbreds in America. Standardbreds are pacers and trotters and pull behind them a cart called a sulky.

Many of the horses racing at the York Fair had been bred a few miles away at the stud. Naturally, any horse from Kentucky raised our competitive spirits to a fever pitch.

It wasn't that we didn't love Thoroughbred racing. We did. But the nearest good track was every bit of forty miles away. Forty miles over two-lane highways took forever.

Betting wasn't allowed at the county fair. That didn't stop anyone.

Children could watch the races from the grandstand. Mother said that was no way to learn about horses. I needed to prowl the backstretch and the shedrow barns.

She threw a burlap rag over my shoulder, took me by the hand and sashayed by the guard. (Rubbing a horse with burlap brings up a satiny sheen to the coat.)

"Julia." He nodded. He didn't blink an eye as I walked through.

The air was golden as only September light can make it. The smell of harness leather, sweat, hoof dressing and liniment filled my nostrils. The perfume of happiness.

People waved to Mom. A man driving by in blistering red silks nodded to her, his whip jiggling with each step.

She pointed out various horses to me. "That one has a kind eye. That one has an offset knee."

I'd ask what she meant and she patiently explained. Mother would have made a fine teacher because she was clear and organized. Actually, she could have been an army general in charge of logistics. Daddy said she had a "figuring" mind.

At the last set of barns Mom stopped at a set of stalls whose stable colors were yellow and brown. A wiry man, not much bigger than myself, was wiping down a dark bay. Mother knew him. Shanks was his nickname. She asked if he'd watch me for five minutes while she went to church. That meant she was placing a bet.

So I sat on an overturned bucket and quietly watched him. He asked if I liked horses and I said better than anything except for cats. I asked him if he was a driver and he said, "Used to be. I'm a trainer now. I can train more horses than I can drive."

"What's your best horse?"

"Come on, honey. I'll show you."

He picked me up and held me so I could look in the stall of another bay mare. She didn't look like much but I said she was beautiful.

"Pretty is as pretty does. That's the first thing you should know about horses. She won her heat earlier."

He named a time but it didn't mean anything to me. She was running later in the big race and he knew she was going to win it.

Mom returned, walking me to the lovely wooden building where the contestants were checked out before they went onto the track. This equine backstage made me so excited I couldn't move. I wanted to drink in every single color, sound and face.

I whispered to her that the bay mare was going to win the big race. Shanks had told me.

"Find out anything else?"

"No."

"That's pretty good for starters."

She placed a bet later that day on the horse, and sure enough, the mare cleaned up and so did Mom.

Haunting the backstretch became something we did together as long as Mom lived—that and going to pickup fights, some of them bare-knuckle.

Three sports Mother knew forward and backward: racing, boxing (especially the middleweight and heavyweight divisions) and baseball.

I liked being useful to Mother. It shaved the edge off when she'd call me "Ill." She was furious at Violet for casting up my origins, yet she'd do it herself whenever I annoyed her. It was confusing. I wasn't about to tell her this was unfair, however, because I knew what could happen. Once, when I was three or four, Mother and I were downtown in York. It was cold. I must have been acting muley and she must have been cold and tired because she hauled me off to the reform school, which was surrounded by an iron fence with decorative arrows on top of it. She told me that was where bad kids were dumped and if I didn't shape up she'd drag me right up those steps and fling me inside. She scared me that time.

But even if I hadn't felt I had to earn my way, not be a burden, I still would have wanted to be useful. It's in my nature, just as gambling was in Mother's nature.

She wasn't a fool about it. True gambling operates on the premise that greed can be satisfied by luck. For Juts, gambling was a flash of excitement, a challenge to see if she could pick the winner. She never bet more than she could afford to lose. She rattled off sums wagered as she rattled off batting averages. She won more than she lost and on this occasion she won twenty dollars. She gave me five dollars, the most money I'd ever held in my hand.

"I can buy my paint box."

"You will not." She glared at me.

"But it's my money."

"You're putting that money in a savings account, which we'll open Monday, and that's the end of it."

There was something about the flush of red in her face that warned me this concerned more than saving money. Even if I had to put the five dollars in a savings account, I felt rich and that felt good.

The magic of that lush fall swirls in my memory like the spun candy of the fair. It was one of the happiest times of my life.

11

The Virgin Mary Pays a Call

Virginia, aunt mimi's elder daughter, gave birth to a third son, Terry. Tiny, resembling his mother in facial structure and his father in coloring, he became the center of attention.

Kenny and Wade and I ignored him. He was a pretty baby but he was boring. We found there wasn't much you could do with a baby except change his diapers. Dad said he'd be big in no time and then we'd have another player for our baseball team. We weren't convinced.

After the birth Aunt Ginny couldn't put weight back on. Usually women blow up like a poisoned dog when they're pregnant but she wore down.

I don't know when they knew for certain that Virginia, at age thirty-three, was dying of cancer. Maybe the boys knew before I did.

You could see her wasting away, but she fought back. She didn't want to take to her bed. Julia Ellen, her younger sister, was away at school, the Immaculate Heart of Mary. When she came home even though it wasn't vacation time, that's when I knew it was bad.

Two occurrences stick in my mind from that time. Dad had me in the car when he drove to Aunt Mimi's. He parked in front of the house. Mother was staying with Sis around the clock. He told me to stay in the car. It was cold. An eon passed, and I got antsy. So I walked home, a few miles away.

One of our neighbors, Helen Stambaugh, saw me walk up the driveway. She called Dad. He came home frantic. I'd never seen Dad lose his temper, and a man that strong ought not to lose his temper. Shaking, he spanked me up every step to the upstairs. I didn't utter a peep. I was too terrified.

I had scared him half to death. The poor fellow, exhausted and sad, had come out from his sister-in-law's house to find an empty car. Had I been kidnapped? Had I been run over on the road? He must have felt as if someone had ripped his stomach out.

The other event happened at Ginny's farm out in Shiloh. A thunderstorm rose up even though it was cold out. Kenny, Wade and I were playing outside because it was too depressing to be in the house. The storm rolled over, and then behind the house appeared a rainbow of startling color. I thought Jesus would slide down that rainbow. We ran in the house to get the adults. They came out on the porch and clapped their hands.

That was the last time I saw Virginia stand on her feet.

Ginny was a quiet, warmhearted woman who was some kind of saint. I mean it. There was only goodness in her. People felt it. She lived for her husband, Ken, and the kids. Ken had survived the front lines at Okinawa, being wounded, coming home to more hard times, having to eke out an existence. Things had just begun to pick up for him at the farm, and now he was losing his wife and would be left with three sons to care for, one of them six months old.

Virginia died at Aunt Mimi's. Cheerful, no matter how searing the pain, loving in the face of her approaching death, that woman taught me courage. You could smell the cancer. It ate through to the surface of her skin. The sickly sweet odor of rot clung to her, and even though Mom, Aunt Mimi and Julia Ellen changed her bandages regularly, the fluids and blood kept seeping through.

Despite the grimness, no one minded being in Ginny's presence. She shared with each of us everything she had: her heart and her unshakable faith in the goodness, mercy and wisdom of God.

As I watched her suffer I felt the reverse. God was a bully. How could he allow Ginny to suffer from breast cancer? I could think of a few kids and adults that I'd have liked to see in her place and I prayed for him to give them her affliction. God didn't see things my way.

Just before Virginia died she sat up in the bed and said she saw the Virgin Mary. The Blessed Virgin Mother was coming to take her from this life. Radiance shone over her face. She closed her eyes, surrendering to this new adventure.

I cried. I cried until I had a headache and was sick to my stomach. While the women prepared the body, I cried and cried. Dad cried, too. Ken was so distraught we didn't see him. I don't know who was taking care of him. Kenny, Wadie and I didn't know what had hit us.

Many people came to Ginny's funeral. Flowers filled the church and a large satin ribbon with *Mother* embroidered on it was on the huge floral blanket covering the casket. Ken Bowers, a powerfully built man, shrank before my eyes. I saw the savagery of grief, but I also saw the power of love. No man looks like that or cries like that if he hasn't loved a woman with his body, his mind, his heart and his soul.

I didn't understand that love but I saw it.

After the funeral we went back to the farm in Shiloh. The adults hovered in the kitchen. Ken wanted the boys with him. I went to find them.

I walked up the narrow wooden steps to their bedroom. Kenny and Wade lay on their beds, and behind them on the wall was the embroidered ribbon that read *Mother.* I had never felt so desolate, helpless, useless. I kissed them and went downstairs.

On the surface, Ken eventually recovered. Some years later he married the woman he'd hired as his housekeeper. I don't think he ever really got over Virginia's death, though. At the end of his life, when he was dying of lung cancer, he visited Aunt Mimi and Mom and cried over Virginia. He cried for the times he'd been mean to her. He cried for the stupid things he'd done, for his hair-trigger temper, for the times he'd hit her, which weren't many but it only takes one. He wanted forgiveness and the Buckingham sisters did forgive him, although Aunt Mimi couldn't let slip the opportunity to tell him only God could really forgive him.

By that time I was a grown woman and I happened to be home visiting Mom. I had always adored Ken. What woman didn't? In his twenties he had looked like that other blond titan, Gary Cooper. And Ken aged well too, like Cooper.

He told me that the pain he'd felt when Ginny died was worse than any pain he'd felt when he was wounded fighting the Japanese.

Pain is a purifier. I know that now. I even knew it then, and yet when I remember those two little boys lying in bed, eyes hollow, the embroidered ribbon over their beds, I still wish we could learn how unique people are before we lose them.

12

Bait Your Own Hook

MOTHER WORE A WATCH WITH A FACE SO SMALL I DON'T know how she could tell time. This was her way of proving her eyes were good. At forty-six she had little cause to worry; she looked like a woman in her early thirties and she acted like one who was fifteen.

The fragrance of honeysuckle pervaded the air. A low fog hugged the rolling hills. Ginny had slipped away from us six months before and we all missed her.

A child's sense of loss is different from an adult's. In some ways it is far greater and in others more superficial. Each time I thought of Ginny I imagined she was playing a harp, wearing a flowing white gown and conversing with the BVM and Jesus.

Uncle Kenny kept his nose to the grindstone. Apart from work, the boys were his focus and Aunt Mimi's too. She was bound and determined that one of them should become a priest, to make up for the fact that her daughters had not taken vows. Even at that age Kenny and Wade's unsuitability for a life of denial and service was obvious.

We hoped Aunt Mimi would take vows herself. Her despotism reached new heights. Certainly she felt the death of her daughter sincerely but she never missed a chance to remind us of her cruel loss. Then again, the Blessed Virgin Mother gave up one of her sons and Mary Magdalene suffered, too. I wondered why suffering was glorified. Crucifixes gave me the creeps. Not only did they adorn every wall of Mimi's house, she had a tiny one on the dashboard of her Nash.

Torn and bleeding Jesus, his eyes rolled to heaven, greeted me constantly. I loved Jesus but I liked to think of him throwing the money changers out of the temple. Aunt Mimi gravitated toward the crown of thorns.

On this early summer morning, Mother checked and rechecked her watch. We were standing at the top of Queen Street Hill, fishing poles and tackle boxes in our hands.

Right on the dot, 6:30 A.M., Aunt Mimi roared out of the fog, stopping at the beer joint that also stood at the top of Queen Street Hill. Since cars possessed speedometers, Aunt Mimi felt one should use them: bury the needle.

We hopped in. I had the backseat to myself since the boys were with their father and Julia Ellen was off doing something exciting. Fifteen years older than I, Julia Ellen dazzled me. She played the piano, she was going to nursing school, she dressed like a model and she had so many boyfriends that Aunt Mimi fretted over it. If she had not been so attractive, my aunt would have fretted even more.

She used to tell her popular daughter, "It's just as easy to marry a rich man as a poor one," and then she'd fling up the example of Virginia's marrying handsome but poor Ken, working her fingers to the bone to make ends meet.

Julia would sass back, "Oh, Mom."

That doesn't sound like sassing, but any independent opinion counted as rebellion in my aunt's eyes.

Needless to say, I wasn't thrilled at the prospect of fishing at Long Level with Mother and the saint-in-residence. Butch came, too; that was Sis's big Boston Bull. He was big as a Boxer and cunning. Mickey loathed the sight of him, never missing an opportunity to swat and run.

Dogs contributed to Aunt Mimi's image. Buster, elegant in his permanent tuxedo, beautifully muscled, did suit her. Hounds would never do and gun dogs had too much fur. She wouldn't waste time combing them out.

Butch and I stared out the back window at the corn shoots breaking through the chocolate soil. The apple trees had bloomed late that year, and white petals covered the ground.

By the time we reached Long Level at the Susquehanna, the fog was burning off the river. Way on the other side, for it's a wide, impressive river, were train tracks.

A moored raft bobbed in the water maybe ten yards offshore.

Mother set up a fishing camp: three chairs, three towels, three buckets for our catch. The hamper of food stayed in the car because of the ants. She said we'd have lunch at the proper time. She and Aunt Mimi shared a thermos of coffee. I had a thermos of hot tea—I loved tea. A cooler of pop sat next to Uncle Mearl's truck, too heavy to haul far.

Mother favored tiny red worms because they wiggled. She declared that fish like wigglers. Aunt Mimi preferred flies and she taught me how to tie them. She liked to watch them laze on the surface of the water. I contented myself with night crawlers. Wigglers were too tough for me to handle. I'd drop them and Mother would get impatient with me for wasting bait.

Mother combed her hair.

"Juts, what are you doing?"

"Combing my hair."

"There's no one here but us," Aunt Mimi said.

"The fish might look at me."

Aunt Mimi laughed. She hadn't laughed for a long time. Then she and Mom dug little holes for the butts of their fishing poles, left them and waded in the water, thereby scaring off any possible strike. They didn't really want to catch anything.

They talked. I swam through the cold water to the raft to throw in my line.

Aunt Mimi said that Delphine Falkenroth had the most beautiful hands, so beautiful that she modeled for glove and hand cream manufacturers in New York City. I tuned out after that and waited for my whale to bite. Not one nibble.

The sun danced on the surface of the water and I looked back at the two women, so alike they could have been twins. Mom was making Aunt Mimi laugh. Some of the terrible gloom was lifting and for a moment I could see what Aunt Mimi had been like as a girl. Standing in the water up to her knees, her skirt rolled up, head back, laughing at Mother, she kicked some water at Mom. Then Mother kicked water back. The Chesterfield sizzled when Mom flicked it in the river. Within seconds they were having a water fight. They screamed and laughed, and I was so jealous. I wanted a sister.

I had one. She was about to show up.

Sleepwalker

PATTY, ACCOMPANIED BY JULIANN, OUR MOTHER, APPEARED ONE summer day. Two years older than I was, dark, quiet and shy, she was going to share my room. That wasn't so bad. She displayed little interest in horses, which irritated me, but far worse, she couldn't play baseball.

Horses, being big, scared people. I figured given enough time Patty would come around and join me in jumping on the backs of the Percherons and Belgians grazing in neighborhood pastures. Their backs were so broad, my legs so short, that I couldn't drop a leg over their sides. I'd grab the mane and bounce up and down to make them go, which meant they'd trot three steps and then go back to grazing. I must have felt like a large fly to them.

Patty had visited us before, when I was very small. I had a dim memory of that, but I must have been around three, because I didn't know she was my half sister. This time I knew.

As I said earlier, Mom and Dad, quite intelligently, told me early that I was adopted, although I can't recall a specific conversation. It seemed like a kernel of information that grew and opened as I did. As time went on I understood what it meant. I was proud of the fact that I had been chosen. Other parents were stuck with their kids.

I called my natural mother Aunt Jule, but I saw her so infrequently that I had no recollection of her other than that she was Jack and Sadie Young's girl. As Sadie had died in the 1930s, I never knew her, but Mother, Aunt Mimi and Big Mimi talked about her as though she were still alive. When you love people that much they are alive, I believe, even though their bodies are gone. Sadie was a shadowy presence for me, a benevolent ghost. Jule was something else.

When she dropped off Patty I scrutinized her every feature. I didn't much resemble her or Patty. Jule was a dead ringer for Jane Russell, not yet popular but soon to be a major star. Everything about her suggested voluptuousness. No wonder she drove men crazy.

Mom said that because Sadie had died when Jule was so young, she had had no guidance. Her father, Mom said, had been too busy running after women—Jack could no more be faithful than a turtle could fly. At least while Sadie lived, he attempted discretion. Once she died of double pneumonia, he caroused openly. Some people blamed his behavior on Sadie's death and felt sympathy for him, said it "took him that way." Mom said, "Bullshit." I said nothing.

Anyway, Jule delighted Mom since she had raised her after Sadie died. The two of them chattered like blue jays. I eyed Patty. She barely spoke to me and not one speck of dirt marred her dress. I would change that. The relationship between Mother and Jule interested me not a bit. My relationship with Patty, however, captured my full attention.

As soon as the parade of manners was done, I shot out of the house. As to the parade of manners, remember, Mother was born in Maryland and we lived almost on the Mason-Dixon line. That meant I'd acquire good manners if it killed us both.

Ladies and gentlemen were judged by their children's doings as well as by their own. Therefore I had to sit down, cross my legs and not speak until spoken to. To this day it unnerves me if a child walks right up and starts chattering. It violates everything I have been taught about how one must literally climb into society, each rung being a further refinement of deportment.

Okay. I sat there. I smiled. Jule, herself a product of relentless etiquette, inquired about my schoolwork. I said I loved school and couldn't wait to start second grade.

This is the way it works. The adult asks questions. The child isn't supposed to ask the adult questions unless it's something like this: "Mrs. So-and-So, your brooch is so pretty. I bet there's a story behind it." We were taught to admire something about a person and to get them to talk about themselves. Once I asked a family friend, Mrs. Myrtle, if she ate a lot of oysters to get her beautiful pearls. When she'd recovered from laughing herself sick, she told me about pearls.

Mother declared it was white-trash to talk about yourself. Not that that stopped her, but the way in which she talked about herself was so original, so irreverent, that she wasn't exactly violating the rule. Because the second rule of how to behave in correct society is that you should be amusing. If you can't be amusing, be pleasant.

Another rule is never to discuss politics or religion, which we discussed endlessly within the family. I hated this part of the parade of manners. I wanted to know what other people thought. Still do.

You are displayed by your somewhat apprehensive parent. If you pass muster, the guest generally says something like, "Well, Juts, I can see she is turning into quite a little lady." Ugh. Or "I have enjoyed talking to you. You're a bright little girl." More tolerable. As soon as you receive the desired compliment your relieved parent dismisses you. Tedious as this ordeal proved, you picked up at least the minimum of social graces. As you grew, these lessons expanded. Finally you entered cotillion. That happened at age twelve. Cotillion is to manners what West Point is to a military life. I was slotted to attend as soon as I turned twelve. (You put up your child the minute he or she drew breath.) It wasn't expensive; in fact, money had nothing to do with cotillion. It was about your place in the community, and if you wanted to succeed, you'd better endure those years of boredom.

This ruthless determination to create ladies and gentlemen was not restricted by race. Not that our cotillion was integrated, it wasn't, but my colored sisters (I use *colored* because that was the polite word then. If I'd said *black* Mother would have washed my mouth out with soap. I'll try to use the word that matches the times) were enduring boot camp for manners. If you ever meet a southerner who doesn't have good manners, it means only one thing: They are trifling people.

If a child failed the parade, the phone lines heated up. Everyone knew. The parent was shamed. No one blamed the child, though. If you had children, it was your job to prepare them to be productive, pleasant people. As Mother used to say, "If I don't correct you, the world will."

Well, I passed the parade of manners, as did Patty.

Once we were outside, Mom and Jule could talk about whatever interested them and we could play. Patty liked to swing, so I pushed her on the swing. Used to boys, I wasn't good at handling a sensitive peer. Cheryl was, though. She came over. Cheryl had two older brothers, which had toughened her up, but she was still "girly." Patty liked her, but then everyone liked Cheryl, and her younger sister, Judy, was getting big enough that she wasn't a drag anymore.

That night Patty slept in my room. I didn't mind but I told Mom I'd sleep on the floor; I wouldn't sleep with anyone in my bed. So I slept on the bedroll with Mickey next to me, and Patty slept in the bed. The next thing I knew I heard a thump. It was pitch-dark. Patty was sleepwalking.

Fascinated, I followed her. When she reached the top of the stairs I was scared she'd fall down. I woke her up and she screamed bloody murder. Mom and Dad clicked on the lights.

I didn't know what sleepwalking was exactly. I explained to my parents as best I could because I was afraid they would think I had beaten her up. The boys and I fought, so it followed that I might take a pop at Patty.

To my surprise, Mother not only didn't blame me, she made us both warm milk. Dad went back to bed.

The next day, Cheryl and Judy came over again. Mother called me inside for a minute while Patty was happily occupied.

"You be gentle with her."

"I am," I protested.

"You've been a perfect hostess." Mother was standing over the sink. The front of her apron was wet, and little soap bubbles floated from the sink. "Patty's bounced from foster home to foster home. It's upset her. She's a sweet child. You take care of her while she's here."

That Mom, Dad and Aunt Mimi could convey Patty's trials to me says something about their ability to communicate. The other great thing about all three of them was they never talked down to you.

I did my best by Patty and then Jule picked her up a week or two later. I kissed Patty goodbye and I never saw her again.

Children are much more resilient than most adults. Forgive me for stating the obvious. An adult would worry about seeing her natural mother, about realizing that Patty was her half sister. I didn't.

Mom was Juts. I thought of Jule as a broodmare. As for Patty, I liked her but I felt no great rush of kinship. My bonds were forged from use, not from blood, although I must have heard Mother and Aunt Mimi intone "Blood tells" a thousand times.

Blood does tell. You inherit your talents and your physical attributes as well as a propensity for certain diseases. That's all it tells.

Love doesn't come via the womb. It comes from work, worry and the willingness to discipline and guide a child. I looked at Jule and felt very little other than that she was nice to me. I looked at Julia and Ralph. They were Mom and Dad. To them I owed honor and obedience. The obedience part was hard.

Have Hotpad,
Will Travel

J ULE FOXHUNTED WITH GREEN SPRINGS IN MARYLAND AND WITH ROSE
Tree outside of Philadelphia. Because of her skill, people welcomed her.

American hunting is quite different from English foxhunting, although
there are some Americans who live to imitate the old country. Our territory is different, and because of that, our farming practices are different;
we never passed an enclosure law, as did England in the seventeenth century.

Foxes will wipe out your hens and geese if you don't supply protection.
Even if you do, they'll get in the henhouse. But here, for the most part,
foxes are not the troublesome predators they are for the English farmer.
Also, we haven't lived in North America long enough to wipe out those
animals who prey on the fox or the fox's prey. We still have balance,
although how long that can last with our foolish development policies is
anyone's guess.

Poor people could hunt here. Slaves hunted as grooms. The mix from
the very beginning was democratic. If you had a fit horse or mule and
could ride, and if you wore clean attire no matter how frayed, you were
welcome.

This quality, this openness is what's best about American hunting. It's
what's best about America, period.

Today, the fox isn't killed. The hunt should more accurately be called a
chase. That doesn't mean an old or sick fox won't get caught, but it's quite
rare. In my youth people did hunt to kill.

I'd wanted to hunt since I could remember. Mother adamantly opposed
it. The reason was not danger; Juts deplored cowardice. She said we
couldn't afford a horse. That was the truth, but I could have borrowed or

rented one. I was willing to sign my life away for hard work at a boarding stable not far from our house, just to ride.

She wouldn't budge. On the other hand, I could ride draft horses all day long, and she was also happy for me to be, as she put it, "a useful groundsman."

This backfired in a strange way that fall.

I loved to read and I loved to draw. If the weather was bad, I didn't mind staying inside and reading. As much as I wanted a horse, I also wanted a paint set. A glimmer of talent provoked Dad to encourage me. Dad could draw anything.

That year at the York Fair I won a paint set, a little oil set with twelve tubes of paint. I won the set because a drawing I had made of a horse, what else, was entered in a competition for grade-schoolers and I won fourth place.

I was ecstatic.

I also had a small square loom on which I could make hotpads out of old dyed nylons and scrap fabrics, which were easy to get. I'd sell them for a quarter. I was big enough to push a lawn mower, so I did that, too. I was going to make enough money to buy a horse.

The Martin Memorial Library of East Market and Queen contained some lovely volumes with colored pictures of great paintings. The Impressionists intrigued me. Not that I knew what they were or their relationship to art history. The colors were pretty. I also discovered Stubbs and Munnings, sporting artists. Since they painted horses I liked them better than anything, and I loved Corot.

I thought I would grow up and paint country scenes and horses and make enough money to buy my own horses. Clearly, I wasn't cut out to be a financial wizard, but Dad didn't pop my bubble by telling me artists starved.

I set up my paints in the basement. The coal furnace was the only other thing down there. I had the entire basement for my province.

I painted whatever I saw for one whole day. I showed my creations to Mother, who evidenced no enthusiasm. She usually praised my efforts no matter how puny. I decided I was really awful and needed to apply myself.

Suddenly Mother lost her temper, marched down to the basement and threw my paints everywhere. She yelled that I was a spoiled brat—I'd better get these ideas out of my head and learn something useful.

Mother's rage put wings to my feet. I raced out of there. She usually cooled off after an hour or two.

I was devastated that she had destroyed my paint set. I was also bullshit mad.

From my perch in the enormous black walnut in the back, I watched her hang up the wash. I jumped down, ran inside, emptied out my piggy bank and packed my loom and materials in a small red cardboard suitcase. I walked to the top of Queen Street Hill and caught the bus heading southeast.

When the bus came to the end of its route, near the Mason-Dixon line, I got of and started walking. I knew where the Maryland border was. I intended to walk through Maryland into Virginia. The sun set. It grew cooler. I forgot about getting to Virginia.

As luck would have it, friends of Mom and Dad's lived in a neat brick house across from a wayside ice cream parlor. I hoped they would help me.

I knocked on the door. Mrs. Rau let me in. I told her that if she'd let me spend the night, I'd make her a hotpad. I explained everything. She ordered one hotpad from me in red and white. I set up my loom in her kitchen and got to work. She disappeared but I was intent on my task and didn't notice.

A half hour later Dad appeared. He thanked Mrs. Rau. I gave her the hotpad. She paid me a quarter because I hadn't spent the night and therefore, she said, I'd earned the money.

I wanted to be with Daddy but I didn't want to go home. I asked him if I could live at the store. Mickey could come too and catch mice, and I'd sweep the floors, put the parsley on the shaved dry ice in the meat case and even help with inventory. I wanted to work. In retrospect I understand that the desire to work was one of my strongest drives. I didn't just want to ride horses, I wanted to work with them. I wanted to paint and I was willing to meet people, sell them my idea and paint their horses. No matter how unrealistic these schemes might have been, they were connected by the drive to be useful and independent.

Dad pretended to consider this. I told him what had happened. I think Mother had already told him, and probably more than she told me. He took me to a little restaurant and the two of us ate like grown-ups. I should add as an aside that children could not eat with adults until they displayed the ability to handle utensils, chew with their mouth closed and listen to the adults. No interruptions were allowed. When Kenny was invited to eat Sunday dinner with the grown-ups I had nearly perished from envy.

Eating with Dad was a big deal. I had passed the test.

He said, "You know that painting of the windmill by the front door?"

"Yes."

"Your Aunt Jule painted that when she was fourteen and she lived with us."

"So?"

"Mom is afraid you will like Aunt Jule better than you like her."

He tried to explain that since Mom couldn't have children, she was worried that someday I'd love Jule more than I loved her. The fact that I displayed a proclivity identical to Juliann's scared her.

Both Daddy and I knew that was silly, but Mother was radical about it.

"What about my natural father? What if I turn out like him? Is that going to upset her, too?"

"Don't worry about him."

"Will you be cross with me if I turn out different than Mom wants?"

He put my hand in his huge one. "You're *my* girl."

I decided to go home. When we walked through the door Mother's eyes were red and she wasn't even smoking. Aunt Mimi and Uncle Mearl were there, too. Mother said she was sorry. I said that was all right and I went to bed, happy to be with Mickey.

The next night, after work, Daddy brought me an ancient black Underwood typewriter with a book teaching you how to type.

I never tried to paint again. I never asked for riding lessons. I continued to hop on the draft horses. I watched other kids ride. I watched the hunt go off. I kept my mouth shut. I made hotpads. I looked for any way to make money and I saved every penny. I taught myself how to type and started writing little stories.

So great was my loyalty to my mother that I didn't buy my first horse until I was thirty-three. I called to tell her.

She sounded pleased. "You got what you always wanted. More power to you, kid."

Funny, though, I didn't take riding lessons until the year after she died.

The Rubber
Tablecloth

MOTHER'S SOLE ENCOUNTER WITH FICTION WAS *GONE WITH the Wind* when it was first published. Three chapters into it she set it aside. Mom couldn't sit still long enough to read anything except the newspapers and her daily devotional.

My ravenous appetite for the printed word baffled her. Not that she was against it, but a love of books was so removed from her realm I could have been studying astrophysics. She'd trot into my basement workroom, examine my library books (all organized by due date), wrinkle her brow and toss another load of coal into the furnace.

Both parents believed that if a child knocks on a door, open it. When I was five I got my library card, although not without a struggle.

The Martin Memorial Library, a brick Federal building on the corner of Market and Queen Streets, had an interior balcony, an iron railing protecting the distracted reader from falling onto the main lobby below. This airy, open architecture, colonial in inspiration, invited me in to read and reflect. No doubt that was its purpose.

The minute Mom took me into the building, I made a beeline for the upstairs balcony. I couldn't reach high, so I sat on the floor pulling books from the bottom shelves. The first one I yanked out was a small, light blue volume with a black Grecian frieze on the top, *Bulfinch's Mythology*. The drawings, such as Icarus falling into the sea, jumped out at me. Mother found *Little Women*. She liked the movie, so she thought I'd like the book. We took the two books to the graceful wooden checkout counter, polished with years of use.

The lady behind the counter had a pen hanging on a chain around her neck. Maybe she was Mother's age. At that time everyone was vastly older than I was. She wouldn't write me a card and she said those books were above my level of learning.

My head didn't reach to the top of the checkout counter. My ears worked fine. Mother waxed impatient. She wanted to see the librarian in charge. The pen lady was the librarian in charge.

"Come here, kid." Mother pulled over a chair, parked it in front of the checkout counter and lifted me onto it. "Read for the lady."

She opened to the first page of *Little Women* and I read. The librarian, none too keen about the disturbance we were causing, was startled that I could read at that age. The brand-new library card, stiff cardboard in a little manila sleeve, was forked over.

Now, I can't pretend that I comprehended the real meaning of the myths or of *Little Women,* but I remembered the stories. And from then on, each Friday or Saturday (depending on the season) I would take the bus with Mom or Aunt Mimi to downtown York to exchange my library books for new ones. Five books was the checkout limit, but Mother limited me to two. That way she didn't have to lug the books around as we shopped in the Central Market or ran errands. Two books, one for each of us to carry, was the rule.

The Central Market and the Eastern Market, still operating today and still jammed with meats, poultry, vegetables of every variety, homemade candies and the locally famous Utz and Bon-Ton potato chips, was a kaleidoscope of sounds, smells and people.

Browns' Meat Market stood to the side with its gleaming white cases displaying prime cuts. Dad wouldn't put a choice cut in his case. Prime or nothing. He selected the animals to be slaughtered. If an animal hadn't the rich marbling he thought it should, he'd sell that meat to another butcher. Only the best for Dad's customers. The Browns built a multigeneration reputation for quality, and I expect they had it centuries ago in Swabia, too.

I'd tear down the aisle, put my books behind the counter and ask Dad, Papaw, Uncle Claude or Uncle Earl if there was a job for me. With gravity they'd point to the broom or a case that needed more lamb chops. Yes, they had a job for me, a big one. I'd fling myself into whatever they asked, thinking I was indispensable. Mother used to remark that I wasn't that eager to do housework.

I could rise to an occasion so long as it didn't include housework. She taught me to clean, but no matter how hard Mother tried I wouldn't go near the kitchen. I didn't want to know anything about washing. Under duress I could iron a hanky.

Aunt Mimi complained loudly and to all that I would fail utterly as a wife. She was right.

Iron-willed as I was, Mother wisely sidestepped the issue. She too was willful, but why lock horns? Or as Mom said, "You catch more flies with honey than with vinegar."

Since I was only too eager to perform outside chores, she taught me how to weed. How to tell weeds from good plants. How to identify snails, birds, good snakes and bad snakes. She taught me to respect bats because they were the farmer's friend. She and I put up a big square trellis we'd painted white. There she planted fragrant climbing pink roses, saving the big red roses for the garden closer to the house.

Tea roses soon covered the side of the garage. I loved irises, so we planted them in front of white hollyhocks.

We drew closest together in the garden or walking a shedrow, but I was closer to Dad. It hurt her, but even if she hadn't tormented me about my birth when she was angry, I still would have been closer to Dad. There are some people in life who are kindred spirits. You meet them and feel instantly close. Had Daddy not been here as my father, he would have become my best friend.

Mother was wound tighter than a piano wire; Dad was relaxed. Mother possessed a rapier wit; Dad, good humor. Mother had to be the center of attention; Dad was content to bask in her glow. Mother owned a ferocious temper; Dad barely raised his voice. Mother was highly and combatively intelligent; Dad had only average intelligence but profound insight into people's hearts. Mother could be cruel; Dad didn't have a mean bone in his body. Mother planned ahead; Dad lived in the moment. Mother was fanatical about time; Dad was habitually late. Mother devoutly believed in the Lutheran Church and its dogma; Dad believed God was in the trees, in the sunrise, inside each of us. And most important for me, Mother loved the idea of a daughter, while Dad loved me.

When I finished my "job" at the meat counter I could run through the market. One special market day stands out from all the others. I wanted to go to the Pennsylvania National Horse Show, which was the following weekend. In those days all horses showed together—hunters, jumpers, Saddlebreds, driving horses, even Western horses. Horsemen mixed with one another, swapped stories and learned, since each of the disciplines is different and demanding. A sensational Saddlebred named Wing Commander had taken the county by storm, and I hoped he would appear at the show.

After I raced up and down every aisle, hung over the balcony (my trick to get attention) and smiled at the Amish ladies and gentlemen, I wandered back to the booth. Aunt Mimi was there. Something had changed. No one said anything.

That night when Dad came home from work the three of us sat down in the living room and Mom and Dad tried to explain the situation to me.

Mom's brother George, or "Bucky," looked like Ronald Colman with black wavy hair. This could account for his woman troubles. They chased him a lot. Seven years younger than Mother, he was the baby and thoroughly spoiled by Big Mimi and just about every other woman who came his way. He wasn't lazy, though, as some men of that kind are.

What I got out of the discussion that night was that Bucky's lady friend in Baltimore was an irresponsible shit. After their relationship fizzled she had abandoned her teenage son by her first husband. Dad said the young man had been sleeping in hotel hallways, trying to work and go to school. He had no money and not much to eat. He'd been existing on coffee.

Both Mom and Dad were calm but upset. Mother said they wanted me to think about sharing my basement workroom with this young man. I'd have to give up half the space and I'd have to share other things, too.

I'd shared with Kenny and Wadie. Sometimes I'd be at their farm, sometimes they'd be at Aunt Mimi's and sometimes they'd stay with us. And I'd shared with Patty even though that hadn't lasted long. I thought I was Miss Generosity.

Dad explained this was a little different because this would be his home, not just a stopping place. He would be a member of our family.

Mother said, "We've got a rubber tablecloth. We can stretch it to feed one more."

And so we did.

Eugene Byers moved in that next weekend. Even as a teenager his voice was so deep, pure and melodic that every time he opened his mouth I fell into a trance. His hair was light brown, blond in summer, his smile was wide and generous, he was skinny but was he ever handsome. He's still handsome.

We had little in common, for he was so much older than I. I was a pesky and sometimes truculent kid, especially if he scooted into the bathroom before I did. I admired him, though, even if we weren't close. He would come home from William Penn High School, open his books at the kitchen table and study. He didn't shirk on the chores either.

Mother fell totally in love with him. He was the son she never had. Maybe it's me but I think mothers and sons are closer than mothers and daughters. She bragged about Gene to everyone. He put on a little muscle with good food, becoming even better-looking, if that was possible. His high-school buddies—he made friends easily even though he was more quiet than boisterous—would hang around. Mom was in heaven. She was surrounded by young men. Gene saved enough from odd jobs to buy an Indian motorcycle. He took Mother for a ride. She hopped on that stunning blue machine, hugged Gene's waist and off they went. Then he gave me a ride, too.

The only time Mother ever fussed at him was when he wore golf spikes and ruined her new kitchen linoleum. Dad just shrugged.

Dad loved him, too. And to my surprise I wasn't jealous. Gene became part of the family so quickly that soon it was hard for me to remember a time without him.

What he felt, I don't know. If he spoke of his mother or father, I never heard it. Even if he hated them, he wouldn't have said anything.

As Mother would advise, "People of quality don't wash their dirty linen in public."

Of course, Gene also endured the siege of manners, but his were already pretty good. I suspect he emerged from the womb a gentleman.

The biggest surprise was Aunt Mimi. She could find fly shit in pepper, but she never found fault with Gene.

She was certainly finding enough fault with me and Ginny's children. Kenny wasn't doing so hot in school. Wade could be sullen. Terry was too little to be trouble, for which she thanked the Almighty daily and within our earshot. Withering fire was reserved for me: I was too clever by half, I wouldn't do housework, I wasn't properly grateful, I resisted the One True Church (this was said when Mother wasn't around), I engaged in too many fistfights. Girls don't fight.

Domineering by nature, she was cranky during this time. I think she was upset because her daughter Julia Ellen, the star of the family, was seriously dating a no-'count. He may have been a no-'count, but he was a real hunk. Julia Ellen relished her rebellion. So did we.

Each time he called on her, we'd plague him until he gave us money to leave them alone. I must have eaten more raspberry ice cream at that time than any child in America, because as soon as he'd slide a dime into my palm I'd dash to the store and buy a raspberry ice cream cone. I might vary that and buy an RC Cola, pour a bag of Planters peanuts in it, shake it up with my thumb over the mouth of the bottle and then shoot the ensuing eruption into my mouth. Sometimes I'd aim it at Kenny or Wade. If you time it right, those peanuts are lethal.

Cheryl Shellenberger moved away at the end of the school year—not far, but when you can't drive and the bus lines aren't very good, any distance over two miles is far.

Things changed constantly. Sometimes I liked the changes and sometimes I didn't.

One day that summer between third grade and fourth grade Mom and I were pulling weeds. A boiling black thunderstorm came up so fast we hadn't time to run back into the house. The three of us—Mickey, old now, was with us—ran into the garage.

Lightning hit a tree at the edge of the backyard and hayfield. The snap sizzled, then the agonizing crack of the tree as it split in two.

As we huddled in the garage Mother said, "Thunderstorms are big shows, like vaudeville. The lightning comes when God flips the stage lights, and the thunder is the angels clapping. My mother and Ginny and people you never knew but I did are up there enjoying themselves."

"Mom, I'm not a baby." I was insulted that she'd tell me such a story to soothe me. I thought the storm was exciting. Children like disasters, but then, such events are much more amusing when you don't have to pay the bills.

"I didn't say you were a baby. It's what I imagine." She felt for her cigarettes, which, happily, were dry. She lit one and offered me a puff. This meant I wasn't a baby.

I never much liked the smell or taste of cigarettes, but I wasn't going to pass up the opportunity to have a puff.

"Don't swallow the smoke. Breathe it in and breathe it out." I did. It wasn't so bad.

She brought it back to her lips, red lipstick staining the pure white paper. "Smoking is one of life's greatest pleasures, but it's not good for you. If you do start, you know a lady never walks and smokes at the same time."

"I know."

"And if a gentleman doesn't light a cigarette for you, forget him."

"Yes, ma'am."

"Never three on a match. Bad luck."

It was bad luck, too. Soldiers festering in the trenches learned that the opposing artillery officer had time to find his range when they let a match flicker long enough for three people to light up. She said boys returning from World War I had told her that.

We chatted until the storm finally relented. I never did take up smoking, but now when a wicked big thunderstorm crashes over my head I imagine Dad, Aunt Mimi and other friends up in heaven applauding Mother, who would surely be onstage, offering her commentary on everyone's individual quirks, and then breaking into a dance.

Tweedledum and
Tweedledee

THE FOURTH OF JULY FOUND THE WORLD, OR THE WORLD AS I knew it, crammed onto Aunt Mimi's sweeping porch. Hanging begonias and ferns, potted plants, sparkling painted furniture and a swing lent color to the expanse, for it was a big porch.

A watering tub filled with cracked ice, beer and soda squatted by the wide steps. Rolling Rock, Gunther's, Pabst Blue Ribbon, Carling Black Label, Budweiser, Miller and the occasional jar of country water (moonshine) nestled next to Coca-Cola, RC Cola, Nehi, Dad's root beer, 7-Up and Canada Dry ginger ale. At this time people didn't drink expensive water with tiny bubbles in it.

Hot dogs, hamburgers, barbecue, German potato salad, pickled eggs, deviled eggs, coleslaw, potato chips, floppy soft pretzels with mustard, baked beans with bacon, corn bread, white bread and pumpernickel covered the red, white and blue tablecloth. When all else failed there were ham biscuits, homemade pickles and fried okra, my special favorite.

The finish of the soapbox derby was right at the corner of Aunt Mimi's house. Only boys could compete, which set my teeth on edge. A few years later Mom, Dad and I would get in trouble for wedging me into the derby while flying false colors.

This particular Fourth of July, Dwight D. Eisenhower was running against Adlai Stevenson for the presidency. Since Ike lived in nearby Gettysburg, some of the Democrats of the county were wavering.

PopPop Harmon, sitting in the swing, remembered when McKinley was shot. Unlike Jack Young, my natural grandfather, he hated politics. Until heart failure knocked Jack down, he plunged into the thick of any gathering, shaking hands, collecting votes, listening to troubles.

Mother, Aunt Mimi and other ladies busied themselves with seeing that guests ate, drank and were introduced properly, though most people knew one another. I recognized some of the night hunters and members of Dad's clubs. Then there was Kenny, Wadie and our little group.

I didn't remember Truman versus Dewey, so this was my first real presidential election. Banners hung from second-story windows, a huge banner was strung over the street, people wore hats with different ribbons according to their candidate because the lesser offices were up for grabs, too.

Bands played and the liquor flowed like water. Floats rolled down the street between the bands, and candidates stood upon them like so many prom queens waving to their court.

Mother was a Republican. Aunt Mimi was a Democrat. Not only did they battle over the Reformation daily, they battled over political issues, too. Always apples and oranges with them. I was sure to get both sides of the story.

However, there was another reason that the sisters allied with rival parties. The story goes that when Thomas Buckingham fled the rise of Puritanism not only did he bring his wits and good looks to the New World in the beginning of the seventeenth century, he brought his cynicism about politics. In each generation the siblings divided up among the competing parties. In this fashion the Buckingham family always had someone in each generation who could talk to whoever was in power. There were only two exceptions. Buckinghams were always Cavaliers, never Roundheads, and during the War Between the States they were Marylanders who stood with the South.

Julia Ellen was to be a Democrat and I was to be a Republican.

I asked Daddy what he thought and he said he always voted the man. Americans liked to vote for generals, he said, but not for admirals. As far as he was concerned, Stevenson didn't have a prayer.

Aunt Mimi overheard this and displayed a sulfurous reaction. She fired off a few choice words that were not "The Lord bless thee and keep thee."

Mother instantly reminded her that Christian charity applied to politics, which made Sis see red. The fur flew.

Aunt Mimi lurched for the garden hose, turning it on Mom and wrecking her hairdo.

Dad, Uncle Mearl and Big Kenny separated them. Dad said politics was just the choice between Tweedledum and Tweedledee anyway.

Everything appeared to be normal. Later Mother, armed with scissors, snuck up behind her sister and lopped off a hank of hair.

Aunt Mimi sat right down on the steps and cried because her "do" was really ruined. Mother's could dry out, which it did; since she'd been giving herself those stinky Toni home permanents, she looked like a frizzy poodle. Aunt Mimi lamented the disgraceful behavior of her little sister.

"Oh, I've tried to bring you around, Juts, but you're beyond hope."

She went on in this vein for some time. Everyone had heard that, so they returned to the festivities. I, however, wanted to hear more.

So she told me that when her mother died, she had asked her to take care of Juts.

Since Big Mimi had dropped dead of a heart attack, I didn't think she'd had time to give earthly directions to Aunt Mimi. I saw no reason to inform her of this fact.

After wearing out that line of talk, she switched back to politics, telling me that the Republican Party was the party of "big business" and the Democratic Party represented the "little man."

Mother had always told me that the Democratic Party started wars and spent money whereas Republicans encouraged business so people could make money.

Finally, Aunt Mimi wearied of not enjoying her own party and with a theatrical small sigh she got up and again began serving her guests. Before the party was over both sisters were arm in arm again.

It kind of made me glad that Patty had left when she did because I didn't think I had the energy to carry on like Mom and Aunt Mimi.

And I certainly don't think that both political parties are like Tweedle-dum and Tweedledee. The difference between the Republican and Democratic Parties is the difference between syphilis and gonorrhea, a statement I am particularly fond of reading when I give speeches.

The Glide

MOTHER BELIEVED IN ENJOYING HERSELF. AUNT MIMI BELIEVED in enjoying herself, then feeling guilty about it. If a celebration wasn't connected to Our Dear Lord or some obscure saint, Aunt Mimi harbored grave suspicions about the frolic.

Those punctuation points of pleasure like the Memorial Day barbecue, the Fourth of July parade, the butchers' picnic in August and the York Fair were eagerly anticipated by Mom and me. Hanover even had a nice horse show, which was exciting.

Softening up her sister started two weeks before the nonholy event. Mother would make a cup of coffee, light a cigarette, then pick up the phone, which was a party line. Every person who wasn't disgustingly rich had a party line. When you lifted the receiver you might hear another conversation. Courtesy decreed you hang up and wait for the line to be free.

Mother perfected the trick of picking up, putting the receiver in the cradle with a click, then carefully lifting it so she could eavesdrop. Since most people on our party line were farmers, she grew bored with weather stories and crop reports. She'd hang up for real.

When she used the phone the reverse was true. Her conversations sparkled. The neighborhood listened in. That infuriated both Mom and Aunt Mimi, who loudly decried the practice even though they did it themselves. The issue had less to do with privacy than with the fact that both sisters wanted to be first to spread their own news.

Mother would say, "Sis, I've been thinking about the butchers' picnic. Butch is in charge of—"

Aunt Mimi would interrupt, "Now, Julia, I told you I don't have time for that this year. I've got to put up my baby corn and . . ."

Women made jams, pickled cucumbers and beets, and boiled peaches in heavy syrup at the hottest, stickiest time of the year. Bad enough that your shirt stuck to your body outside, it was a good fifteen degrees hotter in the kitchen. The vegetables or fruit, once prepared, would be put in Ball jars, which were in three parts. The top would be sealed with wax. A small square of cloth was put over that and tied with twine. The food could last years if the process was properly done.

Mother would listen to the litany of excuses and then beg her sister to come along. "It just won't be the same without you."

"I can't, I've got too much to do."

The next morning this performance would be repeated. The first week of calls and encounters, Mother would always tell Aunt Mimi that everyone would be miserable without her, and Aunt Mimi would use any excuse she had except for declaring she had to go to St. Rose of Lima and do the Stations of the Cross.

The second week Mother would imagine the games that she'd win: bingo, horseshoes and poker on the side. She'd enumerate the dishes she would pick out for her prize, the glasses, maybe even something new and really expensive like a mixer. And she wouldn't mention that we'd miss Aunt Mimi.

The protests weakened on the other end of the line.

Meanwhile, Dad and Uncle Mearl would have worked out the details of who would carry the kids, the blankets and the extra clothes we always took in case someone fell (or was pushed) into the pond. The men worked well together. They had survived many a Buckingham battle, which drew them close together.

The next time Mother saw Aunt Mimi she'd solemnly inform her that she'd figured out how to get all of us kids to the picnic without Aunt Mimi's car.

The day after that she'd casually remark that the picnic fell on the Feast of the Immaculate Heart of Mary and that she, herself, had devised a morning prayer to honor the BVM.

The Thursday before the picnic she'd take the bus down the hill to her sister's, walk in the door and plop the big wicker basket she carried down on the kitchen table. Aunt Mimi, with her good eye for space and design, had a wonderful, airy kitchen.

I tagged along, since vacation Bible school lasted only six weeks and by this time I was free and glad of it.

"Sis, I brought you some jars, wax and twine. I've got stuff left over."

Aunt Mimi would open the basket and thank Mother. Then they'd have coffee while I had lemonade or Coca-Cola.

Pretty soon I'd be hearing, "It's supposed to be dreadfully hot this weekend."

"A real stinker," Mother nonchalantly replied.

"I wonder if I should put off canning for a couple of days."

"Too much heat can soften the brain," Mother solemnly informed her sister.

"Yes, I've heard that, too."

Of course, Aunt Mimi would go to the butchers' picnic.

This picnic stands out for me because Eugene had graduated from high school, class of 1951, and was working in the store. Girls trailed him to the picnic, although he had invited only one. Out of high school for almost a year, he decided to enlist in the army and serve his tour of duty. This was his fling before all that.

The dreadful gloom from the deaths of Big Mimi and Virginia had finally lifted.

A large turn-of-the-century bandstand stood down by a pond. You walked over a curving bridge to reach it. Colored lanterns hung overhead, casting liquid light on the lily pads. It was romantic.

For us kids there were swings, baseball and horseshoes, and dodgeball for the teeny-weenies.

The men pitched horseshoes and played baseball too.

There were also mixed teams so the ladies could play, but this was after the men's game. Mom said the men played for blood. No quarter asked, none given, but after the dust settled the men clapped one another on the back, repairing to the open-air square wooden bar. Injuries heal faster with ice-cold tap beer.

I would accompany Dad to the bar. He'd sit on a stool or stand with his foot on the rail. I'd sit on his broad shoulders or on the bar. I must have been marginally amusing because the men laughed at my chatter. No one looked cross or told Dad to get me out of there.

I also stood on the bar and sang a song about a perfumed Persian cat, the words of which I remember to this day. That must have been a huge hit because the bartender gave me a small glass with real beer as a reward.

Dad told me I could drink it. People didn't fret then as they do now about cigarettes and alcohol. If my dad thought I could drink a small glass of beer, then I could. I did and no ill effects were suffered, nor did I transform into a raging alcoholic.

I rushed back to Mom, Aunt Mimi, Julia Ellen and the group surrounding them to announce that I had drunk beer.

Mother laughed.

Aunt Mimi surprised us by saying, "On a hot day it tastes better than anything." Then she really surprised us by going over to the men's bar, where Dad bought her a big mug.

By early evening we'd eaten ourselves into a stupor.

Before the dancing began, eagerly awaited by everyone but us kids, the band played a cakewalk. Mother and I were a team, team eleven. We won a devil's food cake with creamy vanilla icing. You would have thought we'd won the Irish Sweepstakes because we jumped up and down, hugged and carried our prize back to our gang, where we ate some more.

Mom said the trick to a cakewalk wasn't just being lucky enough to hit the right number, it was in the glide. You didn't walk, you glided. I practiced gliding.

The band played "Red Sails in the Sunset," "Boogie Woogie Bugle Boy" and other songs from the thirties and forties. Kenny, Wadie and I took turns dancing with one another until we got bored and sat on the bridge to listen to the bullfrogs.

We could see the men lining up to dance with Mom. She was a terrific ballroom dancer. Her perfectly shaped legs didn't hurt, either. Aunt Mimi wasn't quite as good as Mom, or at least that's what I thought, but the men crowded around her too.

They enjoyed more admirers than women half their age, but then they always did, even up to the end.

Dad, who couldn't dance, sat on the sidelines and watched Mother be the belle of the ball. He loved seeing her happy. After a time, he came down and sat with us on the bridge.

I remarked that the pond was full of stars. The different-hued lantern lights washing over the water looked like colored comets streaking across the surface.

Everything was perfect.

O Holy Night

MOTHER ACCUSED AUNT MIMI'S CHRISTMAS TREE OF HARBORing cockroaches. At least, I think that's how the fight started. Mother favored long-needled evergreens decorated with multicolored balls and tinsel painstakingly draped over the branches. Aunt Mimi yanked out of her attic each season a medium-sized deciduous corpse wrapped in white cotton. She'd hang Christmas balls on it and Uncle Mearl would put together the train set underneath the tree.

I don't know if Aunt Mimi's cotton-wrapped wonder provided apartments for bugs, but it was looking a little tired.

The season to be jolly catapulted the Buckingham girls into a frenzy of competitive decorating; on top of that, Aunt Mimi had to go to mass every single morning, and sometimes she'd hit vespers too. She must have been exhausted. Every present had to be hand-wrapped, made individual in some way. If you let the store wrap the present, it meant you didn't truly love the recipient.

Then there was the holiday cooking, because everyone kept open house the week of Christmas, plus there were parties to attend every night.

Rich, poor or in the middle, everyone decorated for the holiday. A friend of Uncle Mearl's even put a sleigh with Santa and reindeer on his roof. People sang in the streets, carols blared over loudspeakers and we gathered around pianos, fiddles and even harmonicas to sing together.

We Buckinghams sang more than others, or at least I think we did. Half the girls in my class took piano lessons. I vowed never to do it. I'd play the tuba before I'd itch on a piano bench, crinolines torturing me, while I pounded out "Jingle Bells."

We didn't have money for music lessons, but Mother, ruthlessly determined that I should master the social graces, was an excellent seamstress and she'd been putting money aside.

I promised to start music lessons after Christmas. But we each had to make a contribution to the group. If you didn't play the piano or cook a ham, you had to make something. I wrote a poem, coolly received by Mother, who said I'd cheated because words came easily to me. I should sweat over a group present. Still, she let the poem pass. It was about horses talking at midnight on Christmas Eve.

Aunt Mimi thought I should have written about Jesus. I learned early that everyone is a critic.

Anyway, Mother and Aunt Mimi started hollering at each other in Aunt Mimi's heavily decorated living room—elves peeped out from picture frames, for starters, and even the naked-lady ashtrays, which Uncle Mearl adored, wore Christmas garb. (Aunt Mimi insisted the ashtrays were artistic.) These freestanding Nubian princesses now had wreaths around their necks, their nipples freshened with red nail polish.

Both sisters were probably worn out getting ready for nonstop festivities. However, once a fight was engaged, it had to be seen through to the bitter end.

Mother stomped out. I followed. Everyone else had the presence of mind to disappear. Once they raised their voices a small fit of destruction usually followed. You didn't want to be in the line of fire.

By the time we reached home, instead of being cooled off—and it was a cold walk—Mother was volcanic. She yanked Sis's presents out of the closet and said we were going down to the square to return them.

I was happy to be home with Mickey. Why go back out into the wind?

"Mom, why does Aunt Mimi have a cotton tree?"

"Because she's too damn cheap to buy a tree each year."

"I thought Aunt Mimi had money."

"She has more than we do, kid. Tighter than the bark on a tree."

In truth, Aunt Mimi's resources were modest, but she was a good manager of money, whereas Mother was not. This, too, was often noted by big sister to little sister with predictable results. As luck would have it, Dad, softhearted, would give money to anyone telling him a sob story. He didn't help matters.

"And how come Aunt Mimi uses only one color ball on the tree?"

Sometimes she varied the colors. This was a red year.

"She thinks she's fashionable. I know more about color than she does. She used to go to Philadelphia and New York when she was a buyer for Bon-Ton department store, so she thinks she knows everything."

The wind rattled the shutters. Mother decided she'd go downtown the next day. I asked Mother whether Big Mimi and Virginia would know it if I bought them Christmas presents. Could they look down from heaven and see?

Mother didn't answer. She picked up the phone and called Aunt Mimi. The next thing I knew she was bawling on the phone, and I guess Aunt Mimi was too.

Eugene was in Japan now. Even though Japan had lost World War II and now played permanent host to their American guests, Mother was nervous for him. If they'd bombed Pearl Harbor, who knew what they might do in the future? She cried about Gene's being away.

By the time the tears dried, the girls had made up.

Good thing, because the big Christmas dinner was the next night. The sisters alternated years. It was Aunt Mimi's year. She'd pushed together every table in the house, plus card tables, so that they were in one line extending from the end of the kitchen through the formal dining room and into the living room.

As I could now eat with the adults, I was very excited to show off. Mother worried (and Aunt Mimi worried even more) that I would never become a proper lady. I intended to be the best dinner companion who'd ever existed, and I had read etiquette books at the library. I was armed for any conversational possibility including flower arranging, about which I knew little, but Mother said it was important.

The evening of the dinner, crystal clear and icy cold, presaged a good party. People stamped their feet before walking through Aunt Mimi's wide front door. Dad made orange blossoms, his specialty. Uncle Mearl and Russell, Julia Ellen's steady, stood behind the bar mixing drinks. We kids scrambled, chased one another and played with Butch, who was in a frenzy of excitement. We played with the toy train.

The seating arrangements puffed me up because I was not seated between Mom and Dad. I sat between Russell and Ken senior. Directly across from me was Grandma Spellman, who was so old they shouldn't have been serving her turkey—they should have been giving her extreme unction.

Grandma Spellman was Gertrude Buckingham's mother. Bucky, Mom's younger brother, had married a cultured woman, to the shock of the family. He was rough and ready. Gertrude appreciated the arts, the finer things in life. They were proof that opposites attract, because it was a good marriage.

Grandma Spellman suffered from Parkinson's disease. Her head wiggled and her voice did too. As this was my first meeting with the lady, I had no idea she was afflicted. I thought she was playing with me, so I, remembering my etiquette books, tried to be the most pleasing dinner companion in the world. I began wiggling my head and my voice, too.

Russell couldn't help himself. He giggled. Ken senior, red in the face, looked the other way or he would have laughed, too. My mother finally caught sight of me, jumped out of her chair and literally lifted me up from mine. She smacked my bottom down the hall all the way back to the kitchen.

Not only had I disgraced myself by offending Grandma Spellman, I had disgraced her and Dad. I could march myself up to Aunt Mimi's bedroom and miss the party. No food, either.

Grandma Spellman had a good sense of humor. She thought it was funny and she knew I wasn't mocking her. She troubled herself to get up from the table and plead my case to Mom.

Finally I was permitted back in the dining room. Russell couldn't speak to me, though, because he'd burst out laughing and then Aunt Mimi would be cross at him.

After dinner we sang, I read my poem and Dad and Mom sang "O Holy Night" together. His voice, deep as an operatic bass, and her voice, a mezzo, sounded glorious together. Everyone sang some more and we remembered by name and song those that were dead. Then the children were dismissed to play.

I wanted to make up for my mistake, so I washed dishes in the kitchen with Julia Ellen. She was a cheerful worker and we sang together too. Back then people sang a lot; you sang in the fields, you sang in the evening, you sang at church. It made the work go faster. People don't sing like that today.

The men tossed on coats and stood out on the porch smoking their cigars, pipes and cigarettes. The house, overflowing, would have turned into a smokebomb if the men hadn't gone outside. Mother merrily trotted around, Chesterfield to her lips. She wasn't exposing herself to the cold.

I skipped out, taking a break from the dishes. I saw that Uncle Kenny's eyes were wet. Dad and Uncle Mearl stood next to him, Dad's arm thrown around Ken's shoulders.

I snuck quietly back into the kitchen. Whatever love was, it was more than I could understand.

A Slip of
the Tongue

DAD ALLOWED ME TO HUNT, ALTHOUGH HE WOULDN'T KILL ANY-
thing himself. He went along to watch the dogs or hounds work. I had a
Chesapeake Bay Retriever, Chap, which I trained. They are easy dogs to
work, and I thought I knew something.

Dad drove me to streams and I'd send Chap in after a rubber ball. I
dearly wanted a rifle so I could shoot ducks, but we couldn't afford one.
Dad, a devout pacifist, believed that guns did the devil's work and if you
had to resort to violence to solve a problem, it meant you'd failed. But if
he'd had the money, he would have bought me a rifle. Dad felt beliefs had
to come from inside. He couldn't push his beliefs on me.

He had served in the Civil Air Patrol during World War II. He was
thirteen when World War I ended, so he was too young to participate
except for gathering scrap metal, which the boys did while the girls rolled
bandages.

Sometimes we'd tag along with the pheasant hunters. Setters of every
sort would be out. The Irish Setters, shiny chestnut, dashed quick as
lightning but could be flighty in the field. The English Setters, still fast,
proved more reliable and the Black-and-Tan Gordons, heavier setters,
while comparatively slow, were steady as a rock.

However, the gun dog I loved was the Clumber Spaniel, which most
people take to be an ugly huge Cocker Spaniel. Steady in all conditions,
patient as a saint and with unflagging drive, these animals earn every
morsel of food you give them. On top of that, they are playful, loyal and
loving. I hope to own a Clumber one day and work in the field with it.

One morning Dad and I got up early to watch field trials. PopPop
tagged along, although he much preferred hounds to gun dogs.

When I got home I told Mom and Aunt Mimi everything. Then I

rambled on about who shot John (a southern expression that means you give more information than society requires).

When I'd finished my bucolic rapture Mother informed me that I was to be enrolled in cotillion. Really it was pre-cotillion, just as Brownies precedes Girl Scouts.

The thought of endless ice-water teas (nothing but ice-water was served) and filling out dancing cards gave me the heaves.

Mom couldn't remember if the lessons were to take place at one of the local schools, Hannah Penn or Millard Fillmore, or at Miss Holtzapple's house.

At the mention of Fillmore, Aunt Mimi blurted out, "You can't send her there."

"Why not?"

"Because her brother is there."

Mother snapped, "Shut up, Sis."

Aunt Mimi obeyed her sister for the only time in their lives together. "I don't know what came over me."

"What brother?" I asked.

"Your aunt Mimi's elevator doesn't go to the top, kid. Forget it."

Fat chance.

20

A Froth of Discontent

MOTHER SILENCED MY ENTREATIES BY TELLING ME SHE DIDN'T
know anything. However, she didn't silence herself. Years of endless chastisement by her sister goaded Mother into turning the tables now.

She couldn't contain herself. A friend would drop by for coffee and
Mother would announce that the real reason Sis had wagged her tongue
was because Mother had noted that her cotton-wrapped Christmas tree
was getting tired. After ten minutes on the horrors of the white Christmas
tree, she'd recall how they fought over a cast-iron elephant bank Mom
bought for a nickel in 1908. Her supply of anecdotes was tailored to suit
the appropriate ears.

Meanwhile Aunt Mimi traipsed to mass and confession so much she
wore a path between her house and St. Rose. If a convoy of flagellants
from the Middle Ages had appeared in the town square, she would have
joined them. Her suffering afforded her a variant of pleasure.

As usual, what I thought and felt about this was overshadowed by their
drama.

I knew by this time, 1953, that Mother's need to be the star superseded
her need to be a mother. In a profound way, I also knew I couldn't depend
on her. I was rocked to know that I had a brother, but I wasn't shaken to
learn that Mother hadn't told me.

I bothered her, bugged her, battled her over this one. Once I knew she
was lying to me, I wouldn't be silenced.

Mother's retort was "I don't know" or "Shut up."

I walked down the hill and harassed Aunt Mimi, which sent them both
up in flames.

I pestered Dad, and for once my salvation remained neutral. Mom had
the whip hand over him, but I didn't know why.

Finally Mother, in a gesture of appeasement, cooked me fried chicken and greens with fatback, my favorite dish. As I gobbled away she composed herself. She picked out the fatback from my greens, nibbling while she "explained." I grew more incensed about the fatback than the news.

"When we brought you home with us, Daddy drove over to your father's house. I don't know who your father is because Daddy won't tell me. But he asked him to come out of the house and they talked in the car. Daddy told him never to come around you. He didn't want you upset. Apparently, your father was only too happy to comply."

"What does my father do?"

"He's some kind of professional athlete."

"How old is he?"

"I don't know. Younger than we are, I guess."

"Well, what about my brother?"

"He's your half brother and he's three years older than you are. That's why Juliann couldn't marry your father. He was already married."

"So he's a real shit."

"I didn't teach you to talk like that." She pointed her fork at me. "But I would agree he is not a prince among men."

"Do you know his name?"

"I told you, no." Another hunk of fatback speared.

"Mom, that's mine."

"You can't eat all this."

"I can try." I flared up and whacked at her fork with mine.

Instead of getting angry with me, she laughed. Mother far preferred a fighter to a crier, even if the fight was with her.

"You'd better hop down to cotillion right now, young lady, you need the work." She laughed. "And your brother isn't going to be there. I don't know what gets into Sis. Miss Know-It-All. She's been like that ever since I can remember. It doesn't matter if what she says is true or not. She thinks it is."

However, I knew that Aunt Mimi wasn't lying on this one.

"Mom, I don't believe you."

"About Sis?"

"You know who my father is."

She paused, then her voice rose in that singsong quality that meant she was fibbing big-time. "I really don't." Another moment passed. "Why are you worried about this? Isn't it good enough here? Do you think it's better somewhere else?"

"No. I don't want to end up like Patty." That was God's honest truth. I feared being batted around from home to home, and I saw how sad it was for Kenny, Wadie and Terry without a mother. Then there was the example of Gene when he'd come to live with us. Dumped children were a reality.

This reply halfway satisfied Mother, but she would have preferred a paean of praise for rescuing me from the orphanage and being the world's perfect mother.

"You're a tough little nut, kid" was all she said.

Some adopted children fervently desire to meet their blood parents. I'd met Juliann. I was curious as to what my father looked like since I barely resembled my mother. Other than that, I didn't care. Whoever had given me life hadn't wiped my forehead when I was sick with fever, hadn't baked me my favorite birthday cake, hadn't taken me to the library or the foxhunts. Juliann and my natural father had never told me stories at night or taught me basic dance steps or shown me how to prune roses. They'd never taken me to church or taught me right from wrong: "It's the Ten Commandments, kid, not the Ten Suggestions." For whatever reasons, no matter how sound, my natural parents had abandoned me. No child is so stupid that he or she doesn't know when they're not wanted. Whatever Mother's faults, and by now I could enumerate every one, she packed my lunch for school, she checked my lessons, she listened to my childish enthusiasms.

Dad drove me to the railroad station so I could wave at the people— why this excited me, I don't know, but it did. He took me to various stables so I could learn about the different breeds of horses, and a friend of his who had fine harness Saddlebreds allowed us to watch her train them. Whatever I wanted to do, Daddy found a way. He couldn't buy me things, but he gave me something much better—his undivided attention and love.

I didn't want to run away to my natural mother or father. I didn't dream about a perfect family. No matter how mad I'd get at Mom, I remained loyal to her.

LATER THAT WINTER MICKEY, AN OLD BOY, BEGAN TO HAVE TROUBLE urinating. He'd sit in his dirtbox for twenty to thirty minutes. A tidy fellow, he'd cover the few drops he squeezed out. Since Mickey and I were rarely parted, I noticed right away and told Mom.

She watched him for a day, then made a little cardboard travel box for him with soft towels inside. We walked up to the bus stop and hopped the bus to the vet's.

His office was green and white. We didn't have to wait long. The vet examined Mickey and told us male neutered cats often developed urinary tract problems. He said he could drain out the urine but Mickey would fill up again. If we were willing to bring him down every day, we could keep him alive, but he was old and getting drained like that would be hard on him.

Mother, usually so glib, was struck dumb. She stared at Mickey.

I piped up, "Will he suffer?"

"He'll feel good when his bladder is empty and then he'll feel sick again," the young vet answered me.

"I can't do it," Mom whispered.

"How much is it a visit?"

"Ten dollars."

"Mom, do we have the money?"

"I've got my pin money."

I looked at my best friend. He purred at me.

"Why don't we try it once and see what happens?"

We left Mickey and picked him up the next day. He felt great, but by the following day he was struggling to relieve himself again.

I told Mother we had to put him down. I stayed home from school. Mom called Aunt Mimi and she drove over. We took Mickey to the vet and I kissed him goodbye. He purred at me some more.

Then the vet gave him the shot. We put his body in the cardboard box and got back in the car. Mother cried so hard I thought she would pass out. Aunt Mimi, no cat lover, started crying. I cried too, holding my poor Mick.

We buried him under the lovely crabapple tree in the backyard.

When I remember Mother, I remember her with Mickey. I like to think of her that way and not as the woman who would fly up in a fury and fling my beginnings in my face.

That night, going to bed without Mickey, was the loneliest night of my life.

Bumblebees

POPPOP HARMON, BIG MIMI'S HUSBAND, SLIPPED AWAY SHORTLY AF-
ter Mickey died. I wanted his dogs, Belle and Toby, but Dad said I was too
little to work with such big hounds. That rich son of a bitch, Harve, in
Maryland bought the hounds.

PopPop, like many an old drunk, may not have done much good in his
life, but he did no harm. He was the best hound man I ever saw and I
admired him for it. He was so poor he didn't own a suit to be buried in, so
Mom and Aunt Mimi bought their stepfather a suit, giving him a proper
send-off.

"He made Momma happy for a while," Mother said.

Big Mimi and PopPop hadn't lived together for years when she died,
but they'd stayed on good terms. He'd given way at her funeral, and if the
tables had been turned, she would have given way at his.

Aunt Mimi declared that her mother was a two-time loser. Charles
Buckingham had been a handsome drunk and PopPop Harmon a not-so-
handsome drunk. Then she started on Sadie Huff, Big Mimi's half sister
and my natural grandmother, who, she said, had avoided marrying a drunk
only to marry the biggest bullshitter in Carroll and York Counties.

Mom said it didn't matter. We didn't have to live with any of them.

"Julia, how do you propose to teach this girl about how to find the
right kind of man? Do you want her marrying some charming boozer?
She thought PopPop was wonderful. She never saw him passed out lying
in his own, uh, urine."

"Sis, there's plenty of time to worry about men."

"Blood tells," Aunt Mimi cryptically intoned.

I could have ripped her throat out.

"One man's as good as another," I bellowed. Where I'd heard that I don't know, but it derailed their impending argument.

They hopped to another subject and I walked outside to play with Chap, the Chesapeake Bay Retriever. We plunged into the moist woods. I liked to find the air currents and follow them, hoping to find deer. Sometimes I'd sit for what seemed like hours waiting to catch sight of an indigo bunting or an owl, my favorite bird.

While I was popular at school, made good grades and loved learning, I was most content racing across hayfields or climbing the biggest walnut tree in the woods. With people it was blab, blab, blab. I craved silence and animal sounds. I never took Mom or Dad with me. I didn't take the boys either. We'd build forts or fish, but my secret paths to the fox earths or a red-tailed hawk's nest I showed no one. I didn't trust them not to kill the animals that in a distant way I loved. If you put aside your frittering mind, the part of your brain that's filled with words, you can learn a great deal from animals. Any animal that you encounter is a success. The failures are extinct.

I watched animals prepare their young to live on their own. Vixens would go into a killing frenzy sometimes to teach their cubs. Birds truly would push their young out of the nest.

The world waited outside the door. I wanted to go. I counted the years until I would graduate from high school. Eternity.

The more Mom cranked on me to behave properly, the more I wanted to tear out of there. However, they did beat good manners into my skin and I wasn't even in full-blown cotillion yet. Big cotillion meant dancing with boys. Ugh. Playing baseball or football, that's what boys were for.

Poor as we were, our social equals were the royal family of England, according to Aunt Mimi. Aunt Mimi was hard-working, but she could be an awful snob sometimes. I hated that.

Mother's pungent phrase for Aunt Mimi when she'd climb on her high horse was "She thinks her shit doesn't stink."

As snobby as Aunt Mimi could be, Mom was egalitarian. Color, gender, class meant nothing to her. She could get exercised about religion, but even there she was fundamentally tolerant except where Aunt Mimi's Catholicism was concerned.

I watched, listened and absorbed every conversation those two had that I overheard. I also vowed never to be like either one of them—the usual battle cry of any girl, "I will not grow up to be like my mother!"

That early summer I rode the bus to downtown York. A red and gold

McCrory's five-and-dime stood on the corner. I strolled the aisles. A pretty yellow yo-yo with a black stripe leaped into my pocket.

I love honeybees and bumblebees. I have never been stung by a bee, although yellow jackets and wasps have dive-bombed me plenty. I liked to touch bees' furry thoraxes, to stroke them and sing to them. I can't imagine what an adult would have thought if they'd caught me singing to the bees.

There are many country superstitions about bees. One is that when a family member dies you must go tell the bees. Every time someone died I dutifully told whatever bee I found. I didn't know it meant you were supposed to go to the beeboxes. The bees didn't seem to mind.

This yo-yo looked like a bumblebee. I hadn't a penny in my pocket but I had the yo-yo.

By the time I walked home I was "walking the dog" with the yo-yo. Naturally, it caught my mother's eye. She asked where I got it.

"McCrory's."

"With what?"

"Huh?" Acting dumb didn't save me.

"With what money, kid?"

"Uh . . ."

"That's what I thought." She pinched my ear, hauling me to the phone, where she called Aunt Mimi. In a flash Aunt Mimi and her hateful black Nash appeared at the back door. The next thing I knew I was being marched into McCrory's. Aunt Mimi had the good grace to stay outside. Mother dragged me to the counter. I had to hand over the yo-yo, confess my sin and apologize.

The clerk, a scrawny red-eyed twit, chose to be even nastier than Mother. She said she could put me in jail. Well, I'd have rather been in jail than standing between her and Mom.

After the tongue-lashing, Mother led me out the back door of the store.

"Aunt Mimi is waiting out front."

"She'll be window-shopping." Mom stopped and put her hands on her hips. "Buzz, whatever happened to 'Thou shalt not steal'?"

"I don't know." And I didn't.

"All through your life you'll see things you think you have to have. Next time this happens, try a little game that I play." She walked me around to the street side. "Wait a day. One full day. Then go back and look at whatever it is. You might find that the shine has worn off. Then again, you might find it's even prettier than you remembered. If you can afford to, buy it. Now, if it's something really big, like a refrigerator—"

"Or a horse," I interrupted.

"Or a horse, then wait a whole week and find out everything you can about what it is. You know, does someone sell the same thing for less money? You can't give in to your first impulse. Now, whatever happened to 'Thou shalt not steal'?"

"I forgot it."

"You didn't forget it, you pushed it out of your mind. Self-control, kid."

"Is God going to remember this? That I broke a commandment?"

"Uh . . ." She paused a second, then burst out laughing. "Nah, but Aunt Mimi will never forget it."

And, indeed, she never did.

Laundry

MOTHER WAS RUSHED TO THE HOSPITAL WITH STRANGE PAINS in her bowel. She endured three operations in one week. She had adhesions that blocked part of her colon. Finally, the doctors removed three feet of intestine.

No one thought she would live. I vaguely remembered Mother being in the hospital once before, when I was four. I was afraid then and I was afraid now, especially when Daddy cried.

Mom pulled through. I cleaned house, did the laundry and ironed until she was on her feet.

I felt very important, but I was scared to death that I'd lose Mother. For months afterward I wouldn't let her out of my sight. Going to school upset me. I was sure Mother would die.

It took me a long time to get over that.

Valley View
Elementary School

THE SUMMER BEFORE FOURTH GRADE, 1954, A HANDFUL OF CHILDREN from Violet Hill Elementary School were relocated to the newer Valley View Elementary School, which reposed on a ridge overlooking the farm valley. We lived on the opposite ridge.

I walked through the farm, across the creek and up the hill to Valley View. The children attending this school differed from the kids at Violet Hill. These kids came from money, maybe not all of them, but enough of them to let me know I was not born with a silver spoon in my mouth. They already owned televisions. Their parents drove them in new cars to school. Some children even had swimming pools, a much bigger status symbol in the fifties than it is today.

The other significant change was how incredibly competitive these kids were. They'd jostle for the teacher's attention, they'd cut one another on the kickball fields and they shared few of their material goods. They sucked up to authority.

What a jolt. I don't know if I said two words my fourth-grade year, but I made E's (for "excellent"). Mom and Dad fixed it so I could go to the library if I finished my lessons early, just as they had at Violet Hill.

My athletic ability helped me make friends, but I didn't grow close to anyone. Carol Morton, a blond, outgoing girl, invited me to her house once for a pool party. That was the extent of my socializing at Valley View. I missed the draft horses. During recess at Violet Hill I'd been able to sneak across the playing field, vault the fence and crawl up on the back of one of the plow horses. I missed those horses and I missed my farm school buddies.

More than anything, I missed Mickey.

Mother brought me a tiger, a short-haired kitten, one fall day. Tuffy entered my life and I haven't lived without a short-haired tiger since.

I had Kenny, Wadie and ever-growing Terry. Eugene was far away but okay, so Mother was happy. I worked with Chap, and Dad let me have a tricolor Collie puppy that I named Ginger so I could learn to work with herding dogs, which are quite different from hunting dogs.

I dutifully trudged to school, then ran all the way home. The one outstanding event of those subdued years at school occurred on a crisp fall day when I was in fifth grade. The sow escaped her pen. I had no idea of this as I climbed the farm road up the hill. I heard a dark squeal behind me, glanced around and beheld six hundred pounds of angry bacon heading straight for me. If you're a city person, you may not know that hogs can run faster than you. If they're in a scuffling mood, an enraged hog can hurt you. A boar can kill you.

I dropped my books, running for all I was worth. The farmer was nowhere to be seen. The sow was gaining on me. Thank God for an old oak tree in the middle of the top cornfield. I made it in time and shimmied up, grabbing hold of a thick, low branch to swing up. My vantage point provided me with an excellent view of Tons of Fun. She, in turn, appeared fascinated with her quarry. She didn't budge. I missed school and sat in the tree until early afternoon, when the farmer drove down the road. Poor fellow, he was scared to death when he saw me. My dress was ripped, and scratches added to my allure. He captured the hog, put her back, then fetched me out of the tree. He found my books and drove me home and apologized to Mom.

By now you have gathered that Mother was not the overprotective type. Thank God. There are enough born wimps without making one.

After the farmer left she made me a mayonnaise sandwich and smiled at me. "Good thing you're fast on your feet."

"Yes, ma'am."

"Were you scared?"

"Yes, ma'am."

"You didn't cry, did you?"

"No." I was so insulted I forgot the *ma'am*.

She opened the old Norge and took out vanilla ice cream. I perked up.

"Let's celebrate. I'll make hot-fudge sundaes."

"Celebrate what?"

"A pig in a poke." She attacked the rock-hard ice cream, then turned toward me. "You weren't a coward."

"I was scared."

"Anyone with sense would be scared. A coward lets it get to him. You didn't, so I say let's eat ice cream."

I hoped this display of courage would release me from pre-cotillion and church. I know God means for us to go to church, but did he mean for it to be so dull?

Betting on the Side

AUNT MIMI POSSESSED A HORROR OF SILENCE, WHICH SHE BAT-
tled with endless chat. The Typhoid Mary of the Telephone started her
calls at 6:30 each morning. After she finished with Mother she must have
knocked off everyone in her social and church circle. Then she'd often
hop in her car and head for our house.

Both sisters hungered for information, news and rank gossip. Mother
refused to pass on the gossip. She said Aunt Mimi could do that. Also,
Mother rarely believed much of what she heard.

"Believe none of what you hear and half of what you see," she often
counseled me.

Big Ken was courting his housekeeper, Ceil. Little Terry loved her.
Kenny and Wade had mixed emotions. Aunt Mimi needed to report fully
on those developments. We thought she'd be cool to Ceil, but she surprised everyone by welcoming her. The big issues brought out the best in
Aunt Mimi. The boys needed a young woman's care and love. Ceil, brave
woman, was ready to try.

Julia Ellen was bound and determined to marry the gorgeous but pen-
niless Russell. Aunt Mimi exhausted every argument in her arsenal. She
tried waiting her out. Julia Ellen, usually a docile and obedient daughter,
wouldn't budge.

"She'll ruin her life," Aunt Mimi wailed to Mom.

"At least she's ruining it with someone handsome."

"Juts, you are no help at all. You talk to her."

"I did talk to her."

"Well, talk to her again! She thinks he's Don Juan."

"Don Guano!" I giggled as I slapped more peanut butter on the bread. I loved playing with language and made jokes and puns constantly. Adults often began to grind their teeth in my presence. I thought I was hysterical.

Mother frowned. "Who asked you? If you can't behave, you can take that sandwich and eat outside."

"Oh, Mom."

"And that's another thing, Juts. Calling you Mom. *Mom* is vulgar. It's what the lower classes say. Mother. It should be *Mother.*"

"We are the lower classes," I fired back.

"We most certainly are not. We have slender resources but impeccable blood."

She was so predictable. I sassed back. "The best blood is Teddy blood."

"What is she talking about?" Aunt Mimi was cross.

"Kid, out of here."

I picked up my sandwich in one hand, my glass of milk in the other. At the top of the backyard, where the yard met the hayfield, Dad had built a huge outdoor brick fireplace and grill to display his considerable cooking abilities. I walked up the hill and sat on the side of the fireplace.

Tuffy followed me. Chap, sound asleep in his house, couldn't be bothered to open an eye.

I wondered if Mother was explaining Teddy blood to Sis. Citation's great-grandfather on the top line, the sire line, was Teddy. Mom said Teddy blood was the best. She also bemoaned the American obsession with speed. A horse needs speed *and* stamina. Otherwise, they're like Jaguars, pretty to look at but always breaking down.

Aunt Mimi didn't share Mother's love for horses or boxing or baseball. But they shared a love of color, clothes and interior decoration.

I could just hear Mom explaining the great sire Teddy to a fidgety sister whose main worries were, in descending order of importance: Her candidacy for sainthood; Julia Ellen's marriage; the boys; Mearl's house-painting business; her wardrobe; the irritating appearance of more gray hair than she felt necessary to display.

I also figured she'd take a swipe at my bloodlines, which, although every bit as good as hers, were outside the boundaries of marriage.

As much as the Buckingham sisters did for me—and I was grateful—I wanted to be on my own. I didn't want to hear about my beginnings, a failing attached to me although I had nothing to do with it. I wearied of their pettiness, bickering and power struggles.

As for visiting Mother Brown, that continued to be a season in purgatory. The good thing was that I'd read every *National Geographic* from the 1940s on.

The developers were gobbling up farmland that I loved. The valley below me was dotted with homes, although the farm still held out in the middle. Our road was extended. New homes, much bigger than ours, appeared.

I hated it. I begged Daddy to move near Hanover Shoe Farm. He said we couldn't afford to.

Nothing stayed the same. Even I was changing. Clothes that had fit the year before didn't fit this year. The boys and I traded T-shirts, shorts, jeans among us. Dreams I'd dreamed were supplanted by new ones. I no longer wanted a hotpad business. I thought I'd run a yard service, since I'd made money that spring and summer trimming hedges, planting bulbs and mowing lawns. Small but strong, I accomplished a lot more than grown-ups thought I would, and I liked any kind of outside work, so I did a good job. I'd mow your lawn for a dollar. The dollars rolled in. I was saving to buy a farm in Virginia. That dream remained constant, fired, no doubt, by that first visit back in 1949 and by the one thing my mother said about my father's family: FFV. First Families of Virginia.

I could read anything. I ripped through books, especially history books and military history, at the rate of five a week. I could only go to the Martin Memorial Library on Saturdays, the day I "helped" Dad at the store. Mom still allowed only two books per week from the city library but I could take what I wanted from the school library since she wouldn't have to carry them.

Except now I was big enough to really work. I could keep inventory, sweep the aisles, restock shelves and trim the fat off meat. I was too short to work on the huge butcher block, so Dad stood me on a wooden milk crate to teach me how to do it properly. When I was halfway decent at fat trimming, he taught me how to cut away from the bone. Those knives sparkled from use and honing. I was careful.

He taught me how to grade meat. We also rode around to the various cattle farmers. Grading on the hoof is a lot harder than grading once you've opened up the animal. Dad was terrific at it. The faces of farmers when he rolled into the driveway told me Dad was special. People smiled and laughed. He was liked and respected. I wanted people to treat me like that, too.

The farmers called me "Sidekick."

The boys seethed with jealousy, especially when I made the rounds with Dad. However, Kenny's feet could reach the pedals of the old tripod tractor, so he bragged that he could drive it. It was my turn to seethe with jealousy.

One summer evening Kenny crowed over the fields he'd plowed that day. Wade and I called him a liar, which launched us into a wicked fistfight.

As Kenny was now almost a foot taller than I was, though skinny as a rail, I weathered a few of these blows and then decided to take another tack.

"Kenny, I want proof. If you can drive the tractor, I'll give you my piggy bank."

He let up on Wade. "You mean it?"

"Swear."

"On the Bible?"

"A stack."

"The Catholic Bible, not the Lutheran Bible." He leaned over me.

"Swear on the Catholic Bible." I crossed my arms over my chest.

"Ha!" Kenny was spending that money in his head before he had it.

The grown-ups were on the porch, and we were far enough away that they paid us no mind. As for our fights, we fought all the time, nothing new there.

Kenny crawled up onto the tractor. Wade and I got on behind him. You've seen the ads: "Nothing runs like a Deere." It's true. John Deeres are the best tractors in the world and gruesomely expensive, but they run forever. This particular model, with its two small wheels together in the front, was already close to twenty years old. The tripod design worked fine for row crops on fairly even ground. A pitch and roll in the ground made for heavy going.

Those old tractors didn't have power steering and sophisticated hydraulics. You needed to be strong to steer one, which was an effective deterrent in keeping children off the machines.

I'd extracted a promise from Kenny that if he failed, I'd get to clean out the contents of his piggy bank. Wade informed me the piggy bank was empty. So I bet on his stag-handled pocketknife. I wanted his air rifle, but I knew he'd never part with it.

The deal set, Kenny pulled out the choke and flicked the small lever on the right. The old tractor rumbled; a cloud of black smoke belched from the exhaust pipe in front of us. He pushed in the choke, pushed down hard on the clutch and shifted into what he thought was first gear, but wasn't. He somehow popped it into third.

When he lifted up off the clutch—he was standing up to reach it—he sat down hard because that tractor reared up on its rear wheels, lurched forward and shot down the plowed field.

Big Ken flew off the porch, followed by Dad and Uncle Mearl. The women, smart thinkers, ran back in the house for hydrogen peroxide, methiolate and bandages.

"Downshift," Wade hollered.

Kenny, straining to hold the machine between the rows, couldn't even think of it.

Every time he ran over a row we flew up like birds off a line, only to resettle in our various positions: Kenny on the seat, Wade hanging on behind and me clinging to Wade.

I looked behind. The PTO wasn't turning. I bailed out.

Wade, frozen, clutched his brother's waist. Kenny was running out of field. He turned right to swing back, but he couldn't turn the wheel the whole way, so instead of a U-turn he turned at a right angle and the tractor flew straight for the steep drainage ditch by the side of the dirt road.

I raced after the tractor. I should have been scared for the boys, but I was too busy enjoying the spectacle. I knew Kenny was going to smash its nose into that ditch, and he did. The machine stood up, nose down, then settled with a heavy thump, rear tires spinning, more smoke billowing out of the exhaust pipe. Kenny hung on. The way he stayed in that seat was a miracle. Wade was thrown clear into the ditch.

Kenny, although shook up, was far more worried about his father, who bore down on him.

Big Ken leaped into the ditch, reached up and clicked off the tractor. He yanked Kenny out of the seat, taking the strap to him in front of all of us.

When Big Ken lost his temper, you shut up fast.

Little Kenny bawled. By the time Aunt Mimi reached the ditch some of Ken's anger had abated. Now Aunt Mimi was bullshit mad. She climbed down in the ditch, grabbed Ken's arm and told him to lay off.

He listened.

Dad and Uncle Mearl inspected the tractor. Dad thought Ken wailed at the boys too much, but he said raising a son was a hard business. You couldn't coddle boys, but you didn't want to brutalize them, either. I took from that that Dad was glad to have a daughter.

Mom and Aunt Mimi took the boys back to the house to clean them up, dress their scratches and scrapes.

I squared off at Uncle Ken. "I bet him he couldn't drive the tractor, so you'd better beat me too."

An instant silence fell over the four of us in the ditch.

"Oh, you did?"

"I did."

Dad moved next to me just in case. "Didn't you think about what could happen?"

"No, sir. I was tired of him bragging that he could drive it, so I bet him he couldn't."

"What did you bet?" Ken, shirt off and looking twice as powerful, asked.

"His stag-handled pocketknife against my piggy bank."

"Well, I guess you won yourself a stag-handled pocketknife."

"You aren't going to strap me?"

"No. He didn't have to listen to you. Now go on and get your knife. You tell him I said so."

The men pushed the tractor out of the ditch, no easy task. The front grille was pushed in, one headlight was snapped off and there were other odds and ends of damage. At least it wasn't going to cost a lot of money to fix it.

That night I slept with the pocketknife under my pillow. Mother told me I ought to give it back.

I said I'd won it fair and square. He wouldn't have given me back my piggy bank if he'd won.

I kept the knife.

I did, however, take some money from my piggy bank and buy Kenny a lime-colored plastic squirt gun, which he immediately used on me.

25

The Marrying Kind

S T. ROSE OF LIMA WITNESSED JULIA ELLEN'S BLOWOUT WEDDING TO Russell. Every time Aunt Mimi considered the cost of this heterosexual extravaganza she needed smelling salts.

"They could have just eloped," Mother would say, snapping her back to her senses.

"Julia, don't be ridiculous." Then Aunt Mimi would once again wade into the voluminous guest list.

Not a seat was empty in the church. Julia Ellen truly was a beautiful bride and Russell a stunning groom. Having been a tank man in the army, Russell had a certain manly swagger. He was scared at the altar, though, which I thought funny as I sat in the second row, behind Aunt Mimi, expensive Belgian lace hanky dabbing her eyes. The mother of the bride looked as good as the bride.

Even Dad got misty. I tried to concentrate, but my mind soon wandered. Mother pinched me to stop reading the hymnal.

Once out of the church and in the car on our way to the reception, she dug into me.

"If you throw food, yell at anyone or do one thing rude, you are getting dragged back to the car and you'll stay here. Do you hear me?"

"Yes, ma'am."

"This is the most important day of Julia Ellen's life and I don't want you acting a fool."

"Yes, ma'am."

"Someday you'll be married and you'll want everything perfect."

"Not me."

"Oh, la." She threw up her hands. "Our little hermit."

"I believe her," Dad said.

"Believe her? You encourage her."

"No, I don't." It was rare for Dad to argue with Mother. "Some people are made for marriage and some aren't."

She whirled around in the passenger seat to fix her light gray eyes on me. "This will change when you become a teenager."

"I don't want to be a teenager. I want to be grown-up right away. I don't even want to be a kid now." I was telling the truth.

"Somewhere out there is a little boy who will grow up to be your husband."

"I'd rather have a horse. Teddy blood, Mom."

Dad laughed so hard he dropped a wheel off the road.

"Butch, watch where you're going!" Mother, fussed up from the wedding and helping Aunt Mimi morning, noon and night for weeks, was testy. "This will all pass," she said as she settled back in her seat.

I stood up and leaned over the seat. "Mom, men are too much work."

"Well—I—"

Dad started laughing again. "Honey, I hate to admit it, but I think we *are* too much work."

Mother's lipstick red lips curled upward. "If you love the man, he's not too much work."

"I don't want to cook. I don't want to clean. I hate ironing and I'm not sitting around the house, Mom. I swear." I punctuated this with a childish saying the boys and I said when we swore sometimes. "Ein swine."

"Ein swine you." She flipped her lace hanky at me. "Say, did you see that handkerchief of Sis's?" This was addressed to Dad. "Cost twenty-five dollars if it cost a penny."

"She could blow her nose in a Kleenex."

"She wasn't blowing her nose, she was wiping away tears of joy. You need a lace hanky for that." Mother was fishing for an expensive handkerchief.

"Uh-huh." Dad smiled.

"She was crying tears of relief," I piped up.

"Since when did you get so smart?" Mother studied her handkerchief.

"Since I started listening to you."

They both laughed as we pulled into the already overflowing parking lot, where space had been reserved for us.

"Mom, don't you want to know why I don't want to get married?"

"I heard why." She checked her makeup in the passenger visor mirror.

Mother wore light makeup. Too much meant you were cheap, like wearing big jewels during the day. A lady didn't do such crass things.

"I have other reasons."

"Make it short." She pretended to be interested, which was good of her.

"All that work you do in the house disappears. Daddy's work stays. Like the time Daddy, Uncle Mearl and Uncle Kenny built the fence. It's still standing. The wash just gets dirty again."

"The tulip bulbs stay." Mother rolled her lips together after applying her lipstick.

"She's got a point, though." Dad winked at me in the rearview mirror.

"She'll get a point in her head if she doesn't behave today. If Kenny or Wadie teases you, walk away and don't tease them back. And don't speak until spoken to. You know what's right and wrong. Come on."

I behaved like a perfect little lady, which weighted me down with boredom. Julia Ellen was so happy and people cried all over again at her first dance with her father. Later I danced with the boys. That was better than sitting around waiting for some adult to praise my manners.

Children's pronouncements are often brushed aside, but I meant what I said about getting married. The other issue that bothered me was losing my name. Julia Ellen was now Dubbs. Dubbs is a good enough name, but I liked the name Brown. I was determined to hang on to my last name.

Later that spring the county-wide track meet held at York Catholic High School found me entered in the broad-jump event. I was the only grade-schooler in the meet, but our physical-education teacher had entered me. Mom, Dad, Aunt Mimi and the boys sat in the stands. It was cool and misty. All we had in those days were sneakers like PF Flyers or track shoes with cleats. I wore sneakers since we couldn't find cleats small enough to fit me. I remember hearing my name called over the loudspeaker and then running and jumping for all I was worth. Each contestant got three tries. The girls from West York High, William Penn High, Red Lion, Hanover High and York Catholic were mostly juniors and seniors. I didn't even have a uniform, like the Catholic-school kids' green-and-gold ones. I wore navy blue shorts and a white T-shirt.

I placed fourth in the whole county. When I was handed my green ribbon, my name and the name of Valley View Elementary School were called out and everyone applauded. It was tremendously exciting, but I had to contain myself. Showing off would have brought down Mother's wrath.

Later, one of the physical-education teachers, I think from William Penn, spoke to Dad. She told him I had exceptional athletic ability and she looked forward to the day when I'd be a freshman at William Penn.

Mother liked my small victory, but anything to do with sports made her nervous because of my natural father. Then too, Juliann was a fine rider. However, Mother loved sports—she was a fanatic—and eventually that overrode her fears. Still, she didn't want me to resemble my natural parents in any fashion.

I harbored no illusions of athletic glory. I wanted to play any sport girls were allowed to play, and I played baseball and football with the boys in pickup games. I leaped bareback onto any horse or mule that would stand for it. I'd never ridden in a saddle and knew I wouldn't as long as I was under Mother's roof.

I loved sports. I loved competition. I loved the feeling of speed when a horse rolled from a canter to a flat-out gallop. The only female athletes I'd seen or read about were Babe Didrikson Zaharias, Patty Berg, Pauline Betz and Alice Marble.

Each of those women was by then in her thirties or forties. I knew of no female athlete in her teens or twenties, and I don't think anyone else did, either.

I wanted to support myself. I knew sports wasn't the way, but I was often sad as a child and young woman because my athletic ability couldn't fully flower.

The gods had other plans for me.

26

*Red Sails in
the Sunset*

THE DREADFUL PIANO RECITAL, A FACT OF LIFE FOR MOST CHIL-
dren of a certain class, held little fear for me. We were too poor to afford
piano lessons. Thank you, Jesus. However, we gathered at Aunt Mimi's for
her concerts.

Aunt Mimi, not a hair out of place, served hors d'oeuvres, or "horse's
dubers," as she and Mom called them. Uncle Mearl mixed drinks. If the
weather warranted, the party lingered on the porch. If it was cold, we
huddled in her pretty living room. The kids played catch, tag or hide-and-
seek. At twilight we played kick the can, one of the best games ever
invented. When you were tagged and dragged to "prison," you might be
released if a team member burst forth from hiding and kicked the can
before getting tagged himself. What a glorious sound, that can rattling
across the lawn or down the street.

Fried chicken, ham, barbecue, steaks, beans, coleslaw, deviled eggs and,
even better, pickled eggs were served. We'd sit with our plates on our
knees, eat, laugh and argue.

Eventually a guest would say, "Mary, why don't you play something for
us?"

If no guest parroted these lines, Mother usually picked up the cue.

Aunt Mimi would shake her head. "I can't play. Ask Julia Ellen."

"Oh, Mom, you can play," Julia Ellen would reply.

"No, no, I'll turn on the radio." Aunt Mimi would rise.

"Oh, please, Aunt Mimi."

"Yeah, play for us, Mom," the boys would say. Even though she was
their grandmother they called her Mom, and she could have indeed passed
for their mother.

The chorus would swell. She'd demur. Finally, bowing to social pressure and "only to please you," she'd swoop to the piano, pick up her skirt and fling it over the piano bench as she sat down in one smooth motion.

Then she'd root around for sheet music. Julia Ellen would walk over and suggest a tune. Aunt Mimi would flatten out the music, then, with a dramatic pause, lift her hands and drop them to the keys.

After the new pieces were played, she'd take requests: "Night and Day," "School Days," "The Man Who Broke the Bank at Monte Carlo." She especially enjoyed songs from her childhood.

We'd sing. She'd sing. She and Mother would sing a duet. Then the men would sing. Then Mom and Dad would sing. We kids would sing. Then we'd all sing the chorus.

Between selections she'd apologize for lack of skill, only to be shouted down. Shaking her head in disbelief, she'd launch into another Tin Pan Alley melody.

The Buckingham sisters, hospitable to a fault, battled each other for attention. They loved being surrounded by people. Everyone was married or dating, but some of their friends were gay.

One particular couple attracted my attention.

He owned a popular restaurant in town. A broad-chested man with curly hair, Millard wore expensive clothing. He didn't shop in Hanover or York, he headed to Philadelphia. His wife, Ann, a petite, peppy, really nice-looking woman, was also impeccably groomed. They were everybody's favorite. Witty, energetic and well-traveled, they were also smart enough to allow Aunt Mimi and Mom to be the stars when they visited either of the sisters' homes.

What I knew of the world outside York County and Carroll County was what the World War II vets told me and what I read. Ann and Millard spoke not of war, but of theater, symphonies and clothes.

Mother once told me they were "that way." No one said "homosexual" or "gay" or "faggot" or any such term. Somehow you knew what "that way" meant. In Mother's eyes they were worldly and smart. They married, built a great team. Those two worked a room in tandem and whatever they did on the side was their business.

Mother's attitude about gay people was the same as her attitude about everything: "You lead your life and I'll lead mine."

But you absolutely, positively had to get married. Maybe his lover lived in the house, or next door, or maybe hers did—it didn't matter. You still got married, marched to parties together and worked together for a greater goal. Mother, so shrewd in so many ways, demonstrated yet again why she moved so easily within all social circles and among all types of people. She didn't judge. As long as you displayed good manners, you were welcome.

A gang of Dad's buddies from his youth were musicians, which is funny because Dad, apart from his beautiful deep singing voice, wasn't musical. Most of these men, every one of them heart-stoppingly handsome, were gay. They were all married. Some of their wives were lesbians, some were straight.

Mother's anger was reserved for the men who didn't tell women the truth. If a man told you his true preference and you accepted it, fine. Lying was another matter. She hated liars wherever she found them, except when it came to lying to me about my natural father and siblings.

Curious, I asked Dad what he thought. He shrugged his broad shoulders. "God doesn't make mistakes." How typical of Dad to place this on a different, higher plane.

If any of the gang had showed up with a same-sex partner, I don't know how my family would have reacted. In those days, no one would have dreamed of such a thing. A proper facade was part of good manners.

Neither Mom nor Dad rushed things. If I had a question, they answered it. They didn't burden me with knowledge I didn't yet need or want. Outside sources weren't yet weakening the family patterns. Radio standards were very high, and no one even swore on the air. Newspaper standards were also high, and although television was just starting up in terms of being available to many people, the content was both creative and responsible.

The first television I saw had a screen like a porthole. It held no interest for me. A few years later, though, the appliance stores put televisions in their storefront windows. These TVs had square screens; the reception was better and the shows were on weekly. Mom and Dad bought one.

Television may have changed America, but it didn't change us. Aunt Mimi still played her piano. We still gathered on the porch. The personalities and feuds of Mother's Sunday-school class, class number thirty-six, proved far more dramatic than anything on TV.

We watched the news. Mother loved the morning show with Dave Garroway. I could watch one show a night if I had no homework. Usually I was outside. I didn't watch much.

I loved Lucy. Didn't we all? To see those shows when they were first aired was a little bit of heaven. I laughed until I cried. She can still make me laugh until I cry. Many years later, when Miss Ball was in her sixties or seventies, I met her at the opening of the Academy of Television Arts and Sciences Hall of Fame. I could have kissed her. I didn't. I thanked her for her work and moved along. But I loved shaking her hand, meeting one of the comic geniuses of our time.

Tragedy is easy. Comedy is hard. You've heard it before and it's true. If comedy were easy, everyone would be doing it. It's harder to act, harder to direct and, trust me, harder to write.

Eve Arden dazzled us with *Our Miss Brooks*. The appeal of the show lay in its being set in a school; everyone could relate to school, and the fact that Eve Arden was a beautiful, beautiful woman who played against her beauty was interesting. That technique worked for Lucy, too.

Milton Berle, whom I also met many years later, mesmerized the nation. No one knew what he would do next. We'd sing along with the Texaco lyrics, waiting for the appearance of the star.

Mom and Dad liked *The Honeymooners*. I was too young to really absorb the tension between Gleason and Meadows.

But that was about it. Television was not yet a substitute for real life.

I never imagined that I would write for TV. Of course, there are days when I still can't imagine writing for TV.

The sweet cycle of winter, spring, summer, fall, of Advent, Easter, Trinity, created punctuation points to the year. Recognizing Ash Wednesday or the first Sunday in Advent or Memorial Day made me feel grownup.

Whenever people asked me what I wanted to be when I grew up, I'd say "president" or "I want to be like Bill Hardtack." Bill Hardtack, a jockey, could ride even the devil to the finish line.

The fact that I never said "nurse" or "teacher" was noted. People laughed and told me a woman couldn't be president or a jockey.

Well, we proved them wrong on the latter and we'll eventually prove them wrong on the former.

No amount of buttering me up could sway my opinion. I wanted to do whatever I wanted to do. Mother, subtly or flat out, told me what women could do and could not do. Aunt Mimi waged a full-scale campaign to make sure I knew my place.

Bless them. Their banging and badgering toughened me. I stood up to them. I wouldn't let anyone tell me what to do or how to do it.

Mother used to say in a rising tone, "You're heading for a fall."

I'd snap back, "Least I got on the horse."

She swore that adolescence would change all that.

Dad upset everyone's applecart before I could enter the dreaded teenage years.

Kumquat May

THE WINTER OF 1954–55 BROUGHT MY TENTH BIRTHDAY AND
Grandma and Grandpa Brown's fiftieth wedding anniversary. Since their
anniversary was the same day as my birthday, November 28, Mom and
Dad threw a huge party. I was overshadowed but didn't mind. I had sense
enough to know that fifty years of marriage outweighed ten years of my
being around. Mother Brown, in a buoyant mood, a side of her I'd never
seen, allowed pictures of us together. In ten years I'd never had a photo
taken with my paternal grandparents. Nor did Mom give Mamaw my
school photos. Although she was willing now to forgive my illegitimacy,
Mamaw's interest in me remained constant: none.

She did, however, promise me an iron horse doorstop should she leave
this earth. Robust and confident she was sure her exit visa was in no
danger of being stamped.

What I didn't know was that Dad was planning his first real vacation.
He would turn fifty on August 7, 1955, and a quiet rebellion simmered in
his dutiful breast.

The first glimmer occurred in February. He and Mom arranged for me
to leave school for two weeks. I finished my lessons ahead of time and
turned them in. I was already ahead of the game, anyway. They packed the
car, arranged to have the neighbors feed and love on the animals and off
we rolled down old Route 1.

A cruise through Charleston, South Carolina, showed me that while
Philadelphia contained lovely Federal and Georgian architecture, Charleston gloried in it. Back then the Charleston slums were dreadful, though. I
remember driving slowly down one street north of Broad, and second-
story porches, seemingly hanging by a thread, were filled with people.

Georgia impressed me for the great number of pigs and cows walking along the highway. I'd never seen a place so poor and I stirred up trouble at the five-and-dime when we stopped for lunch. Thirsty, I skipped to the closest water fountain and pressed the button. Suddenly a harpy of considerable proportions bore down on me. This black-haired lady with pointy glasses pushed me away from the fountain so hard I fell down.

"Girl, what's wrong with you?"

"I beg your pardon?" (Pre-cotillion at work.)

"Can't you read?"

"Yes, ma'am." My eyes followed her fleshy arm, fingers pointing to a sign reading Colored.

About that time, Mother, hearing the commotion, trotted over to me. She didn't acknowledge the huffing and puffing defender of the Aryan race. She simply grabbed my hand and escorted me out of that five-and-dime in Macon, Georgia.

Mom and Dad left their food on the counter. I thought I was about to be dressed up one side and down the other.

All Mother said was, "Lardass," referring to the harpy.

Neither Mom nor Dad indulged in philosophical lectures or exhaustive explanations about much of anything. By virtue of attending school in York County, I was accustomed to seeing colored people. No one paid attention to the fact that we were integrated. We didn't even know we were integrated. It was a fact of life. Since schools grew out of their communities, the reality was that the student population was not balanced. At Valley View, when I was in fourth grade, there was one colored kid, in the sixth grade. Two years at that time of life is a Grand Canyon. He was high and airy, being so much older than us "weenies." But his classmates liked him and it wasn't an issue for anyone.

So this first encounter with the virulence of American apartheid scared me silly.

"Some people can't drink out of a fountain marked Colored?"

"No, and you can't sit in a waiting room marked Colored, either." Mother folded her arms across her chest.

"But it's wrong."

"People have their ways." Dad, hungry, was looking for another place to eat. He could eat—never put on a pound.

Mother, cooling down, counseled me, "When in Rome do as the Romans do." She paused a minute and then added, "I don't think it's right, but I don't know what to do about it, and don't you get any ideas because you're too little to do anything about it."

"Mom, what about Jesus at the temple?"

"What about it?"

"He threw out the money changers."

"Yes."

"Doesn't that mean we're supposed to fight when something's wrong?"

"I'm taking you out of vacation Bible school," she laughed.

"Does that mean I can leave Sunday school, too?"

"No."

Sunday school, a series of droning lectures illustrated with pictures of a sanitized Jesus, could turn even the most devout Christian into an atheist. Worse, Christine Welch, in my class, was so pretty, had such cute dimples that the Sunday-school teacher looked only at adorable Christine. Poor girl, her face had to be sore from all that forced smiling.

Then too, how many geraniums can you plant on Easter Sunday? If I received one more potted geranium, I was planning to toss it right at the teacher's head.

We puttered along, Dad glancing at me in the rearview mirror. "Maybe things will be better when you're grown-up."

"Maybe I'll make them better," I bragged.

"Thank God my sister isn't along to hear this. She'd beat us over the head with her rosary beads."

"She'd try to convert the Baptists." Dad giggled. He had the most infectious giggle, especially since it emitted from that powerful body.

"Our Lady of the Rosary." Mom was off and running, and we laughed the entire way to the Florida state line.

Driving to Florida before the advent of superhighways tested your patience, but not as much as finally reaching Florida. You can't imagine how long the state is until you drive it. You drive and drive and drive and it's still Florida.

After spending the night below Jacksonville, which smelled reassuringly like Spring Grove, which is to say like one moist paper-mill fart, we set off in the hour before dawn and Dad picked up A1A. As the sun rose we stopped by a beach filled with sea grape trees and undergrowth. We walked down to the Atlantic, a path of red beckoning to us as the sun peeped over the horizon. A school of dolphins broke the surface of the water. No one uttered a word. We watched as the water streaking off their bodies sparkled in the air like thousands of tiny rubies.

One exquisite sight after another greeted us. Mother fell in love with royal palms—those are the tall straight ones whose bases look like poured concrete. I liked the coconut palms and the flocks of wild parrots.

Fort Lauderdale, a small town with one public high school for whites, one Catholic high school, one private school, and one colored high school, enchanted everyone. It was laced with deep canals and boasted a good harbor in Port Everglades. Mother played on the beach across from Birch State Park. Her figure, and she was about to turn fifty herself on March 6, showed little wear and tear. Wearing her bathing suit, she turned heads, which afforded her no small pleasure. Dad, content as always, was happy because she was happy.

We visited the Hialeah and Gulfstream racetracks. Mom, per usual, talked me into the backstretch. I hoped I'd see my hero, Bill Hardtack. I didn't. I saw good horses, though. The Thoroughbred industry in Florida was just getting under way and would challenge California's and New York's with the great horse Needles. Excitement bubbled beneath the surface. Hialeah, distinctive with wrought-iron work and perfectly mani-cured grounds, contrasted with Gulfstream, whose buildings and grounds weren't as pretty. However, the Gulfstream infield, stocked with pink flamingoes, was gorgeous.

I saw my first polo match in south Florida. Apart from foxhunting, it was the most thrilling sport I'd ever witnessed. After the match, I raced to the sidelines and asked if I could hot-walk the ponies—walk them to cool them down. I did and the head groom gave me a quarter—a quarter for doing something I loved.

Mother kept a diary. Her utilitarian entries are interesting for what caught her attention. *Miami Beach. How do they pay their electric bill? So many lights. It was seventy degrees this evening and women wore mink coats. I wore shorts. Rita only wants to see the horses. Butch inspected two meat markets and three supermarkets today. He wore sandals. I can't believe it. I picked an orange off a tree in February. It wasn't ripe, but still. Butch bought oranges from the Piggly Wiggly, isn't that a funny name? I made the kid eat one. That kid hates fruit. This is paradise.*

Every day she'd scribble in her leather travel book. We crossed Alligator Alley, skimming the tip of the Everglades. Armadillos waddled to and fro. Naples, next on the agenda, was as appealing to me as to Mom and Dad. It was tiny then, a pier jutting into the Gulf of Mexico. One high school and wonderful weather, that was Naples.

We cruised up the west coast of Florida, marveling at Sarasota with its handsome houses, wondering if the bridge over to Tampa would hold, zooming through St. Petersburg, which had so many old people they always took a body count after the movie was over. Just in case.

Then we veered over to Tarpon Springs and Silver Springs and finally we reached Ocala. The limestone soil there is perfect for horses. The big farms were in the process of being created. I loved it. Mother liked it too, but Mother wanted those ocean breezes, so we headed back over to A1A.

Our last day in Florida, Mom cried. She didn't want to leave. We got on Route 301 and headed back home. Just inside Maryland a snowstorm whacked us hard. Dad stopped to buy chains and he and the service station man put them on the car. There was something funny about watching suntanned Dad out there in the snow.

He was steaming. I'd seen my father lose his temper only once before. He cursed the entire rest of the trip back to York, which with the filthy weather and the bad roads took twelve hours when it should have taken four.

The next morning I woke up to find Dad and Mom at the breakfast table. He had one day of vacation left and he wasn't going in to work. That alone was amazing. Ralph Brown, who sometimes worked from 6:30 A.M. until he dragged home at 10:00 P.M., wasn't even calling to see how the store was doing.

Their sudden silence made me think of "little pitchers." Children overhear stuff, and you never know what the buggers will repeat in company.

Mother placed a glass of fresh-squeezed orange juice before me, from the mesh bag of Florida oranges on the counter. The only way I could get the rest of my breakfast was to drink the orange juice, which I unwillingly did every morning.

Dad made breakfast. Mother and I sat there while he served us food garnished with a stream of his early morning jokes, which were so corny, but, well, so Dad.

"How would you like to live in Florida?"

"Me?"

"Is there someone else in the room?" Mother joked.

"Where in Florida? Ocala?" I parried.

"Fort Lauderdale."

"Naples?"

"The west coast is hotter than the east," Mother said.

"Can we go now?"

"As soon as you finish school. That way you can start seventh grade down there and we'll have time to sell the house. And don't say anything yet. We haven't told Uncle Claude or Uncle Earl or Sis. We have a lot to do and some people might be upset. So you let us do the talking."

"Yes, ma'am." Daddy poured me another cup of tea. "Mom, what about Tuffy and Chap and Ginger?"

"Aunt Gertrude has always wanted Tuffy. Dad knows a man who'll buy Chap because you've done such a good job with him, and we'll find a good home for Ginger before we leave."

"I don't want to leave my animals. You drop me in Virginia and keep going to Florida."

"There are lots of diseases in that tropical heat. These animals aren't acclimated to it and they'll get sick." Mother usually didn't use big words like *acclimated*.

"What about us?"

"They say it takes a year for your blood to thin." Dad spoke up finally. "Once we're settled you can have another kitty and puppy, ones that have been born there."

"Well . . . I'll go if I don't have to go to Sunday school. I'll go to church, but I won't go to Sunday school."

"Why don't you see what Sunday school is like there? Maybe it's better."

"Mom, I hate it."

A long, long silence followed.

Mother said, "You're of an age now where you must take catechism classes. I guess that's enough."

"No vacation Bible school."

"I guess not." She laughed, then pointed her fork at me. "But you are enrolling in cotillion the minute we get there, you hear me?"

"Yes, ma'am."

"Butch, do you have anything to say?"

"Where'd she learn to drive such a hard bargain? Must be your side of the family."

"How about a horse?"

"When we win the Irish Sweepstakes. Are you going to eat that sausage?" Mother leaned toward me.

"I'm saving it till last."

Disappointed, she said, "Oh."

Dad got up and fried more sausage.

"Why do you eat all your egg, then all your toast, then all your sausage? You do that at every meal. You have to learn to sample from each food group."

"It tastes better this way."

"It's not proper."

"Well, I'll learn when I get to cotillion—in Florida."

"You know, honey"—Dad placed the sizzling sausages on my plate—"you've got the makings of a first-rate politician."

"Don't encourage her, Butch."

And that's how we landed in Florida.

28

Skinks and
Land Crabs

THERE MUST HAVE BEEN A RUN ON SMELLING SALTS AT THE DRUGstore, because each time Mom and Dad spread the news of their decision, somebody just about passed out. Mother Brown opted for the Bismarck approach: tight lips, iron gaze. Aunt Mimi, once she regained her breath, offered token resistance. Of all people, she was the one I thought would pitch a home-run hissy. Her secret agenda emerged later.

Ralph Brown, that beast of burden who toted his load and everyone else's, quietly but effectively rebelled. He sold out his share of the store. Our house sold in a flash. Before I knew it we were packed and ready to go.

When we took Tuffy to Gertrude, I wavered. Tuffy lived a long and honorable life with Gertrude Buckingham, but I missed her.

Chap and Ginger were already in their new homes, and I received praise for my work with the dogs. I would have preferred my dogs to the praise, but I hoped PopPop could look down on me and smile. They weren't hounds, but still, I'd trained them. I vowed that when I was big and strong, I'd handle hounds.

We sold nearly everything other than Mother's treadle sewing machine and the family heirlooms, my favorite being the one knife with a wooden handle that the Yankees had left after they looted the place in Maryland. They stole the hot stove and then returned to steal the smoke. All we had left after 1865 were a few dishes and odds and ends.

People mumbled that Dad, ancient at fifty, would never get hired. I was becoming aware how frightened most people are of change, how negative they are, too, when someone makes a break for whatever happiness they can grab in this life. I wanted to say, "Shut your fat trap," but Mother would have washed my mouth out with Grandpa's Tar Soap, a particularly virulent brand. So as neighbors and false friends painted a dark picture for my parents, I acted as though I were concentrating on other things. No one said much about me other than that southern schools were dreadful and I wouldn't learn a thing.

Mother, in a rare burst of discipline, kept her own mouth shut. Not that Mother didn't have good manners, she did, but she also had a low boiling point. If you heated her up that far, she'd describe the full extent of your stupidity.

Sis cried and waved us off. The boys were jealous, of course. Eugene, now married, said he'd visit.

The minute we crossed the Mason-Dixon line, which was less than fifteen minutes from home, my mother let out a war whoop that would have made Tecumseh proud. We sang the whole way to Florida.

Our first day in Fort Lauderdale, Mom found an efficiency off Fifteenth Street NE. Sparkling white with aqua trim, nothing could have been more Florida. The owners, a young couple named Skula, had a son my age. In one day we were all best friends, and Mom and Dad remained friends with the Skulas after we found a home to buy. I bought a push mower and hustled a few jobs, which was a lot harder than in York since lawn mainte-nance companies sewed up most of the business. I undercut their rates, begged people to give me a chance. I was a convincing eleven-year-old. I was also reliable and I liked plants. I got my library card at the Middle River Library, the only library in town then, so I could read about hibis-cus, lantana, bougainvillea, citrus trees and the awful crabgrass everyone calls a lawn in Florida.

Mother, feeling I was big enough to take care of myself, took a job at Stevens' Bakery. Dad found a job within a week at Crossroads Market.

Isn't it funny how when you finally break out and do what your heart wants to do, everything falls into place? Within seven days of moving to Florida, and without knowing one person, both my parents had jobs, I had some work, we'd found the Skulas and we had more time together than ever before.

The bakery proved to be a godsend because the Stevens brothers, who owned it, were politicians. Fred was the commissioner of Port Everglades and Bill sat on the city council. Mother was in her element. She adored these men, who were about her age, and she liked learning the bakery business. She'd worked in a silk mill before I was born, and she liked working, meeting people and solving problems. Dad dropped her off at the bakery in the mornings and then drove on to work. He'd pick her up about four-thirty or five o'clock. We spent every evening and the week-ends together. In Pennsylvania Dad used to work through most of the weekends, often even on Sunday. Now he took Sundays off. My parents were so happy. We'd hurry to the beach, day or night, where we'd walk, chase sand crabs and breathe in the salty air.

I wanted a cat and dog. Mother promised me I could have pets, but only when we bought a house.

We looked around. Finally, not far from where we were renting, a new small house was being built. They put the money down and three months later—things go up fast in Florida—we moved into a house that was diaper-rash pink with black wrought-iron shutters.

Mother and I planted palm trees, hibiscus, ixora and a small orange tree. We settled for a queen palm, which had a gray base but was smaller than the royal palms, and I got a coconut palm. The deal was I had to trim the dead fronds, which I did, but the palmetto bugs, brown bombers, that zoomed out of there tried my nerves.

Skinks with electric blue stripes on their sides scurried in the crotons, in the flame hibiscus, everywhere. Land crabs trooped by. Those suckers are formidable.

Every time Mom saw a land crab she'd holler, "Get the shovel." Her reasoning was that they'd undermine your house, and if they grabbed hold of you, you'd lose digits.

It was my job to kill them. She wouldn't. The brittle *thwack* when I'd nail them would bring a cheer from Mom.

Killing snakes, another job of mine, required subterfuge. Unlike most people, I like snakes. They eat pests, as do bats, owls, praying mantises, ladybugs, etc. Why kill a friend? I'd grab the snake behind the head, make a commotion, then release the creature away from Mother's gaze.

The only time I backed off from this mission was if the intruder was a rattler. Fortunately, I only crossed one, and I distracted him with one hand while I cut him clean through with a machete.

If you're really fast, you can grab a rattler's tail and snap him, literally snap him like a whip, cracking his head on the ground. I'd seen a guy do that, but I was sticking to my machete.

I hated living in the suburbs, but I loved Florida. Herds of Brahman bulls roamed a few miles inland—we were only three miles from the ocean. They intrigued me. I knew Holsteins, Herefords, Angus, Red Angus, Jerseys and Guernseys, but the light-colored Brahmans kept you on your toes. For one thing, they are fast. For another, they can be mean as snakeshit. Angus can be mean, too, but not like the Brahmans. I tore across more than one field of Bermuda grass and sandspurs with a bull charging after me. Maybe I was stupid, but I wanted to get close to them, really see how they were put together and how they moved.

Animals that adapted to the semitropical environment were all new to me. I'd never seen a manatee, also called a sea cow. They are so sweet. We used to jump in the canals and swim with them.

I discovered garfish, alligators and barracuda, all to be meticulously avoided. I saw my first sea turtle, as big as I was and weighing more. It was as though Noah had dropped the gangplank from his ark and bid the fabulous creatures disembark in Florida.

Flocks of wild parrots screeched. Ibis, white and black, stalked the canals. Occasionally we'd glimpse a flamingo that had taken a hike, from Gulfstream, I guess.

Foxhunting didn't exist. The only hounds I saw were coonhounds, a nice hound, mind you, but not a foxhound. That upset me.

However, Mother more than made up for it by dragging me to the shedrows of Hialeah and Gulfstream on her odd days off. I'd sit on an overturned bucket watching everything and everybody trooping up and down the shedrow. Taught to look at a horse from the hoof up, I did just that. I bet I looked at as many Thoroughbreds as the people racing them did.

I looked for a good hoof, a short, heavy cannon bone, well-sprung ribs, a big chest (for a big heart), big eyes, big nostrils and room at the throat-latch. The best conformation in the world is useless if the horse can't breathe.

I also learned that some flaws didn't bother me much. A little toe-out or toe-in, what the heck. An offset knee, well, that's a bit worse but the horse doesn't know it; they adjust to their flaw. Some of the greatest racehorses in the world, like Seattle Slew, would not have passed a conformation evaluation.

I also learned who was doping horses, who was fleecing their employer and who was honest—not many of the last, but there were some. The trainers who knew what they were doing had the best feed and exercise programs. Since I couldn't watch the races, I watched horses breeze down the track. If I was lucky, I would be allowed to towel off a horse or hot-walk it.

Sometimes we'd go up to Royal Palm, where I hot-walked the polo ponies. Mostly they were small Thoroughbreds and mostly they were kind, willing animals. Polo ponies taught me a great deal about how tolerant horses can be. Many of those polo players used their horses like bumper cars. That the ponies put up with it just amazed me. I hated those guys.

However, the really good horsemen were like the really good Thoroughbred trainers—they paid attention to the horses' nutrition and training. They rode light. A good polo match is one of the most exciting sporting events in the world. I saw a lot of good polo, and once I learned to separate the wheat from the chaff, I came to respect polo players.

In all equine sports there are people who should not own horses or ride them; it's just so obvious in polo, that's all.

I wanted a horse. I saved my lawn service money but I couldn't begin to get there. Dad bought me a gold English racer. He said the bicycle would have to take the place of a horse until I made enough money to buy one.

Dad always knew how to handle me. Mother would say no, berate me or, worse, remind me I should be grateful and not ask for things. Dad said nothing, but he came up with alternatives.

I still worked on the typewriter he had given me. I graduated to writing stories about what I saw around me. No more talking Easter eggs that hatched brightly colored chicks. The English language, easy for me, none-theless presented problems. You could drown in the pool of words, we have so many. You could also show off. I was at the show-off stage. If there was any way to sound intellectual, I did. Mother threw the stuff in the trash. She was my first and harshest critic—and the most accurate.

"Be clear." If she said that once, she said it a thousand times. Ranked right up there with "Blood tells."

About this time we marched down to Fort Lauderdale High School, where I had to register for seventh grade. The high school was a beautiful old Spanish-style series of buildings connected by graceful arched breeze-ways. The red Mediterranean tile roofs reflected the glare of the sun, and palm trees dotted the acres of ground. One quad, where kids could dance, contained a mosaic with the school symbol, a blue flying *L.* I'd never seen anything so beautiful at a high school.

I wouldn't be attending classes there, however; I'd be bused to the Naval Air Station, site of the takeoff of the famous Lost Squadron. Even though I was officially attending Sunrise Junior High, classes were held at Naval Air. They simply hadn't built the new junior high school yet. An-other school used the Naval Air barracks, too, Rogers Junior High. That wasn't built either.

Anyway, I accompanied Mom down to register, armed with my birth certificate. Here I might add that I tan to a deep brown. My eyes are dark brown and my hair is black-brown. Now there's some gray in it, nature's frosting, but then it was all black.

The lady behind the desk, no doubt hot and tired, checked my birth certificate, saw "adopted," looked me over and wouldn't let us sign up. She said I might be "mixed race."

Mother, stunned, stood there for a second.

"You'll have to move, madam, there's a line behind you."

"She's white." Mother's jaw set.

"Well, now, Mrs. Brown, you'll have to prove this girl here isn't part Negra." This was how she pronounced the word *Negro*.

I leaned over the desk, put my face right in hers and growled, "I'd rather be part Negra than all stupid like you."

I stormed out.

Mother, speechless, followed me out of the building.

"I'll go to the Negro school," I said.

"Oh, no, you won't."

"I don't care."

"Well, I do!"

"I thought you didn't care about that."

"I don't, but I know they get the short end of the stick, kid, and I'll be damned if I let someone cheat my kid out of her proper place. And honey, the Negro folks don't want you. You don't belong there even if you want to go there." She put up her hand to stop the tirade that was building. "I'm your mother and you'll do as I say." Then she sat down because she had started laughing so hard. "Oh, God, the look on that biddy's face!" A flash of propriety. "Don't you ever sass an adult like that again in public, you hear me?"

"Yes, ma'am."

Then she laughed again until she cried. When she finally pulled herself together, we walked into the big church across from the school and Mom asked a woman in the office if she could use her phone. The woman, young and pretty, gladly let Mom dial.

I thought she was calling Dad, something she rarely did because Mom said we shouldn't bother Dad or anyone else at work. Instead she called Bill Stevens at his office. Briefly she recapped the event, then hung up the phone.

The young lady at the desk scrutinized me and blurted out, "She certainly has Caucasian features."

"She ought to, her people came here in 1620. Buckingham."

Most southerners know the name Buckingham.

"Aha." A new emotion crossed the young woman's pretty face. "She sure does tan."

"That she does."

And we left.

A few days passed. I received in the mail my notification of when I was to start school, my bus number, eighty-four, and the time I had to be at the bus stop, 6:30 A.M. I have no idea what Mother told Bill Stevens when she saw him—I guess the whole story about my adoption. But I know he fixed it.

Mother took to calling me "Pick," which was short for *pickaninny*. I didn't mind it; it was better than being called "the Ill." She still called me "Buzzer," but "Pick" was reserved for when she was feeling devilish. Then you knew something was going to happen—like maybe she'd throw a water balloon at you.

Ugliness leaves a mark. I had knowingly encountered racial ugliness only twice up to the age of eleven. If it left a mark on me, what in God's name does it do to children who face it every single day? And how could someone like that absurd registrar's assistant act that way? How sad, miserable and pinched must someone's life be for her to need a crutch like the color of your skin to feel superior to you. Makes me sick.

Offsetting this was Aunt Mimi's announcement that she was moving to Fort Lauderdale. No wonder she hadn't carried on like Aida, or even Bette Davis, when we moved away. She'd been already working on Uncle Mearl. And a few months after that, down came Ken, Ceil, Kenny, Wadie, Terry, Julia Ellen and Russell.

Again, magic held. Everyone found work and everyone was happy.

And, of course, Aunt Mimi called up or marched through the door at the crack of dawn each morning, either on her way to mass at St. Anthony's or on her way back. The Buckingham girls were together again. Could Florida survive them?

Top Dog

BUTCH, AUNT MIMI'S GLORIOUS BOSTON TERRIER, JOINED THE BIG Hound in the Sky. After a suitable period of mourning, she needed another creature to order about. Her daughter, married, could be bullied but not as frequently as before she entered into wedded bliss. Her sister fought back, which provided equal parts irritation and excitement. Her husband, her loyal ally, was not a suitable candidate. I failed the obedience test as well. Surely another dog would fill this void.

Dad brought me a white kitten with gray spots, Skippy. An excellent murderer of skinks and the occasional sloppy blue jay, Skippy followed me around like a penny dog.

I wanted an American Foxhound but ran into walls of resistance. I begged for a Chow Chow, but Mother said that heat would be cruel for such a heavy-coated animal. She was right. I tried for an Airedale, but Mom reminded me we'd need to strip the fur twice a year.

I volunteered to ride around with Aunt Mimi as she searched for the perfect pet. We'd cruise up and down the straight streets—the land was flat as a pancake—and stop by breeders. She'd check out the puppies, we'd climb back in the car.

"Too small. If I stepped on one, I'd kill it." Her verdict on Chihuahuas. "Doggy odor." Her response to a Wire Fox Terrier.

"Why not get another Boston bull?"

"Can't do that." She shook her head sadly. "There will never be another Butch. The dog would suffer by comparison."

I thought about how Aunt Mimi used to stand on the porch and call, "Butch! Come here, Butch!"

Dad and Butch the dog would both race around the corner and up on the porch to greet her. No matter how many times we witnessed this spectacle it made us laugh.

Dysfunctional families grab attention today. Our family carried its share of mishaps, mistakes and outright fights, but in the main, we were happy; we expected to work hard, and whatever good fortune came our way was celebrated. After all, Mom and Dad's generation lived through two world wars and the Great Depression. Those calamities framed their sense of life. They knew horrible things happened for no special reason. *Carpe diem.* And they did.

Our corny jokes, like Aunt Mimi calling the dog and Dad showing up, drew us closer. We played pranks on one another, worked together and buried our dead together.

Aunt Virginia had died young and then Mother's brother, Bucky, died too. The last person anyone expected to go down young was George Buckingham. Colon cancer ate him alive.

Maybe that's why our passions drive us, why our sense of humor is so sharp; we each know we could be erased on the great blackboard of life without leaving but a speck of chalk dust.

Aunt Mimi's passion right now was a puppy. After a few weeks of the canine search of the century, still no pooch. Following each of our forays, I'd report to Mother.

"She doesn't need a dog. She's naturally vicious." Mother would laugh, and sometimes she'd go on to reverse herself. "She wants a dog because she's too chicken to bite someone herself." Like confetti, the put-downs floated harmlessly to the ground. Mom needed to throw things.

A whirl through Burdine's in downtown Fort Lauderdale always enlivened Mom. That woman moved through a department store like an army scout on a recon mission. Rarely purchasing anything, she folded garments back to check the seams, tapped crystal with her fingernail and plopped into every chair, testing them.

This day she found a sundress with a flared skirt and short sleeves cut on an angle. It fit her perfectly. Jumping black poodles decorated the fabric.

"What do you think?"

"You look great, Mom."

"Not bad for an old lady." She spun on the ball of her foot.

She bought the dress after a small period of agony over the cost. We hopped into the car. She'd had it with shopping for the day and the next thing I knew she was roaring up Dixie Highway, turning left into the northwest section of Fort Lauderdale. She pulled up at a lime green house with white trim and shutters. I tagged along.

The yips of puppies greeted my ears. Mother picked out a jet black little guy, a Miniature Poodle. She paid the portly lady and home we drove.

Mortified, I said nothing. A poodle. How could she? Poodles belonged to old ladies with butterfly sunglasses, rhinestone jewelry and high-heeled sandals parading up and down Collins Avenue in Miami Beach.

The little fellow curled up and slept in my lap.

"Does Dad know about this?"

"He will when I pick him up from work."

"Mom?"

"Well"—her voice rose a tone—"the right dog completes a lady's ensemble."

"Oh." No point arguing that one. "Greyhounds are elegant."

"And big, and they chase anything, including Skippy."

"Yeah, I forgot about that. . . . A Clumber Spaniel?" I loved those Clumbers.

"Hair is too long. A Miniature Poodle will suit me fine."

"You know that they aren't really miniature, Mom. This dog will get to be the size of a Toy Schnauzer." I petted his little head. "Maybe fifteen pounds."

"Big enough to get out of the way, small enough to handle." And she added, "They're very smart, so you can train him."

"Okay," I agreed weakly.

She hummed the whole way home, breezed through the door, picked up the phone and invited her sister over.

She greeted Sis with rapture, making Aunt Mimi suspicious. Then Mother walked into the kitchen which she'd blocked off to keep the puppy confined, scooped up the puppy and showed it to her sister.

"You always have to be first!" Aunt Mimi flamed out of there.

"Jealous," Mother giggled.

Fortunately, poodles originally were hunting dogs. I felt better when I learned that. And he was smart. I taught him the basics and I taught him to fetch the paper. Mother loved that dog. She wore her poodle sundress a lot. She began finding poodle scarves, poodle costume jewelry, you name it. Mother became heavily empoodled.

Dad liked the dog, too.

Aunt Mimi, spiked to a competitive pitch, bought an expensive Pekingese. She spent a lot more than she'd intended. Chin had a pedigree as good as that of Bold Ruler, a fabulous Thoroughbred. Black Sunshine, Mom's dog, although handsome and well put together, was not well bred.

What a sight they were, strolling through the Sunrise Plaza shopping center, then brand spanking new, with their canine alter egos. Aunt Mimi favored a thin leash with rhinestones on it to match the sparkling red collar Chin wore. Mother thought male dogs should never be exposed to rhinestones, for it might affect their sexuality. Black Sunshine, a butch poodle, wore a rolled leather collar.

The two dogs often got along better than the two sisters.

On those trips to the shedrows, Sunshine stayed with me on his leash. He liked horses.

Aunt Mimi, who made a show of opposing gambling, allowed Mother to cajole her into attending the races one time. She won over two hundred dollars. She and Mom sang "Shine On Harvest Moon" part of the way home until their voices pooped out. They'd shouted themselves hoarse at the races.

Aunt Mimi's new car (white—the only intelligent choice in Florida) had a good radio. They turned it on and we all heard Elvis Presley for the first time. "Hound Dog" delighted the sisters. One of the lines, "You ain't nothing but a hound dog," became one of their refrains. Mother read about Elvis. She adored him. Aunt Mimi said he was singing "race music," but then proceeded to listen to every new single he released.

They loved him, Patsy Cline, Tennessee Ernie Ford and Dinah Shore. They bickered about how fat Kate Smith really was and vied with each other singing "When the Moon Comes Over the Mountain" complete with tremolo.

We'd be strolling down Las Olas Boulevard, Sunshine and Chin keeping pace.

Mother would start, "Ginger Rogers."

Aunt Mimi would counter, "Eleanor Powell."

"Cyd Charisse."

"Ruby Keeler."

"Ann Miller."

"Isadora Duncan."

"Can't use her." Aunt Mimi stopped in front of the preppy women's clothing store that sold tassel Weejuns, a kind of loafer.

"Why not?"

"She didn't dance in the movies."

"You're saying that because you can't think of anyone else."

"Ha."

I dropped twenty feet behind them. I'd reached the age where I didn't want to be seen with my family, anyway, and when Mom and Aunt Mimi wound up for a donnybrook I really didn't want to be around.

I walked into the store and tried on tassel Weejuns, size 7B. They were twelve dollars. I had five, which I'd saved from my lawn mowing. The rest I had put in the bank.

Old Maine Trotters, Weejuns and tassel Weejuns were the shoes of choice. If you couldn't afford them, you could pass muster with a pair of white sneakers, no socks. If you wore socks in Florida, that meant you were a major weenie. Couldn't carry an umbrella, either, no matter how hard it rained.

I left the store and ran after Mother, who was deadlocked with Aunt Mimi over dancers.

"Mother, will you lend me seven dollars?"

"Seven dollars?"

"I need tassel Weejuns and I only have five dollars."

"Will you clean the jalousies?"

This had to be one of the most hateful jobs in Florida. Jalousie windows have thin louvers of heavy glass, exactly right for the climate, but a royal pain to keep clean. It required three to four hours in the hot sun to soap them up and wash them down, and you couldn't use the hose or you'd soak the inside of the house.

"I'll do them today."

She reached into her skirt pocket and pulled out the money.

"Hey, Pick." She smiled. "Put your best foot forward."

"Oh, Mom." I ran back and bought the shoes as those two laughed at how clever they were.

When I emerged from the store, shoe box in hand, I didn't join them immediately, but walked behind, watching them. I wondered if I would grow up to be like Mother. Surely this is a fear that strikes terror in the heart of every female when she takes her mother's measure.

I swore I wouldn't. Never. Not for a skinny minute would I be like Juts. Ha.

30

School Daze

DOES ANYTHING INTERESTING HAPPEN IN JUNIOR HIGH? IF SO, tell me. I missed it.

31

Pluperfect

P ASSING AND REPASSING, A SOUTHERN RITUAL, SLOWS YOU DOWN while loading you up with all the news that's not fit to print.

Mother and Aunt Mimi excelled at trolling through town. They were newcomers, but their church work and political affiliations catapulted them to the center of activity. Then again, Fort Lauderdale in those days was a sleepy town; there wasn't but so much activity. Drowsy though it was, the inhabitants could be counted upon for their share of drunkenness, car wrecks and desultory infidelity. Naturally, Mom and Aunt Mimi wished to hear every syllable even if they weren't on a first-name basis with the culprits.

I unwittingly supplied them plenty to comment on. The time came when the boys no longer enjoyed my whipping them at baseball and football. My arm alone could make a coach weep. My gender made him weep even more. I could throw anything with accuracy. A lot of good it did me.

Nothing could induce me to join the swim team after eighth grade. Since the school in those days had no swimming pool, we practiced in the Atlantic Ocean. If nothing else, it made us tough. That salt water was cold at six-thirty in the morning, and swimming parallel to shore with the tide sucking you in and out built strong swimmers. After an hour of that we showered at the open showers on the beach, threw on our clothes and hitched a ride back to school. In the afternoon we used the Casino Pool for the miserable drill of wind sprints. My lungs burned even as my teeth chattered. My lungs gave out before my muscles did.

The other thing I loathed about swimming was that I couldn't see my rivals. Well, the chlorine turned one's hair green, but I could have lived with that. I swam freestyle and butterfly and the only reason I hung on as long as I did was that it only cost me a bathing suit.

Finally red-rimmed eyes and chilly mornings forced me to look for another "girls' sport."

Dad dragged me to a driving range. The guy handed me a bucket of balls and showed me the proper grip on the rented golf club. I teed up and whacked that sucker out to the last numbered card. I blasted every ball I could. A few veered to the right, which infuriated me, but most of them sailed straight out and not very high, just like a rifle shot.

The fellow in the little booth allowed as to how I might have some talent. I didn't want to play golf, though. For one thing, it was much too expensive for us. For another, I associated it with old men in kelly green pants with embroidered whales on them.

The only sport left was tennis, which I thought was another weenie sport. At least I could run around and hit things, but it seemed so tame compared to football and baseball. However, if my parents didn't find some channel for my energy, I'd drive them crazy—or worse, run off to Hialeah and try to breeze horses. This thought scared Mother half to death, quite apart from the family history concerning riding.

The danger involved in sitting atop a flying twelve-hundred-pound animal was, as you might expect, exactly what attracted me.

Wherever you find the footprint of a Buckingham, Young, Finster or Zepp, you'll also find a hoofprint. My great-uncle Johnny ran a Thoroughbred stable in Green Springs, Maryland, right after World War II (or maybe it was before the war). At that time, the great state of Maryland (and it is) brimmed with tracks. Johnny kept good foxhunters on the side and went out with Green Springs Hunt, too, really a grand hunt. The law busted him for making book and he lost everything. He sat in the pokey for a while.

Today, they call it off-track betting and the state controls it. So much for free enterprise.

Mother came by her gambling naturally. I don't think she feared that I would gamble because I have no inclination in that direction. I might gamble with my life but I won't gamble with money.

But long before Great-Uncle Johnny cooled his heels in a Black Maria heading for jail, our family trained horses, sold them or showed them. I wonder if that first Thomas Buckingham, running from Cromwell, wasn't really a horse thief. Aunt Mimi must be spinning in her grave that I could even think such a thing. Face it, no one suffered an Atlantic crossing in the seventeenth century unless life had turned unbearable in the old country. What Aunt Mimi told me was that as the younger son, Thomas wouldn't inherit. Well, he could have gone into the church or the military, but Thomas must have had a skeleton in his closet. In the beginning, of course, we were all Europe's rejects and Africa's captured. What a strange beginning for a country.

But underneath, I think, Mother worried that I'd go bad at the track even though she was the one always depositing me there. She frantically searched for some new focus.

The first time I saw the Southside tennis courts, next to Southside Elementary School, I nearly laughed. Of packed red clay, those courts had withstood the abuse of many feet. Except at the yacht club and the country club, there were no other courts. These were public ones.

The skipper of this pathetic ship was a vigorous, good-natured man named Jim Evert. A little bowlegged, heavily muscled, with jet black hair and sparkling eyes, he'd stand out there in the grueling sun teaching classic flat tennis strokes. As some of you know, with the classic stroke (as opposed to, say, a topspin forehand), you have little margin for error, but the payoff comes when the ball hits your opponent's court. That baby will fly.

I had no money for lessons. I watched him. I'd saved enough from mowing lawns to buy a racket from Sears. It cost eleven dollars and was called a Blue Ribbon. It was awful.

Armed with this poorly balanced, nylon-strung block of wood, I would pick up old tennis balls and go onto the courts at the end of the afternoon. I'd serve.

But Jimmy Evert, unknown to us kids, was no ordinary tennis pro. Oh, we knew of his titles, including winning both singles and doubles titles at the Canadian Open in 1947, but we didn't know the sweep of vision he possessed. He convinced the city fathers that Fort Lauderdale needed first-class public courts. Lighted courts. As Southside was away from the center, why not place them in Holiday Park, which was a better location? This was great for me because it meant I could walk to the courts, whereas I had to take a bus to Southside.

Fort Lauderdale built eight clay courts with a green surface. No lights. Those came later. The place was packed morning, noon and night. Within a few years the city added more courts.

The best part for me was the backboard. I could hit to my heart's content. Dad bought me a month's membership, which I think cost fourteen dollars. I didn't know if anyone would play with me.

Jimmy, stern on the outside and a real sweetheart on the inside, found an older gentleman who would hit with me. The fellow was German and a baker. He lavished attention on me. I loved him. I called him Otto to torment him.

Pretty soon other people asked to hit with me, mostly men. I was off and running.

If I lost my temper, Jimmy would haul me off the court. I'd sulk. He was very strict and so was Colette, his engaging, extremely pretty wife. Standards were high. You measured up or you shipped out.

One Saturday I got so mad at myself I threw my racket on the ground and broke it. That fast I was off the court. Jimmy told me not to come back until I repented.

Repented? I was in anguish. I didn't have the money for another racket. Bad though it was, the Blue Ribbon was all I had. I fought back the tears and trudged home to disgrace because Jimmy had called my mother.

People paid close attention to children then. If you were reprimanded at school or at the tennis courts, you were bound to catch holy hell at home. If someone like Jimmy eighty-sixed some cherub today, God only knows what would happen. Chances are the enraged parents would engage a lawyer.

Mother tore me a new asshole, she was so mad. Then Dad, who didn't raise his voice, voiced his disappointment. That hurt even worse.

Aunt Mimi, Uncle Mearl, Russell and Julia Ellen also gave me the benefit of their thoughts: I was a jerk. I thought they were going to take out an ad in the Fort Lauderdale newspaper.

But Otto and my other hitting partners showed me once again that my life is full of loving surprises. I didn't know that Mom knew Hans (Otto's real name). He baked at the downtown store for the Stevens brothers.

At that time he must have been nearing seventy. His abundant hair, glimmering white, set off his bright blue eyes. He had the square build and chin of a Bavarian. He loved to talk about Germany before World War I. Europe must have been idyllic then, between the Franco-Prussian War and World War I. He fought in the First World War, then suffered the punitive peace that paved the way for extremists. When Hitler came to power, Hans left with a little bit of money. He couldn't speak English, but he learned fast. His wife died when he was in his fifties, and for whatever reason he hadn't the heart to find another partner.

Mother paid little heed to my athletic gifts. She couldn't see where they benefited a girl, and realistically she was right. There were no athletic scholarships for women, nor was there respect for talent except for those few men who liked to see a good athlete compete regardless of sex. Hans convinced Mother that I should stick with tennis.

Never one to throw away an advantage, Mother laid down her conditions. "This only goes to show that you need cotillion."

"I said I would go."

"I know. I enrolled you for spring."

"That's a year early. I can't go to catechism and cotillion at the same time."

"You can and you will."

I did.

Hans and the guys bought me a Jack Kramer, 4⅝ grip (I liked big grips), strung with Victor Imperial gut. If I misbehaved again, they'd take back the racket.

Counting to ten became a necessity, but I didn't throw my racket again.

Tennis delighted me. Cotillion didn't.

The guardians of manners, many of whom were UDC (United Daughters of the Confederacy), had bosoms like flight decks. They'd bear down on you at forty knots. If one of those ladies had slammed into me, I'd be blind. These were the days of rocket-cone tits. Jane Russell and Marilyn Monroe reigned.

I poured ice-water "tea" until my biceps bulged. Bring the cup to the pot, never the other way around. Stand when a married lady enters the room. The guest of honor sits at the right of the head of the table. Never wear navy blue before Easter or white after Labor Day.

The rules, memorized and repeated, separated quality people from riffraff. Riffraff was starting to look good to me. After all, Elvis was riffraff, but Mother insisted he had manners. He did, too.

Added on to the weekly session of deportment came the introduction sessions. "May I present Rita Mae Brown to Your Majesty."

I curtsey.

Her Majesty slightly inclines her head and moves on. She may or may not shake your hand.

After Her Majesty comes Her Royal Highness. Oh, God, the endless drills. I longed for Her Lowness.

Finally, the *pièce de résistance* (I emphasize *résistance*): the Christmas Ball.

It was held at the Governor's Club, then the most fashionable hotel in Fort Lauderdale. Each year, various groups would decorate the ballroom, engendering hot competition among the Junior League, the Professional Women's Association, the Pilot Club, and so on.

My first Christmas Ball truly was beautiful. The theme of red and white transformed the ballroom into a winter fairyland, and since there was no winter, the fake ice and snow surrounding an enormous ice sculpture of a reindeer with a red nose was fun.

You had to glide through the receiving line. The mayor was in it. If a lady, you positioned yourself somewhere in the open and waited for young men and boys to fill your dance card. This could be agony, and I imagine it was agony for the boys too. Large fathers resplendent in tuxedos quietly forced boys to sign up to dance with girls they didn't want to go near.

While we girls were hammered into fine gold, the boys were being beaten into precious social metal, too. I think it's harder to be a gentleman. For one thing, a gentleman must always find subtle ways to bolster a lady. She can be a dead ringer for a warthog, but he has to savor her charm. You will never find a southern gentleman who publicly deplores a lady's looks. It just isn't done. What they say to one another in the bathroom is any woman's guess, but in public every single woman, regardless of age or nature's blessing, must be treated as a treasure.

No lady is allowed to sit alone. No lady is allowed to fetch her own refreshment. And no lady is allowed to walk back to her place at the table unescorted.

The poor fellows were run ragged tending to the women. Yankees often laugh at how important it is to southerners to have either an equal number of men and women at a party or more men than women. It's survival. We'd kill our men if the women outnumbered them.

At my first ball, my date, two years older than myself, signed my dance card, then ditched me as he dashed around signing other girls' dance cards. He was learning the ropes, too, even if he was older.

A boy from ninth grade, Mr. Slide Rule, approached me. He smiled. I grimaced. I couldn't endure the pomade on his hair.

He asked for the second dance and his pencil was at the ready.

I refused. This was wrong on my part, because if the boys had to make us feel special, we had to return the favor and act as though a request for a dance were heaven itself.

"Bug off."

"You can't talk to me like that. It's the Christmas Ball."

"Pizza face."

Anita Milsap, standing next to me, heard this insult and turned to me.

"Desist." She actually said "desist."

"I beg your pardon?" Some of the manners were returning.

"Refrain from insulting this gentleman in such a crude manner."

"You can bug off, too. Turdball." At least I didn't repeat myself.

Face red, she tottered off in her low heels to report me to Mrs. T., the Queen of Quite a Lot.

Jerry Pfeiffer, my erstwhile date, thin as a blade, remained ignorant of the growing drama. He wouldn't have cared because he was signing Nancy Meadows's dance card and she was one of the prettiest girls there. It looked like a convention where Nancy stood. A few of the grown men probably wanted to sign her card, too. Fortunately, she hadn't an ounce of conceit over her beauty, and her sense of humor was sharp, even in her early teens.

Mrs. T., trailed by Anita, inquired as to the vulgar nature of my insults. A picture of Mother flashed before me. Juts would kill me.

"I did use foul language. I was wrong and I am sorry." I smiled weakly.

"Mistress Brown"—yes, it really was Mistress and Master—"I will forgive you this one time, but if you lapse again into such common behavior, I will expunge you from cotillion."

The end of social life.

I groveled and trooped through two more years of cotillion until I passed the course. I apologized to Anita, too, who took these things more seriously than I did. She had a lovely singing voice and was in demand at parties.

Jerry Pfeiffer trooped through more than cotillion with me. I was twelve and he was fourteen when we met. I loved him on sight. I must have been blind or a prophet. This skinny boy with the raucous laugh actually grew into a tall, masculine fellow who was as close to me as a second skin.

Our first date, inauspicious, provided me with the spectacle of Jerry straddling the ice reindeer at the end of the party. It was the only time his crotch was ever cold.

Twelve, thirteen and fourteen not only try the patience of adults, they try the patience of the changeling. Your voice changes; girls' voices don't change as dramatically as boys', but they do change. You pack on pounds, then shoot up like a weed. Your face breaks out. You have to use deodorant or everyone around you holds her nose. (Fortunately, Mother, the harpy of hygiene, never gave me the chance to make a mistake.) You change hairstyles hoping to look older. Nothing quite fits right. Your breasts grow and they hurt, too. You look in the mirror and wonder what is going on. Will you ever be good-looking?

Awkward and silly as that time is for every one of us, I enjoyed myself. For one thing, Grandma Brown was no longer on the duty roster. I didn't have to go there on Sundays.

For another thing, I didn't hear about my brother, whom I have not met to this day, nor Juliann's growing family; she had married. My blood family meant nothing to my friends in Florida. They began to fade for Mom and Aunt Mimi, too. Things were good.

I could have used more money, but then, who couldn't?

32

Double Clutch

Sea salt sticks to your skin in Florida, the tangy air invigo-rates you. At night I'd go to sleep, Skippy on the pillow, listening to the wind in the palm fronds, inhaling the intoxicating scent of night-blooming jasmine.

Most Sundays we'd take a drive. Belle Glade, a sugarcane town, was maybe twenty minutes away from Five Points, where my cousins lived. The whole place sits on rich muck. I'd watch young men grow old fast cutting cane.

The heavy odor of the muck makes you drowsy. Some people wouldn't like it, but I did because, for me, wealth comes out of the earth.

A lot of the cane cutters wore their hair in a "big do" style that we called "gassed heads." Seeing sweating, well-built men with rags on their heads gave me the giggles. They looked girly.

If we drove inland from Belle Glade, we'd reach Lake Okeechobee, which is huge. Hardly anyone lived around Okeechobee. I'd stand at the edge of the lake and imagine what it was like when the great hurricane of 1928 scooped up the water, leaving only an empty basin. When the winds reversed, the water crashed back in, killing people who had run into the lakebed, curious.

Most of all, I loved the citrus groves, mile after mile of orange trees. The symmetry pleased me. Oranges in spring bloom made me giddy; the white looked like snow.

Sometimes Mom and I would wander around the inland areas of the state and she'd say, "You're the only kid I know who would rather be in the groves than at the ocean." I love agriculture. Coastal Bermuda grass, so different from red-bud clover or timothy or rich alfalfa, intrigued me.

Mother would sit in the car or lean against a fence while I strolled in a field studying the grass, pulling up a blade to inspect the roots.

As long as I kept her secrets about the track and about boleta, a Cuban numbers game she played, she indulged my farm passion. She even weakened when Uncle Kenny brought home a polo pony from Royal Palm. This old trooper, with two bowed tendons, stood calmly while I hosed his legs, brushed him and lavished attention on him. When Mom wasn't looking I swung up. He couldn't trot or canter with those bows but I hoped I was so light I wouldn't break him down. We walked around with just the lead rope on the halter, no bridle or bit. What a great old fellow he was.

I'd reached the age where people began asking me what I wanted to do when I grew up. I usually smiled and said, "I'm considering my prospects," which would make them laugh.

Older people can't contain themselves. They see young people as dumping grounds for whatever they've learned about life. It's well-meaning but I sat through many a lecture about a suitable career, a suitable mate, etc.

Mother's approach was, "It's just as easy to marry a rich man as a poor one." She echoed Aunt Mimi but I never believed her.

She could care less what I did with my life as long as I didn't cost her money. Her deal was she'd get me through high school and then I was on my own. If I wanted to attend college, I'd better work for it. My lawn mowing brought in some money. I spent very little. But I couldn't imagine earning enough to pay for college. Nor could I imagine marrying some local stud who'd be wearing a toupee by the time he was forty.

I figured I'd have to win an academic scholarship. I also figured I'd nail it. School came easy for me.

But the pressure to conform increased. Outwardly I wasn't a nonconformist. I dressed as well as we could afford. I displayed those hard-won good manners. I got along with kids my own age and with adults. On the surface I was cool. But Mom knew the underneath and so did Dad. I was a maverick. I listened to everyone but kept my own counsel. I was developing tremendous control of my emotions, which were not much on display anyway. But even those flashes of anger at the tennis courts were reined in—I had a ways to go, but I was moving on.

What rattled Mom the most was the fact that I plain didn't give a damn what anyone thought of me. As long as I felt I had behaved in a responsible manner, people could steer clear. I live my life; you live yours.

This detachment challenged her. She'd needle me, and her sarcasm stung. She'd pinch and poke at me for a reaction.

One time she said, "You'll never catch a man by beating him at tennis."

I replied, "Mother, I don't want a man I can beat at tennis."

So she tried another tack. I guess it was one of those days when she missed fencing with her sister, so I was her opponent. "You need to build a man up."

"Why?"

"They're weak. They need it."

"I don't have time."

"And what will you be doing, Miss High and Mighty?"

"Whatever I please, and I won't be doing it with you."

"Who asked you?" she fired back.

I walked away, which burned her up. She came after me and clamped her hand on my shoulder. "Don't you turn your back on me when I'm talking to you. You think you're better than I am, don't you? You think you're better than all of us. When you start putting on airs, kid, you would do well to remember you're Jule Young's bastard."

I'd eaten that crow for fourteen years. "If I thought I was your daughter, I'd puke."

She burst into tears, ran into her bedroom and slammed the door.

I suppose I should have felt guilty or sorry for her, or any number of things that would mark me off as a sensitive and refined soul. I didn't. I was glad I hurt her, and if she pushed me again, I'd hurt her again. I was fourteen years old and I knew I was fourteen. I couldn't have the wisdom of an older person, but I could at least know what my own life was like, and I was sick to death of being told I didn't belong. I didn't want to belong.

My deepest instinct is to go about my business without intruding on anyone else. (It may be one of the reasons I became a writer. Talent alone does not make an artist.) But if you are stupid enough to mess with me, sooner or later I'll put a stop to it.

I had just put a stop to it with Mom.

When Dad came home she cried some more. He asked me to ride with him, so we drove over to the Intracoastal Waterway, the brand-new Seventeenth Street Bridge, to watch the boats.

"Dad, I'm getting out of here the day I graduate from high school."

"You've got some time."

"Yes, sir, but I mean it. And I'm going to college."

A high-masted sailboat approached. We walked back down the bridge and sat on the seawall.

"Daddy, are you mad at me?"

"No." He waited. "Ignore her when she gets like that. She wants to pick a fight."

"Yes, sir," I sighed. It was hard to ignore her when she stood nose to nose with me.

"Honey, you've got a big brain in that head, more brains than I have. Learn to back off and let the other guy win. Sometimes you win when you lose."

I hated this advice even as I knew it to be true. "That like leaving a little money on the table for the other guy?"

"Yep."

Dad used to tell me never to go for the other guy's throat in a business deal. Always leave a little money on the table for him and never, never tell anyone else you got the better of him. It comes back to haunt you.

"Daddy?"

"Uh-huh?"

"Is life always this hard?"

He laughed and put his arm around me. "Think of this as strategy. This isn't really hard. It's maneuvering. When Virginia died—that's hard."

I followed Dad's advice, though I slipped occasionally, especially with Mom. My self-confidence enraged her at times. I didn't think I was arrogant, but she did. I knew what I wanted and I knew I'd get it. I'd do whatever it took to get up and get over.

I wanted to either write or be president. I dreamed of attending West Point, but girls couldn't go. Not being able to study at a service academy upset me. For one thing, the state paid for it. Given our situation, that was a huge attraction. For another thing, I believed combat experience was necessary for a presidential candidate. Truman fought in World War I. Eisenhower was overlord. All I knew were soldiers and I couldn't imagine a person being elected without a war record.

What's sad is that I assumed we'd be at war again soon.

The Korean War was over, but something else was bound to happen. I didn't believe that nuclear war was possible. This was ignorance, of course, but at my age I couldn't fathom the horror of nuclear war no matter how many times I saw footage of Hiroshima. Also, I didn't believe any nation would be dumb enough to drop the bomb.

By fourteen I knew West Point was not going to make an exception for me. A scholarship was a necessity, a scholarship to a good school.

Much as politics lured me, there was something deeper. The arts, any of the arts, set my heart racing, but literature was like breathing. I can't remember not loving the style, the structure of novels, the ideas inside them. Mark Twain was my favorite American author, Shakespeare my favorite writer overall. I read *Diary of the Voyage of the H.M.S. Beagle,* which wasn't a novel, but I thought I should know about evolution from Darwin himself, especially since animals were the key to my life in many ways. Then I launched into *The Origin of Species.* Darwin wasn't writing for teenage girls, but I stuck it out.

I walked to school reciting my Latin conjugations and vocabulary. I sat through grimly boring classes with mostly grimly boring teachers. I walked to the tennis courts and I walked home. I'd do whatever chores Mom set out for me and then I'd go back to my room and read, read, read, anything and everything.

I hid this lust from my schoolmates. Eggheads don't have social lives. I was in the advanced class. Actually, I'd been in the advanced track since seventh grade, so my peers were bright kids. Even so, only the spazzes, as we called them, blabbed about how smart they were. Uncool. Still, I guess uncool is better than no-cool. No-cool was the vocational track. Those kids didn't have a prayer.

The tracking system, flawed though it may be, saved me. If I'd had to sit in class with kids who weren't gifted, I would have turned into a juvenile delinquent.

The hardest studies I had happened to be catechism. Pastor Golder, strict and demanding, never let me off the hook. He made it a point to push me. Church history and dogma require some application. It prepared me for Marx in college. Marx was nothing compared to those early arguments in the first three centuries after Christ's death. I longed for Pastor Neely, who I imagined would have been a lot easier.

Confirmation proved a marvelous day. The end of catechism!

In Florida at that time you could get your learner's permit at fourteen. With that permit you were allowed to drive a car as long as a licensed person eighteen or older accompanied you.

Now that confirmation was off my mind I could concentrate on driving. Remember that age when you were obsessed with getting your driver's license?

Dad would take me out and we'd drive around the back roads. We all knew better than for me to go out with Mother.

One rainy night I was driving back home when Dad told me to turn left on Eighteenth Street NE. He'd left something at the store. I turned. The rain poured down harder.

"Turn around again. We'll go home."

I stopped, put the car in reverse and backed flat into a royal palm. I stopped, got out, got soaked.

"Well?" Dad was straining to see out the back window when I slid behind the wheel again.

"The Leaning Tower of Pisa palm." Palms have tiny root systems.

He covered his eyes with his hand for a second. "Get out of here."

I paused for a moment, then did. We reached Fifteenth Street and started laughing. We laughed until we cried. It was the only time I'd ever seen my father be irresponsible. I don't know why but it made me love him even more.

Mother demanded to know the source of our mirth.

"The kid knocked over a royal palm."

"Oh no." Her face drained. "Is the car damaged?"

We forgot to look. We ran out to the carport. It wasn't.

"Those royal palms cost a fortune." Mother made tea. "Did you talk to the people?"

"I left the scene of the crime."

"You what?" She turned to Dad. "Ralph?"

"It's true. I told her to go." He started laughing. "Honey, I couldn't help it."

Her hand was poised over the teapot. "That wasn't right." The teapot whistled. "I think I would have done the same thing."

This became known as the Palm Caper, a story told and retold by Dad or Mom. It ranked up there with the stolen yo-yo and Myrtle the Girdle.

Myrtle the Girdle referred to a fun-loving lady in Mom's old Sunday school class who wore girdles of considerable strength. Despite their compressive power, parts of Myrtle spilled over. One day at the church picnic I snapped Myrtle's girdle (I was seven) and the whole damn thing blew apart. Thank God, Myrtle laughed. She laughed so hard she fell off the picnic bench. I was confined to quarters.

Every family collects stories, folding them into their memory book like pressed flowers.

I adored the stories from before World War I. My other favorites were about the flapper days. Much as I liked the stories involving me, I liked Mom and Aunt Mimi's "running day" stories better.

For instance, in the late 1920s both Mom and Aunt Mimi worked. Young and pretty, they enjoyed a whole circle of friends and admirers. Lunch break meant everyone met at the drugstore. One particular summer day, Mother and her sister dashed to lunch. They had to cross the railroad tracks. An ambulance was parked at the tracks with a large wicker basket, bloody at the bottom, sitting next to it. A few people stood around.

Remember, a small town. Everybody knows everybody.

Mom marched up and said, "What happened?"

The ambulance attendant informed them a man had been decapitated by the train.

Aunt Mimi wanted to know who it was.

The fellow said they didn't know. The body, wrapped in a sheet, was in the ambulance. He added that the head was in the wicker basket. Mother lifted the lid, reached in, grabbed the head by the hair and hoisted it up.

Aunt Mimi said, "I don't know him."

Mom responded, "Me neither," and dropped the head back in the basket.

They walked on to lunch.

Tough girls. Mom was, too. She could view blood, guts, brains—nothing fazed her.

Well, that became the dead-head story. It turned out he was a drunk who fell asleep on the tracks.

What happens to children and families today who sit around the television? They're watching made-up stories. It's not their experience and it's not truly shared. A human being must learn at a very young age how to connect to other human beings. Our technologies are driving us apart, only connecting us in terms of information, not in terms of emotions.

Furious as Mom and Aunt Mimi made me, they taught me how to link up with other people, to feel for others. Best of all, they gave me their histories, the history of our family. They didn't bother to clean it up. Apart from the thrill of hearing about feuds, duels, sex scandals and eerie events, I learned that people aren't perfect and neither was I. You love them as you find them. Occasionally, they'll love you too.

33

Blue and White

CITATION STANDS IN THE MIDDLE OF A REFLECTING POOL WITH lily pads at Hialeah. This statue inspired me. Getting Mom to drive me there on nonracing days utilized all my persuasive powers, since she only wanted to go where horses were running. I'd lure her by saying there was a daughter of Swaps or Needles in the shedrow. The great horses at that time were Nashua, Needles, Swaps, Native Dancer and Bold Ruler. There were other fine horses but those caught the public's attention.

She'd prowl the shedrow while I scampered off to the part of Hialeah forbidden me.

For those of you interested in horses, let me recount Citation's lineage. Foaled in 1945, he was by Bull Lea out of Hydroplane II. On the top line, the sire line, his great-grandfather was Teddy. Tom Fool, foaled in 1949, another fine horse, also carried Teddy blood but on the dam side.

Citation could run in anything at any distance, which is the mark of the highest level of equine athlete. He could sprint. He could go the distance. He started racing as a two-year-old and lost twice, once in 1947 and once in 1948. He ran and ran and ran.

He missed his fourth year, usually a Thoroughbred's best year, because of injury, then came back in 1950. I was five and a half going on six. I remember he had to carry heavier weights than other horses, who, of course, didn't have his injury; though it had healed, it still affected him. He gave us thrilling races, even the ones he lost. What a courageous horse.

Mom loved Seabiscuit, a grandson of Man o' War, Man o' War himself, Whirlaway and Count Fleet. I loved Citation. I wanted to be as courageous as he was.

Young people search for heroes. The world is full of them but for whatever reason I found few historical figures that inspired me: Shakespeare, Robert E. Lee, Stonewall Jackson, Hannibal, Harriet Tubman and Elizabeth I. What united them was their courage under fire. Shakespeare's courage wasn't as obvious, but I knew enough about writing to see the chances he took, especially with material. If he tipped over the line, Elizabeth might have shut him down or, worse, shut him up.

Movie stars left me cold—a bunch of people flouncing around with makeup on. The women especially seemed irrelevant. They were. The films of the fifties were like one long homoerotic song. The women were caricatures. I might not have put it in those terms at that time. My term was "yuk."

The films from the thirties and forties captured my attention. Those women seemed a little more real. We could watch these films early on Saturdays, when the Gateway Theater had a kids' feature, an old movie and then the main feature for twenty-five cents. The junior-high set hung out there. Lots of the kids made out. The boys accompanying me found out I watched the movies and wanted to talk about them.

But this left me with not much in the way of heroes. Citation it was.

By now I have had ample opportunity to observe the courage of certain cats, dogs, horses and wildlife too. People think animals don't know they can die. They know. I've seen them risk their lives for another animal, their babies or even a human. Love goes beyond species.

THE FALL OF 1959, I ENTERED FORT LAUDERDALE HIGH. BOTH EXCITED and wary, I wondered how I would fit in. The lordly seniors appeared beyond reach. The juniors were a bit more approachable, and we lowly sophomores scurried about doing the upperclassmen's bidding.

Batista, brought down by Fidel Castro, changed our high school forever. The brightest and best of Cuba fled to south Florida. Cuba's loss was America's gain. In the span of a year, our high school welcomed many of these refugees, who were better-educated than we were, spoke better English than we did and nine times out of ten were better-looking.

At that age your deepest desire is to belong to the "in group." The Cuban kids, picked for the service clubs, landed in the center of everything.

The service clubs were Anchor, Juniorettes and Sinawik for the girls; Key, Wheel and Civitan for the boys. One had to be tapped for membership. Few sophomores were tapped unless a big sister or brother happened to be in the club. Usually you cooled your heels until your junior year, hoping you'd make it.

The tapping ceremony, noisy and fun, involved cars, decorated with streamers, greasepaint and funny horns, careening around the town, stopping at the homes of those who would be asked to join. Few kids left home that one Saturday out of each year.

I did. I knew I didn't have a prayer my sophomore year. I walked to the tennis courts.

No small amount of snobbery went into those damn service clubs, which were, as the name implies, expected to provide service to the community outside the high school and were pretty effective in doing so. How many broken hearts and dashed dreams they left in their wake I don't know. But they prepared us for life. You either make it or you don't, and the real world judges you by the standards of the day, no matter how superficial.

I didn't expect much socially since we had little money and Fort Lauderdale High overflowed with wealthy kids, kids who drove to school in brand-new Corvettes, MGs, Austin Healys, Triumphs and Spyders. Convertibles were the thing. Of course, old cars reposed in the parking lot, too.

I walked. It would be a cold day in hell before we had enough money to buy me a car. Even Mom didn't have a car.

Sometimes I'd catch rides with friends. The names of those people seem as familiar to me as the names of my closest friends today, and some of them still are my closest friends: Patrick Butterfield, Jerry Pfeiffer (deceased), Betty Pierce, Connie Coyne, Bill Wilson, Willis Fugate and Judy Bass. Other people like Judy Allen, Jeri Starr, Bonnie Baltier, John and Jeff Barker, Carlos Ullola, Armando Valdez (deceased), Noel Howlett, Tommy Van Allen, Hans Johnson, Sandy Annis and Larry Centers crowd into my mind because they were great fun and because they were kind to me.

My life centered around my studies, tennis and the horses. Overnight the boys became bigger, stronger and obsessed with sex. Astonished by the change in them, I stayed friendly but not romantic. I remember the girls thought Bob McCarty sexy; his younger brother, David, also was very good-looking. Jerry Pfeiffer trailed girls behind him even though he wasn't good-looking then.

Girls whom I thought I knew suddenly turned into simps in the face of these deeper-voiced buddies of mine. Jeri Starr was chased by boys from half the schools in Florida, although she never acted like a ninny.

I liked the Sumwalt sisters, Nancy and Carol, because they acted the same when talking to boys as when talking to girls. It didn't hurt their popularity. I used to giggle watching Noel Doepke restrain a budding

Romeo with an icy smile. Nancy Meadows kept her cool. That was about it. The other girls went haywire. They were as bad as the boys, with the major exception that while the boys directly expressed their interest in sex, the girls were covert. The girls had more to lose. I knew this thanks to the endless lessons concerning Juliann Young.

My sophomore year found me busy, loving Latin II and trying to steer clear of this romance stuff. My hormones hadn't reached a fever pitch. At this point it was easy to sidestep the whole issue.

Also, I am not a romantic person. If the world divides into romanticists and classicists, or Apollonian and Dionysian personalities, thank you Nietzsche, I'm a classicist, an Apollonian, a head-before-heart person.

I feel and I feel deeply, but I rarely act spontaneously and didn't even when I was a teenager. I think first, then act. Only animals cause this process in me to short-circuit, and sometimes I have to think first when it comes to them, too. I can't feed every abandoned animal in the world although God knows I'm trying.

Girls fell in love every other day. The boys, too. People sat in class and made eyes at one another. I couldn't believe it.

If I couldn't believe it, it must have been a razor-blade ride for those boys maturing slowly. There we'd be sitting in a class with a kid who was physically mature, like Clark Blake, next to a boy whose voice hadn't changed. The slow maturers caught rat week in gym class.

There they'd be, exposed to the world in their gym shorts, skinny arms hanging out of a T-shirt, getting the stuffing knocked out of them by a bruiser like Ron Harnett.

Emotionally we roughed one another up too, male and female. Sarcastic comments flew back and forth. If you lost your temper, you lost face. Ideally, you had to top the person attacking you. If you couldn't, it was better to shut up. Thanks to Juts and Aunt Mimi, I excelled. After a time, people realized I could hurt them more than they could hurt me.

More than one kid slunk out of the lunchroom in tears. High school, the great American leveling experience, unites each generation that experiences it: your first football game when your team loses, your first football game when your team wins, first love, first A, first D or F (some of us avoided this one), first inkling that this really was a rite of passage, first understanding of how people behave in groups and first taste of power or lack of it in a group.

My generation, the biggest in America—and it will be as long as we are on the earth—was forced to be ruthlessly competitive. There were so many of us that school times were staggered to fit us in. We competed for grades, for places on sports teams, for one another's attention and affection. Two thousand kids attended Fort Lauderdale High School. My class was over five hundred kids. Sink or swim. I swam for all I was worth.

Unlike most of my peers, I had to excel. I was going to go to college and, I hoped, to graduate school as well. Determined to amount to something, I wouldn't be sidetracked. I didn't drink. I didn't smoke. I didn't fool around. Nobody was using drugs then.

My friends had no idea how determined I was. On the surface I was fun-loving and the best female athlete in the school, better than most of the boys. Only the tanks among them could overpower me. I held my own with the rest and my arm grew stronger and stronger. It wasn't just distance I was capable of, it was accuracy. In tennis I had fast hands and a bomber serve. I was too short to come down over the ball, so I had to rely on muscle.

I confided in no one. That, for better or for worse, remains part of my character. I'll happily tell you what I'm thinking. I won't tell you what I'm feeling until I've known you for about five years and seldom then.

The result of this was that I was reasonably popular, I got along, my teachers liked me and I liked most of them. I pulled a few pranks, the worst being when I dumped a dead fish into the ventilation system, which freed us from study hall and the tyranny of Miss Ida Mae Bryant, pound for pound as vicious as a piranha.

If my sophomore year bolstered me, my junior year was sensational. I aced most of my classes. I was number one on the tennis team. A little girl called Chris Evert used to follow me around the Holiday Park courts because she liked my blue satin Flying L jacket. All those Evert kids were incredibly cute, combining the best of their mother and father. Since she was ten years younger I barely noticed her.

My circle of friends grew. I was invited to the "good parties" although I often couldn't attend because on weekends I worked mowing lawns. Jimmy Evert helped out Pat Butterfield and me by allowing us to roll the courts and sweep lines in exchange for our dues.

The best thing about Jimmy was that he never let you know he was helping you. He had a gift for fixing a problem in your game. I learned a lot from that man and from Colette, too. Everyone loved them.

Jerry, class of 1960, was now attending the University of Florida at Gainesville. He wrote me regularly. I felt grown-up to be receiving letters from a college man.

I hot-walked ponies on Sundays during polo season. Mom flourished at the track that year, and I was becoming a regular on the shedrows. I had crossed the line between energetic girl and young woman. Men looked at me differently. Not once, not for a second, did I hear anything resembling dirty talk on the shedrow. The grooms and trainers respected women. Men acted with courtesy then. No one swore in the presence of a lady unless it was another lady—Mother, usually.

What a golden year, from the fall of 1960 to the summer of 1961; to July 13, 1961, to be exact.

Continuity

NEITHER OF MY PARENTS COULD ATTEND MY TENNIS MATCHES due to their jobs. I'd reached a level where I could compete in the city tournament in my age group and usually fight my way to the quarterfinals or semis. I still had received no lessons. I learned by watching others. Jerry and I played mixed doubles in the summers. We usually cleaned up.

Thanks to Jimmy Evert's fame and organizing ability, the best players would stop and visit if they happened to be in south Florida. Usually they'd hit with the kids. You don't find generosity like that now—there's not much glory in it.

Mo Connolly, Alice Marble, Darlene Hard and Pauline Betz hit with us at various times. Mo Connolly was the only woman ever to win the Grand Slam titles in the same calendar year until Margaret Court astounded the world by doing it many years later. Short, powerful and capable of quick bursts of speed in any direction, Mo had a heart as big as her serve. Her early death to cancer was a loss not only to tennis but also to her community. She was a doer and a giver. Married to a man as kind and upbeat as she was, Mo had it all.

Alice, when I met her, was already in her forties and good-looking in a glamorous way, although the alcohol was telling on her a little. Her ground strokes, classic, sent the ball back to you flat and hard. Just when you got used to the pace she'd change up. Mo, on the other hand, overpowered people. She hit rockets. I've been lucky enough to see many great women players since Mo, but I have never seen a woman consistently hit the ball as hard.

I had managed to make it into the quarterfinals of the city tournament the first year I was eligible for the sixteen-and-unders, which was a tough division in Florida. I was playing kids who'd been taking lessons since they were six but I had something most of them didn't—a wealth of athletic talent. I knew that if nothing else I'd outrun them, charge the net and pressure them every second. And I wouldn't give up. Never.

I'm not a chatty person but I was more silent than usual at home. The only time I get chatty is if I truly adore someone. Usually I'd talk a lot with Dad; I wasn't even doing that. Neither of my parents said anything.

I'd played in the Orange Bowl tennis tournament in the fourteen-and-unders. I'd been stone quiet then, too.

My quarterfinal match was to be played on a Friday. I faced a girl I liked very much. Martha attended Central Catholic High. Tall, composed and genuinely sweet, she had an advantage in her height, which gave her reach. If she came down over the ball and I couldn't set up a lob far back enough, she'd grind me to dust.

The day was hot. I noticed Denise Wall's father (Denise was a shoo-in to win the sixteen-and-unders) sitting on the bleachers. A soggy cigar, part of Mr. Wall's permanent ensemble, was your clue to his emotional state. If he kept biting it so that it would jump, you knew electricity was coursing through him. Jerry and a smattering of others were there. Chris was almost six; her sister, Jeannie, was about two years younger. Chris must have been on sister watch that day because she'd sit in the bleachers and when Jeannie, the little rowdy one, would take off, Chris would run after her. They were a comical pair. I don't remember Drew Evert or Colette being there that day.

Well, anyway, I won the first set, 9–7, I think. I lost the second, 4–6. I was being handed my ass in the third set. I was down 2–5 and it was my serve. I couldn't find the court. At 0–4 I wanted to die. Then, I will never know why, my father squeezed into the bleachers, which had filled up. He smiled at me.

I looked across the net at Martha and the one thought I remember having was, "I can't lose in front of my father."

I fought my heart out. I ran down every point. I leaped, lunged and scrambled. I won the last set 7–5. Martha ran to the net, jumped over, shook my hand and then hugged me, her opponent. People in the stands applauded with enthusiasm. Mr. Wall's cigar twirled like a dervish.

Dad said, "I bet you need a Coke."

Amazed that I had lived through the match, I tottered to the Coke machine, the old kind where you had to walk the bottle through the maze and then pull it up straight. Jerry ran ahead of Dad and bought me a Coke.

Whenever I'm backed to the wall, I remember that match.

Denise won the sixteen-and-unders. She was a better player than I was, a true baseliner, but the defeat hardly stung. I'd gotten that far.

That particular city tournament produced the most exciting tennis match I've ever witnessed. It's strange, I've been fortunate enough to sit in the best seats at Wimbledon, the U.S. Open, the Australian Open (my favorite) and countless other wonderful tournaments, but this match for the women's city title remains untouched in my mind.

Gretchen Summerfield, the first seed, advanced to the finals, and Betty Rinehart, the second seed, made it too. The match, bound to be a good one, pulled a big crowd. The bleachers sagged under the weight. People stood by the sidelines. Kids crouched behind the back, peeping under the green wind nets. One spectator that day was Brian Piccolo, a class ahead of me.

There wasn't a boring point. Tooth and nail, hammer and tongs, those two battled without pause. Gretchen, in her twenties, had the advantage of height and maturity. Betty, at eighteen, possessed extraordinary athletic ability and charisma.

Gretchen, Scandinavian, tall and austere, contained her emotions. Being tanned and blond didn't hurt her. She worked for the parks department running the Holiday Park program for sports other than tennis.

Gretchen, strict and proper, used to correct me regularly. My exuberance rubbed her the wrong way. I didn't like her because of that but I respected her. I'd probably like her much more today because I can understand how trying it must have been to do your job with half the kids in the city running around you, screaming. She recognized my ability and from time to time would give me a tip here or there. I drank in every word because she was good.

Betty, with her curly red hair, freckles, great body and adorable face, was my idol. We all worshipped her. Betty would catch sight of you and smile as though you were the most important person on earth. One of those rare people loved by men and women alike, she happened to be one of the finest natural athletes I have ever seen in my life. Had she been born ten years later, she would have made her mark in either women's tennis or women's golf. She could do anything.

I don't remember breathing during that match. People teetered on the edge of their seats. Even Jimmy came out to watch. I think Colette was the umpire. Colette was unimpeachable.

The match rolled on for hours. Ad in, ad out, deuce, ad in, ad out, deuce. Their shoulders must have ached from serving.

Finally, Gretchen won. Betty bounded up to the net and shook her hand. They walked over and thanked the umpire. You knew that Betty wanted to cry. She didn't. Nor did Gretchen gloat.

I was exhausted and all I'd done was sit there. From the distance of three and a half decades, I can see that match more clearly than ever. It was the first time I recognized fundamental differences in human temperament and worldview. It wasn't a baseliner versus a serve-and-volleyer, it was play-it-safe versus take-a-risk, it was Apollo versus Dionysus. Betty, all out, emotional but never rude, provided high contrast to Gretchen, methodical, patient and cool on the surface.

Had Betty continued with her tennis, I think she would have finally beaten Gretchen in some future city championship. She entered a convent that summer. Before she left she asked me to think of her and she promised to pray for me. The last day Betty played at the courts was her last day before entering the convent. We couldn't write her there nor could she have written back. The finality of it scared me. Even Jerry, a devout Catholic, appeared shaken.

After she drove out of the parking lot, I went back to my locker to pull out my tennis shoes. I found she'd stuffed twenty dollars in the toe—a lot of money then, and Betty was not a well-off girl. That's the closest to crying in public I have ever come. Denise, Pat and some of the other girls asked me what was wrong and all I could do was hold up the twenty dollars.

I have never seen or heard from Betty since. If she remains in the religious life, I hope it is fulfilling. If she has left, I hope she's found peace and love in the outside world.

One summer night I came home late from the courts. Dad, slumped in his favorite chair, was reading the newspaper. Mom recited her list of chores for me. Skippy purred and Sunshine squatted on Dad's feet.

Somehow or other Dad and I wandered into a disagreement. I had never had a fight with my father. This wasn't so much a fight as an argument about Kennedy's policies. He'd been elected the year before. I must have been cranky, and so I said, "Well, Dad, if you're so smart, why aren't we rich?"

Dad didn't reply. He was too much of a gentleman. He should have fanned my rear end. Mother flew up at me. I retreated to my bedroom, certain I was the injured party. You're always the injured party when you're sixteen.

My self-imposed isolation irritated me. I opened my bedroom door a crack. Dad was placidly reading his paper.

I hissed.

He didn't look up.

I hissed louder, which upset Skippy, and Dad glanced back at me. I made the snakes sign.

Mother used to make snakes with her fingers. It's pretty silly but you point your fingers palms down at the offending party and hiss, "Snakes." Usually this was employed by Mother during games of five hundred rummy.

Snakes could be used to hex someone or to bedevil them. It came in handy during fusses with Aunt Mimi unless she used it first. After that your only hope was to reach the garden hose before she did.

The remainder of the evening passed without incident. I should have apologized but I didn't. It takes me a while to reach the apologizing stage.

Everyone went to bed.

A weird red light awakened me about three in the morning. This red light circled around the ceiling of my bedroom. My bedroom door was closed, which confused me, because I never closed that door. The next thing I knew the door was thrown open and Mom hurled herself on me. A figure was right behind her but I couldn't see who it was. I sat bolt upright and tried to push Mom off. She screamed and cried, grabbing at me. Then I saw that Aunt Mimi was right behind Mom.

"Butch's dead!" Mother howled.

Aunt Mimi, the best in a crisis, pried Mother off me. I threw on shorts and a T-shirt. Shaking like a leaf, I couldn't get my sneakers on.

Aunt Mimi, calm, said, "Your father's in the living room. They have him on a stretcher and the ambulance is about to take him away. Do you want to see him before the funeral?"

Mother grabbed me again. "His face is blue."

"No. I don't want to remember him like that."

Aunt Mimi left for a second. I heard the men carry Dad out. I hurried out to the living room. Uncle Mearl, devastated, looked at me. He tried to say something but his hands fell to his sides.

Dr. Easton, a good family physician who'd known us since we moved, told Aunt Mimi to keep Mother on tranquilizers for a few weeks. He handed Aunt Mimi the pills.

No one slept the rest of that night. I called Fairchild Funeral Home. Ron Fairchild was my classmate. I trusted the Fairchilds.

Mother, disoriented, couldn't do much of anything. She didn't know day from night. Aunt Mimi, Julia Ellen, Russell and friends took turns keeping an eye on her.

Funerals require so much work that you're numb but busy. Since Mother couldn't function, the task of burying my father fell on me and Aunt Mimi. We worked closely together. I saw a side of my aunt I'd never seen before. She knew what to do and she was rock solid.

Russell cried like a baby. He loved Dad. We had to wait for Eugene and Dorcas, his wife, to get down from York.

Dad had died of a massive heart attack at 56. He thought he had heart-burn, got up and walked into the kitchen to drink Alka-Seltzer. By the time he walked back to bed he knew it wasn't heartburn. He woke Mom, telling her to call Dr. Easton. Then he crawled into bed. The pain worsened.

My father's last words were, "Juts, close Rita's door. I don't want to wake her."

Mother had also called Sis. Mimi and Mearl, living so close, reached her before the doctor but it was too late. Dr. Easton tried everything known at the time to revive Dad but he finally said to Mom, "He's gone."

That's when she tore into the room after me.

Aunt Mimi and I went through Dad's clothes. He had owned precious little: a watch, a carnelian ring with a Greek warrior's head on it, a sport coat and a pair of dress shoes. He had some shorts and work shirts. He'd poured what little money he had into Mom and me. Dad hadn't wanted anything for himself.

When we took the clothes to the funeral home, he wasn't there. The ambulance driver had taken Dad to Brown's Funeral Home on North Route 1, an easy mistake to make, I guess. Anyway, we finally got him to Fairchild.

Mother laughed through her tears because Dad was always late, even for his wedding. Now he was late for his funeral.

As we rode to the funeral home, Mom, Aunt Mimi and I in the back of a white Continental, Mother said, "I've always wanted to ride in one of these things. Isn't it terrible that someone has to die before you can do it?"

It struck us as funny. We laughed until we reached the funeral home.

In our family, the eldest child covers the body of the deceased parent. After the service I would have to walk up and cover Dad.

What I didn't know was that there would be over three hundred people at my father's funeral.

Stunned by the size of the crowd, since Dad was a simple butcher, Mom mumbled, "Who are these people?"

"I don't know," Aunt Mimi replied.

Betty Pierce, Connie Coyne, Jerry, Karen McCarthy and some other high-school friends attended. In a daze, I half knew they were there and half didn't.

I walked up and covered Dad and returned to my seat.

We then drove to the cemetery for the final interment. All those people drove out with us.

Once the ceremony was over, people came up to me. One black lady, sobbing, said, "Your daddy gave me food." Some other people of color told me the same thing, and so did some white people. I'd had no idea my dad was taking care of people. Mom hadn't known, either.

Other people came up and shook my hand and said, "Your dad said you'd be the first woman president of the United States."

Still others told me how he'd recounted every single point that he had seen of my tennis match against Martha.

Wave after wave of mourners walked over to pay their respects. Even Uncle Kenny was bawling like a baby. Mother had collapsed, and Uncle Mearl, with Russell's help, had carried her back to the white Continental, where Aunt Mimi tended her sister. I was left with the social responsibilities. Wade and Kenny stood at a distance but they were ready to assist.

I hurt so much it was hard to think. I was actually grateful for cotillion because I'd been drilled in proper funeral behavior for Protestants, Catholics and Jews. Form carried me through.

By the time Russell escorted me back to the car, I wondered how I could have been so ignorant of my father's life. Dad acted from his heart. He didn't call attention to his deeds. He touched the lives of many people by helping where he could, handing out day-old bread or slipping someone meat or shoving five dollars into their hands.

He wasn't just there when I needed him. He was there when others needed him.

People arrived at the house bearing food. *Advise and Consent,* a novel I was reading, provided a little comfort. I'd sneak into my bedroom, read a few pages and come out to speak to more people.

The strain, lack of sleep and concern for Mother must have frayed Aunt Mimi's nerves. At one point I think I was talking with a bit too much animation to a few high-school friends and she snapped, "Cool as a cucumber. Well, he wasn't your father."

I said nothing. I was sixteen. The one person who I knew loved me just as I am was gone. I didn't know if Mother would make it. It's a strange sensation, because you're the center of positive attention but the circumstances are dreadful. Maybe I was enjoying myself or seeming to enjoy myself because of that. Then, too, Aunt Mimi and Mother brooked no rivals for center stage. They played tragedy as handily as they played comedy.

I decided I needed a walk. The Florida East Coast Railway ran near our house. I walked over to the tracks. A gleaming red and yellow engine roared by, pulling car after car of passengers.

Staring at the faces in the windows, I was overcome with rage. My father was dead. How could they sit there as though nothing had happened? But nothing had happened—to them. I was a lonely speck standing by the railroad tracks.

And that's as it should be. Life goes on.

I waved; a few people waved back.

Do or Die

MOTHER DRAGGED TO WORK. HOLLOW EYES, NO LAUGHTER, not even a flash of hostility—she was dead in a way, too.

The night after Dad's funeral I had a dream that woke me. I was mowing the lawn. Dad walked toward me from the railroad tracks. He was young again, in his thirties.

I said, "Dad, you're dead. What are you doing here?"

He smiled at me and said, "Take care of your mother."

That's all I remember. But I sat up in bed and knew I was the head of the house. I also remembered with a shiver that about two weeks before Dad died, I'd dreamed of his death. I'd run into the bedroom to make sure he was alive. I'd forgotten about that dream in my relief. Funny, that I would dream such a thing.

We had no money. Even with Dad working, our annual income was two thousand dollars a year.

Aunt Mimi suggested I quit school and go right to work.

Mother was in no condition to consider anything. I didn't want to talk to her about it.

Aunt Mimi leaned hard on me and I leaned right back.

My senior year in high school meant the world to me. I wasn't going to give it up, but I was willing to work after school and on weekends.

Before I could go job hunting, Jimmy Evert offered me more work at the tennis courts. Sometimes I would come in in the morning, before school. The city's tiny budget had a little room for me, or so I thought. Jimmy could well have paid me out of his pocket and told no one. He's that kind of man. His help meant I could have my senior year. Other people surprised me. Adults, as you would expect, had a real understanding of how deep a blow Dad's death was. The men at the courts would buy me hamburgers. One of the ladies made me a pretty tennis dress since I had only white gym shorts and white T-shirts.

Hans made a point of bringing me books.

Without my being aware of it, I was watched out of the corner of many an eye.

God knows I needed help, but I was too young and too dumb to know it. I didn't know what to do with Mother, though. She'd get up in the middle of the night, go outside and call Dad as if she were calling the cat.

Skippy and I would wake up, and Sunshine, Mom's poodle, would be next to her, scanning the yard. We'd open the front door and bring her inside.

Befuddled, she'd implore, "Where's Butch?"

I'd put her to bed but then I couldn't go back to sleep.

True to form, she never missed a lick of work. The house sparkled. She cooked, washed and ironed. She gardened.

She hardly spoke. That shocked me. Even Aunt Mimi hardly spoke.

I buried myself in school. I hung blue and white yarn dolls from Mom's rearview mirror to show school spirit. I knocked out great college board scores, which took some of the pressure off me. I knew that high grades from a southern high school wouldn't be enough to get me into a good college.

My service club, Anchor, offered plenty of activity to keep my mind off home, and as a member of the student council, I had keys to get in and out of school after hours. Sometimes I'd turn a library light on and read. I didn't want to go home.

Other times I'd stay at the Holiday Park courts until the last person left and Jimmy shooed me out.

Around this time one of my girlfriends, and I will never quite know why she did this, told me she was dying. One curveball had beaned me already. Two?

I told Betty Pierce. A few of us huddled together and decided we'd make her senior year great. We had before us the example of one of our husky football players from the class of 1961, dying of leukemia. And one of the most popular girls in school, Vicki Leaird, had died three years earlier because the hospital didn't have an iron lung. Death at a young age was real for all of us.

One night, this girl stayed late at school. She started crying and seemed to feel so awful. I hugged her and told her things would get better. She kissed me and I kissed her back.

It never occurred to me that this was a lesbian act. I didn't think in those terms and I still don't. Determined to put aside sex until I could become financially established, I wasn't going to fall for boys or girls.

She was good company, a hard worker, and I really liked her.

In looking back, it's clear our relationship was so innocent. We wrote one another romantic letters. We kissed and hugged. We hadn't a clue about sex, really, but our relationship was clearly romantic.

As far as I was concerned, I was going to marry Jerry Pfeiffer even though he hadn't asked me. I was quite untroubled by the prospect of caring for two people and I just figured whatever she needed, we'd all pitch in. This kissing stuff was okay. I liked it fine.

Her mother read the letters I wrote her. My mother read the letters she wrote me. Mom, still grieving, was waking up a little. The girl's mother, Mrs. Busybody, visited Mom and told her we'd have to stay apart.

When I came home that night, Mom told me all this. I was mad but not too upset. I told Mom that the girl had said she was mortally ill. Boy, that burned Mom up. But she got hold of herself and didn't call Mrs. Busy body. She let it go, telling me to steer clear—I had enough to contend with in my life. I agreed. Whatever my sexual inclination might be, Mom didn't care. You married, had children, saved face and did whatever you wanted to do discreetly.

Who knows what Mrs. Busybody said to her daughter? The girl panicked and told our friends that I was a lesbian. She, of course, wasn't.

I couldn't believe it. Then I thought about it some more. Maybe I was a lesbian. Mostly I didn't give a damn.

I did what I always do. I shut up.

Snickers and titters followed me. One boy took it upon himself to insult me on a few public occasions. I had always liked him, so I let it go. If he thought he'd scare me into going to bed with him to prove I wasn't gay, he figured wrong.

A couple of my teachers cracked down on me, but most of them didn't pay much attention to what was going on, for which I was grateful.

My senior year turned into one long siege. The tennis coach made me run extra laps. When that didn't break me down, she told me that if I even thought of looking at another girl in the locker room, she'd throw me off the team.

I would have given anything for Betty Rinehart to be out of the convent or Jerry to be home from college.

Mother, on her feet but miserable, crossed swords with me over college. She and Aunt Mimi pounded at me about going away.

I'd had it. I'd applied to Ivy League schools, Duke and the University of

Florida. Duke accepted me straightaway and I wanted to go. Aunt Mimi hit the ceiling. After a fight wherein I was called everything from "ungrateful" to "selfish" and had the usual "You aren't one of us" thrown at me, I left the house and stayed out all night. I slept in the student council room at school.

When I came home the next night, Mother, a bit frightened that I'd walked out, said, "You know how I feel, but if you want to go, I won't stand in your way."

I replied, "How about if I go to the University of Florida? It's not so far away. If something happens, I can take the bus home."

The bus ride back then was about twelve hours—if two roads crossed, the bus stopped.

She thought about it. "Well, that Smith College is awful far away. Even Duke is far away." That meant she liked the idea as much as she could.

I promised her that I'd have greater earning power with a college degree and that she would never have to worry about money as long as she lived.

I kept my promise.

Boiled Peanuts

Each year the senior class at Fort Lauderdale High participated in Senior Work Day. Each of us had to work for a day, and local merchants, fishermen and farmers hired us. What a wonderful way to test the waters of career choices. Some of us worked in clothing stores and bakeries, on charter boats and with printers.

I was governor of the great state of Florida. Farris Bryant, the state's Democratic governor, happened to be in Japan during our Senior Work Day. Before the big day I wrote to ask if I could be his shadow in Tallahassee. I wanted to learn how state government really worked. He wrote back and told me I could not be his shadow, but I could be his stand-in.

The state flew me to Tallahassee, my first airplane ride. I loved it.

I sat in on a legislative wrangle about stone crabs, then a healthy industry in Florida. Reporters asked silly questions. I tried not to be quite as silly in return. Just because I was seventeen didn't mean I was stupid. I'd been lucky enough to attend Girls' State, been elected party whip for the Nationalist Party, and was voted the alternate to Girls' Nation. Killed me when neither of the two delegates got sick.

Then as now, many a legislator is a venal, self-aggrandizing third-rater. Then as now, some legislators and executives love their state and country, are honest and really work. I'd had the example of Jack Young to teach me very early about how politics really worked.

I toured the capitol. The highway department impressed me. At that time, the engineering level was so high it set standards for the country. Florida was the first state to paint white lines on the outer edges of highways to help motorists stay on the road at night. They would also develop a good plan for unpaved roads and a realistic budget for eventually upgrading some of these secondary and tertiary roads. No one could have predicted the population explosion Florida was about to experience. However, if you drive through Florida today, you'll notice that the state roads are quite good. Remember, federal roads are separate from state ones.

The governor's desk, impressive enough, was made more so by the nearly life-size portrait of Andrew Jackson that hung behind it. The hero of New Orleans, thumping crack British troops, was also the first governor of the Florida territory, appointed in 1821. Although he subdued the Seminoles, neither Jackson nor anyone else conquered them. When I was in high school the Seminoles still had not signed a peace treaty with the United States government. McArthur High School, then a new school in Hollywood, Florida, had a couple of Seminole kids. One of the guys played football barefoot.

Tallahassee is the home of Florida A&M and Florida State. It's a pleasant city and I wished I'd had more than a day there.

I flew home in triumph. Mother greeted me at the airport. No bragging was allowed in our family.

"How was your plane ride?"

"Pretty neat, Mom, you've got to do it."

Aunt Mimi piped up, "If God had wanted us to fly, he would have given us wings."

"If God had wanted us to have peace and quiet, he would have removed your tongue." Mother headed back to the old white Plymouth with a plastic orange stuck on its radio antenna so she could find it in the parking lot.

The celestial aspects of flying occupied their attention until we reached home.

When Mom opened the door, the dog scampered out and the cat strolled out from under the hibiscus. Mom paused in the bright sunlight and then she burst into tears.

Aunt Mimi glared at me.

I wondered what the hell I had done. I hadn't said two words.

Mom collected herself, whispering, "If only Butch could see this."

They boohooed, made coffee and then launched into an argument about my proper station in life. Aunt Mimi, furious that she hadn't been able to thwart my plans for college, lit into Mom.

Mother, clever, said, "She'll find a man with prospects at college. Better than working here."

This new concept somewhat mollified Aunt Mimi. Neither wanted to hear the details of my trip.

I grabbed a mess of boiled peanuts and a Coke and walked over to the

railroad tracks. I wondered if I would ever luxuriate in anything I'd accomplished. Well, maybe I'd be proud of myself, but I didn't think Mom
or Aunt Mimi would pay more than passing notice. That was okay. Sometimes it wiped the shine off an event, but I told myself I'd be out of there
soon enough.

I never wanted to be a child even when I was one. I wanted to be
grown, in full command of my body and mind, earning my keep. And I
never wanted to be beholden to anyone.

While I ate my boiled peanuts Mom and Aunt Mimi's argument escalated. I heard Aunt Mimi peel out of the driveway. "Leadfoot strikes
again," I thought.

Did I want to go back and hear the wail of discontent?

I had barely put my foot over the threshold when Mom started shouting. There were the usual accusations about Aunt Mimi's being a religious
nut, about her keeping too tight a rein on her daughter, about her meddling in Kenny, Wade and Terry's upbringing. That was the warm-up. She
opened her second round of fire about Sis's pushing her to get a lawyer.

This was news to me. A lawyer for what?

Reuben and Caroline Brown had died within six months of one another barely six months before Dad died. Dad and I had driven up to the
funerals. I felt bad for Dad even though I had no love for either of his
parents.

Their will stated that their sons, in order to inherit, must survive them
by a year. If not, the estate would be divided among whoever was left. Dad
had not survived them by a year. Their savings, property and worldly
goods went to Earl and Claude.

By the time they died Mamaw and Papaw, not rich, had achieved
comfort. Mom said we would have received ten thousand dollars, a fortune by our standards. Hey, I'd be happy for it right now.

Aunt Mimi, shrewd about business, couldn't get Mom to hire a lawyer
to contest the will.

In Mom's defense, she had no fight in her for a long time after Dad's
death. That first year she was a zombie. Each year after that she recovered
some, until after five years she seemed like her old self. At that time she
couldn't afford a lawyer though, not emotionally or financially.

So I whipped out the phone book, found the name of a lawyer who was
the father of a high-school friend, borrowed the car and hurried down
there. He told me I was underage and had no legal rights. I couldn't
contest a thing.

I left having been taught a brutal lesson about American law: I was a nonperson. I also weighed how much the Browns had disdained me. I was their only grandchild, yet they had evidenced no concern for my well-being.

That floored me. Not because I'd thought they would someday magically start to love me, the stray cat, but because Dad loved me. Dad was the apple of his mother's eye. If he felt I was his daughter, how could Caroline Brown violate her son's wishes?

I was glad they were dead. And so goddamn mad that if they hadn't been, I might have killed them.

I felt sorry for Mother, too. All the years she'd catered to her mother-in-law, done her best to appease the rest of Dad's family—all for nothing. What a slap in the face.

We needed the money. We were scraping by on the day-old stuff that Mom brought home from the bakery, plus hamburger and other inexpensive meats. I taught myself handwriting analysis from books so I could earn my lunch money at school.

Uncle Claude, a lot like Dad, sent Mother half of his inheritance once the will was settled. She put it in savings against a rainy day, which was so unlike Mom that I nearly passed out. She wouldn't give me any for college, though.

Earl, the middle brother, never shared a penny.

But I understood, finally, why Aunt Mimi had blown up when Mom refused to get a lawyer. She loved her sister, knew she was in need, and couldn't do anything about it. She couldn't fight *for* her.

I thought the two Buckingham sisters would settle this. I told Mom what I'd done. She wasn't mad at me. I told Aunt Mimi. She was thrilled, but outraged that I couldn't file a suit due to my youth.

Neither sister would talk to the other, though. The famous "deep freeze."

At first, Mom sang in the morning because she didn't have to deal with her sister the bossyboots. That lasted three or four days. Then she fretted because Russell wasn't swinging by to see her either. He had been stopping by every day since Dad died. Uncle Mearl stayed out of it. He had to.

By the beginning of the second week, the strain began to show. Mom called Aunt Mimi's friends for a report. Sis called Mom's buddies. Neither one would make the first move, lest they lose face.

Russell and I hatched a plan. We were good friends despite the sixteen years between us. Lots of folks speculated that we were having an affair. He was blond and blue-eyed, with the body of Adonis, and I was seventeen, not a beauty queen but nice-looking. After a time even Julia Ellen grew suspicious.

Small towns. Small minds. Of course, I was later to find out minds are equally small in New York City and Los Angeles. Some people live life and others talk about it.

Russell stuck close to me because he was the only person to recognize how deep my loss was and how alone I felt. There wasn't much he could do about it but be there. As I've said before, I'm not much of a talker. We'd snorkel early in the mornings, staying close to shore because the barracudas and sharks were feeding.

One time out there, as the sun was rising, Russell was underwater and I came up for air. And straight in front of me an enormous manta ray rose out of the water, wings curled at the tips, water spraying off in red and gold droplets. Its little eyes met mine. The animal glided over calm waters and then silently slipped back into the sea.

No wonder ancient shore dwellers worshipped gods from the ocean.

Despite the swirl of gossip, Russell came to the tennis courts or drove me to Royal Palm so I could hot-walk ponies.

Both sisters had always IV'd coffee. Prices rose sharply that year because the weather had soured in South America. The "girls" cut back on their coffee drinking to save money, especially Mom, because she didn't have the money in the first place.

Russell and I put together our own money and bought two big cans of ground coffee. He was to take one to Aunt Mimi. I was to take the other to Mom. We'd tell each sister that the other had bought it for her as a peace offering.

Off we went. I handed Mom her coffee.

"You saw Sis?"

"No, I saw Russell. He said it's a peace offering."

Mother squinted at the blue can. "I don't trust her. She's up to something."

"Maybe she is, but you might as well drink the coffee."

"What else did he say?"

"Nothing."

"She'll never admit she was wrong. He didn't tell you one thing that she said?"

"No, ma'am, but you know she feels bad or she wouldn't have spent the money. You know how cheap she is, Mother."

"*Prudent* is her word." Mother laughed, opened the coffee and perked a fresh pot.

Russell sheepishly knocked on the door and let himself in. He put a can of coffee on the kitchen table.

"She said she doesn't want it and you can't afford it."

"That bitch." Mother spat, then stopped. "What do you mean, she doesn't want it? She's giving me two cans of coffee?"

"Uh . . ." The explanation followed.

"You two stay out of my business." She nonetheless served Russell coffee.

She noticed that the other coffee can had been opened. It had a plastic lid on top of it. She picked the can up.

"Put it in the refrigerator to keep it fresh," I said.

"I will." She frowned at me.

After all, that was the obvious solution. One should not state the obvious. But when she pulled the plastic lid off, a palmetto bug, gigunda, flew up out of the can.

"What the hell—" Mom threw the can up in the air, spewing ground coffee everywhere.

"Oh, shit." Russell spilled his coffee.

That fast, Mom jumped into her car.

"Russell, it's World War Three," I said.

We tailed her. She hit eighty at one point, barreling up Fifteenth Street into Wilton Manors.

She was already in her sister's house by the time we pulled into the driveway. We could hear them. The entire neighborhood could hear them. Mom and Aunt Mimi needed cotillion more than I did.

We took a deep breath, then hurried inside. The decibel level dropped.

"Mean. Hateful mean." Mom's eyes misted.

"You threw the can up?" Aunt Mimi asked.

"It hit the ceiling."

"Julia, I told you the ceiling in your kitchen is too low. Well, as ye sow, so shall ye reap."

"I don't grow coffee. This has nothing to do with the Bible, Sis. You're hateful."

Aunt Mimi, struggling to hide her glee, folded her hands. Her composure was harder to take than a full-blown hissy.

Russell and I confessed our part in what we had hoped would be a peacemaking.

Mother, still teary, said, "All that expensive coffee ruined."

"Sweep it up and use it anyway," Aunt Mimi said to torment her.

"I am not drinking cat hair."

"You do it now. You just don't know you're doing it."

This went on. Back and forth. The shuttlecock of contention.

"You always exaggerate." Aunt Mimi rose. "I'm going over there to see for myself."

Three cars drove back to our house—the Pink Pagoda, as I called it.

When Aunt Mimi beheld her handiwork, her calm demeanor exploded into laughter.

"It's not funny." Mother pouted.

Aunt Mimi walked to the utility room and handed Mom a broom. Then she grabbed the dustpan and they cleaned up the mess, laughing all the while.

Neither one ever did ask me about being governor for a day.

Gators

THE BUS FOR POINTS NORTH PICKED ME UP BEHIND HOWARD JOHNSON's just north of where the tunnel is now. The long ride passed through tiny Deep South hamlets—Winter Haven, Leesburg, Oxford. Today people think of Florida as a glitzy retreat for snowbirds. I think of it as God's waiting room. But back then, Florida, an important agricultural state, had more in common with Alabama and Georgia. The panhandle of Florida and the southeastern part of Alabama we called Floribama.

We docked at the Greyhound station in Gainesville early in the morning. I picked up Russell's army duffle bag and walked to my dorm, Jennings, then brand-new. The two- or three-mile walk revealed many small wooden houses and water oaks, as well as businesses splashed with blue and orange, Florida's colors.

My roommate, Faye, a premed student from Jacksonville, showed up the next day. A wild woman, she figured rules were meant to be broken. She immediately set about finding one of the building maintenance people and paid him off, thereby ensuring she had a basement window to crawl in and out of after hours. This was a girl after my own heart.

I pledged Delta Delta Delta sorority, a neat trick with no money, but they needed good students to raise their grade point average. Also, I liked them.

Faye thought sororities a waste of time. Much more interested in fraternities, she passed on being one of the girls. She smoked, she drank, she swore, she exhibited hilarious contempt for authority and she was beautiful.

I made the number-three spot on the varsity tennis team, eventually moving up to number two. Alice Luthy, later Tym, locked in the number-one slot. Since she was a senior, I thought I had a chance for a good college tennis career my sophomore, junior and senior years.

I was part of an honors course. They had selected thirty freshmen for the program based on board scores, IQ and grades. Fortunately we weren't joined at the hip. You might be with the honors group for certain classes, then back with other students for others. It kept us from being too segregated.

Jerry Pfeiffer, in his junior year, number two on the men's varsity tennis team, offered guidance.

For a start, he winnowed out the good restaurants from the bad. This was a greater service than one might suppose because in 1962 most restaurants were awful. Mashed potatoes to the max.

He knew where to purchase liquor since the county was dry. One could drink near beer, a brew with a low alcohol content, but you couldn't drink the real thing. Although I didn't drink, I appreciated his thirst and everyone else's around me.

I learned that the minute you want to make something desirable, outlaw it. Drinking was part of rebellion, part of outsmarting the authorities. All you had to do to throw a great party was smuggle in a keg of beer. The biggest thrill was drinking under the noses of the campus police, who could be relied upon to stop by most parties.

Jerry threw terrific parties. He knew the best people and the best places. Although he hadn't the money for a car, he managed to borrow one whenever he needed it.

The weekend of the Florida State football game, deep in the grape, he bought all the laundry detergent he could find. This bounty he lovingly deposited in every fraternity fountain or pool, city fountain or pool—in fact, any man-made body of water he could find.

As he poured the white flakes into the water he was transformed into one of Macbeth's witches—"bubble, bubble, toil and trouble." He never got over playing that part from the high-school play. That and *Charley's Aunt* seemed always to inspire him.

After Jerry's cleanliness fit, he wanted to lie down in the middle of Route 441 to see if he could stop traffic. Took everything I had to drag him out of there.

Finally, he passed out behind the Beta Theta Pi house. I turned him over to his fraternity brothers.

One of the rites of passage for a sorority or fraternity pledge was being road-tripped. A pledge is a sorority member in the larval state. After existing like a slug for a year, one undergoes tests not of an intellectual nature. Then, wrapped in the chrysalis of sororal conformity, one emerges a resplendent sister with full voting privileges.

Overpowered from behind, with a bag thrown over my head, I was dragged into a car where two sisters sat on me for good measure. This was better than being tied up, so I endured the hip bones.

It was early October 1962 and our entire pledge class was being road-tripped, usually in twos. Twenty of us, carried off screaming (but not too loudly), were deposited down back roads.

If you're a chicken, it doesn't bode well for your future and each pledge knew this.

JoAnn Nokomis and I were dumped on a country road. We ripped our blindfolds off and hoped we'd figure out where the hell we were.

We walked down the gravelly, sandy road toward lights. A small clap-board house beckoned us. JoAnn and I discussed this and decided the sight of two bedraggled Tri-Deltas would scare the bejesus out of the inhabitants.

We trudged on.

Fortunately we wore sneakers, the old white kind, before they looked like space boots. No socks. You couldn't possibly wear socks and be considered a real person. Since I'd known that sooner or later I'd be road-tripped, I had taken the precaution of taping two dimes to the instep of each foot. Part of the road–tripping ritual was that the sisters removed money, pocket knives, anything helpful.

We approached a small gas station. It was closed but that good ole blue and white Bell telephone on a pole (no booths out in the boonies) was operating. So was the Coke machine. Cost five cents.

I called the house. JoAnn and I screamed bloody murder when a sister answered the phone. We told them in gasps that we were dying. We hung up after a particularly wrenching sob.

Then I called Jerry and told him to get his ass to where I thought we were, southeast of town.

A half hour and many mosquitoes later, he appeared along with a few other Betas. We informed them of our ruse.

Stopping at a drugstore in town that was still open, we bought out the Ex-Lax supply. We dropped JoAnn not far from the Delta Delta Delta house. The next night there would be chocolate pudding for dessert. We knew that from the schedule. JoAnn ground up the Ex-Lax and stirred it into the pudding, which had been made that night and put in the fridge. Then she snuck back out and went around to the front. Falling through the front door in her exhausted and disheveled state, she declared that I was lying by the side of the road and she couldn't revive me.

Meanwhile, Jerry and I rounded up lots of Betas, made tons of water balloons and returned to the place where JoAnn and I had been dropped. The boys pulled their cars further down the road, then lay flat in the fields. I sprawled by the side of the road. Sure enough, three cars of frightened sisters soon rolled up.

Now you might ask why none of the sisters called the police. Two reasons: People weren't as quick to seek outside help then, and, far more important, they could get expelled. If I was dead, I was dead. Nobody could do a thing about that. If they were expelled, that would be a disaster.

The sisters had correctly suspected that JoAnn and I were pulling their legs with the phone call, but the sight of poor JoAnn sent them back into the night.

I could barely contain my glee when I heard that first car door slam and a muffled sob as a sister sprinted toward my crumpled form. Within seconds all the sisters were out on the road and whammo, water balloons were flying from all directions.

The only problem with this plan was that I got soaked, too. It was so much fun, who cared?

After much scuffling and laughing, everyone gave up and drove down to a greasy spoon to eat hamburgers.

Dinners at the sorority house were formal affairs. You had to appear promptly at six. You couldn't wear shorts or slacks. You had to wear a dress, good shoes, and have your hair in place. During this ordeal you sang between courses.

We had warned the pledges we liked—which is to say most of them—not to eat dessert. Since pledges were scattered throughout the tables, this wasn't immediately noticeable.

The sisters had a moving experience.

Our pledge class quickly gained a reputation for giving as good as we got. We inspired other pledge classes to carry on, too.

What a silly, wonderful time it was. Innocent, too, in many ways. The worst that anyone did back then was sleep with one another. I sidestepped that because if caught you'd get thrown out of school. They threw us out for such trifles—you could get rapped for violating the dress code.

I hoped I would make contacts and friends at Florida who would go through life with me. Being a freshman, at the bottom of the barrel, gave me an opportunity to scan those above me. I was and remain a careful person when making friends.

For me friendship is as sacred as marriage.

Faye, meanwhile, raised holy hell. I can't keep track of how many times she changed her major. She dragged me to Jacksonville once for the express purpose of getting me drunk. She succeeded. Sick as a dog, I vowed never to do that again. I haven't. Anyway, she always waltzed off with the best-looking guy around.

One night I was up late studying and Faye rolled in around one. Relatively sober, she sat down on her bed. Neither one of us had bothered to decorate our room, unlike most of the girls in Jennings. We spent so little time in there, why bother?

"Brown, you'll make A's."

"Gotta nail it. I'll lose my scholarship if I don't." I knew she knew that but I repeated it nonetheless. I didn't want Faye to think me lacking in *joie de vivre*.

"I think you're a lesbian."

"Faye." I shot her a dirty look.

"You love Jerry, but—?" She held up her hands.

The thought of being a lesbian didn't bother me. But I rarely thought of romantic stuff. By now I'd matured enough to know that being gay killed all chances of material success unless you lied through your teeth. I was poised on indecision—I simply did not know what I was sexually. Nor was I eager to find out.

"Why aren't you wearing Jerry's fraternity pin if he loves you so much?"

"I don't know." I didn't . . . but a swift current of anger picked up my energy.

Getting pinned was a ceremony as thickly sweet as treacle pudding. The whole damned fraternity house trooped to your window in the sorority house or dorm. They stood in a semicircle and lit candles, then sang songs. The adored one fluttered at her window. A balcony might provide a better backdrop for fluttering but a window would do. The real pros cried. The man standing in the center of the circle of light was your beau. After all this choreographed romance, the fair damsel floated down, kissed her man and was pinned above the heart. If she was wearing an inflatable bra she hissed.

Inflatable bras, the rage then, felt natural when you squeezed them. Sadly, no one ever developed an inflatable penis for the same purpose.

I would rather have bled from the throat than put up with being pinned.

Girls attracted me no more than boys, though. Nothing connected me to a sexual level because I ruthlessly suppressed anything that might intrude on my drive to succeed. The first thing I had to do was make it through college with great grades. And while I loved Jerry in that I accepted him totally, I felt no great attraction for him.

Without knowing it, I was surrounded by gay kids. No one told. If only they had . . . but as my experience will soon show, hypocrisy saved them on the outside while destroying them on the inside.

Faye, the most open-minded soul I ever met except for Dad, truly could have cared less. The idea that she might be sharing close quarters with a lesbian was fine with her. She accepted people for what they were; her patience ran thin with the fakes, the liars and the cowards. Why I'll never know, but she liked me and I liked her.

Her circle of girlfriends, all attractive, shared her attitudes. They were good to me.

Faye saw something in me that I didn't see myself and it wasn't just that I might be gay. She saw my focus, my willpower and my tremendous fear of being sucked into poverty. She never made fun of that fear and she never lorded it over me with material possessions.

Another woman who was kind in this latter respect was Bernadette Castro. The heiress to the Castro Convertible furniture fortune, she attended Pinecrest in Fort Lauderdale while I was at Fort Lauderdale High School. She was also an Anchor Club kid. I knew her a little. Cuban, dark, and with a glorious body, she possessed singing talent. Everyone made fun of her because her dad could afford the backup band. But the truth is, she did have talent.

This was the first time I perceived the evilness of people toward the rich. They never allow them to succeed, and credit whatever success they do achieve to their money.

Bernadette ran for the U.S. Senate, on the Republican Party ticket, in New York State in 1994. She couldn't unseat Moynihan, but brava for the run. I was proud of her.

I soldiered on, but I worried about Faye. She was going to get thrown out of school if she didn't work harder.

Apart from Faye's insight, my first year seemed typical enough. I adjusted to being one of fourteen thousand students. I raced through my required courses so I could start some electives in my sophomore year. I ran track and found I had a knack for the javelin. Track and field didn't interfere with tennis.

I thought about Betty Rinehart. I wondered if the convent was what she hoped it would be. I truly missed her.

As for Dad, sometimes I'd walk across the campus and music would ring out from the bell towers. My eyes would mist up. I wanted to write and tell him how much I was learning and how lucky I was to be in college. If he had lived, I would have been at an Ivy League school, but now I was fortunate to be at Florida, a state school.

Mom wrote three letters a week, which floored me. Whence came this maternal burst?

The absolute shocker occurred when Mom drove the whole way to Gainesville. Jerry, as stunned as I was, took her to dinner. Students have little money but the fact that he spent it on Mother made him a giant in my eyes. Mother loved him. Who didn't?

We walked around the campus. I showed her the alligator, sleepy, old, covered in moss and wallowing in a big pond.

She loved the Delta Delta Delta house, built on three levels.

"I feel like a coed." She giggled.

The next night just the two of us ate at a small restaurant in downtown Gainesville. As dinner ended she pulled out her pack of Chesterfields.

"Your father smoked three packs of Pall Malls a day. I think if he hadn't smoked like a chimney he might have survived his heart attack." She paused. "I don't know." Then she ripped up her cigarette pack. "That's it."

Mom, a smoker since she was twelve, quit cold turkey.

When she left the next day, I waved goodbye as she turned south on Route 441. It occurred to me that Mother loved me.

She showed it in peculiar ways, if she showed it at all, but I didn't remember her driving that far for anyone else.

Then, too, I knew the minute she arrived home she'd call Sis and tell her she had been a coed.

Mean as
Snakeshit

CAMP HIAWATHA IN KEZAR FALLS, MAINE, REDEFINED THE WORD *cold*. Summer nights drop into the low fifties, sometimes forties.

Every moment of the day, crammed with activity, counted. The counselors—I was head tennis counselor—were as regimented as the kids, but we could sometimes go out at night if permission was granted.

Jerry, a tennis counselor at Camp Wigwam, forty miles away, borrowed a car on a mutual day off. We would drive to Portland, a lovely city, home of Longfellow. I dragged Jer through the poet's home, we ate lobsters by Penobscot Bay and we window-shopped.

He would return to Gainesville for his senior year, then apply to other schools for graduate work in chemistry. We talked about an upcoming tennis tournament in Fryeburg, Maine, where we'd be playing mixed doubles. Then after the sunset we drove back to camp.

The windows open, the smell of the pines drifting into the car, we laughed about our campers, other counselors, each other. We both gave as good as we got.

"I'll miss you when I'm gone."

"Won't be for another year," I answered, unromantic per usual.

"You could transfer to the University of North Carolina, that's really where I want to go. Chapel Hill is a great place."

"Anything's bound to be better than Gainesville, the bedpan of the South."

He laughed. "Do you still want to go to graduate school?"

"Yep."

"Can't you sit down and write without it?"

"Sure I can, but if I can go, I ought to do it. I'm not going to keep up my Latin once I leave school, and I need it."

Jerry had studied four years of Latin at Fort Lauderdale High. He knew the importance of Latin. If you don't know Latin, you don't know English. I needed Greek also, but I was delaying that as long as possible.

"If we got married, we could live together," he said. "I'll get a good job as soon as I graduate and I'll put you through graduate school."

"I don't want to get married."

"You love me, don't you?"

"Yes. I always will."

"Well?"

"Your parents are Catholic, we're Lutheran. I've lived with that fight all my life and I will not raise my children Catholic."

"That'll kill Mom," he mumbled.

"See what I mean?"

"She wouldn't have to know until we had children."

"And I won't get married in the Catholic Church. We marry in my church."

"Oh, God," he moaned.

"Exactly."

We drove back to Camp Hiawatha in silence. I kissed him and walked back to my bunk.

The next afternoon, he showed up again; he'd snuck off work.

"We could be atheists," he greeted me.

My cherubs were hitting crosscourt forehands to one another.

I walked over to him. "Jerry, what are you doing here?"

"Asking for your hand in marriage." He looked as solemn as a heart attack.

"How about my foot?" I joked.

"I love you. I don't want to spend my life with any woman but you."

Much as I loved him, I didn't feel in a nesting mood. All around me engagement rings sparkled as college seniors panicked.

"Now or never."

"No."

"Then I'm dating other women," he threatened.

Threats don't work with me. "Go ahead."

"Goddamn it." His face reddened.

I laughed at him, which made him madder.

He left, and I returned to my kids.

Jerry made a show of dating other girls. I didn't budge.

The green of the leaves darkened, the sun set a tad earlier. Camp would soon be over. The kids overflowed with tears, they kissed and hugged one another at campfire, at color war, wherever. Today someone would read lesbianism or male homosexuality into their actions. But children from age eight up to sixteen express themselves. They knew they wouldn't be able to drive to see one another. They could phone one another since they were all rich enough, but still, they had no control over their lives. A camp goodbye was worth a few tears and kisses until next year.

The ceremony that brought these emotions to a fever pitch was the fire-lighting ceremony.

A big pile of firewood sat in the center of four smaller piles, east, south, north, west.

A child chosen from each group would go over to one of the small piles.

"I light the fire of friendship." They'd boohoo before she finished the line.

Then the west girl would light her fire, which stood for courage or whatever.

As the four fires burned, a counselor or camp director would make a short speech about stellar personal qualities, then put the torch to the big pile.

The bonfire blazing, Tondelayo, in Indian deerskin, would beat her tom-tom, dancing and singing. The joke was, of course, that Tondelayo was the name of the native girl improbably played by Hedy Lamarr, in *White Cargo,* a movie set in Africa. Our Tondelayo, bedecked in fringed and beaded deerskin, may well have had Indian blood in her veins, but she didn't melt into the forest at ceremony's end. She hopped in her car and buzzed off.

As the bonfire crackled, the kids sobbed their little hearts out.

The last day of camp some parents picked up their children. Other kids boarded buses to Newton, Massachusetts, where their parents would fetch them amid cries of how much they'd grown and how tanned they'd become. More tears and kisses as the children said goodbye to one another and goodbye to freedom from Mom and Dad. Sometimes they'd grab on to a counselor, vowing eternal devotion. Mom and Dad would have to pry the child away.

Jerry and I also disembarked at Newton, hopped the MTA to Boston's main train station and caught a train to New York. Once at Grand Central we had half a day before going over to Penn Station to board a train for Florida.

Grand Central exudes energy and warmth. The ceilings draw your attention upward to the constellations painted on them. The staircase at the western end seems fantastic the first time you see it. It's a wonderful example of public architecture.

I wore tennis shoes, the old white kind, and a shift dress. He had on a pair of khakis and an ironed shirt. We walked over to the old Penn Station, without doubt the most beautiful train station I have ever seen. Vaults of glass curved overhead, and the light streamed down on you even as crowds of people hurried by. A breathtaking structure, it had to have been as extraordinary as the Crystal Palace was in its day. Unfortunately, Penn Station was later destroyed by the wrecker's ball to make way for a building notable for its ugliness.

We walked, winding up in the theater district. A well-dressed woman standing in front of the theater where *How to Succeed in Business Without Really Trying* was playing noticed us. She couldn't use her tickets. She gave them to us. We hadn't any money to spare, which she recognized. She heard our accents, smiled and wished us well. It was our first Broadway show. The minute the orchestra struck up the overture I was in heaven.

That was my introduction to the kindness of New Yorkers. I could barely understand a word they were saying. They tended to shout and rush about. No one said hello to anyone else. Definitely no passing and repassing for these Yankees. And yet, it was love at first sight for me—a continuing love affair, although we've suffered rocky moments.

During the long shuffle back to Florida I thought about the city. I was going to study there. Aqueduct was there. (A place without horses was inconceivable.) No hounds, though. That bothered me, but I figured I'd drink up everything I could for as long as I could, then go back home and find hounds aplenty.

I told Jerry. He didn't say anything for a while. He knew I wasn't given to idle statements. If I tell you I'll be at your house at six in the morning to shoot you, I'll be there at six in the morning with a gun—as we say down home.

"I can't go to school in New York," he finally answered me.

"Well, I can't go now. I meant for graduate school."

"That's not so bad." He exhaled. "I can live in New York for a while. I'm not raising children in the city, though."

"I'm not giving birth to Yankees, so don't worry about it."

"You were born seven miles north of the Mason-Dixon line."

This fact delighted him since he could throw it in my face whenever I became too grand and too southern.

"Eat shit and die."

He murmured, "I love you," laughed and fell asleep until Washington.

He did love me, too. He'd known me since I was eleven. I didn't have to explain myself, not that I was inclined to do so. If he'd wanted a sweet, sugar-pie, you're-my-big-man kind of girl, he would have easily found one. He was becoming a hunk. Not that he had a handsome face, he didn't, but his body was prime beef and his sense of humor prime-time.

He wanted a partner who'd stand by him and stand up to him. In that sense, I was perfect. And I was loyal.

Since I wouldn't sleep with him until we were married, he'd find a tart and go to bed with her. That was okay. I thought then (and I think now) that our country is silly about sex.

In America sex is an obsession. In Europe it's a fact of life.

I fall into the fact-of-life school of thought. People do what they do and it's none of my business. To base the most important decision of your life, or one of them, on sexual attraction alone is pure-D foolishness. Marry in haste and repent at leisure.

He could do whatever he wanted to do as long as he didn't rub my nose in it.

Monogamy is necessary for the greater social good but contrary to nature. We each struggle with the conflict.

Jerry didn't struggle. He indulged himself thoroughly. But he was about to shock himself and I was the cause.

If we'd both known what was going to happen to us that year, I wonder if we'd have gone back to Florida.

Guts and No Glory

EVERY NOW AND THEN, LIKE MOM, I HAVE A BRAINSTORM. SOME-times they work and sometimes they don't. When they don't it's usually funny to everyone else. It's funny for me years later.

My sophomore year I decided to declare a major in physical education. I wanted to be a gym teacher like I wanted cancer. However, you had to have a certain number of physical education credits to graduate, and varsity tennis for girls wasn't part of the deal back then. I wanted to get to my electives for my junior and senior years without the interruptions of re-quired courses. I'd switch my major to English the beginning of my junior year.

I thought I was being very smart. I exulted in my ploy. I exulted until the first day of gymnastics when a tanned, drop-dead-gorgeous blonde walked down the aisle for class. I couldn't breathe. I couldn't take my eyes off her.

Julie Swensen exerted an attraction I'd never felt before.

I didn't care what anyone thought about me. I did care what they thought about her. I tried to be restrained.

We'd double-date, me with Jerry. Her twin, Geneva, would sometimes go along with her boyfriend, whom she later married.

Julie, a year older than I was, was a tremendous athlete. I'd never seen uneven bars. She competed on them in the Junior Olympics. Apart from Betty Rinehart, she was the first woman I'd met who had as much athletic talent as I did. Swensen excelled at everything.

Once I recovered from the shock, I decided that if she was better, I ought to learn from her. I was better than she was in field events, but what she had, in everything she did, was an animal grace that is equal parts sex appeal, physical power and charm. The French have a term for someone like that—*animal de luxe*.

One rarely sees this quality. Ava Gardner had it. The young Jean-Paul Belmondo had it. It's not about beauty, it's about something much more seductive.

I visited her home in Lake Worth for Thanksgiving, a subdued holiday since John F. Kennedy had been shot. We were watching the news report when Jack Ruby shoved a gun in Oswald's gut, launching him into eternity. The world had gone crazy. We were old enough to feel terrible but young enough to quickly return to our individual pursuits.

Julie was and remains unassuming, self-effacing and self-reliant. She loved her family and over the decades I never once heard Swensen utter a rude remark about any family member. This was in sharp contrast to my family, where titanic battles followed by hilarious recountings of the hostilities occurred with alarming regularity.

Every family contains stress points. Most of us can't resist blowing off steam when a parent, sister or brother irritates us. Julie refused to criticize even when a person deserved it.

She was a lot like Dad. Jerry was more like Mom.

Perhaps in the early years of our romantic life we bounce between parental models until we finally figure out what works for us. Then, too, each one of us has to contend with cultural pressures. In the late fifties the ideal woman was Marilyn Monroe: vulnerable, ditzy, overtly sexual and with a voluptuousness that bordered dangerously close to something maternal. The male heroes, best represented by Gary Cooper, had to be tall, taciturn, able to handle any and all external crises, unable to articulate deep feelings.

Few of us in our teens and early twenties were Marilyns or Garys. Few of us comprehended what it meant to be emotionally responsible toward another human being. That's what years are for: to teach us.

The surprise was that I liked physical education more than I'd thought I would. Physical education majors aren't bright the way, say, political science majors are bright, yet they can be highly intelligent. The body is their metaphor. Once that sank into my head, I observed them and sports with new eyes. The movement was the message. Winning and losing, at the deepest level, is a side issue. It's about how the body defines space. In team sports a ballet of competition unfolds. The team athlete needs not just physical skills but also social skills, because you can't succeed without cooperating.

Much as I looked forward to declaring my true major in the following year, I was absorbing a great deal from this one. I had decided I wanted to double-major in English and agriculture. There were few women in agricultural departments then. Not only did I face derision about my choice, but my honors professors sang a siren song about how brilliant I was and how I should not waste my time and talents.

Brilliant is as brilliant does, but in college people focus on your ability to master intellectual material. For me, that's like falling off a log. It doesn't, however, mean that I am smart. It only means if you sit me down with a nuclear physicist, a historian or even a mathematician, I'll "get" what they have to teach very quickly.

Swensen lacked this. But let her see a motion and she could reproduce it instantly. That's kinetic intelligence.

In kinesiology class we had to write term papers breaking down the motion of catching a softball above the shoulder height, at the waist level and then below the waist.

Julie could no more write this paper than she could fly. First off, she hated to write. Second, why write about it when you can do it? I've always thought she was dead-on about that.

I knocked off my term paper in an afternoon. Then I tackled hers. The challenge thrilled me because I would have to write in a style foreign to me and write well enough to pull a B but no better. If Julie had turned in a flashy term paper, the red flags would have gone up.

As a writer, I found that the task appealed to me. I knew I could imitate. I'd devoured Gertrude Stein and could parody her easily, but then I guess that's not too hard.

Anyway, I worked into the night and got punchy. I inserted a sentence into her term paper that nearly got both of us canned. We turned in our papers and thought that was that. Julie, of course, didn't bother to read "her" term paper.

The next week Julie found me at the tennis courts. Since she rarely visited practice I hoped she was starting to like me.

She'd been called in by her advisor in the department, Ruby Lee Pye, who read the offending passage out loud.

The passage read, "If the balls are above waist level, consult a physician immediately."

Swensen must have turned three shades of red. Fortunately, her advisor liked her, as did everyone, and forgave her.

By the time Julie finished her story, Jerry was in tears from laughing. Then Julie started laughing.

"Did you tell them I wrote it?"

"No."

Then I laughed, too.

We both could have been expelled for my prank. And I was full of them.

I started a rumor that if you engaged in illicit sex, your urine would turn blue. Naturally, I started this right at the Delta Delta Delta dinner table. Within a week the dreaded new VD story swept the campus. Nothing happened.

I waited. A month later I snuck into the Beta Theta Pi kitchen. I had begged Jerry, the Master Beta, to cook up a dye that wouldn't harm anyone but would turn urine blue. Aided by the Master himself, I dumped the stuff into the iced tea vats. Every fraternity and sorority dinner was accompanied by iced tea. Then we bribed the cooks at the ATO house, the Delta Tau Delta house, Phi Delta Theta, Kappa Alpha Theta, Chi Omega and of course Delta Delta Delta. Chi O gave me chills, since they were perfect southern belles. I could hardly wait.

Didn't take long. By that evening some of my sorority sisters were weeping in their beds. Hardly a light shone from a Chi O window, and the Phi Delts sat glumly in their yard. Jerry and I cruised around to inspect our handiwork. We knew who was sleeping with whom anyway, but this put the cherry on the ice cream sundae.

The infirmary was packed.

It was pure bliss.

That success emboldened me. I unscrewed shower heads in Jennings dorm and put the dye in there too. That nearly tripped me up . . . all those blue girls traipsing around campus while I stayed white.

By now Faye, fed up with school, sought another adventure. Her father bought her a 180 SL, white. Having a Mercedes today is a lovely thought. Imagine having one as a nineteen-year-old!

Faye and I wore out a set of tires cruising Alachua and the surrounding counties. The combination of great-looking Faye and the car snapped heads around. Me, I was along for the ride, but I knew if I could get the opportunity to talk to someone, they might pay a little attention to me.

Faye and I snuck out of Jennings through the window one night in search of booze. Alachua County was dry. This drove the money to the nearest wet county, Marion. She had enough fake IDs to fool the FBI. The way Faye's mind worked she would have made a superb agent. There wasn't a building she couldn't get in or out of, a rule she couldn't bend.

She pulled up to a liquor store in Ocala and bought a bottle of bourbon. She consumed a large quantity of it before we hit the county line. I took over the driving duties. I always thought people liked me, since I was included in activities, but maybe it was because I stayed sober. At any rate,

Faye had a crush on some medical student. We cruised his off-campus residence. He wasn't there. Disappointed, she polished off most of the bottle. By the time I coasted into the dorm parking lot, lights off, Faye had passed out. The first order of business was to stay quiet. I coasted in, barely making a parking spot. I quietly got out and silently closed the door.

Faye, tall, had folded herself into the 180. Unfolding her required ingenuity and strength.

I'd learned the fireman's carry. I hoisted her on my shoulders, tottering to the basement window. I opened it, climbed in and leaned back out. She was a heap on the ground. I whispered her name. Not a flicker of an eyelid. I climbed back out and pulled her to her feet like a rag doll, leaning her against the window.

Nothing awakened her. I tipped her over the window. However, she filled the space, so I couldn't climb in to pull her through. The other windows were locked. After all, she'd only paid for one window.

I dropped my shoulder under her butt and lifted. Slowly but surely I inched her through the window. I heard a soft thump when she landed on the other side, headfirst.

I clambered through, nearly landing on her.

She'd picked up a few scrapes in the process.

Four flights of back stairs awaited me. Again, the fireman's carry. By the time I reached our floor I thought my quads would give way. I dumped Faye on her bed and collapsed on mine.

She woke up the next morning and beheld her scrapes and bruises. "Brown, what did you do to me?"

"Rented you out to the Kappa Alphas."

She flounced down the hall to the showers, her humor restored when she returned.

Whatever Faye was searching for wasn't at the University of Florida. She left before the end of the semester. I decided I couldn't stay in Jennings without her. It was too expensive, and too depressing to walk into the room *sans* Faye.

I moved over to Broward, an older dorm, the butt of campus jokes. My roommate there had a boyfriend who played the piccolo in the Marine Corps band in Washington, D.C. I don't remember her name because I think we spoke two words (which were not unfriendly, but we had nothing in common). She was obsessed with her boyfriend and played Marine Corps music morning, noon and night. There are worse sounds than military music, but I am hard pressed to think of one right now.

I hung out at Jerry's apartment, the library, Julie and Geneva's apartment and the tennis courts. The sorority house was fun, but I was out of it more than in it because a new regime had taken over, one that actually believed all that gooey crap they tell you when you're initiated.

Have you ever noticed how you can look at something and not see it? Full of ideas and activities, I hadn't taken a hard look at the physical education department, which had a large quota of covert lesbians on the staff as well as among the students. I knew some of the girls were gay. I liked them.

A student could be expelled for being homosexual and a professor could lose her job. In the sixties and before, in order to attend the University of Florida, a state university, you had to sign a contract, the last clause of which was the morals clause. You could be expelled from the university for immoral behavior. The sexual revolution was still on the horizon.

This clause made kids hypocrites. The human animal is tremendously sexual at that time of life. Nature intended it that way. Society needs to delay the natural process because life is currently so complicated one is still learning fundamentals into one's early twenties. Starting a family at fifteen is no longer a good idea, even though it may be better from a physical standpoint.

Few students were expelled for sexual activity unless they literally did it on the lawn.

Drunkenness, publicly deplored, was also publicly ignored. Florida football games greatly added to the fortunes of the Busch and Uihlein families (both beer magnates) as well as the distillers of various grades of bourbon. Few students were expelled for drunkenness.

Steroids were used in football and other men's sports. No one noticed.

The duplicity of social behavior was lost on none of us. We had all learned the great rule of southern life even if we hadn't attended the boot camp of manners, cotillion. That rule was: You can do anything you want so long as you display good manners.

Simple as this rule is, it does have variations that illuminate the southern mind. For instance, everyone knows that running around while you are married breaks your spouse's heart. The trick is to be discreet. If your spouse finds you and shoots you, you are at fault, not the spouse. The law may say otherwise, but the social and emotional reality is that people side with the injured party. If you got an ass full of buckshot, it was what you deserved.

Another rule: Certain activities and even conversations belong behind closed doors. That's what closed doors are for!

You can never be ugly to a social inferior. This marks you as trash no matter how exalted your bloodline, how heavy your wallet. You won't be excluded from society, but behind your back you will be called into question. And what people say behind your back marks your true place in society.

Gossip fuels all personal relationships, whether it's in the Pentagon or in your town. There's good gossip and bad gossip, which is why what people say behind your back is crucial.

If people say, "She'll never reach law school," that is negative and reveals as much about the speaker as the subject. Every southerner knows that, which is why we listen so carefully to one another. We listen for people to betray themselves. If it's one negative story after another, over time we draw the conclusion that the speaker is angry and weak.

So the dance of manners is much more than superficial, it's the structure for exchange. But you must know how to listen. This is why Yankees fail so miserably in our party of the country. I mean party, too.

The Yankee, compelled to tell you how terribly smart he or she is, appears the reverse to us. After all, a smart dog buries its bone.

Mother said, "The difference between a Yankee and a southerner is, a Yankee will tell you how smart he is, a southerner will tell you how smart you are."

The other towering mistake is that a Yankee deals in ideas, while a southerner deals in personalities. If you wish to create social change here, you do not march on the state capitol. You find the governor's mistress or sister or daddy. Then things change without appearing to change.

The best world would be a balance of ideas and personalities. I haven't found that place yet, so I'll stick with what I know: Dixie.

Dixie was about to tear me a new asshole. I tripped on that invisible barrier, which made everyone panic. Have you seen those invisible fences for dogs? They work. The dog rushes out to chase a car and hits the invisible fence, which gives Fido an unpleasant shock. A live but humbled dog sits down and rethinks chasing cars.

Human and social interaction is like that. There are invisible fences.

I hated duplicity. My natural instinct is to crush hypocrites. I still struggle with this. I must learn that they too serve a function. As Milton said, "They also serve who only stand and wait."

The function the hypocrite serves is to reinforce the ideal order while breaking the code surreptitiously. What makes people hypocrites is that either they believe the ideal is correct, even if they can't live up to it, or they don't believe a word of it but they don't want to get caught. They are motivated by guilt and fear.

You can only deal with hypocrites by giving them a way out. I didn't and I paid for it.

All those drinking, fornicating and sometimes cheating (on their exams) kids knew something I didn't: Don't challenge authority unless you have a chance of winning.

I never slept with Julie Swensen. She wasn't interested in that. I never slept with anyone in college other than Jerry and we were extremely careful. You couldn't easily get contraceptives then and an abortion was out of the question. We lost a lot of young women to coat hangers. It was a war in a way.

I hated that, but the reality was that if I got pregnant, I would bear the child. My career would be interrupted. I would bear the stigma, too, although Jerry would have been only too happy to marry me.

I hadn't slept with any women at all. My high-school relationship, which I thought was racy and sexual, really wasn't. Hugging and kissing seems like sex when you don't know any better.

My trip wire involved integration. The integration laws, recently passed, meant that any public institution that did not comply with the almighty federal government would lose the almighty federal dollar and probably be sued in the bargain.

The University of Florida in 1962 took the shattering step of admitting five Negroes. The word was no longer *colored* but *Negro*. These students were stuck in a corner of a dorm together.

At first I was unaware of their isolation, but my political science professor, David Chalmers, made certain we knew of it. Most white students didn't care. A handful of us did, especially two young men—brothers— Judith Brown (no relation) and I. We were horrified. There may have been other students who joined in later, but by that time I had left Florida so I can't cite them.

A wade-in occurred at the St. Augustine beach—beaches were still segregated. The two brothers got in trouble on that one because they joined the handful of adults, black and white, who integrated the beach. They may have even gone to jail for a night. I do remember that their father was ripshit mad. It hurt both young men, but they were courageous people. There may have been other students, but I don't know.

I sometimes attended student meetings. There weren't even ten people there, and the group had no name. We uncovered some unsavory facts. For instance, part of the slum housing in Gainesville was owned by university administrators and city fathers. If a Negro family slipped behind in the rent in the winter, the doors would be removed from their home. It doesn't get as cold as in Vermont, but it gets cold enough.

The facts piled up like dead leaves. We were young, idealistic and very naïve. We started making noises.

Jerry, furious, wouldn't speak to me. At that time in his life, Pfeiffer had no social conscience. His task was to get to graduate school, which would be followed by a high-paying job. Black folks would have to take care of themselves.

Eventually, we became a thorn in the side of the administration, a tiny thorn, but back then university officials were not challenged or chastised by students.

As a scholarship student I was vulnerable. I didn't believe it. I really thought that because our ideas were right and reflected what America was supposed to be, a place for everyone, we would solve this problem before my junior year.

I talked to other students and faced outright hostility or apathy.

The girls in the physical education department evidenced disinterest concerning racial injustice. No one connected it to any other kind of oppression. The gay women had no insight at all into their political situation. Everyone thought they could "pass." I'd gone with them to gay bars on the weekend. I knew who was sleeping with whom. I never gave that knowledge a second thought except I knew I must never tell.

My sorority sisters were horrified by my civil rights activities. I was dismissed via a little handwritten envelope in my mailbox, silver, gold and blue border, Delta colors. That angered me, but I could live with it.

Unbeknownst to me, the university was stealthily aiming to rid itself of these pesky political mosquitoes.

I was called into the office of one of the deans.

"What is this trouble you have with girls?" she asked me.

"I beg your pardon?"

She proceeded to inform me that my scholarship would be revoked if I didn't "straighten up and fly right."

If I was to remain at the university, I would have to undergo intensive psychological counseling. She handed me a slip of paper and told me to see the psychiatrist right off.

I didn't cuss her. I did, however, inform her that I'd rather die than be a closet dyke like herself. I walked out and I think she nearly passed out.

I walked to the psychiatrist's office, then on the eighth floor of the J. Hillis Miller Health Center. A Turkish doctor talked to me in his office. His English wasn't good, but his intentions were clear. These cases can be cured. I had scored strangely on my Minnesota Multiphasic Personality Inventory. It suggested a high percentage of lies.

He had all my documents. He explained that the battery of tests we took to gain admittance to this wonderful state university were for our own good.

I immediately understood the real reason for those tests. They had you coming and going.

I did what I always do when I'm on uncertain turf. I shut up.

After an hour of heartfelt counseling as to my appropriate sexual classification and gender behavior, I left.

I opened my dorm door and before I closed it, three students from the physical education department jacked me up against the wall. I knew these girls. I liked them. Two were bawling like babies and one was so mad I thought she would kill me. I offered no resistance since I had no idea what had happened.

They had heard that I'd ratted on them.

Ah, yes, the dean had been a fast worker. She had undoubtedly called the head of the physical education department, or an underling, who must have told one of the lesbian professors that I was a lesbian in hot water and might reveal all. The department surely knew who on their staff was lesbian and who wasn't. The lesbian professor, to protect her ass and the kids, told the kids that I was disclosing the names of gay students to the administration to "save myself."

I hadn't uttered one word. I wouldn't. To this day I have never said who was or wasn't gay in the physical education department from the fall of 1962 to the spring of 1964.

When they left, I cleaned up my trashed room before my roommate could return, but later I discovered she'd been transferred to another room. The danger of rooming with a lesbian was too great. She might be warped forever.

This hurt less than you might suppose. No more piccolo music.

I had a test that afternoon, a big class in one of those amphitheater lecture halls. I walked into the filled room. People laughed at me. Some hissed. No one would allow me to sit next to them. I sat on the floor and took the test. I knew I had aced it.

I also knew the grade would be a D or an F.

I might be stupid going into a situation, but I don't stay stupid for long.

After the exam I walked over to Jerry's apartment. He was studying for exams. I told him what I knew. And I told him I'd have to leave the university. If I didn't, they'd fail me and I'd have a hell of a time getting a scholarship somewhere else.

He hugged me and said he'd take me home. I told him he needed to study. He'd be home soon enough. I was fine.

I packed Russell's duffle bag and caught the bus for the long, long ride home.

I remembered Citation. He had courage. I'd try to have some, too.

When I walked through the door, Mother was outraged. She called me every name in the book plus a few creative ones. I thought "scum of the river" had a ring to it.

Some sweet soul from the university had called Mother to tell her that I was a lesbian sleeping with Negro men.

Which made her angrier, the gay part or the race part?

Neither.

I had jeopardized my education. (This amused me since she had never approved of it in the first place.) I was dumb enough to be open about lesbianism, in that I could love a woman as easily as I could love a man. Lastly, the South was indisputably wrong about the way in which people of color were treated, but one little white girl wasn't going to change it.

"You could have been killed!"

Mom didn't scare easily. She was scared now.

I hadn't thought about being murdered. I figured they'd give me warning. The Klan was strong in north-central Florida. When I considered it, I had been warned.

I asked Mother if I could move back in and pay rent to her. I'd been paying a small rent, twenty dollars a month, since I was fifteen. I couldn't afford to furnish a place and I couldn't afford a car. We settled on fifty dollars a month, which was a lot of money.

I asked if I could borrow the car. She had calmed down. I accepted her rules—no race politics under her roof, no girlfriends. If I was a lesbian, I could damn well hide it, and she preferred that I marry. I told her Jerry kept asking. We hit the rock of his being Catholic.

"Not again," Mother moaned. "Can't you find an Episcopalian?"

"Mom, I don't think I can find anyone. It doesn't feel right."

"Well, shut your goddamned trap." She handed me the keys.

I drove down to Holiday Park. It was about eleven at night. I sat in the bleachers and looked at the lesson court. A policeman chased me off about midnight.

So I drove out to Davie, parked by the side of the road next to a field and called to the horses standing there. They walked over, big eyes hopeful for a carrot. I smelled their sweet breath and listened to their nickers.

I wondered if I would be branded forever. Was this like Hester Prynne's scarlet letter? Would I wear a lavender *L* tastefully embroidered over my heart?

If I was going to be hung for a sheep, then I might as well be hung for a wolf.

Would my University of Florida file follow me, preventing me from matriculating at another university? I was smart enough to know, no degree, no decent job.

Was I supposed to become a hairdresser or a florist? Then, too, those stereotypes were about men, not me. I supposed I could become an undertaker. The dead don't care.

What was left?

It was so awful it was funny.

After a few tears of self-pity I figured I could go to Broward Junior College. If I could get in, it would mean that my Florida failings wouldn't haunt me forever. Since Broward was part of the state system, if they refused me I'd know that I'd have to leave the state—and even that might not work. Who was to say if an out-of-state school would want me? But one way or the other, I'd know if I was marked.

I figured if I could get in, I'd get my associate's degree, then transfer to a four-year institution and maybe even go to graduate school.

If everything blew apart and I was condemned to the shadows as a sexual pariah—just for speaking out loud about it, not for doing it, for Christ's sake—I knew I could work with horses. I could muck stalls with the best of them, hose legs, wrap bandages, clean tack. If lucky, I could attach myself to an accomplished horseperson and learn. I knew enough about the horse world to know that hard work and knowledge counted for far more than sexuality.

Then, too, the horses would like me for me.

40

Sandspurs and X rays

BROWARD JUNIOR COLLEGE, A COUPLE OF BUILDINGS AND A MESS of sandspurs, offered little by way of aesthetics, yet a lot by way of education. Most of the students worked full- or part-time. Money wasn't an issue. No one had any. There was barely enough to buy the baseball team uniforms. The professors, no doubt seriously underpaid, overperformed. My favorite was Neil Crispo, a political science professor. He could prod, cajole, trick even blockheads into original thought.

After the University of Florida, J.C. might seem a comedown and I suppose technically it was. I liked the place. I liked the students and I liked my professors.

Four of us chipped in together to buy gas for Carol Warner's car. In one of my classes we got to talking, and a few other women listened in and we formed a driving club. Carol, the big wheel because she owned this ancient piece of machinery, is now a respected educator in Colorado. If anyone had told me then what she would become, I would have collapsed laughing. Warner, respectable? She was a stand-up comic. I figured she'd go to Hollywood. She made the better choice.

The year rolled by uneventfully because I took a full class load, worked in a nearby gym after class and then walked home or took the bus. Sunday, my one day off, I mowed Mom's lawn, trimmed her hedges, did whatever needed to be done around the house. I inherited Dad's jobs. Every now and then I could borrow the old Plymouth and head to the Royal Palm Polo Club to hot-walk ponies and watch good polo.

Jerry, in his first year of graduate school at the University of North Carolina, wrote regularly. Chemistry came as easily for him as English, history and political science came for me. He liked the combustibility of chemistry. My favorite science was physics. His favorite humanities course was Latin. He was a better Latin student than I was even though we both made A's. His Latin was grammatically perfect and precise. My translations veered toward fluid English. I never minded boogering the grammar. This used to infuriate my professors, who would force me to produce a grammatically exact translation. Then they'd let me fiddle with it.

Our minds meshed in an unusual way. In the areas where he was precise, I was imaginative. In the areas where I was the queen of organization, he was the spontaneous one. Although the creative one in a traditional artistic sense, I was truly the logical, pragmatic one. He was emotional, romantic, impulsive at times.

How UNC survived him I don't know. He was wild. While I was wearing out sneakers walking to and from work, he was throwing tacky-waitress parties. You had to come dressed as the tackiest waitress you had ever seen. I don't think he ever gave a party that didn't dissolve into an orgy.

His letters, filled with piquant detail and written in his left-leaning script (he was left-handed), described his friends and enemies with a jaundiced eye.

After he debauched a large number of the fair sex, he turned his attention to his own. He wrote me that since I might be a lesbian, then he might be a homosexual, and even if he wasn't, he'd try anything once.

He cited me as telling him, "Don't die wondering."

I wasn't sure that my quote related to his current fuckathon, but it pleased him. The human mind can rationalize anything.

He promised I was the only woman he would ever love.

Interestingly enough, I never made a similar promise. His jealousy about men friends—not even lovers, but friends—erupted on the page and in person. I made the mistake of writing him that I liked Steve Cairns, a basketball player at Broward. Jerry couldn't wait for Steve to enlist in the air force after junior college. I prudently never introduced the two men to each other.

Steve was conventionally heterosexual. I was not. Had I been stone straight, I would never have been conventionally heterosexual. He was a good young man, and being great-looking didn't hurt him, either. But our romance couldn't flower. We wanted different things.

I'd met a few gay women at the junior college. Being gay or straight didn't seem to be a defining factor at Broward Junior College. Getting good grades and transferring on was paramount, and everyone was working, putting aside money.

During this time, Mother held her breath, fearing that Aunt Mimi would hear of my possible queerness. "This wouldn't happen if she was

your blood child" is really what she feared, because Aunt Mimi would
have the whip hand.

A few times I borrowed Mom's car to go to a dance bar in western Fort
Lauderdale. Val's, a big barn, hosted mostly gay men with a sprinkling of
fruit flies (straight women who hang out with gay men) and the odd
lesbian. I was the odd lesbian. I danced with the boys, watched them drink
and pair off, and then I'd drive home at sunrise.

Through Bill Stevens, her boss, Mom knew every cop and minor public
official in Broward County. The police cruised the parking lot writing
down license numbers. Unless they could catch someone in a homosexual
act, there wasn't much they could do except harass. However, one of them
told Bill I was down at the bar and Bill told Mom.

If you've ever seen a fighting cock in the pit, you've seen Mother. She
flew all over me.

"What's the cop going to do, Mom, put it in the paper?"

"No, but people talk."

"Talk is cheap," I quoted back to her. It did not produce the desired
effect, a glow of maternal appreciation for how much she'd influenced me.

"Don't sass me. I am still your mother!"

"Yeah, that's a misfortune we both share."

She cracked me one. Mother, quick with her fists, rarely hesitated to
use force when argument failed. I ducked and turned my back because I
hate getting hit in the face. She hurt her hand so bad it swelled up and
eventually turned black and blue, which meant I had twice the amount of
housework to do.

Forget borrowing the car. She did take me down to a used car lot. I saw
an old Buick convertible for eight hundred and fifty dollars, but that might
as well have been eight thousand dollars. I found a Buick older than that, a
1955, still out of reach. I'd kill for that car today. Weren't the portholes
terrific? I loved the big chrome smile of the Buick.

Thanks to the miles of walking, though, my legs drew whistles.

Mother took in laundry, ironing and mending to augment her income.
The mortgage payment was sixty-six dollars a month, so my rent covered
most of that. We had to eat, maintain a car and feed Sunshine and Skippy,
who gave Mom more comfort than I did.

Mother and I battled off and on. About everything. She wanted me to
be like her. I couldn't. Her gifts weren't my gifts. Mother must have
believed I would be a duckling, imprinted at birth to waddle after her like
Julia Ellen trailed after her demanding mother.

Julia Ellen, hands full with work and a son, absorbed the strain of trying to please a mother and a husband, the two vastly different. Uncle Mearl might have dampened Aunt Mimi's meddling ways, but then he'd have been stuck with her ire.

Aunt Mimi, while siding with Mom on any issue concerning me, enjoyed my reduced status far too much. She knew I'd had to come home to save money. She didn't know the rest of the story. Mother harped on my profligacy, and if there was one subject Sis expanded upon, apart from religion, it was "A penny saved is a penny earned." I had not been a spendthrift. I burned at her chastisement but I said nothing.

What good training for my later life. I am adept at deflecting attention away from the real issue to a lesser, still real issue. Time and again I would need to be the whipping girl to give other people the room to succeed.

You learn to bury your ego. Since mine was inextinguishable, like JFK's flame, I needed this lesson.

Fortunately, another event pulled Mother away from berating me for dancing the night away with a bunch of gay men.

Easter dinner, held at Sis's that year, brought the whole crackbrained crew together. If nothing else, it was good for a laugh. Uncle Mearl had bought Aunt Mimi a home organ—a good one, too. Various keys produced background rhythm such as brass, strings, a bossa nova beat. Aunt Mimi, enchanted with the banjo effect, regaled us with "Tiny Bubbles" against this background. This was after we pleaded, begged and otherwise adored her. Once she had banged out a few tunes she would plop her grandson Michael on the bench. Another one to inherit the considerable musical talent in the family, he outplayed his grandmother, who pretended she was pleased. She was pissed.

This led to a recitation of her back operation, which must have occurred when the earth was cooling. Anyway, it occurred either before I was born or when I was too little to take proper note of its impact. We heard every detail, from the washing of the back to kill bacteria to the first slice of the knife. You would have thought she was conscious. On and on this medical adventure unrolled. We smiled. We tried not to check our watches. Mother tapped her foot on the carpet. Why anyone has a carpet in Florida is beyond me. Aunt Mimi felt more is more.

There I sat as the Jesus-with-thorns picture opened and closed its eyes. Christ kneeling at Gethsemane reminded me that we all pray to have this cup pass our lips. Then again, the Crucifixion meant the cup didn't pass. Surrounded as I was with ample dolorous evidence of our good Lord's corporeal suffering, I realized in a flash why Aunt Mimi decorated with torn and bloody Jesus: She intended for us to suffer.

Can't say she didn't warn us. Well, she rattled on. Mother, having surrendered the limelight for nearly an hour, folded her hands in her lap, not a good sign.

"Didn't you say the pin they put in your back is gold?"

Nodding vigorously, Aunt Mimi indicated with her thumb and forefinger how big the pin was. "Gold. The body accepts it better."

"I'd like some for outside my body," Mother replied, which drew snickers from the rest of us.

Aunt Mimi, loath to stop, waved off her sister with a hand motion and fake smile. "Oh, Juts, you're such a card. Eighteen-karat gold." She twisted around and pointed to the spot in her back.

Mother rose, heading for the bathroom. To fool us, she opened and closed the door. She tiptoed into Sis's bedroom, where she opened the chest of drawers. I heard her open it, but Sis, in love with her own voice, missed the telltale squeak.

Within a minute Mother strolled back, that nonchalant expression playing across her face that I knew meant "Duck!"

She carried a manila envelope of considerable size.

"I believe your X rays are in here." She wiggled the envelope.

"Give me that." Sis lunged for it.

Mother sidestepped her, pulled out an X ray and pointed to the rod, clearly visible, while Sis kept batting at her.

"It's black!" Mother triumphantly announced.

We leaned forward for a better look. I grabbed the X ray from Mother, pointed to the spot and passed it on. It was black as the ace of spades.

Aunt Mimi, empurpled with rage, shouted, "You've spoiled my story!"

"No, I separated fact from fiction."

The rest of us screamed with laughter. Aunt Mimi didn't know that gold would show up black on an X ray. If Mother knew she kept it to herself.

Mother flounced out. I followed. Aunt Mimi's threats wafted out the front door.

"Windbag." Mother cheerily smiled, checking the rearview mirror as her sister doubled her hand into a fist, shaking it at her.

Mother giggled, hooted and guffawed the short distance home. I laughed, too. Watching Mother get someone's goat was worth the price of admission.

Mom was her old self again.

41

Fly the Coop

THE LADY CUSTOMERS AT THE GYM COLLECTED PLANE FARE SO I could fly to Philadelphia to interview at schools. I'd applied to schools out of state for my last two years.

Despite my good fortune at Broward Junior College, I still mistrusted the state school system. For one thing, the South changed slowly, reluctantly. I didn't think I could live with the daily dose of racism and sexism so common at the time.

Not that I had truly analyzed sexism. I hadn't. I just knew I didn't cotton to being talked to as if I were an amusing, bright child.

The reports from the University of Florida turned my stomach. The two brothers who had taken so many risks for integration had been locked on the eighth floor of J. Hillis Miller Health Center, the nut floor. One of them killed himself. I don't know how. A suicide verdict makes me suspicious, especially in a person as outgoing and stable as he appeared to me.

If he was confined to the mental ward, didn't they search his room? How long does it take to kill yourself without a knife or a gun? Didn't anyone look in on him? I find these questions disturbing.

Was it a case of "Let's teach this white boy a lesson"?

Whatever he suffered externally or internally, I don't think we will ever know. I have always hoped that his brother will write the story of those dreadful days. Obviously, the people involved in official capacities aren't going to write it.

When Jerry told me he didn't know the details either. The whole thing was hushed up immediately.

The reason I harbored suspicions and still do is that the first thing the university did to me when I rattled the cage was try to make me out to be a person with gender problems.

I may have been only nineteen at the time but I wasn't a complete idiot. I knew how the Soviets declared dissidents mentally ill. They locked them up and threw away the key.

How could I be sure that wasn't happening here?

My own troubles at the University of Florida and the subsequent stories I heard concerning politically active students taught me that the generation above me was so corrupt they would kill (in one form or another; one doesn't kill just the body) young people who challenged repressive policies.

I point the finger here at that older generation. We weren't killing one another. It wasn't youth versus youth. It was age versus youth.

Age and treachery will always overcome youth and skill—for a while, anyway.

Not every veteran of World War II, Depression survivor or even World War I veteran (although they were moving off the stage politically) believed in harmful policies. Not every fifty-year-old was a devotee of the Ku Klux Klan or other forms of keeping people "in their place." As the handwriting appeared on the wall toward the end of the sixties, many older people recoiled from what they read there and they too protested. But these were the early sixties. There were precious few of us and we were young.

Our youth made us vulnerable. We were perceived as the most spoiled generation to be born up to that point. We were. Even I, raised as poor as I had been, harbored high expectations about my future. I was told this was the greatest country on earth: the home of the free and the land of the brave. I was told any kid could grow up to be president—unfortunately this appears to have been true. I thought if I worked hard I'd own my own home, have a truck, a washing machine and a dryer, indoor plumbing (I was raised around lots of people who didn't have it, remember) and finally a television.

I didn't create these expectations. They were given to me. My generation was sold a bill of rights, a bill of wrongs and a bill of goods. We were ruthlessly singled out to be advertising's patsies. The number of products aimed at us as children and then young adults was staggering. You pestered your parents to death and either got what you wanted or got a smack in the face.

I believe this unremitting barrage of advertising created as much cynicism in my generation as Vietnam and later Watergate. It also created a reaction, a revulsion toward material splendors, toward commerce. In later years we surmounted the revulsion, consuming as voraciously as the generation above us, but for a time, perhaps ten or fifteen years, we actually asked pertinent questions about the proper use of resources and the ultimate aims of corporations. Is profit enough?

Given every opportunity by government, state and federal, and often by our parents if they could afford it, we could easily acquire a college education. When we used that education to point out grotesque social wrongs, our elders were outraged. It never occurred to them that they created this exact response.

From such small ripples as the suffering of the brothers I knew at Florida, a sea change would wash over America.

In 1964 I had no idea how successful such new ideas would be. To believe in racial equality in any part of America branded you as some kind of loony, at best a dreamer.

The hatred of white people for white people who opposed racism carried no subtlety. Given that federal grants were now attached to integration policies, a few of the smarter administrators at southern schools had learned to dissemble about black people.

Also, there was little glory in Yankees coming down to protect white kids from our enemies. Those idealistic people from New York and Massachusetts wanted to march with black brothers and sisters. They wanted to sing protest songs and take risks. They could go home. For us, it was home. A few Yankees were killed and it took white Yankees being killed before the nation woke up to how sick racism is. My God, blacks were being killed all along. The southern whites who sympathized with black people were driven out of town.

This is not to say we could have won without those northerners. I mean won in the sense of the Voting Rights Act of 1965, etc. There's a long way to go emotionally. I felt that southern whites working for equality and racial justice were thrown to the dogs, or maybe the death of this young man sits heavy on my soul and I couldn't see beyond it. A young man, full of promise and goodness. I couldn't believe my eyes when Jerry wrote me the news.

I will always be grateful to the University of Florida for teaching me that those in power will do almost anything to stay in power. They will lie, cheat, steal and occasionally kill or drive people to their death. It matters little if they have a program to better the community or not. Once a person or group has power they do not willingly give it up. You must seize it from them.

Today, the University of Florida is a far better place than I knew it to be, but it took a shocking death to push the university forward. The generation that administers the school now is one that saw the South torn apart in the sixties. That won't happen again, even though there will always be people who want to turn the clock back.

Maybe Mother wasn't a fraidy-cat. Born in 1905, she'd had a longer time to see how people acted. When John Kennedy was shot I called Mom. Our government had survived other assassinations of presidents. That didn't worry me. I couldn't understand how it could happen here in my time.

"Honey, I remember the sinking of the *Titanic*. The Hindenburg flew over once. I remember the St. Valentine's Day Massacre." She paused. "After a while you accept disasters."

"He's the president."

"Nobody can control anything. That's what I think. You get up every day and take your chances. It's a big country and there's a lot of crazy people. Hell, I can breed better dogs than we can breed people." She laughed.

"You don't breed dogs."

"I used to breed chickens."

We were in the middle of a gruesome event and she made me laugh.

She was right. If the president of the United States can't be safe, neither can we. You take your chances. But you can minimize your chances. By speaking out, attending meetings and rallies, I was exposing both of us to danger.

Mother wasn't against fighting racism. In her mind, though, those of us who spoke out acted like a bunch of kids. We sought to attract attention to ourselves, which is, after all, what youth does. The whole world has existed without you, and you want to announce that you are here. We announced it loud and clear.

She knew that solving this problem would take more than using personality, more than letting the mayor know you were best friends with his mistress, etc. This would take a critical mass of people to pull down those in power.

The question was, how could we arrive at that critical mass if we didn't speak out? She wasn't even opposed to speaking out, but she didn't think kids ought to be doing it. Once mature leadership stepped forward we wouldn't be so exposed, not only to our enemies, but to our own lack of experience.

She hadn't known my friend at the University of Florida but she mourned him.

"At least he died for something and wasn't run over by a drunk."

"Do you think when your number's up, it's up?"

"Sure I do." She chewed on a pencil.

Ever since she'd given up smoking she had a tendency to chew things. At least she never gnawed the furniture legs.

What Mother didn't take into account was that mature people had too much to lose by opposing racism. Kids could take the risk.

I kept my promise, though. I didn't mix into politics while living with her.

When I interviewed at Temple University I was told point-blank they didn't want me. The University of Pennsylvania was a bit more discreet in their rejection. Discouraged, I hopped on the train at Thirtieth Street Station, a gorgeous structure, landed at Penn Station and walked down to New York University. I don't know exactly why I picked NYU. It was my last hope.

Dean Henry Noss interviewed me. I told him what had happened at Florida, why that one semester of grades was bad. My grades from the junior college were good, my board scores from high school helped. Dean Noss, a square-built man with a warm face and an engaging manner, knew York and Lancaster counties well. He figured, if nothing else, I possessed an ironclad work ethic. He admitted me to New York University. I would have to take a series of tests since NYU felt southern schools so beneath them, my transcript might as well have been tissue paper. I would also have to take a year-long course in remedial speech because my accent was thick. I liked my accent, but I swallowed my pride.

He rummaged around and found a tuition scholarship for me. I'd have to work for lodging and necessities. That was nothing new.

God bless Henry Noss.

I walked back to the train station, rode back to Philadelphia and flew home.

Once home I had no money to get back to New York.

When I filled out scholarship forms my senior year in high school, our family's annual income had been $2,000.00. With Dad gone it had plummeted. Women's wages were half men's wages. With both Mom and me working we could barely pull it together.

Aunt Mimi taunted me and yelled at me. What would happen to Mother if I went to New York?

By now Mother, feeling stronger, told me she wouldn't hold it against me. I should go. Her life was over. Mine was beginning.

"Your life's not over." I was shocked when she said that.

"Without Butch it is."

"Mom, Dad would be upset if he heard you say that. Wherever he is, he wants you to be happy. Don't give up."

"I haven't given up. I just don't think I'll feel that way again."

"Maybe not, but you can still be happy. And you can still marry."

"Never." Her lips clamped shut. "I'm not taking care of some old man."

I laughed. "Okay. I wouldn't want to take care of one, either."

"Their parts drag the ground. Remember how Mother Brown's boobs hung halfway below her belt?" She warmed up. "She could have lifted and separated, you know. Well, men's parts are just as bad. I couldn't bear to look at it."

Off and running, she treated me to a discourse on the shortcomings of the male member, on baldness and dentures. Convinced that women age better than men, she crowed about how many of her friends were widows, proof of our superior engineering.

Jerry drove over. Mom gave him a beer and then proceeded to tell him that when he was old he'd pee all the time. Drink the beer now and enjoy it. Just as Jerry left, Roger Davis, another boyfriend, drove up. She regaled him with biological details also.

It was some time before Roger returned.

Jerry, accustomed to Mom, picked me up weeks later, on a sweltering August day. He had been hired to drive a car as far as Statesboro, Georgia. We'd have to make our way from there to New York. He was going up with me and then he'd return to Chapel Hill in time for school.

Aunt Mimi wouldn't say goodbye. Mom put my duffle bag in the trunk with one box of books. That was it. I didn't have a winter coat or one sweater to my name. My net worth was $14.65.

I had no place to live and no job.

We dropped the car at Statesboro and stood on the road, thumbs up. I wouldn't recommend this today. We zigzagged up the coast, finally landing in New York.

We both knew Frank Aybar, who had been the music counselor at Camp Hiawatha. He lived in Forest Hills, a neighborhood in Queens, and Frank's mother said I could stay there for a few weeks. She took me to Forest Hills to play tennis. We squeezed in a game before preparations for the U.S. Open. The stadium at Forest Hills, covered in ivy, exuded a quietness and charm no longer in existence in tennis. The locker rooms squeezed the skinniest, the clubhouse was small, the courts were grass and the members dressed beautifully on the courts and off. Watching a match at Forest Hills defied time. It was as it had always been: a visual ballet of two figures in pristine white set against rich green.

Once big money entered the game, vulgarity became the rule, not the exception. In 1978 the U.S. Open moved from Forest Hills to Flushing Meadows, aptly named. The worst sin, though, was abandoning the grass surface three years earlier. The argument was that maintaining a sufficient number of grass courts for such a huge tournament was not feasible. The English do it and they have less money than we do.

Real tennis is on grass. No amount of advertising and TV coverage can change that.

Mrs. Aybar, petite, energetic, speaking with a hint of a Spanish accent, combined Latin charm with Yankee pragmatism. She and her husband, Francisco Sr., were driven out of the Dominican Republic during one of its bad times, I guess in the 1930s.

Intelligent, sophisticated and not averse to work, the Aybars flourished in New York. In the few weeks I lived with Frank and his parents, I grew to appreciate the structure of their life. It was close enough to that of the South that I didn't feel like a fish out of water; form counted for much. There was a certain way you did things. Period.

Spanish-speaking peoples exhibit a flair quite unlike their northern neighbors. They dress, walk and talk with vitality and style. They are their own works of art.

The duplicity that Americans find in Hispanic culture is similar to what northerners dislike about the South. Your public face may not be your private face. Life is theater. The family comes first. (Yankees give lip service to this, but southerners know that for most Yankees, the job comes first.)

I attended mass with Mrs. Aybar and was sure to write about that to Aunt Mimi, hoping she'd let up on me and stop bitching and moaning to Mother.

I got a job as a waitress, found a one-room flat on Fifteenth Street between Seventh and Eighth Avenues. I talked the landlord into waiving the security deposit, no small feat in the city. I had just enough in tips to pay my first month's rent because I worked any hours I could get.

One afternoon, coming off a shift, I walked up Hudson Street where Jane Street intersects it and saw two teenage girls coming in the opposite direction, sniffling and crying. They carried a wicker basket with a towel over it.

Not yet accustomed to the ways of the city, I stopped to offer assistance.

They flipped back the towel, exposing four tiger kittens about four weeks old. An animal shelter was three steps from where we stood and their mother was forcing them to give up the kittens.

The mother cat was from Israel. That's what the older girl said, although I don't know why that was so important to her. They therefore were Jewish kittens.

"Which one is your favorite?"

She handed me a tiny gray tiger with an extra toe on each front paw. This extra toe was angled away from the other toes, giving the kitten the dexterity of a thumb.

I carried the small bundle home in my shirt, bought milk and baby food. I warmed the milk and fed the kitten off my fingertip. She learned to drink out of a bowl in no time.

I couldn't think of a name for her. That evening she jumped from the tub to the sink and down to the edge of the toilet. Like many new creatures, she thought the surface of the water was hard. She put out a paw and tried to walk on water. *Plunk.* A furious howl greeted this attempt. I scooped her out, dried her off and named her Baby Jesus.

We went everywhere together. She rode in my shirt or in the Greek cloth bag I carried. She couldn't come to work with me, but she attended NYU. She slept. My professors didn't notice. I got a better job at the university business library—I hated waitressing. I filed Standard and Poors, spending most of the time in the stacks.

Baby Jesus showed an interest in business. My boss never did discover she was with me. As long as the books on the carts were filed, she didn't much care what was cooking.

I loved that cat the way I love tulips and fresh-cut hay. She was a natural wonder to me, like a melon moon rising in an August sky.

I had little time to make friends. I had no money to spend. My rent took everything. I ate on five dollars a week and some of that went to the kitty. I would call Frank Aybar and his mom occasionally.

The apartment was too expensive. I knew I'd have to move. I couldn't find anything affordable and I still needed a winter coat. So I bought the coat, moved out and slept in an abandoned car on University Place. The university opened early in the morning, so I could use their bathrooms to clean up. I kept looking. After a week of this I found a fifth-floor cold-water flat over on East Fifth Street, between First and Second Avenues.

Awful, but cheap. I moved in. No furniture. Just a duffle bag, a carton of books, a cup and plate, one set of utensils and Baby Jesus. I found a sofa on the street and another student helped me move it up all those flights. I acquired bits and pieces of furniture because I found out what garbage day was in the various neighborhoods. Rich people throw the best stuff out. So I'd prowl Park Avenue and the East Sixties. I still have the sofa, two chairs and a chest of drawers from those days. They're beautiful.

Mother wrote three times a week, again surprising me. I wrote on Sundays. I made enough money to get a phone. I called on big days like her birthday and I sent home fifty dollars a month to help with the mortgage. Once I had to send her two hundred because the city dug up the sewer lines and made people pay for the lines in front of their house. That was a rough couple of months for me.

My grades were good enough to keep my scholarship in full force. That first semester I thought these rich kids, many of them products of fine private schools, would flatten me, but I ran with them and generally ran up front. Then again, I had to.

I took political science with Conor Cruise O'Brien and read Marx, all of it. What leaden tripe. How could that silliness dressed up in Germanic garb seduce Russia, China and Eastern Europe?

I read Edmund Burke, finding a kindred spirit. I read Thomas Paine, liking him less than Burke, but in his work there was a hope, an energy that my forebears obviously found irresistible. I read Carlyle on the French Revolution and I read *Danton's Death,* which stayed with me. It was the beginning of modern history, and the guillotine casts a shadow even at night, even today.

Irrationality frightens me even when it's funny. That a nation as elegant, advanced and altogether extraordinary as France could devolve into mass executions, then lurch into a military dictatorship, alerted me to the harsh truth that no people, no nation, is immune from insanity. The English civil war, which drove my people here, was no picnic but it was nothing compared to the French Revolution.

I drew the conclusion that no group can refashion culture, society, politics. You can have a cataclysm that changes the outward form of government and that kills millions of *your own people* but it will never work.

The leaders of the French Revolution were, for the most part, brilliant men, intellectually astounding and dumb as a sack of hammers about people. They paid for it. But so did everyone else.

My favorite person from that time is the Marquise de La Rochejaquelein, who led rebellious Vendeans against the revolutionary soldiers and lived to tell the tale. She knew bullshit when she saw it.

Thanks to Conor Cruise O'Brien, I discovered the political framework that the Western world uses. The ideas of the revolution, the aftermath and the counterrevolution still operate today. Everyone acts them out in one form or another.

The good professor drew different conclusions than I did, formed from his Irish background as well as his time in Africa.

My political philosophy, simply put, is "Better the devil you know than the devil you don't." This doesn't preclude significant change; it means only that change must begin from within, then move outward.

Change starts with you. If it is imposed on you from above, you may comply, but you will smolder. A time will come when enough people, like green hay, burn slowly inside. Soon the whole damn barn burns to bits.

Undergraduate years were a grind, but I gained the polish I needed to move on to a larger arena.

New York University, Washington Square College, may be a second-string Ivy League school, but in the Classics Department and English Department in the middle to late sixties it was first-string. Surrounded by excellent professors and ruthlessly competitive students, I learned more than I ever could have learned at the University of Florida at that time.

My Latin improved to the point where I could think in the language nearly as effortlessly as I thought in English—I don't mean Medieval Latin, but classical Latin. My Greek, at best, was perfunctory. It's a difficult language, but also I never had the feel for it that I had for Latin, which sounded like frozen jazz to me: cool, elegant, many-layered.

I studied Shakespeare with Professor Richard Harrier, a pure joy. I studied Chaucer with Professor Robert Raymo, not such a joy. He made fun of my jeans and white T-shirts and told the class he'd seen cotton pickers better dressed than I was. Humiliated, I fought back by reading Middle English with real rhythm and grace. He still didn't like me and grudgingly gave me a B after some C's to scare me. Although insensitive as a man, he was a good Chaucer scholar and I was fortunate to study with him.

I progressed to honors English and two honors Latin classes. Larissa Bonfante, from Turin, spoke the most perfect Latin I have ever heard. She made chills run up and down my spine. Bluma Trell was good, too.

Kenan Erin was my archeology professor. He led me to Iris Love, the flamboyant, funny and leonine archeologist in charge of the dig at Knidos. I'd hop the subway to catch the lectures which she occasionally gave to Frederica Waxberger's classes at Brooklyn College.

Nothing in my past prepared me for Iris, fluent in multiple languages, wearing clothes better than a model and fond of repartee. I melted each time I saw her.

She treated me with respect, which was more than some others did. She didn't mock my southern accent. I have yet to meet a southerner who doesn't despise Yankees for this mockery, especially since our English is much closer to seventeenth-century English than the rest of America's.

That's important since the English language reached its full power and depth at the end of the sixteenth century, flowering into the seventeenth. The stuff is more powerful than heroin if you live through your mind, as I do.

Iris, in her early to middle thirties, spoke to me as though I had a brain in my head. She never commented on the fact that I always wore the same pair of sneakers, jeans and white T-shirt. I'd made enough for a pea jacket and one dress marine tunic from the army-navy store which got me through fall and then winter.

She moved in rarefied circles to which I was not privy, but from time to time she invited me to functions filled with glittering lesbians, one of whom, Jo Carstairs, even owned her own island. Jo Carstairs's grandfather had been John D. Rockefeller's secretary. He looked, listened, invested in Standard Oil, and got rich. Iris took special pains to introduce me to the others, most of whom accepted me at face value. Louisa Carpenter, then in her early seventies, was inadvertently amusing when she said to me, "If only you could have seen the good that Mussolini did for the Albanian orphans."

I guess there's good in everyone, even the man who destroyed large chunks of Italy, that most seductive of countries.

In those days, no one admitted to being a lesbian. Iris, bold, never said she was, but then she never said she wasn't. That may not seem like much now, but it sent a powerful message then.

I loved Iris for her spontaneous generosity, and my good fortune remains in enjoying her friendship. She is still teaching me what it means to be descended from the Greeks and Romans culturally and metaphorically.

Larissa Bonfante, my classics professor, endured my schoolgirl crush with good grace, as did her irrepressible daughter, Alexandra. Why Larissa didn't slap me in the face and toss me in the snow I don't know, except to say that the world is filled with people who are wise enough to understand when you don't know much.

Another person I met at this time who would enrich my life like a gorgeous cheetah was Liz Smith. Florence and Aileen, two middle-aged ladies who gave me a room in their Bridgehampton, Long Island, house, would take me to the restaurants and dance palaces at night. I put down the brick around their pool and did yard work on the summer weekends. These two were the original Laverne and Shirley. Florence, a bundle of nervous energy and snappy one-liners, cooked for us and mothered and scolded me and anyone else within earshot. Aileen, calmer, given to ripostes concerning the eternal foolishness of politicians, ran a magazine in the city. How I accomplished anything on those weekends I don't know, because they kept me laughing constantly.

One evening they took me to Pat Chez (pronounced "Patches"). Filled with the wealthy, the beautiful and the accomplished, this was the place to be in the Hamptons. An Arabic theme dominated the bar, with huge pillows on tiers for seats in the dance section. Swooping fabrics hung from the ceiling like a tent.

As I observed this from a top tier, a blond, tanned, lean lady with a smile as big as Texas walked into the room with a handsome fellow on one arm and a good-looking lady on the other. Aileen introduced me to Liz Smith, who upon hearing my accent (fading, but still there) turned on her full-wattage Fort Worth charm. I've loved and lusted after her ever since.

Each time I see Liz it's as though I'm seeing her for the first time. She never disappoints. Her sharp humor deflates the pompous. Her many kindnesses to others will never be reported since she performs most of them quietly. She swims in a small pool filled with barracudas yet doesn't lower herself to their standards. People in publishing, film and TV suck up to her because of the power of her column. It doesn't turn her head.

Liz never looked down her nose at me for my poverty. She concentrated on what I could offer, which was humor and good conversation.

Another good friend of mine from those days, Susan Suitman, would take me to dinner because she knew I couldn't afford a full meal.

My senior year at NYU I became involved in Columbia University's first gay student group. This was the first such group in the country. Stephen Donaldson (that was the pseudonym he used), a Columbia student, approached the school chaplain, John D. Cannon, who agreed to advise the group. That took guts. At the initial meeting there were fewer than ten of us. I was the only woman. I knew they could have cared less about gay women, but I'd gained a reputation as a pragmatic political operator and a prankster based on one incident at NYU.

All schools have a job day for seniors when DuPont, Corning, United States Steel, etc., send representatives to certain key schools. The CIA had come to NYU to recruit students into the agency.

The Vietnam War was just nudging into the nation's consciousness in 1967. A few of us were alert to its ruinous possibilities. Unfortunately, we were young. No one else seemed a bit interested in the fact that we could get dragged into a ground war in Asia.

I'd studied General Joseph Stilwell on my own; I am a fanatical military history student. Never as celebrated as Eisenhower, Patton, Bradley (the most extraordinary man), Marshall or MacArthur, Stilwell fought a dogged campaign in Burma. He not only did his job, but called the situation in China correctly. No one listened of course, as they were enamored of Chiang Kai-shek. When was the last time you heard that name?

My study of Stilwell impressed on me that Asia is a morass. Napoleon, making that point, threw away one of the greatest armies in all of recorded history.

Wasn't anyone reading the paper now? Our "advisors" to the Vietnamese multiplied like salmonella in bad chicken. After the advisors came a few troops to bolster the native troops.

The FBI was largely focusing on those few students sounding the clarion. There must have been all of fifteen of us at the time.

Students wanted to protest, make a fuss. I begged them not to do it. Instead I made long, trailing banners that read "Wipe out the CIA" and "Wipe out the Feds." When the banners were draped over Main Building at the northeast corner of Washington Square Park, they looked like giant rolls of toilet paper, which was the idea.

The janitor tore them down in a jiffy. They had little impact, but I'd like to think they had more than a handful of pickets toting signs would have.

And so I gained a reputation for being creative, for catching the opponent off guard.

At Columbia, the gay students had no program. And why should they? There was no precedent. At the beginning, Stephen Donaldson's idea was that it would be good for us to gather together, and we might find areas where the university could help us.

This was 1967. Our efforts appeared on the front page of the *New York Times*. The school lost over one million dollars in alumni funds in a month. They panicked, but they didn't shut us down.

The reason was simple. Columbia exploded like a grenade. Within months of our organizing the Student Homophile League (a terrible name), Columbia's students overran the school and shut it down. The Students for a Democratic Society were enraged by the Columbia administration's plan to build a school-only gymnasium in Morningside Park— land that was not part of the Columbia campus. Since none of the residents of Harlem would be permitted to use the facility, the SDS considered this a racist plot hatched by Columbia. When the administration refused to hear out the SDS's complaint, students occupied school buildings for so long that the school was closed for the rest of the spring semester.

Columbia has never recovered from that time. It used to be brave about selecting students the way Bryn Mawr and Dartmouth are brave: They take chances on the individualist, the iconoclast. Not anymore. Columbia is vanilla pudding.

While this was going on, I would occasionally run into Iris Love, who wanted to make certain my studies didn't suffer. They didn't.

Liz, on the other hand, challenged me. "Why do you have to tell people you're gay? What purpose does it serve?"

"It's wrong to lie."

"Keeping quiet isn't lying."

"It's lying by omission."

She'd poke me, push me, act like the reporter she was.

Thanks to her I began to address this issue of invisibility in a broader sense, not just from the standpoint of the individual but also from the community.

As succinctly as I can put it, a community is a collection of individuals who work for the common good. We don't always agree. Here in Virginia, where I live now, you can put two people in a room and get five opinions. But we know there are huge issues where we must pull together: a clear program for national defense, an educational system competitive with the rest of the world, job opportunity, affordable food and a little help for those in trouble.

The Constitution should protect us, but it doesn't. It didn't protect Medgar Evers. It didn't protect the young man who died at the University of Florida.

We've got work to do. If you're working with people, you'd like to know a little about them. Straight people happily discuss their spouses, their children or, if unmarried, their hopes for same. The gay person, locked into silence in order to survive, either lies outright or says nothing, which in itself arouses suspicion.

I believe a community has a right to know a bit about its members. Who's single? Who's married? Who's ill? Who needs a leg up? Who needs reprimanding? These exchanges bind us. Under every healthy community lies a net of concern, even affection.

A community is weakened by any member's lying, for whatever reason. You usually uncover the lie in a crisis, which makes it twice as bad.

What does it say about a community if it rewards lying and punishes the truth? This is the moral conundrum each gay person must face. The time has come for all of us to face it.

"Don't ask, don't tell" goes beyond insult; it breeds hypocrisy. If you foster hypocrisy on one level, you'll foster it on another—like looking the other way about drug addiction or child abuse.

We need to know who we are in order to work together.

The United States used to be so powerful, so rich it could afford to assign certain groups to a discretionary labor force or push them all the way to the margins: people of color, people who spoke Spanish (or French in the far north), women and gay people.

Those days are gone. We need everyone and the best from everyone. We aren't going to get it by telling them they are so meaningless, their lives so worthless, we don't even want to hear about them.

If it weren't for Liz, I wouldn't have seen this problem in its broad context even though I knew my Edmund Burke, who wrote eloquently about how the bonds of family led to the bonds of the town and finally to the nation-state.

The process of identifying with others, of belonging, is fragile. The wonder of it is that so many gay people want to participate despite their wounds. One could say the same about any of the shoved-aside groups.

The message of inclusiveness created by Washington, Franklin, Jefferson, Madison and other of our founders lives. No one, no group, has ever been able to destroy it. We hold these truths to be self-evident, that all men are created equal.

Liz, Iris, my other professors strengthened my mind just as Mother had strengthened my resolve. If I could survive Mom, I could survive anything.

Good thing, too.

Horse Shit and
Greasepaint

THE THEATER BLAZED ON DESPITE THE DEEPENING DEBACLE IN VIET-
nam and the prairie fire engulfing American colleges. I walked everywhere, the distance from the East Village to the theater district keeping me
fit. I wore trenches in the sidewalks in front of the various theaters. The
ladies who seat you, the ones who look as though they're wearing doilies,
began to recognize me. Since I couldn't afford tickets, I'd ask them if there
were empty seats in the house. Occasionally they'd allow me to take the
seat. More often they'd wait until intermission and then let me come in.

In media res, in the middle of things, is how *The Iliad* begins. I learned
plots *in media res* because I'd reconstruct the first act, training that has
served me well since structure is the base of the triangle that becomes a
novel or a play. The other sides are character and spirit. Rarely are the
three in balance.

At this time I read and reread (and still do) the plays written during the
fifth century B.C. in Athens. The plays surviving from that period represent
the best of the best. I'm sure audiences snoozed through dross then, too.
But what has survived over two thousand five hundred years is the pinnacle
of literary creation, of theatrical creativity.

In case you don't know theater history, you're in for a treat. I hope you
read the plays and histories someday. But in the beginning, plays were
written for two great festivals, the Dionysian festival and Lupercalia. A
playwright wrote three connected plays with a satyr play, their version of
the cartoon before the feature. The plays, dedicated to specific gods, were
to entertain and draw you closer to your compatriots and put you in awe
of the power of the gods. Each selected play was assigned a choregus, who
funded the production or raised the funds. Then as now, this cost dear.

Pure art, art separated from the marketplace, is a Victorian myth. In Western life, the theater and literature are not far removed from the obel, the talent (Roman money, giving us the word *talent,* obviously), the franc, the mark, the pound, the dollar.

Academic writing may be "above" commerce, but the rub there is that so few people ever read the work or know of it.

Luckily I saw every show on Broadway, off-Broadway and even off-off Broadway. Since New York University has an excellent theater and film department, I could sit in on their classes occasionally.

I remember Al Pacino in *The Basic Training of Pavlo Hummel,* Barbra Streisand in *Funny Girl.* The established stars were Julie Andrews, Carol Channing, Robert Morse, Ethel Merman (still kicking), Elaine Stritch, Richard Burton. Mike Nichols and Elaine May, Lenny Bruce, Mort Sahl, Joan Rivers pushed stand-up comedy into new realms. Because they played more intimate houses I could never get in to see them, so I listened to their records. You could listen to records in music stores then. The clerk might not allow you to hear the entire record but you could listen to one riff. I didn't own a record player or radio. In a strange way that may have saved me artistically. I never fell victim to fashions. And no one made judgments for me. I approached each work pure.

Judson Memorial Church, on the south side of Washington Square, produced Aristophanes's *Peace.* A bawdy, broad production with next to nothing in the way of sets, it was hilariously funny, as is all Aristophanes, but it was also poignant. The playwright wrote during the Peloponnesian War, which was tearing apart Athens and draining Sparta, too. Written in the fifth century B.C., *Peace* felt as if it had been written for us. It had.

The Classics Department produced a tragedy in Attic Greek. Less than one hundred of us attended, but seeing and hearing Euripides in his language intoxicated me. To my ear, Greek sounds harsh. Lots of *k* sounds, and it's aspirated, which means you sort of swallow a little breath, then spit it out. Japanese is a bit aspirated, but Attic Greek wins the prize for this strange technique. But hearing the language in its original rhythms, in the different voices of the characters, was one of the great revelations of my life. Language is music.

Scansion is rarely taught in high school now. I don't even know if colleges teach it in poetry classes. If you want to write or if you care about language, learn to scan. You will soon see how sounds are built, how they flow together or stand apart to communicate to you, to express whatever idea or emotion is necessary. The sound is every bit as important as the sense.

I had to go to another language to learn that. You and I are so accustomed to the rhythm and melody of English, we aren't aware of it. We can't hear it as building sounds anymore.

French would seem the logical choice, but don't look there. The sensuousness of that tongue will distract you. I'm not saying don't learn French. I'm saying, that if you want to hear this symphony of sound, seek a less golden tone.

Well, I found it in Greek, a language I don't especially like. With Greek, I could lose the sense in a minute because the language is so difficult for me, especially Attic Greek (old, old Greek).

I arranged my classes so I could go to the theater more. Dreaming of writing for the stage, I soaked up everything.

I watched as many movies as I could, sitting in on film classes. I loved the silent movies best. Still do. No one can touch Mary Pickford for luminosity or Douglas Fairbanks for masculine grace. Mabel Normand and Marie Dressler make your sides ache from laughing. Charlie Chaplin is hailed as a genius. I suppose he is, but I think Mabel was better. She had fewer chances than Charlie, though, and she found the wrong men and the wrong substances to play with. My favorite director was Mack Sennett. D. W. Griffith and Eisenstein impress me, sit me down with their majesty, but the sheer energy of the comedies, the wild movement, is what delights me. Isn't that what it's about, pictures that move?

Once sound arrived, the camera moved precious little. Great films managed to get born, *Dinner at Eight* being one of my all-time favorites. Seeing Marie Dressler and Jean Harlow in the same picture is a little bit of heaven. Once the sound equipment improved we got more movement again. I love John Ford, Ernst Lubitsch, Billy Wilder.

I'd stand in front of the Thalia, that wonderful revival house named for the Muse of comedy, wait for the exit doors to swing open and then slip through with Baby Jesus. We'd hide in the bathroom, coming out when the feature started. I first saw *Alexander Nevsky* there.

The hardship of New York forced me to think quickly, act fast. Once I was hungry, sick hungry, and I rummaged around garbage bins outside a pizza parlor on Macdougal Street for crusts. The fellow inside, a young Italian man perhaps five or six years older than myself, saw me, brought me inside and made me a pizza.

I'm convinced my guardian angel is Italian.

The city itself is theater. Each neighborhood shows you a cast of characters, vibrant, contradictory and alive. Little Italy and the Feast of San Gennaro drew me each year—I loved the parade of the BVM with dollar bills stuck on her. I considered dressing in robes and attaching a halo to my head to see if anyone would stick dollars on me. Yorktown, clean, quiet and substantial, was the German neighborhood with Hungarians on the edges. The East Village, filled with White Russians, moved at a Slavic pace. Everyone had a personal story of how they escaped the Bolsheviks.

The East Sixties, province of the elegant WASPs, attracted me. I liked to stroll along Madison Avenue and imagine how much each woman's earrings cost. The brownstones exuded privacy and comfort.

A white person could go to the Apollo Theater in Harlem for talent night. 125th Street bloomed with activity and people impeccably dressed. I saw Father Divine as well as Martha and the Vandellas. Martha made a better impression.

I never ventured into Spanish Harlem, not because it was especially dangerous but because I didn't speak Spanish and I didn't want to make an ass of myself.

I roamed West Seventeenth Street in Chelsea where lots of Puerto Ricans lived. Two blocks up from where I'd first lived, on Fifteenth Street, it was another world. I eventually moved over there with a classmate, Ed Slough. The Spanish men kept an eye out for me. I learned to love those guys. Often if I returned home late at night, one of the older gentlemen would escort me to my door, tip his hat or put his finger to his temple, bow ever so lightly and wish me a good evening, in either English or Spanish.

My favorite neighborhood was Murray Hill, then mostly brownstones with few high-rises; it had a cozy feel. I used to trip along, Baby Jesus with me, peering in windows and making up stories about the residents.

Knowing I would die without horses, I found a stable on Little West Twelfth Street where the police department kept their horses, mostly Morgans. (There's another stable in Central Park, but the people there weren't as friendly.) The cops let me groom, pick out stalls, bandage. Since it was a hop, skip and jump from school, I hung out there. None of my friends knew. They weren't country people, so there wasn't much point in telling them.

Kauffman's and Miller's, the tack stores, were close to each other on East Twenty-fourth Street. Charlie Kauffman would greet me at the door just as though I were his biggest-spending customer. Charlie had hair then. Recently Kauffman's closed their doors after their move to lower Park Avenue. Charlie and his father still ran the business, the fourth generation to do so. What a loss. I can't imagine New York without Kauffman's.

Knoud's closed, too, a pricey saddlery on Madison Avenue in the Sixties.

Homesick for the South, I'd stand outside Princess Pamela's or the Pink

Teacup. Once Eddie and I sold our textbooks so we could afford a meal of fried chicken, greens with fatback, grits and spoon bread.

Jerry endured my roommate but lost few opportunities to poke fun at him. Even though Ed was gay, Jerry loathed any other man in my life. Jerry's sexual life was homosexual now but his social life was heterosexual.

His explanation for this duplicity cracked me up. "If I can't marry you, I don't want any other woman."

I used to tease him about what a lame excuse that was. If he was queer he should be queer, not drag me into it.

We could say anything to each other and did.

I was ruthless about his ten-minute boyfriends. Jerry was attracted to dependent, terminally cute men who proved to be as demanding as a woman. The more helpless the twit, the more Jerry swooned over him.

Prudently I kept any man I was dating away from Pfeiffer. Given my studies and my work, I only occasionally went out, usually with another classics student.

As for the ladies, Jerry repeatedly picked out women he thought would be perfect for me. They were female versions of his boyfriends. After trying to make conversation with a few of these lovelies, I realized boredom can kill.

I begged him to stop playing Cupid.

"If I don't do anything, you'll become a nun."

"Very funny."

"You have to go out."

"I can't afford to go out."

He thought this was wildly funny but it was true. If you ask someone out, male or female, you have to pay. I could barely feed Baby Jesus and myself, much less take someone to dinner.

Unlike Jerry, I didn't like random couplings. I can't go out with the intention of romance or even sex, which is easier to locate. I like to meet people through common interests.

For him the common interest *was* sex. I thought he was superficial and told him so. He thought I was enjoying my virtue entirely too much. We were both right, I expect.

Jerry visited each Thanksgiving and sometimes for other holidays. His wit captivated everyone. He'd stay with a friend or with me, then prowl at night. Jerry would check out bars, the trucks over in the meatpacking district—wherever there was the hope of a handsome man with a giant cock, he'd show up.

I'm no prude and I don't believe you're going to love everyone you sleep with, but I worried that he was exposing himself to danger. Who were these people? Maybe that was the thrill. Sometimes he'd make friends with one of his tricks, and they turned out, uniformly, to be nice men, as opposed to the boyfriends, who were awful.

It was a game. These squeaky-clean, handsome men, holding good jobs, would don torn blue jeans or leather and go out at night. They were parodies of masculinity and therefore vulnerable. If you wish to know the flash points of a society, look at the outer fringes. The outrageous behavior is the shattered reflection of something buried deep inside the norm.

These guys weren't butch bullies but they wanted to pretend they were.

Jerry was enchanted with the charade.

I was enchanted with reality. The more a person poses, the less I have to do with them.

Although a few lesbian bars existed, there was and is no female equivalent to the relentless sexual hunting of some gay men. Back then it wasn't just some—it was everybody and his brother.

I visited the Sea Colony once, a bar in the West Village. People divided up into butch and femme and that's not me. I left and a girl jumped me out on the street. I have no idea what inspired her to try to beat me up. She was a good-sized black woman. Maybe she'd heard my southern accent and thought I was a racist. She picked the wrong girl. I whirled around and ran backward, squashing her against the side of the building. She let go of me with an "ooof" and I walked home.

Another bar, Kookies, drew a younger crowd, less into role stuff. The owner, a straight woman with a pile of blond hair, liked me. She knew I hadn't a sou.

I'd buy a Coke and she'd let me eat all the peanuts in the bowls. One Thanksgiving she gave me a turkey. I kissed her and thanked her and ran the whole way home.

I'd never cooked a turkey but I could sure try. Baby Jesus and I ate that turkey for ten days and made soup from the bones.

One day my cousin Wade visited me. Wade had joined the marines. His father wasn't happy about it. I'd heard from Mom that Big Ken had claimed he'd shoot anyone who came to get Wade when his draft number was pulled, which it was. Wade didn't go down to register and sure enough, they came for him. I don't know what happened but I think Wade, who had a cool head on his shoulders, must have talked his dad out of resisting and saved Big Ken from jail. Anyway, Wade volunteered for the marines like his dad, which settled the mess.

Big Kenny, awarded a Purple Heart for the horror he lived through in

Okinawa, conceded the point, but he told Wade to get a skill that would keep him out of combat.

Wade became a diesel mechanic, which should have kept him behind the lines, but you could never be sure. He didn't know where he was going to be posted except that he'd be somewhere in the Pacific.

Suddenly Vietnam wasn't so far away.

43

Pea Brains and Pissants

NOEL COWARD SAID OF CHRISTMAS, "THAT TERRIBLE PALL OF goodwill is about to descend upon us again." I agree with this fellow Sagittarian.

New York City during Christmas jolts money out of your pocket better than an earthquake. When I lived there the constant advertising, spectacular window displays and over-the-top decorations at Rockefeller Center inspired nausea, since I couldn't buy a damned thing.

When I could, I'd volunteer to drive a car to a southern city during Christmas. There were a lot of drive-away companies then. Someone would fly to Miami and need their car delivered. This was the only way I could go home. Baby Jesus and I would crawl down those parts of I-95 that were finished until we reached the Pink Palace, the Ixora Express, the home of skinks, parrots, palmetto bugs and Mom.

Perhaps the monochromatic tones of Manhattan dulled my senses, but each time I visited the maternal unit that house became pinker. Finally I told Mother to tone it down—or grow bougainvillea over it.

Aunt Mimi's houses changed color like chameleons. Her first color was lemon, reflecting her tart years. Her next color was charcoal with white trim, reflecting her sophisticated years. Lastly she opted for white with aqua trim, reflecting her prudent years, since white needed repainting far less often than the other colors.

Mother complained that Sis was losing her nerve, settling for a white house. Too boring. The world should be in pink, like her, of course, or deep yellow. Then again, a pale lavender brightened up the subtropical neighborhood, and there was always that standby, lime green.

Aunt Mimi had carted her cotton-wrapped Christmas tree to Florida, horrifying Mother, who declared it a health hazard. This further provoked Aunt Mimi, who retaliated by rising above her little sister's childish pranks.

That would never do.

Perhaps they indulged in this animosity due to the welcome news that Wade was in Okinawa and not, so far, in Vietnam. What an irony that Wade should wind up on the island where his father had been pinned in a foxhole occupied by three dead Japanese soldiers. Uncle Kenny said the worst moment was when his boots smashed through the rib cage of one of the dead men. He was not one to dine out on war stories. As an adult I was beginning to understand why.

Now that neither sister could be drained by genuine worry, life could return to normal, their version.

Since Mother couldn't get a rise out of Sis over the allegedly bug-infested tree, she whipped out to the Sunrise Shopping Center to buy a new pair of glasses—wire-rimmed spectacles, the counterculture look then in vogue among the young. Afterward she buzzed over to Aunt Mimi's to show off her purchase.

"You look like a teenager. You're too old for that," said Aunt Mimi, who favored pointy glasses with rhinestones in the corners.

"Jealous."

"Act your age."

"You know, Sis, you haven't been the same since seeing Mary Pickford in *Pollyanna*."

"What's that got to do with the price of beans?"

"You were overly influenced by the wicked aunt."

"Juts, you're soft as a grape. Now act your age and take those ridiculous glasses off."

"Pea brain." Mother twirled her purse. Since it was big enough to flatten an elephant, this was no mean feat.

I helped myself to a Coca-Cola in the refrigerator since they were warming up and Mother did not yet need my strong, silent support. As I had just arrived the night before, I figured that once they wore themselves out, Aunt Mimi might remember to ask me how I was, how my studies were progressing. I was staying on at NYU for graduate school and since they were taking only one in sixty applicants, I felt grateful to be there.

No such luck.

I hadn't paid attention to exactly what they were saying so I don't know how they quickly leapfrogged from low-level sniping to all-out war. By the time I reached the living room Mother defiantly stood in the middle of the room and Aunt Mimi had retired to her favorite chair as though to a queen's throne.

"You're full of shit."

"See, that's what got Rita in trouble in the first place, your vulgar language and your refusal to take the child to the One True Church. God as my witness, I tried. I even took her to mass when you were busy."

"I didn't appreciate your giving her rosary beads." Mother dredged up an incident from when I was six.

They never forgot a damn thing.

"Why am I in trouble?" I asked like a stupid ox. I should have kept my mouth shut.

"I know of your cross to bear."

"Huh?" I squinted at Aunt Mimi.

"Shut up, Sis. You don't know jackshit."

"That is twice you have used that nasty word under my roof and during the high holy days. Juts, Juts." Sis shook her head, delighting in her moral superiority.

"You're both nuts." I sat in Uncle Mearl's chair. He was out painting houses and making a good living at it, too.

"Don't sit down," Mother commanded. "We're going home."

"I know all about it." Aunt Mimi gazed out the jalousie window as though communing with a higher power. All she needed was backlighting.

"You're all hat and no cattle," Mother bluffed.

Aunt Mimi leveled her pretty gray eyes at my brown ones. "You're a homosexual. I know everything."

"I am?"

"See?" Mother shot me one of her dagger looks.

"You don't lie any better than she does." Mimi indicated her precious baby sister.

"I'm not lying. I'm not a homosexual. I have a whimsical disregard for gender." I thought that was a refined way to put it.

"That's worse. Make up your mind." Aunt Mimi pointed a knitting needle that she had pulled out of her basket, which always sat next to her chair.

"Aunt Mimi, I'm trying to get my Ph.D."

"That doesn't prevent you from sleeping with women."

In fact, it had not, but those moments had been so few and far between and of such short duration that I hardly thought they defined my entire personality.

"You don't know anything." Mother warily moved toward me.

"Tell me the truth," Aunt Mimi demanded. "I'm the one who held you in my arms all the way back from Pittsburgh in the blizzard. You owe me the truth."

If there is one phrase I despise, it is "You owe me." However, Aunt Mimi had a point. I did owe her. You can't participate in any group of people, much less a family, if you aren't truthful. Nor can you be part of a community without incurring obligation.

"Oh, little Mary Sunshine, saving the world." Mother grimaced, edging for the door. "Come on."

I stood up. "Bye, Aunt Mimi."

"Well?"

I echoed Popeye. "I am what I am."

She took this as confirmation. "I knew it! I'll pray for you. I'll light a candle for you—"

"I'd rather you lit your hair." Mom snatched my wrist and hauled me out of there with astonishing force for a woman past sixty.

As we rolled over the little bridge leading from Aunt Mimi's subdivision, she grumbled, "This will be a hell of a Christmas."

"Can't be any worse than the Christmas after Daddy died."

"That's the truth." She pulled into the parking lot of the drugstore out on Route 1. "I wonder who's been running their mouth."

"Wade," I said.

"What'd you tell him?"

"I didn't tell him anything, Mom, but he visited me in New York. He's not stupid. Anyway, people have been saying that about me for years. I guess I look gay, I don't know."

"You don't look gay. Athletic, yes. I wish you'd marry and go about your business."

"I know."

"I'm going to have to live with this."

"It's better out in the open."

"No, it's not. She'll trumpet this to the whole world. Both her girls married beneath them. This is her revenge. I was determined you'd do better than Virginia and Julia Ellen."

"Mom, keep your voice down."

She purchased eyedrops and then harangued me as we walked to the car. "You don't have to tell."

"If you're that ashamed of me, I'm not coming home anymore."

She let it drop. When we walked through the door the phone rang.

"Hello." Mother listened, then stuck her tongue out. "I take it back, then. You're not a pea brain. You're a pissant."

The rest of the vacation involved various family members checking in to see if what they'd heard was true.

Meanwhile I washed the windows, reorganized the storage space in the carport, put down fertilizer for a Eureka palm Mom said she had to have, and played with Baby Jesus.

Aunt Mimi, unable to stay away, drove up the day I left to say goodbye and breathe a sigh of relief. She worried that I'd slept with Russell when I was in high school. Now she knew that wasn't true.

I was insulted. Mother laughed. Thanks, Mom.

"I know this breaks your mother's heart but in some ways it's good. There won't be any unwanted children," Aunt Mimi piously intoned.

"I didn't say it broke my heart." Mother swung her leg over the arm of her favorite upholstered rocker, the one with swan heads carved on the armrests.

"Julia, it has to. No grandchildren. No son-in-law to help every now and then."

"Help with what?"

"It's so nice to have a man around the house," Aunt Mimi sang.

"Men are a lot of work," Mother said. "Anyway, Sis, who knows what the future will bring?"

"I'll have grandchildren and great-grandchildren and you'll be left all alone."

"She's got me," I said.

"What good are you in New York? You'd never walk away from your real mother," Aunt Mimi said.

Here it was again: I wasn't "one of them." Under the circumstances, it seemed a blessing. I shrugged, which irritated Aunt Mimi more. Miffed, she declared I'd come home one day with my tail between my legs, I'd never amount to a thing . . . my real mother had never amounted to a thing, either, and my real father had had a great athletic career, which he had proceeded to drink away.

Another slip of the tongue.

"Shut up, Sis."

"Alcoholism gallops in her—" She stopped. "You don't drink?"

"No, but if I lived around you I would," I said.

"That is impertinent."

"Well, honey, safe journey." Mother propelled me to the car.

They both knew who my natural father was. I had been sure of that from the moment of Aunt Mimi's slip before we left for Florida. I didn't dwell on it, though. I chose to focus on what was in front of me, not what was behind me. Whoever he was, he didn't give a fig for me, so I didn't see why I should give a fig for him.

What bothered me was their lying, that and the fact that once again Aunt Mimi had given me a slip for Christmas, something I never wore.

Mother gave me freeze-dried cashews, which I loved, a pair of Levi's 505s, 28 waist, 31 leg, and socks. Since she lived in Florida she couldn't get me a heavy sweater, which was what I needed.

And Aunt Mimi always left the price tag on the slip. You'd open the present, she'd see the dangling tag (which she had altered to make the slip seem more expensive), then she'd jump out of her chair with a "Silly me." After a great show of embarrassment she'd remove the tag.

That bothered me.

As I ate a pickled egg Mom had packed for me and fed Baby Jesus some of her fried chicken—Mom cooked the best fried chicken in the world—I cruised along. Somewhere between Brunswick and Riceboro, Georgia, it occurred to me that those two were a novel, or a series of novels. I wanted to call it *Looney Tunes* but Warner Brothers might not like the idea.

I figured in time I'd find out what to call the book.

Smart Girls

THE END OF THE SIXTIES, THE BEGINNING OF THE SEVENTIES, ARE currently in vogue again. Why? The original was bad enough. The murders of Martin Luther King Jr. and Robert Kennedy unhinged the doors of repression and rage. Fourteenth Street in Washington, D.C., resembled a war zone.

New York City, to everyone's shock, remained relatively calm. Perhaps Manhattanites were anaesthetized by the vile fashions of the day. How many pretty girls could you see wearing clunky shoes, big pointy collars, plaid pants, white lipstick and Sassoon haircuts before it dulled your senses?

While the citizens did not torch city hall, they were not inactive. New York and Washington, by virtue of their location, size and highly educated populations, became centers for the antiwar movement. Chicago, San Francisco, Atlanta and Boston contained masses of young people marching, thinking and writing for underground papers, but New York and D.C. were central to everyone's development.

Richard Nixon presented a paradox: brilliant but unprincipled. At least, that's how I read him. No one suggested that the president was dumb, yet he seemed curiously unable to comprehend how his actions would be interpreted by others. Being an experienced pol, he couldn't fathom the idealism of millions of young people. Sometimes I think Richard Nixon was born old and that the lack of a young, impossibly idealistic time in his own life harmed him in ways no one could see at the time. He appeared the most Machiavellian creature. He wasn't that old when he became president, but to my generation he seemed antediluvian.

The men surrounding him oozed out of the Dark Ages. They didn't understand that a sea change was occurring, not just here but in Europe too. The Nixon administration underestimated America's young protestors just as they later underestimated the persistence of reporters to dig out the real story.

What I hated most about those days was the nation's temporary loss of its sense of humor. Even the music was angry.

How bizarre that a time so opposite to my own temperament should throw up me, a spark in the conflagration.

I'll spare you the tedious arguments, meetings and dreadfully dull position papers. Position papers, not clothes, made the man and later the woman.

The language used was wrung of any juiciness. *America* was spelled with a *k, Amerika,* like the Germans spell it. When I turned in my first article to *Rat* magazine I was instructed to use a *k*. Each article was to point out some injustice. Since we'll never run out of injustices, regardless of the century, *Rat* never ran out of material.

Graduate school, the antithesis of undergraduate school, bored me. In undergraduate school I'd been encouraged to learn. In graduate school, or at least in the English Department, the attempt was to turn out cookie-cutter scholars. All we did was rip apart texts. In my day the fashion was New Criticism. This is an idea so patently foolish I can't believe anyone paid attention to it. The idea, simply put, is that you must approach any text without reference to the time in which it was written or the life of the person writing it. *A Comedy of Errors* is read as a play to be examined for plot, character development, evolving metaphors, etc. I should think a scholar or writer would do that naturally, but not to take into account that it was Shakespeare's first play seems idiocy to me. The real point of New Criticism seemed to be providing work for critics.

When you read a novel, view a painting or listen to a symphony, you bring all your powers to the experience. Why futz around with somebody to interpret it for you? When I write a book review I try to be very careful and not interpret the book but rather place it in a literary context. I realize most book reviewers are journalists, not novelists. Their function is commercial, fundamentally; buy the book or don't buy the book.

The desire for direct experience is part of what shook the Catholic Church. When the Bible was printed on the Gutenberg press, that most revolutionary moment, mass communication was around the corner. You no longer needed a priest to intone the liturgy in Latin, you could read it yourself in the Vulgate (your language). No wonder the Protestant Reformation came after the spread of literacy.

The arts are the same. You don't need an intermediary. You need training, you need to know history and other works of art. You don't need anyone else to do it for you.

In some ways the explosions of the late sixties and early seventies are similar. A large number of American youth, thanks to the availability of higher education, wanted to participate in government. The doors were locked.

If we hadn't protested about the Vietnam War, I think we would have protested about something else.

We were doing exactly what we had been taught to do: think for ourselves and exercise citizenship. When we were pushed aside, the eruptions occurred.

The events around the Democratic convention in Chicago in 1968 need not have happened. I'm glad they did. They forced us to see how ossified and divided the entire process of selecting a candidate had become.

The Republican convention in 1972, although less violent, was equally instructive. The mere fact that we were outside and Nixon was inside presented us with a clear picture of what we had become: a nation divided, a nation of insiders versus outsiders.

My involvement grew from Dad's reading me the opposing editorials when I was little. I witnessed my parents as active citizens. Aunt Mimi, too, worked for her party. It wasn't anything you thought about or expected credit for. You just did it.

"You have a duty to act and no right to expect approval," Mother used to tell me.

She might also have added, "You have no right to expect understanding."

The Student Homophile League, my first foray into politics at a student level, subsumed by the Columbia riots, tossed me into a larger arena.

That women were used as cheap labor, messengers and coffee makers, as well as sex partners, could not have been more clear or more painful. As the quote goes, "I want to make policy, not coffee."

Whether the leader was Rennie Davis, Abbie Hoffman, Eldridge Cleaver, Huey Newton or someone else, the reality for the women was pretty much the same as it was for the Democratic and Republican women in the traditional parties. The difference was our men were much younger and dressed down, an affectation only a rich kid would find cool.

Most of us women had read enough history to know how Lenin, Mao and Castro sold out women. We didn't even have the chance to get sold out. The men were so ridiculing or hostile to our suggestion that we share this political burden together that even a fake gloss of equality was out of the question.

Women bolted from the New Left. I thought of it as Left Out.

While the black movement kept up a front of unity, we knew the struggle was hot there, too, and in many ways it was far more personal and damaging, since the men would argue that for a woman to think of herself was to abandon her black brother. I have never understood why the argument doesn't work in reverse.

The white boys, initially, were too cocky to think our defection had hurt them. The black movement, far cannier on this question, tried manfully, and I mean manfully, not to let a hint of feminism leak in or out of the tent.

What happened once the women evacuated was that the New Left disintegrated. It didn't happen in a day or even a year, but the loss of that many people, that much energy, hurt them.

The New Left died the day Nixon resigned the presidency. To all apparent purposes, they had won. In fact, they lost. Shorn of numbers and weakened by internal strife (boys don't learn how to negotiate until it's too late, it would appear), they couldn't capitalize on Nixon's exit. They never took their place at the table. Only a handful ever were elected to public office.

The crux is that while everyone celebrated that the system worked—a president had resigned, and the transfer of power had been smooth—the New Left should have mounted a massive attack on that very system. The system didn't work. The system was corrupt.

Instead, everyone fell for the line that Nixon was corrupt. He was no more corrupt than some who had gone before him and a good deal less corrupt than others.

Nixon became the scapegoat for every jerk who wanted to save his congressional seat, for every newspaper editorialist who wanted to celebrate the cleansing power of journalism in driving out a president.

While the nation patted itself on the back, nothing in our political structure substantially changed.

But we changed. The women changed. Something good was coming out of this Feydeau farce. We no longer believed that government was good. We believed we could broker with government, even a corrupt one, but that five-year period from 1968 to 1973 changed women forever. Even the backlash against feminism was determined during those five years.

I wrote for underground newspapers. No pay. I sent copies of my articles to bigger underground newspapers, hoping to get published in them. In this way I had made a name for myself by age twenty-four. It couldn't be done today. It's much harder for a young writer to find an audience.

I attended a very early NOW meeting in late 1968 or early '69. Ti-Grace Atkinson spoke. Betty Friedan was much in evidence, as was Flo

Kennedy, the lawyer with the sharp tongue and no-bullshit approach. Flo wore white Courrèges boots. I can't think of her without thinking of those boots. I never figured out how she kept them so clean in New York City.

Being the youngest person by at least ten years, I kept quiet and listened. Perhaps fifty or sixty women attended. Most of them were professional women wearing pretty Emilio Pucci dresses. They knew their careers were stalled for no other reason than that they were women. Of course, they also went home at night and cleaned house, washed laundry, organized social calendars and took care of the kids. No wonder they were angry.

The ten-year age gap between Betty's earliest foot soldiers and me loomed large. These women had bought the myth of fulfillment through others. In their thirties they had discovered it didn't quite work that way.

I had never believed those fairy tales. Juts never once hinted that a man would ride up on a white horse and take care of me forever. She declared I'd have to take care of a man and that men were boys grown large. This was not an appetizing prospect for one as ambitious as myself.

Some of my generation believed marriage would be heaven. Others didn't. I couldn't imagine the women I'd worked with in the antiwar movement, or the beginning creators of a more radical feminism, believing a husband would cure all and bring home the bacon, too.

What happened to Betty's generation, as well as to thousands of years' worth of women before her, was that men didn't keep their end of the bargain. Men left.

Why was everyone surprised? Did they really believe the bogus Victorian ideal of a cozy family, a haven from the world?

America contains strange contradictions. One is that we worship the Declaration of Independence but blanch at the thought of certain Americans being independent. Another is that we pride ourselves on being a democracy but we create few safe public places where people can practice the mixing that is so important to democracy. Europe abounds in beautiful public squares where people promenade, eat, talk politics and flirt. By contrast, the American, hermetically sealed in her/his car, drives home. We get our knowledge of each other through television. Our architecture and city planning divide people rather than bring them together.

This isn't to say that other countries don't contain contradictions, too. I've mentioned but two of ours. Still, our odd separation by income, race and gender makes us ignorant of one another.

The act of women gathering in one room to discuss being women in a political context was exciting. Elizabeth Cady Stanton and Susan B. Anthony had started the ball rolling in 1848 at Seneca Falls, New York, but six wars diverted its momentum. The Depression didn't much help either.

The hypocrisy of the Vietnam War helped us to see other hypocrisies. Then again, I know of no war started by a woman unless you count the Trojan War, and Helen may have gotten a bum rap.

Not everyone in that room knew their history but everyone in that room knew they were getting the shaft.

Betty Friedan, forty-seven then, couldn't contain herself. She glories in intellectual battles and once that mouth starts running it's hard to turn it off.

As I was young, poor and southern, I held little appeal for her. Once I started working on NOW's newsletter with Dolores Alexander, the first professional executive director of NOW's national organization, I was marginally interesting.

I have often wondered if Betty Friedan and Yasir Arafat are the same person. After all, have you ever seen them together?

Imperious, not fond of give-and-take, she considered NOW her baby. Given the smashing success of *The Feminine Mystique,* she felt she could lord it over the rest of us.

The media attention she'd received had given her valuable experience. She understood how reporters framed questions to make you look idiotic or good. She knew short answers were better than long ones but she never could give a short answer. She had a lot to offer everyone. She offered it nonstop.

Flo Kennedy, a gentler soul despite her rapier wit, understood the nuances of political argument and media attention every bit as well as Betty did, but Flo could tolerate dissent. Even better, Flo could learn from it. In the early days of the second wave of the women's movement, Flo learned faster than anyone. She mastered sound bites before anyone called them that. She hit home and she hit hard.

Intrinsically democratic, Flo went out of her way to hear other points of view. As the only African-American in our group, she could have succumbed to being "professionally black." She never did. She never let anyone reduce her to another kind of stereotype, the glorious black sister who surmounts all obstacles, knows all things. Flo was and remains a complex human being who never, not even once, lost sight of the big issues.

She'd drive Betty crazy since Betty wanted blind obedience, no matter how many times she invoked the words "democratic process." But Betty couldn't do without her. Flo had legal knowledge and Flo made Betty look golden on the race issue.

My grandparents, Reuben and Carrie Brown, on their wedding day in 1901.

Jack Young, my natural mother's father, in 1940. A local power in the Republican Party, he was "the biggest bullshitter in York County," according to Juts.

The Buckingham girls in 1905—from left to right, Maizie, who died of diphtheria, Juts (my adoptive mother), and Mimi. Juts retained that wide-eyed, curious look all her life. Likewise for Mimi's pout.

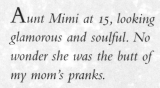

Aunt Mimi at 15, looking glamorous and soulful. No wonder she was the butt of my mom's pranks.

Juts at 14, in 1919. She liberated the parasol from her sister Mimi because she wanted to look like a lady of means. Mimi pitched a fit, Juts hit her over the head with the parasol and broke it. Mimi's head was fine.

James Gordon Venable at age 21, in 1935. My natural father was a professional weightlifter. I never met him.

Juts's younger brother, George "Bucky" Buckingham, was the best-looking man I have ever seen.

The two Butches! My dad, Ralph Brown, and Aunt Mimi's dog.

At 16, my natural mother looked mature beyond her years. Juts always said Juliann was a brilliant girl.

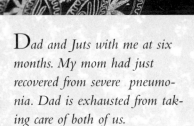

Dad and Juts with me at six months. My mom had just recovered from severe pneumonia. Dad is exhausted from taking care of both of us.

The family at Big Mimi Buckingham's farm in 1945: Eugene Byers is kneeling, far left; PopPop Harmon is kneeling, far right; Big Mimi is in the second row, third from left; my mom is next to her; then comes my aunt Mimi, far right. I'm the baby held up in the back.

*M*e in 1948—age 3 1/2 or 4. *I've just graduated from baby Sunday school.*

*M*om with Tuffy, late 1940s or early 1950s. She's wearing one of her famous poodle dresses.

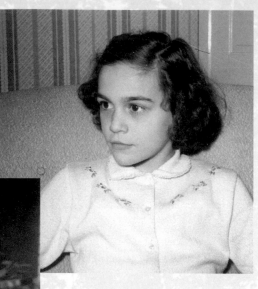

*M*e at nine. I had no choice but to be good since Mom was so bad.

*A*t ten years and ten months (I counted) with Tuffy. I've never lived without a tiger cat. Life without cats is not worth living.

*A*t age ten with Ginger. Dad said I was too young to work with hounds. I learned to love collies.

My senior year photo at Fort Lauderdale High School.

Mom at the Foxfield Races in Charlottesville, 1980: She has just fleeced half the spectators at the steeplechase meet and is celebrating.

In the mid-70s, I addressed a
political rally in New York City's
Central Park. My new shirt came
from singer Lana Cantrell, who
took pity on me for my wardrobe.

With Gloria Steinem around
1971, in New York: Her breadth of
vision and depth of commitment
to all women have always impressed me, but she is also a most
lovable woman.

At thirtysomething, Jerry Pfeiffer was a whirling dervish of activity with a mouth that never stopped.

April 1981, in the gardens at Flordon, near Charlottesville, Virginia, where Martina and I lived. I love to garden. Eleven days after this was taken, Martina skedaddled to the next great love of her life. Adios to Martina and adios to the gardens.

Clare Leach, me, and Margot Kidder at my 40th birthday party, which was a fund-raiser for the women's resource center FOCUS. Margot jumped out of a wrapped box—my birthday surprise.

Tuxedo, rescued from
starvation and disease,
January 1995.

Sneaky Pie signs her first book
contract in 1988. Gordon
Reistrup, then my assistant, has
a firm hand on Pie.

Summer 1994: Taddy snatches
my straw hat. I had sat down to
rest after a long, hot afternoon on
the tractor.

Pewter, Sneaky Pie's plump sidekick, takes a snooze after solving yet another mystery.

Corgi to the rescue! This is the real-life model for Tee Tucker. How can you not love a corgi?

Tuxedo living the good life with Rookie, his best friend and a one-cat demolition derby.

Muffin Spencer-Devlin, the pro golfer, and me after her first foxhunt, in October 1996. The fox survived and so did she.

January 1996 at the Rockfish River near Tea-Time Farm. It was a winter of whopping snowstorms.

Elizabeth (Betsy) Sinsel, me, and Tassle, who did not want to pose.

(Photo by Sue Gerhart)

Betsy Sinsel and Cindy Chandler. Cindy is a gardener extraordinaire and a wonderful friend.

At a December 1996 book signing: I love meeting my readers. They are interesting people, thoughtful and good-natured.

The opening hunt at Oak Ridge, October 1996. I'm surrounded by beloved hounds and brave people. It doesn't get any better than this.

Wendy Weil, my agent, and her husband, Michael Trossman, in 1997. We've gone from being agent and client to being dear friends. I can't imagine life without Wendy and Michael, whom I refer to as the King of Testosterone.

With Joan Hamilton and Betty Behave (the mare) at Kalarama Farm in Springfield, Kentucky. Joan and her partner, Larry Hodge, are two of the best friends I have in this life. Through my friends God has blessed me.

Me and Lynne Beegle (right) coming in after a hard chukker, summer 1996. Nobody is rich—it's sandlot polo. We have great fun.

The wind machine used for this photo drove me to distraction. Mother hated this picture. "False glamour!" she pronounced it. She was right, but a girl needs a little false glamour now and then.

(Copyright © Skrebneski)

In Betty's defense, she hadn't an ounce of racism in her, but Flo made NOW appear more ecumenical than it was. Apart from Flo and me, everyone was white, well educated and middle-class, and there's nothing wrong with that so long as you acknowledge it. NOW pretended to represent all women. Still, this was the beginning of things, and a bit of overstatement isn't the worst of sins.

By this time Ivy Bottini, a mother from Malvern, Long Island, had discovered NOW. She and Dolores Alexander represented a far less rigid type of feminism. Up until then, the show had been a three-way game of kickball between Betty, Ti-Grace and Flo.

Betty was enamored of the media, most especially herself being interviewed. While she created a compelling portrait of her generation for women of her generation, she mistakenly thought this illumination would arouse them from their torpor. When this did not immediately transpire she cast her glance toward the legislative process, a drain if ever there was one.

Ti-Grace Atkinson, on the other hand, possessed a much broader intellectual view of women's political involvement. She knew her history, she knew her political theory. While not averse to action, she wanted an intellectual understanding first. As time went on this program became grander and more airy. She was younger than Betty and a step closer to my generation.

Their clash was inevitable and both wanted the blessing of Flo Kennedy, who was far too smart to get sucked into a triangle. She remained her own woman, which is to say she was more practical than either Betty or Ti-Grace; furthermore her knowledge of the law made Flo especially strong. She believed we could use the law itself to force open doors. Not that she was opposed to an intellectual understanding of oppression, and not that she was opposed to contacting the media or to generating legislation, but in the beginning her focus was more on the law.

Ti-Grace, being southern, could respond to Flo better than Betty could. Betty was like most Yankee liberals; in the presence of a person of color they flutter with guilt or bogus admiration. Suddenly they understand your suffering. Not only do they want to share it, they want to vamp it. There must have been times when Flo felt like the movement poster child. Fortunately, she could see the humor in it. Neither Betty nor Ti-Grace is particularly strong in the sense-of-humor department.

As nearly everyone was a liberal Democrat, weaned on the New Deal, there was no leavening point of view. They believed government could redress wrongs. I thought government interference did more harm than good regardless of the issue. I mistrusted their agricultural policies as much as their foreign policies. But I kept my mouth shut. No one wanted to hear what I had to say.

Jerry, now working for DuPont, was in New York often. When I tried to discuss the issues of female equality with him, he demonstrated the point by cutting me off.

Jerry's line, close to Samuel Johnson's, was that women didn't need to be equal, they were superior. Patriarchy was revenge for that superiority. Men had to keep women in line.

"The cream rises to the top. You don't have to worry," he'd tell me.

Jerry betrayed no sense of community. His view was that if he took care of himself, he had fulfilled his obligation. Everyone else could damn well take care of themselves. I got mine, you get yours.

In the last few years Jerry had become a cognizant schizophrenic in that he was straight as a stick at work and gay as soon as he left it. He thought he could get away with it. Everyone thinks that when they're young. What he didn't realize is that you pay for that kind of compartmentalization. In the long run you are a house divided and, as proclaimed in the Gospel according to St. Mark over two thousand years ago, "a house divided against itself cannot stand."

He'd hear none of it. We fought constantly.

He continued to stay with me often, thrilled that my friend Ed Slough had moved to Chicago. The two men, birthdays one day apart, couldn't have been more different.

Ed enjoyed hearing about the political battles and the issues of women's rights found a resonance in him.

Jerry was becoming a corporate man. Ed stayed his own man.

And I was very much my own woman, which made me an equal-opportunity offender.

Betty, disenchanted with my speaking up at meetings, started to maneuver me out. Subtle at first, she dropped that pose when I raised the specter of lesbianism at Helen Leeds's apartment during one meeting in 1969.

No longer able to endure the constant bitching about men, I piped up, "I'm tired of hearing everyone moan about men. Say something good about women. I'll say something good. I love them. I'm a lesbian."

They just about tore their Pucci dresses jamming the door to get out. Betty approached apoplexy. It wasn't long before I was out on my ass, but I had the pleasure of sneaking an article into the NOW newsletter on why I was hitting the bricks.

I was no worse off than before. Exciting as these new ideas were, they didn't put a penny in my pocket. Poverty teaches you many things, not the least of which is that it stinks.

I took to calling NOW by a new name: NOW WHAT? I also warned Ivy Bottini and the other lesbians that they would be purged. Depend on it. They didn't believe me. Within six months they were erased from the books.

Betty furiously accused me of harming NOW. This pressure to shut up and pretend to be straight followed me wherever I tried to work on feminist issues. Betty, at least, was straightforward about it once she knew she had won the battle.

She won the battle but she lost the war. She didn't know it yet.

The bad thing about my NOW mess was that I was isolated. I could live with that, but it made political work difficult.

And I knew I was right. If straight women treated gay women the way men treated women, why should we work with them?

I was young. I enjoyed being right far too much.

If nothing else, the NOW debacle proved to those women party to it that I had a realistic grasp of politics and power whatever the arena. I earned a grudging respect when the other lesbians were purged. No longer did they dismiss my analysis of a situation out of hand. But since they were all in the closet at that time, they didn't help me either.

Baby Jesus loved me, and I had the police horses to visit. I wrote constantly and worked at whatever jobs I could find. I wasn't heartbroken but I was bloodied. I was hungry a lot, too.

I visited Aqueduct and wished I could find work with the horses. I rejoiced in hard physical labor.

I couldn't stay away from the fight. For anyone reading this who didn't participate in those political events, it must seem strange that we would sacrifice financial gain, career and comfort for an idea. Today we live in cynical times. The energy, the desire and the excitement drew me back. The closest comparison I can make is the raw electricity backstage before the curtain goes up.

The curtain was about to be raised for me.

45

Enter, Stage Left

I COULDN'T VOTE IN NEW YORK UNTIL 1968. I REGISTERED AS AN independent. Mother and Aunt Mimi both growled at me.

"You can't vote in primaries," Mother complained.

"Waste." Aunt Mimi kept it simple for a change.

The way the old Buckingham discipline was supposed to work was that I should have registered Democrat and Julia Ellen should have registered Republican, so Aunt Mimi and I would work together and Mom would work with her niece. In this way no one became overly enchanted with party ideology and one branch of the family wouldn't be opposed to the other.

As I've already mentioned, the entire point of this system was that the family in each generation should be able to work with whoever was in power, whether Whigs or Tories, Democrats or Republicans. Each age group would be involved so we could speak to our peers. The survival of the family motivated the process. The underpinning of the arrangement was a healthy mistrust of public political pronouncements.

So great was the competition between the sisters that Mother's attachment to the Republican Party became genuine just as did Aunt Mimi's to the Democratic Party. This allowed them new fields to fight over and the reliability of a fresh battle every four years.

Mother, outraged that I had denied her a crony in rounding up votes, wouldn't write to me for a few months. How dare I turn my back on the Republican Party? And Julia Ellen was registered as a Democrat. If Sis could keep her daughter in the fold, then so could Juts.

I'd tease her and say no true southerner could register Republican, and she'd say that she had always been a maverick. True enough.

However, she had difficulty accepting that I, too, was a maverick.

I had the disconcerting habit of thinking for myself, a quality that endeared me to no one. The emerging feminist movement asked for conformity just as did the Republican Party of the time. Their prevailing agenda was that all women were sisters, we all worked together, we were all straight and we could change the world for the better.

The economic competition between classes was swept under the rug, as was anything that jarred this smiling image of the true feminist.

Betty Friedan's version maintained an ascendancy thanks to the publicity she had received for her book six years earlier. The underbelly of the movement was the women who left the antiwar movement, most of them ten to twenty years younger than Betty. Due to youth, lack of contacts, lack of reserve funds, those women and their ideas did not surface until a few years later.

As it turned out, this was a good thing.

Thanks to Marx, Darwin and Frazer, the big three of nineteenth-century thinking, personality in history was pushed into the shadows of study. The Germans and Italians in the 1930s shuddered in a convulsion of great-man worship, giving the democratic school more reason to shy away from the study of personality's effect on history. The French fell prey to the great-man idea during the time of Napoleon, too. It seems to go in cycles.

The cheapest way this tension is expressed is: Do the times make the man or does the man make the times?

Substitute *woman*.

I don't know. But I do know that an individual's temperament and character affect people, programs, results.

Betty's personality was and remains domineering. Her brilliance deluded her into thinking she was always right.

Ivy Bottini's sweet temperament prevented her from believing that people who were nice to her face would stab her in the back.

Ti-Grace's heavy reliance on her intellectual gifts, as well as on her willowy southern figure, her extreme femininity, eventually rendered her ineffective. All of her charm and physical attractiveness, so potent with men, fell flat with women.

Flo Kennedy, the most realistic of the earliest leaders, survived as a political player until the vicissitudes of old age somewhat slowed her down. I say "somewhat" because she's in her eighties and has a cable TV show, *The Flo Kennedy Show*.

Those ladies represented the aboveground feminists in the late sixties and early seventies. The media liked them insofar as they were presentable, conservative in dress and speech. They conformed to their generation's notions of femininity. Femininity and masculinity are social constructs. Female and male are biological. We don't have to learn to be men or women but we do have to learn to be ladies and gentlemen.

The next generation, not yet known to the public, contained Robin Morgan, Shulamith Firestone, "Martha Shelley" (I never knew her real name), Barbara Kaminsky, Charlotte Bunch, Sally Miller Gearhart and myself.

I was the least of these. My New Left credentials were shaky. My civil rights credentials were better, but since these women had emerged from the New Left they cared little for a white southerner's troubles in the South with the exception of Sally Gearhart. They were white, middle- to upper-middle-class, articulate, angry, attractive, bursting with the energy of youth.

Once eighty-sixed from NOW, I attended Redstockings meetings, a New Left small group much given to ideological harangues, where I met some of these women as well as Susan Brownmiller, who went on to write *Against Our Will,* a book about rape as relevant today as the day she wrote it. Susan was not by temperament an activist. She was the classic observer.

The other women had marched and been galvanized by the Vietnam War. They hated Nixon, hated the government as it then stood, and believed the government was willfully lying to the people. They were right.

My involvement was less ideological. I hated the war because I didn't know why it was being fought and I didn't want Wade shot to shit in a rice paddy. Nor did I want Jerry drafted, although with his chemical expertise he appeared safe for the time. The government determined they needed him here.

Being a country girl, my passions hardly meshed with their passions. I understood them. I had to in order to survive.

Apart from the usual Marxist dogma—not that everyone was a Marxist—they read R. D. Laing, Noam Chomsky, Herman Hesse, Frantz Fanon. They smacked of the classroom and too many debates at hip bars.

To the best of my knowledge not one had worked with her hands. No one, save myself, had been raised on a farm. No one, except Sally Gearhart, then living in San Francisco, was from the South.

After digesting the required texts of the New Left, they finally got around to reading the works of the women responsible for the first wave of feminism. No one will accuse Susan B. Anthony or Elizabeth Cady Stanton of being literary wonders but they wrote clearly enough. Simone de Beauvoir was dragged into the mix. When French existentialism first appeared in Boston Harbor, it should have been dumped into the water just as we once dumped British tea. Although infected with this theatrical ennui, so inappropriate for an American, Beauvoir could write. *The Second Sex* is worth reading.

I dutifully read all the above but I branched out to study the lives of Victoria Claffin Woodhull and Tennessee Claffin, those wild sisters who upset every applecart. They felt more familiar and I'm attracted to people who *do* as opposed to *talk*.

While I had little in common with these young women, I liked most of them. I enjoyed listening to their debates for about half an hour, and then the unreality of it wore me down.

I believe an ounce of work is worth a pound of theory.

Back then it was mostly theory since no one wanted to risk anything until the ideology was absolutely in place. While a plan of action must be based on some undergirding of thought, isn't it better to base ideas on experience instead of vice versa? There were times when I felt like a medieval student listening to professors argue about how many angels can fit onto the head of a pin.

What motivated them was different from what motivated me. These women wanted to be right. They wanted to be morally unimpeachable. And underneath it all they wanted to be loved. They didn't see themselves as competing with the Jerry Rubins of this world for influence; they wanted to share.

I wanted power. I didn't care if I was loved. I would prefer to be morally unimpeachable, but human beings, myself included, rarely come unsullied. Life leaves its marks on you.

My urgings to build bridges to working-class women were politely listened to and immediately disregarded. I thought we'd create far more credibility by building day-care centers, establishing food distribution centers (trying to dispense with the middleman) and conducting voter registration drives than by presenting flawlessly argued position papers.

I was regarded as a redneck although a surprisingly intelligent one since I could follow their thoughts and read without moving my lips.

They even laughed when I accused them of having subpoena envy. You weren't anybody if you hadn't been subpoenaed to appear in court. The heroes for them were the Chicago Seven. My heroes were Harriet Tubman, Hannibal and Robert E. Lee, people who risked everything for beliefs much deeper than politics.

Anyone who disagreed with doctrine was called a fascist, a covert sexist or, my favorite, a running dog of capitalism. This latter phrase was a favorite of the Socialist Workers Party especially, although that group couldn't crack the feminist movement. Thank God the girls were too smart to let those leeches in.

Everyone said the Redstockings had no money. They had enough for dope and stereos. This isn't to say that every young woman was rolling her own, puffing away, but the acceptance of marijuana was part of the rebellion.

Marijuana was supposedly a liberating weed. I don't know since, as I've said before, I'm not atrracted to alcohol or drugs. They don't feel good in my system, so why bother? Most of my generation, male or female, was puffing at something.

No matter how you look at it, I didn't belong, although the Redstockings were polite even when I raised the issue of lesbianism as a legitimate oppression. They took it in stride. They had no intention of considering the reality of a gay woman's life but at least they didn't ask me to leave. My being drummed out of NOW gave me a certain cachet. But cachet doesn't yield results.

I was going to pull together gay women. This would be a neat trick since, as far as I knew, it had never been done before in the context of mass organizing in all of Western history. There were a few groups from the fifties, Daughters of Bilitis, cumbersomely named after the Pierre Louys poem, and the Mattachine Society for the men. Those groups might as well have come from the Paleolithic Age. They had served a useful purpose for those involved, especially giving one another emotional support, but they were not much use to us now.

No one had ever directly appealed to gay women. I knew better than to appeal to gay men. I saw how quickly the Student Homophile League at Columbia had cascaded into cruising.

I don't care who sleeps with whom or how many whoms, but a political purpose is just that. The boys were lightweights. At that time they didn't truly understand their own oppression. They just didn't want to get busted in tearooms. This changed, thank God, but it took years.

In terms of political understanding, the gay women were and remain ahead of the men. The men have been better able to organize via the Democratic Party because they have so much more discretionary income. If you doubt that women are not being paid equal wages for equal work, don't listen to me, get the figures from the Department of Labor. Better yet, ask your friends.

I started walking from bar to bar. Since I prefer rising early in the morning, this was hard on me; the bars don't begin to hop until ten, sometimes eleven. I left leaflets everywhere. I asked Redstockings to refer people to me should they know of anyone. I put up signs in the student union at NYU. Forget Columbia. It lay in tatters.

Thirty women came to the first meeting, held at my house. I had to find another place. The Lutheran church on Christopher Street just off Seventh Avenue let me use a room once, as did NYU. Judson Memorial helped and Washington Square Church also allowed me a room once. I was running out of spaces.

One man told me that if I stopped canvassing the bars (I was urging people not to drink) he thought he could help me out. There was an old-fashioned firehouse for sale south of Houston Street.

I knew I'd been hurting business in the bars just a tad. The bars then were owned by that well-known society of Italian men who swear their organization doesn't exist. These men also would find you a prostitute, purvey drugs, loan you money at high rates and sell you the Brooklyn Bridge, should you admire it.

He thought he could cut me a deal with that firehouse if I'd stop hitting the bars and especially if I would stop warning that alcohol and drug addiction rates were higher among gay people than among straight people.

As much as I understand suffering, I don't understand numbing your nerve endings. You can't fight when you're dulled.

I declined this possibility without rancor. I could have used his protection but the association would do more harm than good.

A week later I left the Sea Colony, where I had handed out mimeographed sheets concerning the next meeting, which would be in a church in Chelsea. I heard a crack. A bullet hit a brick in front of me to my left. The brick dust flew out like paprika. That was it. No other shots.

I ran around the corner, flattened against a building in the dark and waited. No footsteps. No slow creep of a car. I was safe. I'd been warned.

Shortly thereafter the firehouse was taken over by the Gay Liberation Front, a men's group which had a few women members. Those women soon came over to us, not because the firehouse wasn't a wonderful place, it was, but because men cared nothing for their issues, telling them so loudly and often.

Lois Hart led the women over. Dead now, she was in her middle thirties then, a woman with light, bright eyes. Her approach to life was through the prism of psychology. We couldn't have been more polarized.

Since Betty Friedan had dubbed us "the lavender menace," we took the name. Lois was a painter by profession and contributed a great deal to the group even though I sometimes could have crowned her. The consciousness-raising sessions alone were sheer torture. We'd sit around in a circle and everyone had to pull from the depths of their liver what they felt on a given topic. The topic could be your mother or Richard Nixon.

I thought I would die.

I used to write Mother about these groups and Mom would write back, "Join the Republican Party. Then you'll get something done."

I'd write back, "Mom, the Republican Party isn't going to take in a lesbian."

She'd airily reply, "You'll win them over. You're too smart to keep down, Big Brains."

She'd dropped calling me "the Ill" and had come up with "Big Brains," although her favorite still was "Buzzer."

I often wonder what would have happened if I'd followed my mother's advice, because if I have nothing else to offer, I do have energy and a strong back.

But it was becoming harder and harder to find any good or honor in the current Nixon administration. The lies were so palpable you could taste them. Meanwhile more and more Americans were shipping out to Vietnam.

Although oil and water, Lois and I worked together fitfully. The best job we did together was attending the Second Congress to Unite Women, in May 1970, to which we were pointedly not invited.

We printed "Lavender Menace" on lavender T-shirts. Walking quietly down the aisles, about twenty of us took over the congress and patiently, without theatrics, informed the hordes of straight women why it was in their best interest to accommodate all women, even us.

Our position paper, "The Women-Identified Women," hit this congress like a bombshell. Seven of us worked on it.

The message of this paper was that women needed to identify with women, not with men. Sounds simple enough, but from the time we are born, man is the measure of all things. Women pull away from other women, giving men and male institutions their best energy. The result is that our issues die on the table. As Alice says in *Alice in Wonderland,* "The rule is, jam tomorrow, and jam yesterday—but never jam today."

This congress was being covered by Marlene Sanders for ABC. The congress included a symbolic session with women cutting off their hair onstage. I thought that was silly but it had a powerful resonance for many of the women there.

Mother screamed with laughter when I told her. She understood why long, flowing hair was a symbol, but Mother was never one for symbols. You want to win, you do two things: find a raw nerve and put a match to it, then get out the votes. The old girl knew her stuff.

A lot of the film footage disappeared from the congress. I was always credited or blamed for this act. I'll never tell.

What I will tell is this. Marlene Sanders was and is one of the best reporters in the business. Her rise to the top was anything but easy and as she aged she was yanked from in front of the cameras. No one yanked Walter Cronkite. Realizing that too much of the reporting on feminism was being done by men, she actually understood the issues.

However sympathetic Marlene may have been, the selection of images would have been made by her boss. Then, as now, ratings count, not truth. I had no doubt that television news producers would have selected either the most frivolous or the most inflammatory images available.

Remember the march on the Miss America Pageant in Atlantic City in 1968? The media portrayed those women as bra burners. The hype stuck. I've got news for you. Not one woman took off her bra and not one bra was burned at that march.

This complete misunderstanding of our intentions by the media nearly derailed the entire women's movement. The organizers of the Second Congress, who chose not to invite lesbians (unless they were in the closet), were dumb enough to invite the media.

The reason we showed up in lavender T-shirts was to let them register, visually, who we were and what they had to lose by not inviting us, because we were presentable, dedicated and ready to work hard for women's issues.

How can you freely exchange ideas, argue differences, when a camera is filming away?

The film never made it to the studio. If nothing else, this theft gave more women time to realize the media had to be handled carefully by people who knew what they were doing.

As to how Marlene Sanders felt, she must have been devastated.

That congress shot me up and out as though from a cannon. Women knew who I was. My deeds flashed across the country to other women. Whether they scorned or admired me, people began to realize I had a few things to offer. Those who loathed my ideas began working overtime to trivialize me.

They chose the obvious—sex. My detractors painted me as a female Don Juan. This had the reverse effect. Rather than making me seem hateful, it made me all the more alluring.

If only I had slept with half the women I was accused of sleeping with—but then I'd never have gotten anything done.

Since the common view of lesbianism is purely sexual, using sex to tar and feather a leader makes perfect sense.

And of course, my own ego got in the way. Who wouldn't want to be thought of as a charming, seductive, irresistible force, with women falling at my feet—or perhaps somewhere a little higher? I did nothing to combat the rumors. I was as dumb as the women who invited the media to the Second Congress to Unite Women.

At least they could put that behind them. I still have this myth to face.

For the record, I am very resistible.

In fact, I was a lesbian in name only, too busy to practice what I preached.

What did I preach, though? Sex? No. I don't believe that sex is a topic for political discussion. Harming people because of their sexual preference is.

Do you think a person wakes up in the morning and says, "I'll be gay today? I will call down upon my head the hatred of the New Right, the horror of my family and the dissolution of old friendships. Why, I can hardly wait"?

Get a grip.

Jerry hated what I was doing. A conservative who still thought he could hide his gayness, he told me to leave well enough alone. If I married him, we could pass. This sudden reversion to marriage was due to his feeling pressure at work. He figured the women's movement was so tangential that even if a coworker realized who I was, Jerry could laugh it off. He'd have to buy me some nice clothes, though. His wife couldn't look like a remnant from the military. I hadn't a penny, and I bought used clothes from the army-navy store before it was chic. That too provided fodder for the mill. Surely this must be some lesbian fashion statement.

Good God.

I'd walk home after these meetings glad to curl up next to Baby Jesus. I slept on the floor on two blankets. If the night was bitter I rolled up in them, with a third thrown over me, and sometimes my pea jacket over that.

Baby Jesus, not some big-boobed babe, was the love of my life. She didn't care that I was poor. She didn't care that I was under siege much of the time. After all, if I'd kept my mouth shut, all would have been well. This was my own doing. Politics is a rough arena. She purred at the sight of me. Some mornings I'd wake up and four or five mice would be geometrically lined up for my applause.

That cat made me laugh. The bloodletting was hard.

I was learning bruising lessons before I was twenty-five. But the cat was what got me through it all. She knew it would pass and that human endeavor generally turns to dust.

The horses in the police stables meant more to me than most of the people around me. Those soft brown eyes made everything okay.

I never spoke of my faith. For some reason the two are one in my mind. Whenever I doubt the existence of God or the Goddess, I look at horses. Only God could have made a horse.

I am not a conventionally religious person. I'd like to be a member of the Society of Friends, but I don't measure up to their high standards. Some of the Browns' ancestors were Quakers. And, of course, so was Dolley Madison, a person whose life I often study.

But I'm equally happy to worship at St. Rose of Lima Catholic Church or Christ Lutheran or St. Paul Episcopal. The denomination is less important to me than the act of giving thanks with other people.

What better place to give thanks than a stable? It was good enough for Jesus, who made his first appearance in one!

46

Footlight Parade

ANSELMA DELL'OLIO, JACQUELINE CEBALLOS, SUSAN VANNUCCI and I started the New Feminist Repertory. It was better than the endless, mind-numbing ideological debates of the women's movement.

Jacqui, in her forties then, was the business brain. She found the Martinique Theater in the old Martinique Hotel at Herald Square. A dumping place for the elderly and mentally infirm, clinging to their government checks, it was an unlikely place for a theater.

Anselma, wildly beautiful, told the rest of us what to do. She also starred in most of the skits. Susan, married to an understanding man, worked like a dog. So did I.

Since the others were afraid of heights, I changed the light gels, made friends with the stage manager, blocked actors, worked at the odd, unglamorous jobs. I loved it.

I'd been fired from my job at a small publishing company, where I wrote press releases, photo captions, you name it, because the publisher read an article of mine in *Rat*. He blew up. I'd been proofreading a tome for what seemed like the thousandth time when the pink slip came.

As it so happened, the company's most important writers were expected that day for a meeting on the revised edition of the book I'd been proofing, their baby and gold mine. The publisher, a cheery-looking fellow with rosy cheeks and a circlet of gray hair around his pink pate, told me to pack up and get out. His looks belied an autocratic temper.

Having little to pack up, I was out of there in a flash, saying goodbye to the friends I had made in the small company. I did, however, go to a joke store around the corner and buy a big plastic ass. When the boss strolled out for lunch, I slipped back up, put the ass on the back of his door and left.

I knew he'd close the door when the writers arrived, and I hoped they'd have a giggle. I also hoped the publisher would suffer an instant coronary.

He didn't, but the results proved amusing, according to my buddies at work. He raged through the place, finally deciding the Puerto Rican fellows in shipping had done it. Whenever he couldn't find a culprit he blamed it on the Puerto Ricans.

Now I worked at the theater full-time. I hoped we'd make enough in ticket sales to pay my rent. Baby Jesus worked with me. The place, infested with mice and worse, was kitty paradise.

At that time agitprop theater was the off-Broadway rage. We produced not three-act plays but skits. We did produce one short play that was provocative. We opened at the Village Gate on May 19, 1969, and made the front page of the *New York Times* Arts & Leisure section the day before. Being involved in two projects that got serious attention from the *Times* bolstered my confidence among the heathen Yankees. I might not talk as they did, but I made things happen.

Modest though the receipts were, they allowed us to move to the Top of the Gate. Anselma, beauty to the max, charmed Art D'Lugoff, the owner. He let us follow *Jacques Brel Is Alive and Well and Living in Paris*. No longer dodging the sad assortment of characters at the Martinique, we reached a bigger audience.

Since I sat in the pit, ready to prompt, during performances, I was everyone's understudy. Having no desire to act, I never imagined I'd be put to the test.

I was. I walked out in a weekly agitprop piece and said my lines. The audience howled. Each time I filled in for someone, I got laughs.

Anselma, displeased, found other understudies.

For whatever reason, I have a comic presence. Mom had it, too. It helps to explain why I'd land in hot water at those interminable meetings and odious consciousness-raising sessions. I was not properly miserable and I did not see the world as a terrible place.

We ran short a piece one week and I dashed off a five-minute bit. Huge laughs. I dashed off more and soon I was responsible for all filler.

I wrote one-liners, topical jokes and small character pieces. I was flat broke.

If I took a waitressing job I'd have no time to work with the theater. One summer I worked for the state in an after-care clinic for patients released from state mental institutions. The work was beyond depressing. Contrary to popular myth, crazy people aren't funny. My best buddy there, a delightful young woman, Candy James, helped dispel the gloom. I don't know how she stood it. After that summer I couldn't go back.

I worked at Hearst one summer, too, but I'm not a corporate type no matter how attractive the paycheck. I was stuck.

I called Aqueduct to inquire about breezing horses, grooming—anything. I was hired at my interview but declined the job once I realized I'd have to leave the theater, hop the subway and get to work by dawn. I needed some sleep.

At that time the city embarked on a massive housing rehab campaign. Old brownstones were being gutted and rebuilt with public monies. Landlords would receive incentives to rebuild inexpensive housing.

I bought a red wagon and began going into the buildings before they were totally gutted. The stuff the contractors threw out was a sin. I found old wall telephones, mercury-center doorknobs, brass hinges, brass locks, beautiful old stuff. I even found a pair of well-preserved spats in a torn-out chimney once. I guess they'd been used to fill up the flue when the building switched to oil heat.

I'd take my wagon of goodies down Hudson Street and sell to the antique dealers. I kept up my practice of haunting the ritzy neighborhoods on garbage day, finding chests of drawers, chairs and mirrors, which I resold.

I made enough to cover my rent, which was $112 a month for a cold-water flat, bathtub in the kitchen. Usually I made enough for one hot meal a day and cat food. The cat food always came first.

Scavenging gave me an appreciation for solid construction. Some of the old buildings, those Federal ones built between 1800 and 1830, used construction techniques similar to Amish barn building. A few even had large round wooden pegs driven into the joists instead of nails. Often the masonry work was exquisite.

The Victorian buildings had more modern materials. In those days the carpentry, especially the fine work, was done by Czech immigrants, the stonework by Italians.

Scavenging posed a few dangers. Once I emerged from a building down in the meatpacking district, my wagon filled with crystal doorknobs. A roar, followed by a wave of dust, scared me good. The whole floor had collapsed.

If I'd been trapped in there, no one would have found me until the next morning, if then. I checked floor beams after that.

I saved and bought a membership to the Metropolitan Museum of Art.

I am still a member. The scavenging work had piqued my interest in decor. I soaked up everything I could about Chippendale techniques versus Sheraton, and so on. Today the Met's furniture wing is spectacular and worth a trip across the country. The museum is worth a trip regardless of your interests.

Few museums were dedicated to the living arts. It was catch as catch can.

The theater was exhausting. How could I or anyone make a living in theater? I couldn't sing, dance or act. Worse, why be in front of the footlights? I much preferred being behind them.

My pieces drew good responses, and I thought I could write for the theater, but research told me I'd starve. I'd starved enough. And experience was teaching me that I was so totally different from the feminists as well as the gay men that I'd be knocking my head against the wall.

One experience from those days stands out especially. I was walking in the Village with Martha Shelley on an evening in late June 1969. She was squiring two ladies from out of town. Even though it was nighttime, the heat was still rising off the pavement in waves.

I often took Christopher Street because it was a shortcut; like Greenwich Avenue, it ran on an angle. There were bars on Christopher, but mostly for gay men. Sometime during this stroll Martha and her guests parted company but Martha and I continued to walk. The statue of hateful General Sheridan (he ravaged the Shenandoah Valley) loomed ahead near the intersection of Seventh Avenue.

A Black Maria could be heard tinkling. I don't remember seeing it but I saw other police cars. The next thing I knew, hordes of men exploded out of Stonewall, a bar. Within seconds, like a flash flood, men poured toward the spot from all around Sheridan Square. Buildings disgorged their occupants.

Parked cars were overturned like toothpicks.

There stood Martha Shelley and I in a sea of rioting gay men. Exhilarating as their wrath was, I wondered what they'd make of *us*. In such violent circumstances lengthy explanations don't work.

"I'm your friend" seemed wishy-washy.

Also, I heard sirens. "Martha, we'd better get the hell out of here."

She concurred. We backtracked as fast as we could, winding up at the Women's House of Detention—no longer standing today—on the corner of Greenwich and Sixth Avenues. But the mass of furious people spilled over there, too. The women in the House of Detention began rioting. We heard one voice in particular screaming, "I want to be free. I want to be free."

Then a burning mattress was shoved up against a barred window, high up. Any minute now police were going to be diverted to this spot.

Martha and I split up. She ran east. I ran north, then west. I made it to the Greenwich Village–Chelsea border, Fourteenth Street, before the cops cordoned off the Village.

Thrilled as I was that gay men had finally fought back against the medieval practice of vice raids—rounding up and jailing men who did nothing more than gather for a drink and cruise one another—I knew that riot wasn't my riot.

Once any underclass expresses itself with violence, a few things are sure to follow. First come the police. Next come the lawsuits. Third comes increased vigilance on the part of the police, and finally come the drug dealers.

I saw that when Watts and Fourteenth Street in D.C. exploded. If you lived through that time, didn't you wonder why it became quiet so quickly? And didn't you wonder why an eight-year-old kid could find heroin with no problem but the authorities never could?

Drugs make some people feel better. The whole war against drugs is without moral authority, coming from a government only too happy, at one time, to do business with General Noriega.

Accusations are now made openly that our government supplied the drugs to Watts and Fourteenth Street!

I am not a person given to conspiracy theories but I do think this sordid chapter in our nation's recent history worthy of intense scrutiny. Since so many careers could be dashed by such scrutiny, I wonder if this will happen before the guilty parties die of natural causes.

The sudden calm after those riots beggars description.

Strange to say, a sudden calm did not descend over gay men after Stonewall. There are some obvious reasons why gay men did not lapse back into quiescence. They were white and well educated. For men like them, being arrested in 1969 because of gathering in a bar was so patently absurd, many of them wouldn't shy from pressing the city government, even if it meant "exposure." The whole point of a vice raid was to cow them into submission by threatening said exposure.

Well, a lot of them had developed a set of brass balls. City Hall's strategy wasn't working. You could almost hear the bureaucrats. "Jesus, the faggots are fighting back."

Over the decades so many gay men had been shaken down by cops or by lawyers who specialized in getting them off the hook that an abundant body of evidence was available for anyone who wanted to find it. These men knew that paying through the nose to keep your name hidden was part of the bargain.

Blackmail infuriated them as much as the raid did.

But also, it was time. Simple as that. You can only push people around so long, despise them so long, step on them so long, before they snap.

The way in which I was held back differed in one dramatic manner. I earned fifty-nine cents to their dollar. Had I been arrested I would have sat in jail. Lawyers knew women had little money. Why bother with me? I couldn't pay for a lawyer's Mercedes.

It's doubtful that the police are going to raid a women's bar or any gathering of women.

People assume, but men in particular assume, that women won't be violent as a group. The terrible thing about the way in which their minds work is that they probably won't take women's issues seriously until we snap just the way the men did during Stonewall . . . or the way the women did during the bread riots of the French Revolution.

Once you establish your destructive potential, men listen. Of course, it depends on how you do it. The Stonewall riots were not directed against another large group of people. They were directed against the police during a vice raid.

Huey Newton signed the death warrant of the Black Panther Party when he sat in that plantation wicker chair, weapons in hand. That photo made many young black men proud. It also gave those policemen who were racists and those nonpolicemen who were racists the exact image they needed to rouse white people. It preyed on their fears.

A gay riot directed at the police did not alarm the average straight person. It seemed to have nothing to do with them and it didn't, except that they tacitly went along with the vice raids. But they were safe.

I could hear the sounds from the Village that night.

Time for a change, inside and out.

47

O Canada

OUR FAMILY TOOK TWO VACATIONS DURING MY CHILDHOOD. The first one, when I was six, was to Wildwood, New Jersey. It is fixed in my memory because I met a blind man, Ralph, and his seeing-eye dog, a German Shepherd named Pal that I loved. The Florida trip constituted the second flight from daily responsibility.

My third vacation, hard on the heels of nonstop political drama, came at the invitation of Cynthia Funk. Tall, stately and very intelligent, as one would expect of a Funk (Funk and Wagnalls Dictionary), she possessed something equally valuable, a serviceable car. She invited me to go with her on a camping trip to Nova Scotia.

Jerry, shuttling between Wilmington and New York for DuPont, asked to work for two weeks straight in New York so he could care for Baby Jesus, by now tremendously spoiled.

If you've never driven up the coast of New England in early fall, it's the apotheosis of that season—towns with white church steeples peeping through the treetops, perfect squares surrounded by clapboard houses and small businesses.

New Englanders, chilly by southern standards, believe in order, productivity and sticking with your own kind. You see more redheads in this region than anywhere else in the country, or so it seemed to me.

The coast of Maine veers eastward into the Atlantic Ocean. Having seen only sandy beaches, flat as a pancake, I found that the rocky beaches had a raw quality that appealed to me. The scent of sea mist clung to my skin.

We boarded the ferry to Yarmouth and were blessed with a smooth, though coldish, crossing. What a way to first see Nova Scotia, in full autumn foliage. Reds, oranges, flaming reds, dark russets and shocking yellows covered the hills. Green pastures rolled down to the ocean, and farmers gathered the last hay crops.

I felt at home. Nova Scotia is Canada's South. Poor, looked down upon by the other large and mighty provinces, its people have a quiet strength, a quick good humor that comes with hardship. At least that's how it was in 1969.

We'd pitch our tent and shiver. The mercury dipped into the forties at night, but during the day it climbed back to the sixties. We rumbled down dirt roads, visited tiny roadside churches with only ancient, huge wood-burning stoves in the middle of the church for heat.

Saving our pennies, we'd eat sparingly or nothing at all during the day so we could order lobster for supper. The best lobster I've ever eaten was in Nova Scotia.

My love affair with Canada and its inhabitants started on this trip, and it's a love that intensifies with each passing year. By now I've visited every province that borders the United States. I haven't gone into the far northern territories. Canada's West is as wild as our own and British Columbia is God's gift to the world, deep blue waters rolling up to a shore with snow-capped mountains in view. Zeus has probably vacated Mount Olympus for British Columbia.

Time pressure kept us from going to the northern tip of Nova Scotia, but we covered the southern end.

I made a point to get out and talk to men plowing with Percherons. Grandpa Brown used Percherons, and they're my favorite draft animal. The horses I saw were working horses. I didn't see any show horses or even hunters. I'm sure they're there.

Many of the people knew their family histories and happily shared them. And the English they spoke—clear, concise and perfectly enunciated—was heaven to a young writer's ears.

If I ever get disgustingly rich, you'll know it because I'll buy a cottage in Nova Scotia, to which I'll repair during our seething August summers in Virginia.

Today Cynthia Funk lives in Virginia Beach, has a daughter and has made a good life for herself. I wonder if she ever recalls that Nova Scotia sojourn. I'll always be grateful to her for introducing me to Canada. I'll always be grateful to Canadians for being their original, refreshing, perfectly mannered selves.

Anyone who thinks Canadians are like Americans probably thinks Germans are like Austrians. They're another breed of cat.

Nova Scotia sharpened my hunger for the countryside, my nagging sense of loss.

When I returned, Jerry happily greeted me. Baby Jesus, a monster in residence, had driven him crazy. She shredded his papers and sang off key, and for her finale she saved the bookshelf trick. I used orange crates for bookshelves, stacking them one on the other. She'd wiggle behind the books, kicking them out with her hind legs. Her favorite time for this stunt was in the middle of the night, when she would send a thunderous cascade of books down onto the floor.

The circles under Jerry's eyes testified to his lack of sleep.

"You'd better never leave this cat again," he warned me.

I did so only one other time. Her revenge was vicious then too—she deposited feces in the bowl of the Smith-Corona typewriter. The moisture rusted the long metal strikers of the keys.

The bad thing was I had to buy a new typewriter. The good thing was, I bought an electric typewriter. *Mirabile dictu.*

Blonde Bombshell

GLORIA STEINEM, BLONDE, GORGEOUS, SMART, CHANGED THE
feminist movement. She was a Johnny-come-lately to those of us who'd
been scarred by the NOW wars, the struggles with gay men just to see our
issues recognized and, of course, the unremitting hostility from the press.

She used the media better than anyone thought possible. She knew
what she could present and what she couldn't. She knew that how you
look is more important than what you say, sad but true. She was so beautiful, men couldn't dismiss her.

As in any small pond with a few big frogs, she stirred resentment. Not
from me. I'd never been so glad to see someone in my life.

I trusted her. Why, I don't know. Southern manners enable me to get
along with just about anyone if I have to, but I trust few people. Those I
do trust, I trust with all my heart.

My instincts told me to get out of her way and to help in whatever
manner I could. She needed little from me. I represented a fringe group at
that time. However, she didn't dismiss me or the women from the New
Left. She heard everyone's point of view.

She came at just the right time. She soothed other women by her
noncompetitiveness and ripe sense of humor. She attracted acolytes. That
mystified me. I have never attracted an acolyte in my entire life, then or
now. Somehow my lone-wolf quality shines through and people know I'm
not going to meet their emotional needs. I don't know if Gloria meets
people's needs, but they sure get something out of their contact with her.
For one thing, she makes them think. Gloria pushes people on. It's one of
her best qualities.

I asked her what she thought of gay women.

"Women are women." That was that.

I watched with glee as she twisted interviewers around her little finger. Wherever she moved, cameras followed. Apart from Jacqueline Onassis, she must have been the most photographed woman in America.

As she took over New York, I left. The timing felt right. The women's center on Twenty-second Street flourished in large part due to its board of directors and to June Arnold, a Texas girl with lots of money and keen business sense. Women in Media, a group to spawn writers, newscasters and journalists, was up and running. The first rape crisis center was on stable ground, with absolutely no help from the police; back then, if you were raped, the police assumed it was your fault. Underground newspapers grew fat off advertising. Universities had women's groups. I helped organize Vassar's feminist studies group, led by Christine Acebo, Lita Lepie and Carla Duke, a gathering of the brightest young women.

Their enthusiasm was infectious and fun.

Many people worked hard during those early days of the feminist movement.

Mom would say, "You're less important than you think and more important than you know."

I don't know how important our work was, but I did my part and I was fixing to do more.

I'd spent my teenage years and early twenties criticizing the government.

What did I really know?

After all the bitching and moaning, I figured I had to see for myself.

I moved to Washington, D.C., that northernmost southern city.

Martha Shelley helped me move, a great kindness. Baby Jesus bitched and moaned the entire way.

When Martha got on the train to go back to New York she said, "I feel like I'm leaving you in the belly of the whale."

If Jonah could survive, so could I.

49

Lazy as Sin

Building a city on lowland invites steam heat in the summer, raw, foggy winters and bloodsuckers by the squadron, both mosquitoes and humans. Philadelphia was our nation's first capital. Since Spain controlled Florida, the City of Brotherly Love truly was smack in the center of the East Coast of the infant United States. It was the financial center, shipping center and cultural center. Putting our government there made supreme good sense.

However, our first president, not overly fond of Philadelphia, desired a capital free from the taint of the Revolutionary War. Philadelphia, which had helped finance the war, paradoxically was a hotbed of Tories, people loyal to George III.

I suspect the real reason was that the site of the new city was but a day's comfortable ride from Mount Vernon. Washington deserved whatever he wanted. Without him we'd never have won the war or the peace.

The Washington, D.C., that I came to was far different than the warm, open city of Harry Truman, that most accessible and human of twentieth-century chief executives. Washington displayed the stigma of a siege mentality. Cops rolled around in cars, a lot of them. A guilty conscience gripped this pretty town with a clammy hand. The Nixon administration knew to its bones that the war in Vietnam was foolish, wrong and totally immoral. They threw lives away to save face.

It wasn't a secret that Nixon didn't want to be the first American president to lose a war. LBJ hadn't either. Of course, it wasn't a legal war since Congress had never declared the damn thing. Sordid, twisted and violating the fundamental tenet of our government, which is that the people, not the president, declare a war, the miserable conflict dragged on.

My cousin Wade, a diesel mechanic, had still escaped frontline duty.

Despite Washington's symmetrical, beautiful plantings, the reds and golds of late summer flowers, I couldn't square up the city I was learning with the city I visited in my childhood.

I found a house, 217 Twelfth Street, SE. I was the only white person for five blocks. I lived next to the Inspirational Church of God. Choir practice enlivened my nights. Without a TV, which I hadn't seen regularly since 1962, I'd sit on my stoop, listen to the choir and chat with my neighbors.

Capitol Hill, a poor district, was ignored by the city. Washington, not a state, goes on its knees for a budget from Congress. Since congressmen go home to Nebraska or Arizona, they don't give a fig for most of the city. Georgetown got what it wanted, but then plenty of congressmen and Cabinet officials lived in Georgetown.

My neighbors, wise in the ways of the city, took care of themselves. Our neighborhood was clean; flowerpots sprinkled with color added to the flavor. We kept a sharp eye for plainclothes policemen who trolled through the neighborhood. Every time the Black Panthers made an announcement anywhere in the country, the cop patrol picked up. It was actually funny since the police were white. Did they think we wouldn't notice?

A tiny yard enclosed with a fence gave Baby Jesus fits of happiness. She played in the grass, jumped up for butterflies and brought me many grasshoppers. I started a small garden, a joy. I put in spring bulbs while Baby bent her gray-striped head over each hole. She'd rummage around with her paw to make certain it was suitable, then I'd drop in the bulb and cover it over.

I walked constantly, just as I had in New York. I'd stop in the Treasury Building, the Health, Education and Welfare Building, the House and Senate offices scattered on either side of the Capitol. I enjoyed the Capitol itself, a relatively simple structure rebuilt after the British burnt it in 1814.

What overwhelmed me, however, was the sheer, disgusting laziness of most federal employees. I'd walk into a building and a gaggle of people, old and young, women and men, would be behind the information desks, talking to one another. You'd ask for assistance. Maybe they'd come forward. Maybe they'd make you wait.

It didn't matter what federal building I entered, with the exception of the Supreme Court; those people were on the ball. But everywhere else, you'd walk in and the people working there didn't give a damn, although some of the aides in the various senators' and congressmen's offices "hopped to."

The waste infuriated me. You and I were, and are, paying salaries for people who could not care less. And once hired, they were impossible to fire. Mistake number one. Even the main post office, over by Union Station, was in slow motion.

I couldn't believe it. Nor could I believe the disrepair and filth in Union Station. Once a majestic building, it offered most people's first look at Washington, and it was a haven for druggies, drunks and ladies of questionable repute. The ceiling was grimy, stained from leaks. The windows probably hadn't been cleaned since Truman left office.

Union Station, now rehabilitated, is a wonderful place to visit. That's to the good. As for low-level bureaucrats, I can't say much has changed. When you encounter someone helpful, who likes her job, you're gratified.

I wondered how anything got done in Washington. In New York people hustled. They hustled back home in York; it might be a tiny town, but people worked hard for a living. I couldn't understand the why and how of the laziness, the attitude. I wondered if it was the demoralizing times. Since things haven't changed that much today, it really has to be the system. People are not held to rigorous standards.

Shocked as I was at the slovenliness, I was equally amazed at how easy it was to meet people. I didn't know a soul when I moved to Washington. I'd saved up enough to live for three months, so I was casting about for a job.

I tried the Arena Theater, but they didn't need anyone and my repertory theater work didn't qualify as solid experience.

While I pounded the pavement I met Senator Edward Kennedy. I stuck my head in his offices and an aide allowed me to speak to him. He was courteous, spoke forcefully about ending the war, and when I asked him about job security for gay people he didn't bat an eye. I know I had to be the first person to ask him that. This was shortly after Chappaquiddick, and people were saying Kennedy was finished in politics, but I found him smooth and well prepped.

I met Walter B. Jones, Jr., a congressman from North Carolina who sat on an agricultural committee that interested me. He, too, was courteous.

I met Patsy Mink and Martha Wright Griffiths, both in Congress. There were precious few women in the House then.

Nothing prepared me for Senator Hubert Humphrey.

Remember, I had the sparsest wardrobe. My jeans were clean and pressed. I had a few shirts, a pair of sneakers and my marine tunic and pea jacket for colder weather. That was it. Between sending money to Mom and paying rent, the last thing I could afford was clothing.

So I presented myself at Senator Humphrey's office in my sparkling T-shirt, Levi's and white sneakers. He had the flu and had just walked into the front office. His aide glanced up at me as I walked through the door.

Dabbing his nose, he reached out his right hand. "Hello."

"Senator Humphrey." I shook his hand. "I hope you feel better."

His voice was raspy. "Flu. What can I do for you?"

"I write for underground newspapers." The truth. "I'd love to see how the government works from the inside. All I've done is criticize it from the outside."

Without hesitation he said, "Stick with me."

I tagged after the good senator for the entire day. Even with the flu he was a whirlwind. He knew everybody by first name. Not just other senators, but doormen, guards, other officials' aides. Furthermore, he liked them. You can't fake that. The man loved people.

The flu chased away his appetite. Around two in the afternoon, I must have looked peaked. We were on the grounds behind the Capitol.

"You must be hungry."

"I'm okay."

"Go on, grab a sandwich and meet me back at the office."

"I'm afraid I'll miss something."

He studied me, then handed me five dollars. "Go on."

"I can't take your money, Senator."

"Sure you can. Who's paying my salary?"

I ran over behind the post office since I couldn't eat in the congressional cafeteria without Senator Humphrey. I grabbed a Coke, a hot dog with mustard, a fave forever, and ate it. Then I ate another hot dog since I wasn't sure when I'd get the chance.

Senator Humphrey didn't want his change back. He knew a poor kid when he saw one. But how kind of him not to make the five dollars seem like a handout.

He worked until sundown, when the flu worsened. Sweat poured from his head. His face was red.

When he left he shook my hand and said, "Think twice before you take potshots."

And I do.

Hubert Humphrey would have made a dynamic, strong president. The state of Minnesota was fortunate in their senator, as were the rest of the states. His vision was bigger than the pork barrel.

While Senator Humphrey was the exceptional senator, he was not the exception that proved the rule.

Over and over, I discovered that American public officials are accessible. This is a democracy. You can see your congressman and senator without a great deal of trouble. You can see other senators and congressmen, too.

If I were admitted to a senator's office now, it would not be unusual.

Some of them read, and those who don't might have dimly heard my name once upon a time.

But then, I was twenty-four. It's doubtful those men had read feminist ideological papers. Still, I got to talk to them.

I even met Justice Douglas, who had read feminist writings. His young wife, Cathleen, was interested in the movement, so they had both read up on it. He "got it." What a mind. Most men his age were refuting anything to do with the women's movement, the antiwar movement, any struggle. They had retired and were concentrating on lowering their golf handicap. Justice Douglas seemed like a man in his thirties. The contest of ideas kept him young, I think; he loved what he was doing.

During my first year in Washington I witnessed the biggest protest against the war—orderly, impressive and making travel impossible. I wondered at these thousands upon thousands of people who traveled at great expense to make their feelings known. Many were young, but by now, middle-aged and even older people had joined the protest movement. The loss of life could no longer be covered up and America was *waking* up.

I fell in with the Vietnam Veterans Against the War, because of Wade. I felt closer to the men who'd actually been there.

A ceremony behind the Capitol had the vets marching in single file. Then they would stop and toss their medals into a drain grate. Some men rode in wheelchairs. Others were missing arms. Many, thankfully, were able-bodied. All were angry.

My heart stopped when a mother, not even forty-five, spoke to the crowd. She held in her hand the Congressional Medal of Honor, the beautiful medal with the sky blue ribbon and white stars. Her son had been awarded it posthumously. She threw the medal down the grate. The crowd roared.

For days and weeks afterward I saw that medal flying through the air. It is the highest military award America bestows. The list of men who have earned it is slender. I kept hearing the clink as it hit the grate and then finally dropped through and I wondered about the young man who had died for it, never knowing, of course, that he would win this medal for uncommon valor.

If he were my son, I don't think I could have thrown away the medal, no matter how much I hated the war. Then I thought of German veterans of World War I selling the Blue Max for bread.

The grotesque murders ran together in my head. It didn't matter which war anymore. It didn't matter which side. People died for nothing. At least men could enlist and see combat. The women and children died like rats in bombed sewers. I'd rather die with a rifle in my hand.

Despite what history books may tell you, there has never been a good war. If we go to war, it means everyone has failed. Negotiating may lack glamour, but given what war has become, there's no glamour there either.

That medal of honor flying across the lawn stays with me. I don't know the name of the man who died for it nor do I remember his mother's name. But they gave me something valuable: the knowledge that when it gets bad enough, the American people will finally set things to rights.

Unfortunately, we always, and I emphasize always, wait for a crisis. But finally we do it.

Senator Kennedy wore his brother Joe's flight jacket. He walked down into the mobs and talked to the vets. This was at a time when he received death threats daily.

I thought then and I think now that he carries a heavy burden, the memory of three extraordinary brothers. Probably all he ever wanted to be was Ted Kennedy.

Other elected officials came to the crowd, which the *New York Times* estimated at between two hundred thousand and five hundred thousand. You can never trust the numbers reported.

At any rate, there was a mess of people and the situation could have become volatile. The senators and congressmen who walked among the people could have been fingered as part of the problem. They took a risk, not just in potential violence, but the minute they showed their faces they joined Nixon's enemies list, officially or unofficially.

They came anyway and I think they learned, as did the people who spoke with them. Maybe the entire government was not the enemy. Maybe we could work inside as well as outside to stop the war.

And once we stopped the war we could finally turn our gaze inward and start cleaning up our own backyard.

After the march was over and the people cleared out of the city, I took a bus up to York, then transferred to a local to Hanover. I got off in the square and walked out to Hanover Shoe Farm.

Baby Jesus rode quietly this time in a little plastic travel case. As soon as I was off the bus, I put on her leash and we walked together. When she complained, I'd pick her up. We must have walked fifteen miles that day.

I don't know why, but I wanted her to see where I was born.

The sun sparkled on the meadows where the foals and mares were turned out. Baby climbed up a fence post. A foal walked over to inspect. Baby Jesus had never seen a horse before; I doubt the foal had seen a cat, and certainly not a cat as grand as Baby Jesus, by now a full-figured girl.

The cat held her ground as the foal approached. They touched noses. It was one of the happiest moments of my life.

50

Equal Rights and
Equal Wrongs

ONE FORTY-FOUR CONSTITUTION AVENUE, A LOVELY RED BRICK Georgian known as the Alva Belmont house, sits right on top of Capitol Hill. Mrs. Alva Belmont gave the house to the National Women's Party. Alice Paul, two years older than God (actually she was eighty-four), lived there.

Although she couldn't walk easily, her mind flew ahead of her feet. In fact, her mind grew stronger even as her body failed her.

In 1968 I had met her as part of a delegation with Anselma dell'Olio, Jacqui Ceballos and Susan Vannucci. The New Feminist Repertory ladies had descended on Washington.

Seeing her again, shortly after I moved to D.C., it was apparent that time was running out for this grand old lady of feminism. Alice Paul had inherited the mantle of leader of the party from Elizabeth Cady Stanton and Susan B. Anthony.

Impeccably mannered—you had to be in her day—well groomed, well spoken and wise in the ways of Capitol Hill, she was a natural leader for legislative change.

The big blow came for Alice when her cohorts accepted winning the vote in 1920 in exchange for dropping the push for the Equal Rights Amendment. If you remember Abigail Adams's letter to John in 1776 concerning women's rights, "Remember the ladies . . . all men would be tyrants if they could," the struggle for the vote consumed 140 years. Those girls were tired and they wanted to sit down.

Alice and the radical wing soldiered on, trying to secure passage of the Equal Rights Amendment. While she managed to get this introduced each session, it would die in committee. The Democratic Party gave lip service only.

My hour with Alice involved listening to her tell me how a bill gets through the legislature. I knew the process, but one doesn't interrupt an old lady when she's on her pet subject.

Alice paid attention to bloodlines, another feature consistent with her generation. Mine passed muster. I was a WASP and a Buckingham to boot.

The few new female faces in Congress, Bella Abzug, for one, gave her hope. She wanted to live to see that amendment tacked on to the Constitution. She didn't.

I agreed with Mrs. Paul. And I worked for the amendment in those early years.

But the longer I thought about Alice Paul's life work, and the longer I roamed around Washington, the surer I felt that the timing was wrong, not the amendment itself.

I was supporting myself with freelance editing jobs and I'd mow your lawn for you, too. Sometimes I wonder that I didn't go into the gardening and lawn care business—I'd been doing it since I was big enough to push a mower.

The feminists in New York and the other big cities talked to one another. I talked to my neighbors, working-class black women. I talked to my mother and Aunt Mimi. When I bummed a ride into Virginia or Maryland to visit a stable, I'd talk to the "barn rats," the stable help.

Most of them had never heard of the Equal Rights Amendment. When I explained it they weren't violently opposed, but their primary concern was being able to make a living.

The more I knew of Washington, the more I saw how out of touch the government was with the people. The war threw that into high relief, but the Nixon administration was out of touch on so many issues. I doubt any administration could have survived the tidal wave of change sweeping the country. It wasn't just the war, it was the Pill, it was television intruding into people's consciousness in ways no one quite fathomed. It was a generation in their late teens and twenties who said, "You told me this was the greatest nation on earth. Why, then, do we have racial suffering? Why is there an undeclared war in Indochina?"

The sainted Jack Kennedy couldn't have weathered this sea of change any more than Nixon did.

There have been other times in history when a generational gulf has created desperate problems. In Weimar Germany, the generation that fought World War I was more liberal than their sons, who dragged Germany into World War II. The French Revolution was fueled, for the most part, by young men, which also explains the hideous excesses. Youth may be brilliant, but experience is worth as much as brilliance and a society needs older people for balance. Our own revolution was better balanced by age, which may explain the stability of the process. True, the Articles of Confederation fell flat, but no one lost their heads over it. No one was hanged during the Constitutional Convention.

Compromise saved us, and compromise is the work of mature people.

The women's movement was a force of young women. Apart from Alice Paul and Betty Friedan, the burgeoning ranks were women from their late teens to their early thirties. It's difficult for women with young children to be politically active, so once people settled down many of them dropped back—not necessarily out, but back.

The other drawback was also peculiar to women. Since we had been denied participation in the political process up to 1920, we had no one to help us. Margaret Chase Smith, the great senator from Maine, was nearing the end of her distinguished career. We had maybe four women in government who could show us the ropes.

Our mothers and grandmothers couldn't help us. They weren't hardened in political wars. Even my mother, who had a keen understanding of the political process, had never held elected office. She could give me the benefit of her experience but she couldn't tell me what happens once you're inside the system.

We might as well have been standing in the middle of the Mojave asking for rain.

The mistakes of the feminist movement in the seventies and eighties were the mistakes of youth. And thank God, they weren't mean-spirited mistakes.

My chilling realization about the ERA's bad timing first swept over me as I watched Fairfax Hunt take off one crisp October morning in 1970. Children, adults and older folk trotted off as the sun turned a light frost to dew.

Three generations. We had one. That's when I knew the Equal Rights Amendment couldn't be passed at that time. I gave the benefit of my illumination to everyone, including Gloria.

This is the only issue on which Gloria and I have disagreed publicly. The disagreements we have in private are more in the nature of a city person's view of life versus a country person's.

Gloria, Bella, Betty, all of them, were married to the damned Equal Rights Amendment.

My argument, simply put, is that you can't work for a constitutional amendment without years, decades of local organizing, paying special attention to state legislatures, which are usually more conservative than Congress.

And you can't expect women to rouse themselves across the land without delivering services to them, whether it's in the form of child-care centers, rape crisis centers or legal services for those in need. You've got to give in order to get.

The South was the key to passage of the amendment. Too many feminists held the attitude that southerners are backward, so why bother with them? Then, too, coming from me the argument was seen as special pleading for my region.

The rest of the country mistakes the South's deep hostility to legislation, national or state, as backwardness. Old, silly laws are left on the books, and some are plain horrible, but the point is, they're not enforced. The South's attitude is "Let sleeping dogs lie."

We should know. When our state legislatures passed radical laws for secession, we southerners paid with our lives, our fortunes, our futures.

The easiest way to explain the War Between the States is that the South was right in the beginning and wrong at the end. We were constitutionally correct in our right to secede and we were right in our resistance to the industrial North's attempt to destroy our agrarian economy. But we, especially the Delta, clung to slavery. For that we deserved to get our asses kicked.

Anyway, I knew those old boys needed attention. By virtue of being southern men, they were not automatically opposed to the amendment, contrary to what the Yankee girls thought. But by virtue of being southern men, they needed lots of female attention on this issue and perhaps on issues that might be important to them.

You can't just blow people off and then expect them to come around when you need them.

Another factor is that in our political history, Americans have only amended the Constitution twenty-seven times and two of those amendments involved the Volstead Act, Prohibition. An amendment is the largest political action that our nation can take, and feminists wanted to *start* with an amendment.

Gloria conducted herself with grace, as she always does, but I was riddled with blasts from other women.

First they'd accuse me of splitting the movement over lesbians in the ranks. Right, let's accuse the oppressed of causing the oppression. Now I was going to ruin the movement by opposing the Holy Grail, the Equal Rights Amendment.

I understood their need for a show of solidarity. I promised to be silent on the issue—and silence is usually assumed to be assent—in exchange for fighting openly for gay women to be part of the feminist movement.

I was right about the Equal Rights Amendment even though I wish I had been wrong.

The Death Drill

BABY JESUS AND I VISITED MOTHER FOR HER BIRTHDAY, WHICH WE tried to do each year.

I regaled her with stories of my political fisticuffs. She regaled me with the latest family dirt. Julia Ellen and Russell weren't getting along. Kenny Jr. was getting serious about a girl and thought he'd marry her. Wade was on his way back, praise Jesus; he'd served his time and would not reenlist. Kenny Sr. was being chased by a rich woman he worked for and his wife didn't much like it. Aunt Mimi was considering moving to England and shoving Elizabeth II off the throne.

After racing through the family, Mother started on her friends. A lady she worked with was so fat that she huffed and puffed with each step. Working in a bakery weakened her resolve to lose weight. Then there was Pastor Golder, who was entirely too serious about church dogma. Mom wanted to sing and she'd heard enough sermons to last the rest of her life. At this point she interrupted herself and rendered a few heartfelt bars from "Holy, Holy, Holy," which then melded into "Beautiful Savior," Dad's favorite hymn and one we'd sung at his funeral.

I knew what was coming. We'd been there umpteen times. The dreaded death drill was upon me.

"Now when I die"—she hopped up, dragging me into her bedroom— "open this drawer."

I opened the drawer of her fat-bellied dresser. "Mom, you have the neatest drawers."

"Organization saves time. Here's the key to the strongbox." She lifted out a tiny, shiny key and then marched to the closet, opening the door. "Here's the box." She pointed to a mint-green box. "Get it down."

I stood on a chair and lifted it down. She opened it. "Here's the insurance policy. Here's everything you need." She rifled through the papers, picking out each one, explaining again what I'd heard over and over since Dad's death in 1961.

When Dad died, Mother had thought she'd go too. However deep her grief, her love of life won out and she was radiantly alive or irritatingly alive, depending. But his sudden death had inspired the death drill. She was determined that when the awful event transpired I would not be at a loss. No matter how ravaged by sorrow, I'd know what to do.

"Now, I don't want a big funeral. Feed me to the fish."

"Mother."

"If I have cancer, I'm walking into the ocean."

"Will you stop?"

"No, I won't. It's foolish to stay alive when there's no joy in it and when you're not going to get better."

"Don't fret, Mom, only the good die young."

"Aren't we smart to our mother."

"You're healthy. If I start acting too nice, it means I think you're sick."

She considered that. "Let's go to Saks."

"Mom, I am not standing in front of that perfume counter while you spray on every perfume there."

"Party pooper."

"We could go to the tennis courts."

"Why?"

"You've never been."

"I'm not sitting in the hot sun."

I locked the strongbox and put it back on the top shelf of the closet. "We could pick up Aunt Mimi and go to Saks."

I knew they'd content each other, and I could wander off.

That fast Mother was on the phone: "Sis, comb your hair and put on your lipstick. We're going to Saks and Rita's taking us to lunch."

What a chiseler she was.

They could eat. On her second piece of apple pie, Mother launched into the death drill, which Sis had heard a million times too.

"Julia, don't be so morbid."

"I'm not morbid, I'm practical. You've got lipstick on your teeth."

Aunt Mimi wiped her teeth. "I told Julia Ellen once what to do."

"She'll never remember it. Repetition."

"She'll remember." Aunt Mimi opened her purse, a large affair, and retrieved her lipstick. "You know, I think I'll buy that color I was looking at."

The color was cerise. Ugh.

"I'm leaning toward Persian Melon myself," Mother said.

"You need a tan and only field hands have tans."

"What about Coco Chanel?" Mother replied.

"Who cares what some Frenchwoman does?"

"Only the whole world."

Aunt Mimi ignored this, turning to me. "Do you really believe that women are equal to men?"

"Under the law, yes. In reality I don't think anyone is equal to anyone."

She didn't want a real discussion, she wanted to inflict her opinions on me, which was fine. I'd been hearing them all my life. She leaned over conspiratorially, which meant Mother leaned too. "Now you listen to me. Women are not equal to men. We are superior. Any woman worth her salt can wrap any man around her finger, and I'm not talking about sex. I mean you run them. You hear me?"

"Yeah."

Mother smiled.

"You tell those girlfriends of yours to dump this whole Equal Rights Amendment idea. Just can it. I don't want to talk to a man as an equal. I want to control him. If I'm an equal, then I have to treat him as an equal. Never." She rapped the table. "Men are here to do our bidding. You just leave well enough alone."

"Yes, ma'am." I knew better than to enter into the "men as our beasts of burden" discussion.

"Why are you agreeing with me? To get me to pipe down?"

"No, I agree with you."

"You do?"

"Yes." I elected not to tell her that I agreed but for vastly different reasons and that I thought the Equal Rights Amendment would be a good thing at some time.

"Well." She exhaled, disappointed to win without a knock-down–drag-out. "I knew you were smart, book-learning smart, but you're learning about the way the world works, aren't you?"

"Learned it from you and Mom."

They beamed.

"Well, I'm going to buy that lipstick," Aunt Mimi said.

"Makes her look like a bled pig," Mom said under her breath.

"What was that, Juts?"

"Nothing."

Purdah

I CAN'T REMEMBER MEETING CHARLOTTE BUNCH, ONE OF THE BEST thinkers in the women's movement. It seems she's always been in my life. When I made her acquaintance in D.C., she anchored the antiwar movement there and was married to Jim Weeks.

At that time, in 1971, she was Goody Two-shoes. The years have given her a leavening cynicism but her basic impulse is still to overflow with the milk of human kindness.

Initially, I thought this was a pose. It truly is Charlotte. I respected her mind, one of the best tactical political minds I have ever encountered. I loved her for her kindness.

Jim Weeks impressed me not because he was smart—most of the young politicos were smart—but he too was a kind person. He also grew a red beard yet his hair was black, an eye-catching combination.

Jim was so nice that Charlotte grew restive. Had he deviled her more, they might have remained locked in wedded bliss. Theirs was a remarkably civil parting, which speaks volumes about both of them.

Charlotte's growing feminism sent her in a new direction, me. We'd sit up until all hours of the night talking about how to reach women. How could we make them aware of the special obstacles awaiting them in politics, whether protest or traditional? Then there was the small matter of not being hired for the well-paying jobs. The only other woman I had ever talked to who understood politics from both sides of the fence, party and protest, was Gloria.

I must now take credit for a harebrained idea. I'd apologize, but why? I learned. Sometimes you have to fall flat on your face to learn.

I thought that if women were lesbians, their best energy would go to women; they would become woman-identified instead of identifying with men, who clearly did not have their best interests as a class at heart. A man might have an individual woman's best interests at heart, but not women in general. Unfortunately, this hasn't changed much.

If women were lesbians, then they would work for the freedom of all women. Now I hardly wanted all women to be lesbians. That would be too boring. I only needed a critical mass.

Charlotte, while less enthusiastic than I, eventually rolled along on my wave. We founded the Furies Collective.

Anybody who was anybody lived in a collective or a commune then. Often they operated as political cells. Other times they existed so people could save money. No matter what, the concept galvanized hundreds of thousands of young people, much as the utopian movement galvanized our ancestors in the nineteenth century, the Shakers being the most outstanding and long-lived example.

We all thought we could create a better way to be with people. We thought we could eliminate the power struggles and free our best energy to heal our country.

You may laugh now, especially if you're older than I am or quite a bit younger, but we were patriotically motivated. I cannot overemphasize how much we loved our country and how dismayed, frightened, disgusted we were at the turn of events. Like Saturn devouring his children, the United States was killing its young people at Jackson State and Kent State. Sure, we didn't die by the millions, like the Russians from 1917 to 1945, but none of us ever expected the National Guard or the police to fire upon us. The older generation never warned us that freedom demands vigilance and sacrifice.

Although I had been raised poor and my parents were much older than my contemporaries' parents (Mom and Dad were born in 1905, remember), even I believed that all we had to do was point out a problem and it would be corrected.

I never believed our government would kill us. Once they did I woke up fast. We all woke up fast. No longer was the administration something that needed correcting; they needed to be removed.

I will believe to my dying day that our efforts helped end the war in Vietnam. Watergate accomplished the rest.

But at this time, we would go for a walk and an unmarked car would cruise alongside us. Our phones were bugged. And our taxes paid for this foolishness! I wasn't followed every day and neither was Charlotte, but anytime there was a demonstration the goons would show up.

In a way the drive for communal living was born from this chaos and fear. We needed structure. We needed to watch out for one another. We needed to train ourselves to be rigorously nonviolent. That's a hard one for me because if you push me hard enough, I'll haul off and knock you one. Growing up the only girl among the boys, I learned to inflict pain in order to be left alone. If I hadn't, the boys would have squashed me like a bug.

Our collective would be a lesbian one. We named ourselves the Furies after the avenging angels who pursued Orestes for killing his mother. The Furies asserted motherright. Also, what a lovely way for me to show off my Greek and Latin.

Initially twelve women gathered together and we lived together for over a year. Tasha Byrd, Ginny Berson, Sharon Deevey, Susan Hathaway, Lee Schwin, Helaine Harris, Coletta Reid, Jennifer Woodull, Nancy Myron, Joan Biren, Charlotte and myself.

I knew little about anyone's personal life. Actually, you had no personal life. You worked at our newspaper, our home repair class, our car repair class or canvassing the bars. You worked all the time.

Our newspaper, called *The Furies,* shocked the conservative wing of the women's movement. I don't think they believed lesbians could be literate and they never expected us to stick together as a group. But we knew when someone's boot was on our neck and it didn't take a genius to write clearly about it. God, those ladies were outraged. Actually, their fussing was rather delicious.

Gloria's faction, far more flexible, understood our analysis of how we were kicked around, but while not as old as many of Betty's followers, Gloria was ten years older than I. That's a large enough gap to engender a slightly different viewpoint on events, different flash points of recognition. Those of us born in the middle forties to middle fifties were experimenting with communes, political protest, music and, for some unfortunately, drugs. Gloria's generation, born in the thirties, for the most part wasn't part of the wave.

Already established in careers and relationships, they couldn't uproot all they had accomplished materially.

While slightly older people understood the impulse to live in a commune, they didn't share that impulse.

That I was willing to try, introvert that I am, illustrates the passion of the time, the raw excitement of ideas exploding out of an emerging generation.

We thought we were changing the world. I don't know if we did but we changed ourselves. Since we are the largest generation to be born during recorded history, we probably did change the world by virtue of what we did among ourselves. All those communes, underground newspapers, marches and resource centers began to affect aboveground media perception. Over the span of less than a decade, we traveled from being perceived as dirty, druggie hippies to exposing the moral catastrophe that was Vietnam.

In terms of women, what we did achieve has been taken for granted. Many of our goals are a fact of life now, just as public education is a fact of life. Who can recall the central figures in the struggle for universal public education? We have so swiftly absorbed some of the central tenets of feminism, such as equal pay for equal work, that we have forgotten how difficult achieving those victories, or even partial victories, was.

Sometimes I think, also, that we purposely don't want to remember our recent history as regards women. It's like sand in our eyes. An entire mental construct has faded away, except for right-wing pockets. There are still some people, men and women, who believe women are second-class citizens, a discretionary labor force (last hired, first fired), should be barred from certain careers, etc. They're small but noisy. History has already brushed them aside in America, which may explain why they are so emotional. Losers squeal. Winners head into the future.

If nothing else, the South taught me that. We not only carry the scars of the War Between the States, we've tattooed them with bright colors. The North could care less.

The trivialization of women through sexualization is still a major obstacle to equality. It would appear that any form of sexuality offends the right wing. For those of us not living in constant fear of pleasure, this issue raises interesting questions about the nature of mating. All mammals devote a period of their lives to mating behavior. We're no different. Our central problem is we've created societies that worship productivity; the idol capital means more than human relationships. Mating takes time. It is antithetical to a society organized to deliver goods and services. One of the ways to delay that natural process is to place all the sexual responsibility on women, to compartmentalize the fireworks of hormones in both sexes. So a real man goes to work. The job always comes first. Finding the right woman or even the wrong woman must take place after he's turned out his quota of widgets for the day. It's quite confusing.

Until the women's movement addresses the entire displacement of sexuality in modern societies, it can't begin to resolve the remaining inequalities toward women.

In the beginning we could only see our own problems. We're far enough along the way to examine the entire issue of how lives are thwarted for commerce and commerce alone.

In the late 1960s I was already thinking of these issues. The women in the collective, the women in the movement generally, focused exclusively on a few issues. They were important issues, but we came to be defined by those issues alone, for example, child care. Our path to addressing topics such as the military-industrial complex was shut down. A few of us could have spoken to those issues, but in the beginning the only thing women could focus on was that pain peculiar to them as females, that distinct oppression.

The horror of any form of oppression is that it creates a reverse narcissism.

Any manner of treating people, any people, as inferior blights them. The resentment and hate growing from such treatment can never be underestimated no matter how successfully it is masked. Sooner or later, an inciting incident will blow the lid off. The fact that men are so smug about women's continuing nonviolence astonishes me. It's kind of like the old-time whites in the South assuming that "their Negroes" were "sweet." I don't mean to imply that racial oppression is identical to gender oppression but I do mean to say that all forms of oppression create various coping mechanisms, the foremost being that you only tell the oppressor what s/he wants to hear. You tell them the truth only when you have a critical mass behind you.

I learned some of these things in the Furies Collective by observing the behavior of women who felt powerless. Not every woman in that collective felt powerless, but enough did to give me a real eye-opener as to what a distorted worldview can do to people. Oppression always distorts. A few women, not everyone, saw themselves as victims no matter what the circumstances. Here they were in an all-women collective and they still perceived themselves as victims. One of us would have to be the bad guy so they could continue to be the innocent trampled-upon.

I was so carried away by the drama of the epoch, by the desire to do something positive for my country, that I violated my deepest instincts, which are to write in solitude and to live on the land with animals.

Here I was stuck with a bunch of women in sticky, hot Washington: Of Humid Bondage.

Baby Jesus despised the collective even though I loved on her constantly. Some of the other women lacked proper catitude, and no one thought it was funny when I set a place for her at the dinner table. She had to eat on the floor.

Charlotte and I, finally exhausted by all this togetherness, bucked the group. We modified our plan; you could have personal property, up to a limit, then you had to share. I hadn't a cent, so I wasn't affected—except I did want my own toothbrush. It was different for Charlotte, who had a fellowship at the Institute for Policy Studies, for Susan Hathaway and for a few of the others with resources. They were good about sharing, a lot better than I would have been if the shoe were on the other foot.

Surprised at our national presence, we worked even harder. What we learned in our time together must be different for each woman.

I learned that I can work with anyone, even people I can't stand. But I also learned that if you don't have to, why do it? Life is ever so much more pleasant if you like the people around you, and the bald truth is that even though I shared space with these women, I barely paid attention to them. I can't say that I did like them. They were serious, as in achingly intent. How I sat through those meetings without cracking jokes, I don't know. Life is too important to take seriously.

I was pretending to be something I wasn't, a 100-percent true-blue martyr for the cause. Maybe I could muster 50 percent, but not 100. I loved literature too much, as well as Bach and Mozart, Cézanne and Cellini. In short, I am an aesthete, and if nothing else, my experience in the Furies smacked me square in the face with what must have been obvious to everyone but me. I crave the arts the way I crave good horses.

To make matters worse, I carry a whiff of charisma. I don't know how I got it. Is it like the flu? Can you catch it by standing outside in the rain? All I know is if I stand up and speak, people pay attention. They may not agree with me. Hell, they hardly ever agree with me because I'm usually two or three steps ahead, which makes me far less effective than if I were right in step. It's a quality that has cost me dear in Hollywood, too. It does little good if you can see the future yet not be able to make others see it. I'm not being smug. I can usually see ahead. Of course, the next question is, can I see what's under my nose? Sometimes, yes. Sometimes, no.

I called the ERA right. I called the splits in the women's movement not just right but on the minute. I was pretty clear about what would happen to the black movement and the antiwar movement, not just because I was so almighty smart but because I studied history. I've never stopped studying history. Most people, not just the Furies Collective, thought this uproar was happening for the first time. It wasn't, but it was happening in different ways. No event is a duplicate of another event.

Naturally I was full of myself. I have never lacked self-esteem. In fact, if you need some, I'll give you some of mine.

Jesus, I was so sure of myself I must have driven them crazy. Except for Charlotte, most of the women didn't have a clear or positive sense of themselves then. Their resentment festered.

Worse, I announced that the two children in the collective ought not to be there. I had good reasons for this. I never trusted we would be physically safe, though I never directly expressed this. Not that we were violent. We didn't espouse violence, but the violence against black leaders and New Left leaders had escalated. I feared it would affect us sooner or later. You simply do not expose children to risks like that.

Anyone who has a rosy view of motherhood is exceptionally blind. While children give you incredible gifts of love, of seeing the world anew, they ought to be your number one priority. If you can't give them that primacy, don't have them. It's cruel.

We shared responsibility for the children, but I think now, and I said then, it's wrong. Children can't be raised by everyone. We weren't an extended family, we were a political collective. Maybe those societies that Margaret Mead studied share child rearing, but we weren't living in Samoa.

The women with children should have left. As the demands of our many projects sapped them, they should have seen that. Eventually they did, but not until after a fair amount of shitfire and abuse.

The first people purged from this barrel of laughs were Sharon Deevey and Joan Biren. They were already a couple when they joined the group. They spent more time with each other than with us. Small wonder. They must have been as bored and antsy as I was.

Out they went.

I was next. I was a leader in a leaderless group. I'd gotten ideas above my station. Out with me.

I don't know when I've been so relieved. They threw me out, which meant I didn't have to make the decision to leave. I don't know why I would have felt so guilty about leaving them. Hell, by this time I couldn't stand them.

Charlotte stayed on until the group fizzled.

For all our silliness, we accomplished some important things. We stayed true to our vision of nonviolent protest. Gandhi created this. He gets all the credit. But it's hard for Americans. In a perverse way we worship violence. From the days of our first landing, from the novels of James Fenimore Cooper, we absolutely worship violence. It isn't a dark tangent of American life, it's central to our concept of who we are. This nation was born in blood. We can't get away from it. First we killed the Indians. Then we killed the French in the French and Indian War. We whacked the British twice (they started it). Then we managed to endear ourselves to the Mexicans. Not long after that we slaughtered one another in the worst war of our history. Recovered, sort of, from that grotesque episode, we displayed adventurism in the Spanish-American War. And in rapid succession we've engaged in World War I, World War II, Korea, Vietnam and the Gulf War. The Gulf War was covered by the media like a football game.

We cheered smart bombs.

Far better had we cheered smart people.

If nothing else, the Furies stayed true to a nonviolent concept of cleansing and confrontation.

And the collective also alerted other gay women to the shattering knowledge that they weren't alone. Today it's almost impossible to feel the resonance of that connection.

With the delightful exception of Charlotte, who never stops thinking, the only other Fury I have seen since then is Sharon Deevey, a nurse who lives in Cleveland and whom I still count as a friend.

There are few people who will stay by you for your entire life. To expect that I would make lifelong friends from a superficial connection is a mistake. Politics is not compelling enough to bind you to people for life. The Furies taught me that, and it has continued to help my perspective about people in politics. I know, nine times out of ten, that when the political project is finished, so is the relationship.

I moved back into 217 Twelfth Street, SE. Baby Jesus preened with my undivided attention.

I decided to write a novel. Everyone said how hard it was to write one, journalists especially. I figured, what the hell. If I fell on my face, I'd pick myself up and do something else. What was the big deal?

With Baby Jesus lurking behind my typewriter, batting the paper, I fired off *Rubyfruit Jungle*. It made me laugh. I needed one.

MAYBE ONE OF THE REASONS I NEEDED TO LAUGH WAS THAT I HAD COME to the dolorous conclusion that American women are not serious about power.

Harsh as this judgment sounds, let me explain. Politics is war without killing. You want your program to succeed. It's a battle and often that battle is filled with bravery, cowardice, greed and heapings of dishonesty. It's a bare-knuckle fight for power. You want the power to enact your program. If you're a lightweight, you want the power for self-aggrandizement or money. The real warriors fight for their program just as military warriors fight for territory.

While a few women in history were able to battle, such as Elizabeth I of England or Catherine the Great of Russia, the political experience of women has been no experience. They haven't learned how to fight. The process is repellant to most women. Of course, it's so cheap now I think it's repellant to most men.

Women are not accustomed to an arena in which people would willingly destroy another person's reputation just for two years in Congress. The vengeful nature needed to succeed, the constant dissembling, eludes most women. And you absolutely must hurt the people who hurt you, or you look weak. If you look weak, you accomplish nothing.

My experience is, once an opponent or outright enemy gets hurt they treat you with respect. All animals understand pain.

It really doesn't take brains to be a politician as much as it takes stomach. Both would be nice, but in America we have accepted diminishing returns in this arena. I'm not sure why. Many reasons, I guess.

For women to be serious about political power they must demolish their political enemies as the liberals demolished Judge Robert Bork during his confirmation hearings to fill a vacant Supreme Court seat. That was a lesson in naked revenge exacted by the Democrats on the Republicans.

I'm not commenting here on Judge Bork's viewpoints. I'm commenting on the campaign against him.

The theater of the Bork hearings seemed to be about a Supreme Court nominee. That was the text. The subtext was about power. The Democrats served notice on the Republicans: If Republicans wanted to get any person confirmed or any program accomplished, they were going to have to find a middle ground on which to meet the Democrats. The way things were going, neither party was likely to get anything out of the famous pork barrel.

The Democrats' success, limited, was success nonetheless.

That's politics. I could cite Republican retaliations but you expect me to do that. Each side has to inflict enough damage on the other side to create pain. Once enough pain has been absorbed, the "reasonable" minds in the party will call for bipartisan cooperation.

Of course, this is a grotesque waste of time, energy and money. As a people, at this moment in our history, we seem willing to watch this sorry spectacle and to feel superior to it. I expect we will change the process when we are ready.

The point is, until we can change the process we must participate in it if we are to accomplish anything politically. If you want paid paternity leave, then you have to fight.

Bad as this process is, wounded as you will become, it is still better than not fighting at all. Not fighting doesn't make you morally superior. It makes you a victim. You get chewed up like dog meat.

Until women realize that some pain is better than more pain, we aren't going to get but so far politically. I should amend that to *many* women. Clearly individual women understand the process and will fight for power. Elizabeth Dole certainly understands the process. Madeleine Albright understands the process.

Until millions fight back, I can only conclude that American women, as a group, are not serious about political power.

Assholes Anonymous

ANGELS CAN FLY BECAUSE THEY TAKE THEMSELVES LIGHTLY. I WAS flying with *Rubyfruit*. I love writing fiction. Comic vision is natural for me—not necessarily comedy, but comic vision, which entails an entire worldview incorporating pain and tragedy.

Thanks to Charlotte, the Institute for Policy Studies granted me a one-year visiting fellowship at $7,000 a year. I figured once they knew me I wouldn't be visiting long. The institute, founded by Marcus Raskin and Richard Barnet, is in essence graduate school for the New Left. Marc and Dick had both worked in government for a time. But they were interested in moving beyond the anticommunism touted by the liberals in office. So they founded IPS as a haven for New Left and radical thinkers like themselves. Since I am an old-fashioned American centrist I knew I wouldn't dazzle the guys at IPS. I just hoped I could hang on long enough to write my novel and learn something from them. One need not agree with people in order to learn. I don't agree with Otto von Bismarck but I've learned from his life and work.

IPS, nestled hard by the National Democratic Women's Headquarters on New Hampshire Avenue, burst at the seams with people and activity. Karl Hess, a former speechwriter for Barry Goldwater, and far more of a structured anarchist (sounds like a contradiction but read Karl, you'll see it isn't) than a leftist, became a friend for life. He understood technology and people, a rare combination.

Arthur Waskow can only be described as a radical Talmudic scholar, although he wasn't a rabbi. He brought a deep spirituality to political questions; he brought the best of Judaism. He taught me to wrestle with God.

James Ridgway, as young as I was among these older men, was working on coal mining problems at the time. What I adored about his lectures was that they were based on specific events.

Marcus, on the other hand, floated above us all with his philosophical approach. Given his time in the Kennedy administration, we knew he could deal in spades when he had to but his true inclination was philosophy.

Dick Barnet was just beginning his study of how the multinational corporation would change the world, which resulted in the publication of *Global Reach*. Dick's writings are accessible, well organized and hit the bull's-eye.

The black radical contingent at the institute included Frank Smith and Ivanhoe Donaldson. Ivanhoe was later to go down in ignominy. In 1986, he pleaded guilty to stealing from the District of Columbia government and served three years in prison.

Frank and Ivanhoe's relationship with the white fellows, lined with tension and suspicion, taught me not to bite the hand that fed me. These men, each so different from the other, felt forced into an alliance against the white folks. Or at least that's my analysis, I could be wrong. Frank was a genuine idealist underneath the steely, quiet cynicism. Why he thought we didn't know that mystifies me. You can hide the fire but what are you going to do with the smoke?

Ivanhoe dazzled everyone. His fall from grace reverberated in our minds when it happened years later. He was so special, so magnetic. Maybe everything fell into his lap and he forgot the struggle. I don't know. Or maybe, as we say in the horse world, he broke bad.

Charlotte, the resident feminist, both challenged and charmed the men. The challenge was that these guys, the wunderkinds from Harvard, etc., were hearing feminist thought for the first time. The charm was Charlotte herself. You had to like her. She was engaging and nonthreatening.

I'd pop in most every day for a few hours, sit in on a lecture or conference. Often a congressman would call for information on an odd subject such as the cost of setting up an oil refinery in Saudi Arabia. The various fellows over the years covered the world, literally, in their knowledge. Being at the center of the exchange was exciting.

I had a crush on Bob Borsage. I made my feelings manifest by ignoring him at every moment. His view of the people and events at IPS delighted me because he had critical distance. He must have learned it from his father, Frank, the famous film director who even directed Mary Pickford.

The swirl around me helped me write my first novel. Not one thing in that first novel suggests heightened intellectualism or political thought. IPS gave me the high contrast I needed to find my true fictional voice.

Up until that time, I'd had two books of poetry published as well as grim political essays and articles in underground newspapers, but it wasn't my voice. The writing showed promise, but how many young people with promise break out? Precious few.

The glorious thing about the institute was I didn't belong there anymore than I belonged in the Furies Collective. The dislocation and loss, the constant feeling that my pants were on backward, drove me to what did fit, fiction.

I owe a great debt to Alexis Smith, an actress from the forties and fifties. She appeared in movies like *Night and Day,* solid movies with handsome leading men. When Hal Prince staged Stephen Sondheim's *Follies,* a cinematic musical that had an impact on how plays were staged ever after that, he brought back Alexis for the starring role. It was a good cast, Dorothy Collins, Yvonne DeCarlo, John McMartin and Gene Nelson.

I saw the show in 1971, on a trip to New York, and fell in love with Alexis, as did everyone who saw it. I wrote her a letter and she responded. I visited her at the Winter Garden theater, and she took me to dinner after the show. She was wise, warm and direct. She told me to forget politics. Many more people can be politicians than can be fiction writers.

Wearisome as my crush must have been for her and her husband, Craig Smith, she nudged me along. She never said anything antigay. She never commented on my obvious poverty. She delighted in my tales of Mom and Aunt Mimi and she seemed to understand how much I loved animals.

I have never felt such lust in my life as I felt for that gorgeous creature. She bore it with good humor.

In a way I wrote *Rubyfruit Jungle* for her. I hoped I would prove her confidence in me not unfounded. And I finally had sense enough to realize I couldn't keep up with her. She was at the top of her game and I was just starting mine.

She would never love me but she saw a flash of talent. That was better than carnal love.

Writing fiction brought me to my great love: the English language.

THE ENGLISH LANGUAGE HAS CREATED A VAST BODY OF LITERATURE IN our native tongue. That may sound odd but if you think about it, Medieval French is a kind of lax Latin. English literature as we know it starts with *The Canterbury Tales.* Most scholars will tell you no, it started with *Beowulf.* I dispute that. *Beowulf,* redolent with Teutonic attitude, written in Anglo-Saxon, is important, but *The Canterbury Tales* is English to the core. Between the time when *Beowulf* was composed, sometime around 1000, and the late fourteenth century, when Chaucer roistered forth with his energy, insight into character and use of sophisticated structure (it's a pilgrimage, remember), something revolutionary had happened in England. The people became English and the language soared to the heavens, the dialect of London gaining ascendance over the other dialects.

That's what I found. My home was the English language and my particular path was the same as Chaucer's: comic vision. Comedy, in the grand sense, is the richest vein of English. The language breathes, expands, turns golden with comedy, for an English sentence is capable of conveying irony, pathos, wit and humor simultaneously. Think of some of Shakespeare's comedies. Hell, think of the tragedies too. When Hamlet is about to stab Polonius to death behind the curtain, he says, "How now? A rat? Dead for a ducat, dead!"

This prince, so often portrayed as a sensitive, suffering young man in an existential crisis (please, Louise), is really a brute.

What about Noel Coward's *Private Lives*? It's easy to hop from Shakespeare to Coward because Coward wrote the second most famous balcony scene in the English language. I'm assuming most of you have read or seen the play *Private Lives*. If you haven't, you're in for an exhilarating experience.

The line "Strange how potent cheap music can be" is mean, hysterically funny given the circumstances, poignant and above all true. One simple line.

English is at its highest and best use in comedy. Unfortunately, comedy is much harder to write than straight prose or tragedy. And fewer people understand true comedy. Everyone understands slapstick, but real comedy presupposes intelligence and the ability to discern not just different levels of language, but different levels among people. Comedy is always set in society. It's about people as they live. Tragedy can be one man against one god. Technically, that's much easier.

Tragedy massages the human ego even as comedy deflates it. While you're weeping for just blinded Oedipus you're drawn into the nobility of the tale, a human crosses the gods even if unwittingly. Tragedy pits us against large foes and the trip wire is our own character. Still, falling afoul of Zeus or Athena or Hera ennobles the human.

In comedy we fall afoul of one another. Comedy depends on social life, on our behavior in groups. In tragedy you can observe one human against the gods. In comedy it's one human versus other humans and often one man (or woman if I'm writing it) against her own worst impulses.

The English language is one of the superb inventions of the human mind. It is and always will be the perfect language for comedy. The homonyms alone can send you into peals of laughter.

The other reason that English is made for comic vision is the temper of
our people. English-speaking peoples are wary of emotion. We prize logic.
Comedy depends on our hubris, on that absurd conceit that we can think
our way through life.

All English speakers are set up from birth for a fall, that moment when
you realize you might be smart but you've still fallen flat on your face. For
us, this is the beginning of wisdom.

The other aspect of comedy that suits me is the sheer drive, the strong
sense of self-confidence one needs to write it. It's what has gotten me in
trouble, too. We still haven't reached the point where we are sure we like
self-confidence in a woman. We'll accept violent self-centeredness, especially in beauty queens and movie stars; the more superficial they are the
more we accept it. But a truly self-confident woman, one who looks you
straight in the eye and doesn't lower her eyes in a nonverbal (and cloying)
nod to your superiority, if you are male, is unnerving.

Suited though we are to comedy, since the dreary days of Cromwell and
his Puritan myrmidons, tragedy has been in the ascendant. People want to
see others suffer. They're getting their wish. I suppose it makes them feel
superior.

Well, whatever the reason, our society now values sorrowful tales heavily laced with violence. The French call it *nostalgie de la boue,* nostalgia for
the mud.

I actually knew that when I started my first novel. I hadn't studied
Latin, Greek, Anglo-Saxon, Middle English and the merest hint of French
for nothing. I knew our traditions. I knew my tool. I didn't necessarily
know structure, but I could learn. At least I knew a story had to have a
beginning, a middle and an end. These days you can't take even that for
granted.

Virginia Woolf has a lot to answer for with that damned stream-of-
consciousness technique. She could do it. Nobody else can, really.

And then there are all the *Ulysses* imitators. Dear God, please send them
back into the pubs. Could Joyce have known what he spawned?

You find when you write a novel that once you've established your
worldview, you have a temperament. Since I crave Shakespeare's comedies, Aristophanes's comedies, Molière, Sheridan, Wycherley, Pope, Goldsmith, Gibbon (it's prose, but what prose!) and Twain, that establishes my
temperament.

It doesn't mean I hate *Paradise Lost* or *Light in August,* but those works represent a different temperament, a much more emotional one. Milton and Faulkner were wounded men, deeply feeling men. You might not think it upon first reading, but read those works again.

Times have temperament. This explains why artists go in and out of fashion like clothes. Thornton Wilder was a very good writer. Not of the first water, but damned good and worth reading. Who reads him today? Wrong temperament, but he'll come back when the times change, and I wonder if Willa Cather and Edna Ferber will come back with him.

Temperament. Henry James's *Washington Square* moves me in a way that Malcolm Lowry's *Under the Volcano* does not. Both are exceptional works.

For whatever reason, my first novel—written on a door laid across two black file cabinets with a big red stripe painted down the middle—arrived at the right time, in the right temperament.

Rubyfruit Jungle studied the struggle of an individual to be an individual. This is one of the oldest themes in Western literature: the individual versus society. Think of *Antigone*. It's the same subject but in tragic form.

In order to become a useful person to the group, Molly Bolt must first defy the group mentality to find herself.

Of course you shouldn't notice this theme. If you do, it means I've failed. When you read my novels the first time, if you bother to read them at all, I would hope you'll be transported into the worlds these characters inhabit and I pray when you're done you'll know those people. They will now be part of your family.

Not that anyone wanted to publish *Rubyfruit Jungle*. Far from it. I sent it to agents in New York. A few people told me to send it to one particular agent, said to be gay. Anyway, with hope, I packed it off.

I took the train up a month later; a month seemed a reasonable time to read my novel. The agent threw the manuscript at me. You would have thought I'd tossed a canister of mustard gas into her office. She called me a pervert, telling me to get out of her office. She was so deep in the closet my novel must have given her the vapors.

I eventually gave up on agents and sent it to Simon and Schuster, Random House . . . really, the list is as long as your arm. I couldn't get arrested.

Eat your hearts out. *Rubyfruit Jungle* is still selling and it could have been yours.

June Arnold, the Houston heiress, and Parke Bowman had started a small feminist publishing house called Daughters, Inc. They paid me a thousand dollars and printed five thousand copies of the novel. I sent half the money to Mom, but not the book, which Daughters brought out in 1973. Pretty soon Daughters couldn't keep up with the demand. Without one ad, one review, one anything, the book, sold out of the back of cars, or by mail since big bookstores wouldn't carry a line from such a small publisher, chalked up close to 100,000 copies.

Both women wanted to publish new fiction. They didn't want to be servants to *Rubyfruit Jungle* even if it was selling. They also published my second novel, *In Her Day*. The demand for that overloaded their circuits.

Originally they had wanted to publish five new books each season, ambitious for such a small house. They were the first feminist publishing company that I know of, which also complicated their business life. Their mission was to let women's fiction see the light of day.

At that time, most commercial women's fiction offered women as men wanted to see them—*Valley of the Dolls* kind of stuff. Big numbers, no soul.

Ironically, my success was interfering with June and Parke's mission. They could publish me or publish new writers.

They asked whether I minded if they sold me out, so to speak, to a company that could handle the demand. It was okay with me.

Several years after publishing *Rubyfruit,* they sold the rights to Bantam Books. Elly Sidel, curly-haired and wildly funny, bought the book for Bantam, which was then a reprint or paperback house. Bantam is now also a hardcover house.

Although they didn't have to do it, June and Parke split the paycheck with me. June had inherited a great deal of wealth, and like most Texas folks, she was extremely generous. Parke, or Patty, didn't care about money one way or another. I remember standing on the corner of Seventh Avenue near Bleecker Street, outside the Daughters office, with a check for $125,000 in my hand. It seemed like a dream: Poverty that grinds you to dust, and suddenly a mess of money.

I walked down to the main Chase Manhattan Bank in Wall Street and opened an account, even though I was still living in Washington. I didn't take a cab. It hadn't sunk in that I could afford one.

When Mom finally read the book she was all beshit and forty miles from water.

"Everyone will think I'm that mean mother," she wailed.

Mother could be mean as malaria. She could also be funny, but in the novel I concentrated on the malaria.

Mother could pitch all the hissy fits she wanted. She was in Florida. I was in D.C. and damn glad of it. If I'd lived within shouting distance of her, she would have shot me.

Once I paid her outstanding bills, her attitude changed to one of sweetness and light.

When you write your first novel your family snatches it up, eagerly

searching for themselves and horrified when they find what they're looking for.

So I didn't put any part of Mother in my second novel. She didn't speak
to me for months after that.

As for Aunt Mimi, she lost no opportunity to sob at how I was ruining
the family. For her my novels were a dehydrating experience.

Jerry said I'd obliterated all chances of a political career as well as any
other kind of career. No one would hire me. He'd be my friend for life,
but he wasn't taking me to any more company dinners.

Gloria Steinem liked the book.

Charlotte Bunch liked it, too.

Eugene, Kenny, Wade and Terry have never said a word to me about
any of my books, which only goes to prove what I've always suspected:
"real men" don't read fiction.

Rubyfruit brought me notoriety, a ton of hate mail, numerous threats on
my life including two bomb threats, increased outrage from the conservative wing of the feminist movement and scorn from the radical dykes.

Straight people were mad because I was gay. The dykes were mad
because I wasn't gay enough.

The only creature to take it all in stride, apart from myself, was Baby
Jesus.

54

A Hop, Skip
and a Jump

I WROTE *RUBYFRUIT* IN 1971. DAUGHTERS PUBLISHED IT IN 1973 AND Bantam reprinted it in 1977. Soon after the Bantam deal I found a very young Wendy Weil to be my literary agent. She worked for a well-established agent, Julian Bach, in those days.

Belonging to a kicked-around group means enduring unpleasant events, whether it's having an ugly word flung at you, being denied a job or housing or being cast aside even from social discourse. I experience such unpleasantries. Perhaps you have as well. Irritating, painful and sometimes dangerous as being an outsider can be, poverty is worse.

My life changed the day I finally had money.

The several years following 1972 weren't entirely uneventful, but hustling for funds, working and trying to write often drained the days of their luster.

A few memories remain, such as studying in Princeton's library. A friend in the archeology department got me a library card. I'd moved to a small farm in Cranbury, New Jersey, to be close to Princeton. The campus, beautiful and serene, allowed me the luxury of enjoying it without having to go to classes. I proofread novels at night for money. No one cared if a proofreader was gay.

The chapel at Princeton was my second refuge. The stained-glass windows are exceptionally fine for a small church.

In spring the wisteria with pendulous lavender blossoms drapes over the stone buildings. Aaron Burr's father was president of what was then named the College of New Jersey. Burr himself attended, as did James Madison. Since I respect James Madison, I paid attention to Princeton. The past is never dead for me; it rides on my shoulder like a becapped and jeweled monkey.

I felt alive again being on a farm, although a farm in New Jersey is different than Hanover Shoe Farm—smaller, different crops. Folks down the road had horses. That's what really mattered.

Baby Jesus loved it. She'd sit under the purple morning glories covering the tractor shed.

Once my research was over and I'd finished *In Her Day,* I had an opportunity to teach a semester at Goddard College, in Plainfield, Vermont.

Goddard was as close to an experimental college as one could get. The faculty was interesting, many of them genuine academics but willing to try new things. *Rubyfruit* attracted them. Probably it was the only college in America that would have taken a chance on me.

I loved teaching. I know writers are supposed to hate it, but watching another person handle the language delights me. They all come to writing classes in college worried about character development and plot; some are already thinking about an agent. The cart's before the horse. They know nothing about their tool, English. You've got to crawl before you can walk, so I took them right back to nouns and verbs, active voice versus passive—as a writer sees language, not a grammarian. A writer doesn't need to know the subject of an elliptical clause. It's nice but not necessary. What is necessary is to *hear* it. Language is music, and few languages are capable of such wide cadence as our own.

As I knocked around from pillar to post, from Plainfield, Vermont, to New York City, to Cazenovia, New York, I learned to rise at five or five-thirty in the morning, write until I had to go to work and then come home and write until I fell asleep.

People make demands on you. Not being a social person helped me write. Over the years I've disappointed many people by not attending parties or dinners. I hate those affairs. If an event doesn't involve work, theater, horses or hounds, I don't want to go. Because I wasn't social I made few friends. It's no different today. I'd sooner bleed from the throat than go to most cocktail parties, and fund-raisers are a descent into hell.

I'll do it if I have to or if I'm the point person raising the funds.

What I do love is having tea with a friend. Because I want to know what people think and feel, I like intimate gatherings. Teatime is my favorite time of day, the best time to see people. Also, since I don't drink, having tea spares me the ordeal of dinner, where you run the risk of your dinner partner or partners bending their elbow and becoming increasingly less witty. A few people become more witty with alcohol—precious few.

What strikes me most about those floating years between the first publication of *Rubyfruit* and the release by Bantam is that they had little emotional effect on me.

Even a year's stint in Boston, an exquisite architectural jewel, left hardly a mark. The one thing I most remember from my time in Boston was the corruption of Elaine Noble, the first openly gay elected person. She did business with crooked folks and turned state's witness to escape any charges that might be brought against her. What sorrow she brought on herself, and what sorrow she brought on all those who elected her.

Boston brought me Santa Ferari, Ann Lewis, and Ann's brother, Representative Barney Frank, each of whom I see intermittently, usually at one of those fund-raisers I don't much like. While Ann, then deputy director of Clinton's re-election campaign, and Barney are acquaintances whose political acumen is never to be underestimated, Santa had become a friend. She raises funds for a house where women with AIDS can live.

Our friendship had an unlikely beginning; we both dated the same woman, the above-mentioned Elaine Noble, called by us and others "Ignoble."

Before Elaine took her waltz with the sleazy boys, she worked hard. Full of energy and that bombast so peculiar to professional politicians, she helped me buy two buildings on Marlborough Street near Massachusetts Avenue. In the early seventies they were cheap. Broke as I was, Linda Damico—a saint, really—lent me five thousand dollars for a down payment. I met Linda at a summer school for feminists called Sagaris. I'd helped found it but didn't administer it. She was one of the students, a quiet, thoughtful person, a true thinking person.

These two buildings brought me $225,000 worth of debt. Finally I was in business. You're nothing in America if you don't have debt. All those years that I paid cash, had no credit cards, was clean as a whistle, were utterly worthless in our perverted economy. Now I had a shitload of debt, and all of a sudden the banks loved me.

Elaine Noble helped me find the buildings, she put me in touch with John and Linda Lecoq, the owners, and she took a share of the properties. Years later I sold those two buildings as the co-op boom was starting. I did okay.

While my romance with Elaine was short-lived, I wasn't upset. I rarely was, because I neither understood romantic love nor wished to understand it. It looked like neurosis shared by two. So when the bloom was off the rose I was fine. This relaxed attitude was not always shared by the other party.

Elaine, however, could not have cared less. She was wrapped up in what appeared to be the beginning of a good career and was meeting lots of women who were falling all over her. My southern worldview, with its emphasis on honor in capital letters and underlined three times, wearied her.

Santa, with her green eyes, rapier wit and good looks, caught her eye. Well, to tell the truth, Santa caught everyone's eye. Elaine was happy that I didn't throw roadblocks up as she drove in the direction of the appealing, alluring and available Santa.

Poor Santa. She was the one who bore the brunt when Elaine's dealings became public. All the more painful since Santa had given her ample warning that if she continued doing business with the wrong people her career would flame out.

Elaine's apartment was on the ground floor of 401 Marlborough Street, and mine was on the floor above it, in the rear. We had keys to each other's apartments, but this turned out to be more useful for her than for me. Since she was out all the time, I endlessly walked her Welsh Terrier, a dog with an inexhaustible voice.

One evening I came downstairs and she was sitting with a state senator who had a reputation for financially advantageous deals allied to political favors. When he left I said, "Elaine, you'd better be careful. You're running with the wrong people."

Flushed, she replied, "You'll never get anywhere in politics. You need a little shit to fertilize the rose."

I told her if she cut a deal with this particular politician she'd better move out of the building. She moved next door, and soon after moved in with Santa.

But the damage was done. It took a year for the fertilizer to become public knowledge.

Elaine was the second person to tell me I'd never make it in politics. The first was Robin Morgan, who said, "You don't know how to dissemble."

The terrible thing is, they're right. In order to succeed, you have to lie.

If I didn't lie about being gay at a time when you could be shot for it, worst case, or ostracized, more common response, why would I lie about anything else?

That doesn't mean I don't forget things or repress others or plain make mistakes. If you have total recall, I feel sorry for you. Repression is like nicotine—it soothes in small doses. Also, if you have total recall you will be bereft of friends. No one likes to be reminded of exactly what they did at Old U at that wild fraternity party.

If my mind is clear, I will not lie. I guess I won't be your president or even your senator or state senator.

From Boston I moved to Cazenovia, New York, where I taught for a year at the Women's Writers' Center, housed in Cazenovia College.

Cazenovia, twenty miles east of Syracuse, glistens with white clapboard houses, stone houses, big houses on the lake. It's gorgeous. The upstate New Yorkers are like New Englanders, taciturn, distant, wary. Once they decide they like you they are friendly. It's the reverse of the South, where everyone is warm on the surface. No wonder Yankees get so confused. They think we're fakes because we're so welcoming while they associate that warmth with family or years of friendship. Our rules are different, that's all. Underneath we take just as long to size someone up, but we don't feel the need to stick people out in the cold while we are making up our minds.

Another huge difference is that a southerner hates to say no. We have evolved elaborate ways to refuse things or offer criticism without saying no or being unduly harsh—in public. At home and with your best friends you can be scalding. Yankees feel as though they've fallen into a vat of marsh-mallow because they're curt with one another and feel no need to smooth things over. It's a generalization but more often true than not. It's an odd Yankee who does the two-step of refusal without seeming to say no.

Here I was amidst the infidels, the people who had carried off the family silver. I looked for our pattern but didn't find it.

A local realtor, dead now, complained to the president of Cazenovia that I was teaching lesbianism. The president gave her a copy of my course list, which included lots of Euripides, and told her she was off the mark.

The funny thing was, I'd never met my defender. For him it was a matter of principle even though I was employed not by Cazenovia College, but by the Women's Writers' Center.

This was the first time a straight man had stood up for me.

The second wonderful thing was the Genesee Valley Hunt. I could see the hunt off. They go early up there because of the cold. They start cubbing in August, and hunting is over by Christmas.

Upstate New York has good horses, all breeds. The state legislature has passed legislation to make the state hospitable to horsemen. Consequently, there are large breeding operations, especially for Thoroughbreds and Standardbreds.

There's polo at Skaneateles and driving everywhere. The estate, Lo-renzo, at the west side of Cazenovia Lake, hosted a driving competition while I lived there.

Another wonderful thing was that Mom visited me. She had visited me once before, in Boston, but it took less effort to get her to Cazenovia in June when the weather was perfect, the nights crisp and the days warm.

Mother and I walked everywhere. We gardened. We rode out to stables looking at horses. We ate her fried chicken and greens, drank vats of ice-cold Coca-Cola and found that we could be good friends.

One evening we walked along the two gardens that ran the length of the yard, which had to be about a quarter of an acre. A lovely apple tree graced one of the gardens, a small ruins by the canal, the other. We heard a sorry mewing and found a long-haired calico, a half-grown kitten, under the apple tree. Undernourished, full of fleas, she was not an impressive sight. We raced her to the vet, cleaned her up and introduced her to Baby Jesus and her sidekick, Frip, a big black and white cat who had joined the family, too.

Cazenovia, as Mom named the cat, grew into an animal of such beauty people would stop and stare at her when they first visited me.

I hated to put Mom back on the plane to Florida. It was the first time I realized how much I loved her.

She may not have been the best mother. She was certainly a strict disciplinarian, and her remarks cut to the bone, but she was the only mother I knew. Her visit to Cazenovia brought out a softer side. Maybe I'd matured enough to let her be and maybe she'd matured enough to stop giving orders.

I sat down and wrote *Six of One,* a novel about Mother and Aunt Mimi starting when they were children. I cleaned it up to get it published!

ANYONE CAN WRITE ONE BOOK. ALMOST ANYONE. FEWER PEOPLE CAN write a novel, as fiction is difficult. The true test is writing the second and then the third work of fiction. By the time you fire off that third one, you're either a writer or you're not. If you don't know it, everyone around you does. A fiction writer lives or dies on the page.

Six of One lifted me up and over. I was the real deal.

And with the royalties from *Rubyfruit,* I could sit down and think about what I wanted to do next.

I didn't have to think long. Marion Rosenberg, who once worked for Elliot Kastner, the producer, invited me to Los Angeles to sniff around the film business.

The five preceding years hadn't changed me inside. It took Hollywood to do that.

Dead Fathers

MOTHER'S STATIONERY, BRIGHT YELLOW WITH CORAL LETtering, brightened the mail. Her letters stood out from the others like a goldfinch amidst the sparrows.

Packed for California, ready to go, I picked up the mail that had dropped through the mail slot, carefully removing it from underneath Baby Jesus, who craved paper. If you put a postage stamp in an empty concert hall she'd sit on the postage stamp.

I opened Mom's letter first. An obituary fell out for James Gordon Venable, world-class weight lifter and part of the Bob Hoffman team at York Barbell in Pennsylvania.

Mother wrote, "He went to his grave with a secret. This was your father." She declined to elaborate. I had known she knew who he was all along.

The Venable name, one of the great names of Virginia, sounded lovely even if I couldn't claim it legitimately. Like all southerners, I knew the great family names: Custis, Valentine and Byrd, to name a few. Nathaniel Venable founded Hampden-Sydney College and Colonel Charles Venable, aide-de-camp to Robert E. Lee, stood by his side at Appomattox. After the war he became a mathematics professor at the University of Virginia. It's a family with a history of service.

My natural father's wife survived him, as did a son.

I called York Barbell and talked to John Terpak, an Olympian from 1936 who had worked with Gordon, as he was called. He said everyone had adored Gordon. He was a great guy with a drinking problem. In the end it killed him. His liver gave out. Mr. Terpak wasn't surprised when I told him I was Gordon's natural daughter. He remembered Gordon's troubles in the mid-1940s and he said that's when his drinking increased. Mr. Terpak said I could drive up and meet him at work.

John Terpak himself was in his seventies. Fit, energetic and handsome, he looked better than most men in their forties. Another great one from that time and group was John Grimek, also a sensational-looking guy who hits the iron just like he did in the old days.

Bob Hoffman was dead by then, as were many of my father's cronies. Mr. Terpak recalled the days when they all built York Barbell in the depths of the Depression. Gordon, a gifted athlete, boxed, lifted weights and missed the 1936 Olympics by a few pounds. He peaked during the war and by the time the Olympics were reinstituted he was over the hill. Until 1943 he was heavyweight lifting champion of North America.

After his competitive career was over, Gordon edited magazines, notably *Strength and Health*.

He had wondrous hand-eye coordination. At the risk of bragging, so do I. I come by it honestly.

"You look like Gord" was all that Mr. Terpak said to me.

My father had betrayed his wife and then abandoned my mother. He deserved no credit for either. However physically strong he was, he was weak.

I guess if you're going to hate people for being weak you're going to hate most of the world because we're all weak in some fashion or another, at one time or another.

I prayed for his soul.

I never met my paternal half brother. He and his mother, if she's still alive, probably don't know I exist. I suppose if they read this book they'll know but we're all too far down the road for it to make much difference.

Mother should have been hit upside the head for her thirty years of lying to me, but her fear that I would ditch her overwhelmed her usual good judgment on the larger emotional issues.

The funny thing is, you'd think I would be the one to fear being ditched. I called Mother and told her what I'd learned.

"He was thirty. Juliann was eighteen. He should have known better."

"Did anyone talk to her?"

"You try talking to someone in love. Nothing you can do but let them learn the hard way."

"Guess they both did."

"He got off scot-free."

"Who knows, Mom? Maybe he suffered inside. People cover up pretty good."

I heard a suspicious puff. "Yeah."

"Mother, are you smoking again?"

"No" came the not very convincing reply.

"I smoke Montecristos when I can get my hands on them. I can't say anything."

"Oh boy, Cuban cigars. Your father loved those cigars."

"Romeo and Juliet, and when he couldn't buy a good cigar he contented himself with White Owl."

"I didn't like those." She paused. "You have anything else to tell me?"

"No. Done is done."

"Yeah, that's how I look at it." Another puff. "You got a girlfriend yet?"

"Nope."

"You aren't very successful as a gay person, are you?"

"Mother, I haven't had time."

"Before it used to be 'I haven't the money.'"

"Right. I don't think I can live off love. I'm not getting involved unless I have resources."

"Got some now."

"Yeah, but I need the time to establish my career."

"Did I do something wrong?"

This was a shock. Mother never did anything wrong and if she did she never admitted it.

"I can't afford to talk on the phone that long."

"Ha. Ha," she drily replied.

"I'm not ready."

"Think all this stuff about Gordon and Juliann set you back? You sure shy away from settling down."

"No. Anyway, how could it? I didn't know about Gordon."

"I don't want to die and have you alone in the world."

"You're too mean to die. I've always been alone."

"You need someone to take care of you."

"Mother, for God's sake, that's the last thing I need. And with my luck, I'll wind up taking care of someone else. I can't do that. I have to write."

"I got those release forms you sent me."

Harper and Row, my publishers in hardback for *Six of One,* insisted that Mother and Aunt Mimi sign release forms before they published the book because they feared lawsuits.

I told my editor, Harvey Ginsburg, "Where I come from we don't use lawyers, we use guns."

He laughed but insisted the papers must be signed.

"Sign them and send them to Harper and Row," I told Mother.

"You'd better come down here and we can talk about it."

56

Two Old Bandits

MY DETOUR TO FLORIDA ON THE WAY TO CALIFORNIA IRRI-
tated me. I'd bought a used Rolls-Royce because everyone who'd ever
been to Hollywood said, "You are what you drive." Then, by God, I'd be
the best.

Mother's first order of business was for me to cart her butt all over south
Florida. There wasn't a crossroads we missed from Five Points to Coral
Gables. We'd reach a stoplight. She'd press the electric window button,
and the glass would purr down. She'd start a conversation with the victim
in the adjoining car. I could have killed her.

She loved the Silver Shadow. I liked Silver Clouds better but they're
harder to drive, so I'd bought a newer Silver Shadow, a metallic sand with
a coral pinstripe.

I drove her to church. I drove her to the grocery store. I drove her to
work. I drove her to the beach. I drove her to Aunt Mimi's. That was
jubilation. I drove her to Julia Ellen and Russell's. I drove more miles than
if I had driven straight through to California on Route 10.

Time was pressing. I urged her to sign the release form. She picked up a
Bic pen, sat at the kitchen table and held her hand over the dotted line.
She put the pen down. Picked it up again.

Pen poised in midair, she said, "Honey, I could sign this so much easier
if I had an emerald-cut diamond on my hand."

She skipped to the car. I drove her to her favorite jeweler. She picked
out a sparkling emerald-cut diamond, not too gaudy. The carat size of a
diamond depends on your hand size as well as your pocketbook. Anyone
wearing a gigunda diamond, too big for her hand, is marked a crass.
Mother might be crass but she wasn't going to look it.

She put the diamond against her wedding band. We drove home. She signed the release form.

"Mom, you were supposed to help me with Aunt Mimi. She hasn't signed anything yet and I've got to boogie."

We hopped in the car, a wonderful car but too flashy. By now I realized I would have preferred a Bentley. Of course, even being able to own a car was magic.

We reached Aunt Mimi's. She lay in wait. I was handed an ice-cold Coke. Pickled eggs and fried chicken awaited me. Aunt Mimi, a good cook, sat me at the head of the table. She and Mother sat on either side of me. Her smooth macaroni salad tasted like ambrosia. Her fried chicken, same recipe as Mother's, crunched. She had even taken some chicken off the bones for the cats back at Mom's. However, she called Baby Jesus "B.J." since she thought the cat's name was sacrilegious.

"B.J. will love this. Frippie too."

Needless to say, I was suspicious.

Aunt Mimi sipped an iced tea. "You know, kid, getting old is hard. I can't work like I used to. Neither can Mearl, and we have to help out the kids from time to time."

"Aches and pains."

"The day will come when Mearl can't make the good living we're used to—"

"How much, Aunt Mimi?"

"Why, I am offended!"

Mother kicked me under the table. "What she means to say, Sis, is she loves you so much. After all, you were the one who drove in the blizzard and held her all the way back from Pittsburgh."

"That tiny undernourished baby." Aunt Mimi got misty.

Why was I going to Hollywood? Clearly, these two were Academy material.

"Aunt Mimi, I am eternally grateful. Why, I wouldn't be where I am if it weren't for you."

She beamed and shoved another piece of fried chicken my way. "I'm no slouch myself. Why, if I were a young woman, who knows what I'd do."

"You'd be the best." I sighed a big sigh, hoping I could get out of there without being skinned alive. "Well, let me send those release forms up to Harper and Row."

I finished my food while Mother brought me my purse, ostensibly so I could find a pen for Aunt Mimi but really so I could fish out my flattening checkbook.

I wrote out a check for $2,000. That may seem a small sum. Money was worth more then. Why is it that money keeps getting devalued? Think what $150,000 was worth in 1831. Weird. Anyway, judicious hints from Mother let me know that was what was left on Aunt Mimi's mortgage.

I know she never told anyone, but she and Mother celebrated plenty. They'd put one over on the college-educated kid. I knew it was coming. What the hell. It gave them far more pleasure than if I had just paid up without the theatrics.

Before the kitties and I finally left for the West Coast, I had to go through the death drill one more time.

As I walked to the car Mother busied herself making kitty nests in the backseat. We put a dirt box on the back floor on top of plastic sheeting.

Baby Jesus enjoyed riding in the Rolls. She didn't much like other cars but she tolerated the Shadow. Frip and Caz despised it. They'd cry until they fell asleep.

We also put a travel box, door open, on the backseat so they could go in and out. It made the two nontravelers feel safer.

I kissed Mom goodbye. She had packed a big basket for me. Aunt Mimi gave me a round plastic Tupperware container filled with her macaroni salad. I was supposed to return the Tupperware, of course.

"Kid." Mom stood by the driver's door, her hands on her hips. "I love you."

"Love you too, Mom."

Then she waved me goodbye with her left hand turned toward me, palm inward, so the diamond would spray rainbows.

57

18th Century-Fox

THE UNITED STATES UNFOLDS LIKE A TREASURE CHEST OF SOILS, crops, small towns and big mountains. Doesn't matter whether you take Route 10, Route 40 or Route 94 way up north, you leave the dense hickory and oak forests of the eastern seaboard, plunge into the Appalachians, once taller than the Rockies, and come out in the rich valleys of Ohio or Tennessee. Delta soil, rich as gold, puts envy in the hearts of those of us who farm. The Mississippi floods cyclically, but each time she does she makes up for her damage by leaving those rich alluvial deposits.

America is a series of river crossings; those rivers made us rich. They left the soil that has made us the breadbasket of the world, whether it's the James or the Ohio, the Mississippi or the Missouri. The great rivers define us and made transportation possible until the railroads revolutionized life in the 1830s and 1840s.

The flat plains appealed to me, the blue sky overhead startling by its vastness. Most coastal Americans don't like the Midwest, but I love it. But then I love farming.

Each region of our country is distinct but the people are good. Didn't matter if I was in Kansas or the sparse expanse of New Mexico, people are good.

I'm so busy now I can't drive across America or Canada like I used to do. About once a year I'd take a train or the car. It's the old story. When you have the time you don't have the money, and when you have the money you don't have the time.

Baby Jesus rode in my lap. Sometimes she'd sit on the pillow next to me so she could gaze out the window. When we finally dropped down through the San Bernadinos, the megalopolis spreading before us, I was amazed at how much we've done and how fast. In 1910 California's population was 2,377,549. Los Angeles had 102,479 people.

It was about to be bumped up in 1973 by one human and three cats.

Californians like to think they're worlds apart from Florida; they are not, at least not in southern California, because northern California is a different state. The architecture surviving from the turn of the century and the twenties is identical. Those small wooden bungalows with big awnings to ward off the harsh sun, the Spanish haciendas with red tile roofs, the nasty ranches from the fifties. In Los Angeles you have mountains behind you, whereas in Florida you have alligators, armadillos and cottonmouths. In California the cottonmouths were people.

The sun bleaches out color quickly in both places, but California, semi-arid, luxuriates in crystal-cool nights.

While I belong in the Blue Ridge Mountains, certainly no farther west than Lexington, Kentucky, I like southern California. I wish I could have seen it in the teens and the twenties when Douglas Fairbanks Sr. and Mary Pickford rode through the orange grove on La Brea.

Despite the grotesque development, the callous disregard for flora and fauna, remnants of the early beauty remain tucked away in canyons or in parts of Griffith Park.

Aunt Mimi worried that the Big One would hit and I'd sink into the Pacific.

"Don't worry," I said, "the fish will reject it."

She thought I was making light of the San Andreas Fault, but people worry too much. If it hits, it hits. There are worse things that can happen to you than a natural disaster. Granted, the natural disaster might kill you, but in the long run the things people do to themselves are far more damaging than what nature dishes out.

THE FILM BUSINESS IS *SUI GENERIS.* YOU CAN BE A BIG NOISE IN REAL estate or newspapers or ball bearings, but it won't prepare you for film or TV.

Nor will all the film classes at all the schools in America, including my alma mater, New York University, one of the best, or USC or UCLA. Until your ass is on the line you'll never feel the heat. You're sitting on a stove.

The first person I met, pure serendipity, was Ronnie Shedlo, a producer who had been Errol Flynn's last secretary. He wore around his neck a gold button from one of Flynn's jackets with a beautiful inscribed *E* emblazoned on it.

He regaled me with tales of his boss and the studio days in Hollywood, which I quickly began thinking of as "Hollyweird." He trooped me through 20th Century–Fox, Marion Rosenberg in tow, as they were old friends. He even drove me out to Flynn's last house up in the hills.

I loved Fox. I secured a pass thanks to Ronnie and cruised in with my Rolls-Royce. I drove an important car, therefore I had to be important.

The soundstages do to me what Westminster Abbey does to tourists. I get chills in a soundstage, empty or working, and my mind can write and shoot a film in ten minutes. If only the body could keep up with the mind—or more accurately, if only the money men understood that to make money you take risks, in material and in people.

They never will get it. I learned with lightning speed that everyone can say no in the film industry but fewer than five people have the balls to say yes.

This town runs on fear. In the beginning, Mack Sennett, D. W. Griffith, Charlie Chaplin, Mary Pickford, Douglas Fairbanks Sr., Mabel Normand, the Gish sisters—they were young. They made it up as they went along. There were no rules. Even the producers, the money men like Goldfish (later changed his name to Goldwyn), Lasky and Zanuck—they were young, too, for the most part. Their energy exploded out across the country. You can't watch the silents without feeling that energy. Even the producers loved the process. They knew how to make movies. Today, once the camera is rolling most producers are lost, and I guarantee you the boys at the studio are more than lost. They couldn't find their way around a shoot if you put a compass in the heel of their boot.

Ronnie Shedlo told me, "They can all read but they can't shoot. That means they chew up writers. They take it out on the writer. Cover your back."

It was blue-chip advice.

The second person who helped me was Ernest Borgnine and his beautiful wife, Tova, whom I had met at a party. Mr. Borgnine hasn't a snobbish bone in his body. I'd written three novels by that time, the last of which, *Six of One,* had made it onto best-seller lists, but I was hardly on anyone's A-list. He could have cared less. I interested him and Tova. They're thinking people.

"The better prepared you are, the more flexible you can be," he once said to me.

I always thought that Borgnine was born to play Mussolini. I saw the cable movie about Mussolini with George C. Scott in the title role, and while Mr. Scott is a grand actor, Borgnine should have played Il Duce.

But then again, Ernest Borgnine can play anything. He's a real actor. So many others are only stars.

While I was learning the ropes and sometimes hanging on them, I found a house on Outpost Drive thanks to Delphine Mann at Jon Douglas Realty Agency.

The cats liked it. That sealed the deal. Better to be west in Los Angeles than east, but I liked the hills and Outpost felt more like an older California, the one I missed by virtue of birth.

Since I had next to no furniture I pioneered the minimalist look. I really hate that look but when money's tight you might as well make a virtue of necessity.

Stairs in the back led to the top of the canyon, where I could sit and watch the blue Pacific. Baby Jesus walked with me and we'd sometimes sit there until the big fog bank rolled across the waters at about five in the afternoon. Frip and Cazenovia, too lazy for the climb, reposed in the gazebo below.

The funny thing is, I don't think I could afford that same house today, prices are so outrageous.

The hunger in Los Angeles for product makes you feel like the main course at a vampire's banquet. I knew I could write terrific screenplays but I had to learn to translate my ideas. I pitched and pitched until I could do it without wanting to throw up.

At first I resisted the idea that a movie story should be reducible to one sentence. For instance, *War and Peace* could be pitched as "A man can't understand women but learns to understand war in Russia of 1812." How about *Bambi*? "Little fawn learns man is evil and grows up to protect his own."

You can probably come up with better ones than I can. Reducing a complex novel to one sentence shocks those of us who revere texts. In Hollywood they revere nothing—not even money, because they waste too much of it to really love it. If I ran a studio or a mini-major like Orion they'd be running in the black pretty damn fast because I know where the slush funds are flowing. I hate waste as much as I hate penny-pinching. You can make a profit and treat your people to some luxuries without being wasteful. When you wind up writing a contract for a star that requires you to pay for his or her twenty-person entourage, you're wasteful and stupid. Stupid because if you do it for X, then Y has got to have it, too. Waste in capital letters, and honey, that's not the half of it—but you didn't pick up this book to find out how to run a studio efficiently and profitably.

It all comes down to trust. If you don't trust your talent, you can't maximize your assets, and in film the assets are the *talent*. It's so simple.

Back to the one-liner. A movie, unlike a novel, cannot be complex. A great novel can have a main story line and three to six subordinate story lines with characters developing and changing in each one.

The absolute best you can manage in film—and this is pushing it—is one main story line and two subplots. You're much better off with one main story line and one subplot.

I finally did learn how to reduce the story. It's harder to reduce the main character but you can do that too. Writing for film, then, is like an accordion. Once the bandleader nods at you, you can open the instrument.

Where was my nod? I was ready, willing and able.

It came from exactly where you would think it would: Roger Corman. If Academy Awards were presented for giving people a start in this business, one would go to this remarkable Oxford scholar. He makes cheap movies. They have strong stories, appealing unknown actors and first-time directors. The product does not look like a 1940s MGM film, with a focus so deep you fall into Arizona. But you watch them because of the story.

Frances Kimbrough, his right-hand assistant, convinced him to take a chance on me. I was cheap—I worked for scale. We all did. I think even George Lucas, Jack Nicholson, and the list goes on and on, at one time worked for scale. In my case it was $12,000 minus 10 percent to Nancy Hardin, who was my film agent for five minutes. She left the Ziegfield Agency and I landed in the lap of Maggie Field, who was even younger than I was but took good care of me.

Frances, the Mother Teresa of fledgling screenwriters, taught me the format. My first screenplay, *Room to Move,* was about a truck driver who wanted to be Fred Astaire. My second screenplay for Roger was *Sleepless Nights,* a spoof of horror films, which years later was taken off the shelf and made as a straight slasher movie, no humor, called *Slumber Party Massacre.* I wish they'd had the guts to do the send-up version because it was pretty funny, on the page anyway.

Then I wanted to do a film set in a small southern town about four girls graduating from high school. Think of it as a female *Diner,* since the only way you can describe a movie not made is to describe one that has been made. It isn't *Diner,* of course, but has the same kind of feel, only in my case lots more sass. After all, Mack Sennett is my favorite director.

This project didn't get off the ground. I still don't know if Roger lost interest or if I wanted too much money.

I figure I'll make it one of these days because it's a timeless story: coming of age.

While I piloted muddy waters, Wendy Weil in New York remained my chief navigator. She offered a sane and classy counterpoint to the ruthless self-aggrandizement washing over me in California. Huge egos floated into meetings daily, egos unrelated to accomplishment. Worse, this was the time when middle-aged men started attending meetings in expensive workout clothes. They looked as though they were swaddled in parachute cloth. I resented the hell out of that. Business is business. Just because you're in southern California doesn't mean you don tennis warm-up clothes for a meeting. Putzes.

Putz is the operative word. I found to my dismay that I would be in a room full of men, yet be the only person with balls. If that doesn't kill your libido, nothing will. Much as I love women, I am not immune to the charms of the opposite sex—if they act like men.

Then came the purses. I'd walk into a meeting and some twit with a skinny leather tie would be rummaging through his purse, a rectangular leather affair a bit like a messenger's pouch from World War I.

This has nothing to do with being straight or gay. In truth, the straight men acted nellier than the gay men. It was quite confusing to a country girl.

Once I understood that no one knew what the hell they were doing, life became easier. I didn't expect anyone to exhibit even the minimum of taste; I certainly didn't expect them to read anything other than synopses (called coverage) of novels plus, of course, the trades, *Variety* and *Hollywood Reporter*. If somebody's name appeared in George Christy's column, they were in heaven.

Few places in America are as vulgar as Los Angeles. Even Dallas shows more restraint. The more vulgar it was, the more I loved it. It truly was funny because so much energy was expended on being so tacky. I conjured images of my cotillion drill sergeants swooning with the vapors on Little Santa Monica Avenue. It's not just people who are garnished; the architecture appears to have been designed by children: giant hot dogs for roadside eateries, pink elephants over a bar and so on.

What's funnier than the looming hot dogs or pink elephants is Rodeo Drive. There's nothing more idiotic than this attempt at aristocracy. Because everything is offered to you at ten times over cost—and sometimes more—it's supposed to be high-tone. Add to that the hilarity of people tiptoeing along the sidewalk as though they were in church. Money doesn't talk, it tiptoes.

The ultimate aphrodisiac: a suntanned bullshitter cruises up to Cartier in his rented (although we don't know that) Corniche, top down. He double-parks, dashes in, dashes out, big Panther watch glistening on his wrist. The whole point of Rodeo Drive is not just that you spend money but that other people must see you spend money. Commerce is confused with power. The power to buy is only that. Real power is saying, "Three hundred thousand troops will be shipping out to Bosnia." If they ship out, you have power.

I'm not sure anyone in Hollywood understands this, which may explain why they stay in their enclave. Leave and the illusion of power is shattered. The movies aren't just about an illusion on the screen, they're about the illusions of the people who make them: people who couldn't make it in Omaha.

Now, the fact that most people in the film business are rejects of one sort or another provides the fluctuating energy. Los Angeles, continually washed over by America's rejects, misfits and erratic geniuses, beats to a zigzag pulse. Whereas New York City, undergirded by old families as well as waves of immigrants from within the country and without, pulses with a much steadier energy.

I'd like to think I'm one of those erratic geniuses, but I may be a misfit. In that case, it's Miss Fit to you.

No one really belongs. Even if you've made ten hit movies or written ten, you can be replaced, and in time, you can count on being bounced out. When you define yourself by your work, then you're a product. For better or for worse, everyone is a product, everyone has a shelf life, and most relationships are about what you can do, not what you are. There's freedom but there's no stability. Los Angeles is the exact opposite of Japan.

If you have strong internal values, you'll survive. If not, you'll disintegrate and no one will give a damn except the tabloids.

While everyone in Hollywood gives lip service to celebrating individuality, they run with the pack. If Westerns make money, everyone makes a Western. Since no one has the balls to try something new or reinvent something old, they exhaust the genre. Those guys then get bumped off and a new set comes in and repeats the process. Nobody learns from film history.

The pack mentality makes for interesting encounters. My first big meeting at 20th Century–Fox involved three producers in their thirties. They had offices on the lot but were not 20th employees. I listened as they discussed a thriller. Four small dishes, like soy sauce dishes, were filled with what I thought was salt. They drank their morning coffee and sniffed this salt like snuff. I was so dumb I didn't realize they were jamming cocaine up their noses and had thoughtfully provided some for me. The thriller never materialized. None of these men were addicts but cocaine was the hip thing. The pack mentality was not invented by Los Angeles, but it's so over the top there.

One thing I picked up pronto was that there was an "in" drug crowd opposed to those who did not take drugs. Since I didn't take drugs I was hired only once by the "in" crowd. It was a harrowing experience. These two young men, the producers, never shut up, they contradicted themselves constantly, they sweated profusely and their emotions flew around like a balloon losing air.

I hope these boys have grown up. There are a lot of people in Hollywood who have cleaned up and have created better work because of it. But the drug crowd usually won't hire someone who isn't one of them. Anyone who thinks otherwise is smoking opium, forgive the pun. And anyone who thinks drugs still aren't a part of the business isn't looking. The people taking them have gotten better at hiding their problems.

Another worrisome habit was sex as metaphor. No matter what meeting I went to, bragging rights became part of the exchange. I listened. They bragged. There I'd be, talking about the project, focused on the task, and the producer would say something like, "This scene is a dry hump, let's get more juice in it." This coming from the mouth of a chub who couldn't hit a baseball if it was pitched underhand to him.

Perhaps because these men assumed I was exclusively gay, they felt compelled to treat me like one of the boys. If so, no wonder the boys made such bad movies. When you're that insensitive to the people around you, chances are you're also insensitive to material. Or maybe they were serving notice about how potent they were. If so it failed. Men who yak about sex betray their fragility.

The women I met were incredible, though. Sherry Lansing had just taken over 20th. She was good enough to see me and I was impressed by her directness, her ability to communicate clearly and her knowledge of the world she lived in. She was able to succeed without succumbing to the bullshit.

Joan Tewkesbury wrote *Nashville* and other films, too. She is funny, warm and technically skilled as well as imaginative (the latter two rarely are twined), and I adored both her and her husband. Watching Joan watch a movie is almost better than watching the movie itself.

Cruising up the coast to see polo matches helped me keep life in perspective. As long as I can be near a horse, I won't mess up too badly.

As I sat on the sidelines I had no idea that a few miles north, in Montecito, lived a woman who would be one of the great loves of my life and who would teach me not just about television but about myself.

It happened because of my Rolls-Royce.

A Rolls-Royce and Love

MARLO THOMAS HOSTED A STUPENDOUS PARTY AT HER BEVerly Hills home to support the Equal Rights Amendment. The amendment, passed by Congress, was now in the process of being ratified by the states. If fewer than three fourths of the states ratified it, then the amendment would not stand.

The feminist euphoria intoxicated liberals and middle-of-the-roaders. As I said before, I didn't believe that the amendment would pass in the South. However, a show of support was important.

Marlo Thomas rounded up women and men in the industry willing to attach their names to the controversial amendment. Since most people are chicken, and actors especially, how she managed this beats me.

Let me digress for a moment about why I think actors are chicken. For any role in any movie, play or television show there are hundreds of people who could perform the part. Disposability makes people fearful. For an actor, rejection is personal. It's your face, your body, your voice that's rejected. This does little for your sense of security.

On the way up, if you're fortunate enough to move up, a prudent person keeps politics out of the picture. Since you can so easily be replaced, why run the risk?

There are those who groan when an actor espouses a cause or political opinion, yet say nothing when the head of United States Steel does the same. Why is it okay for the industrialist to be an active citizen but not okay for the actor?

Naturally, this attitude grates on my nerves, but there is a cracked logic to it. Illusions again. If an actor speaks as a citizen, s/he moves forward as a real person. And we don't want them to be real. We want them as fantasies, as their last role, as our dream lover or whatever. An actor walks a fine edge. If the public turns from them as a person, it's a sure bet producers won't hire them. Great talent is no defense, Vanessa Redgrave being an obvious example.

However she did it, Marlo brought together hundreds of people, most of them young, at a time when few would admit to feminism; they risked being branded as lesbians. If Betty Friedan and Co. hadn't wimped out of the lesbian issue and turned on us, the media wouldn't have been so successful in exploiting the label.

Benjamin Franklin said, concerning the Revolution, "We must all hang together, or assuredly we shall all hang separately." Our political enemies as well as reporters out for a good story knew how to rattle people. Betty, by going public about "the lavender menace," handed them the issue on a silver platter. It's one thing to fight amongst ourselves, it's another to do it in public. Her mother never told her not to hang her dirty laundry in public.

Hundreds of people crowded onto the deck built over Marlo's pool. Robert Altman and Chevy Chase cut a swath through the ladies. Their support was genuine and much needed.

Shirley MacLaine held court, ignoring anyone she didn't think important enough for her attention. That meant she spoke mostly to Gloria Steinem and Bella Abzug. When Gloria introduced me to her, Shirley pointedly turned away. At that point in her life, Shirley apparently didn't shake hands with lesbians, especially if there were photographers in evidence. Gloria, looking embarrassed, then introduced me to Marlo Thomas, who, having a set of brass ovaries, couldn't have cared less. She was gracious.

Another gutsy lady was Joan Hackett. She sat at a table, smoking her pipe, laughing uproariously. She had read *Rubyfruit Jungle* and was happy to talk about that and anything and everything. Her early death to cancer was a loss to those who appreciate good acting as well as to the feminist movement.

But Shirley MacLaine shocked me because she's from Virginia. Did she leave voluntarily or did the matrons drive her out due to bad manners?

Kate Jackson, from Birmingham, did shake my hand when we were introduced but quickly moved on. It could have been that she knew who I was and also didn't want anyone to take a photograph of us together, or it could have been that she was so hot at the time, thanks to *Charlie's Angels,* that everyone wanted her attention. At least she didn't pretend I wasn't there. I gave her a lot of credit for being there in the first place.

Other women apart from Gloria and Marlo noticed I was being frozen out. Lily Tomlin pushed her way through the crowds, kissed me, put her arm around me and said, "How good to see you." She shamed the others. Lily, an original on every level, has a fighting heart. She guided me to a table of older women, one of whom headed a talent agency.

They invited me to sit down. I was certainly glad to do it. I'd sucked up my fill of cowardice and rudeness.

A reporter from the *Los Angeles Times* sashayed over to our table and said, "This must be the lesbian table."

I replied, "No, the other lesbians brought their husbands."

He got the hell out of there. Good thing. I'd have decked him. The ladies at the table laughed. Married or divorced and none of them actors, they didn't give a damn.

Marlo Thomas gives everything she's got when she believes in a cause. Most fund-raisers are deadly dull. This was a terrific party. The hostess spared no expense.

I watched the throng. Getting knocked around in movement fights toughened me, but then, those were intellectual battles. You could stand on your hind legs and slug it out. Betty Friedan never pulled her punches. She was up-front. By contrast, many of these people were engaged in cover-your-ass behavior. It had to do with their concept of their careers and not with personal or political beliefs. I preferred Betty. A fight can enable you. This felt cheesy, the fear. I was hardly the only lesbian or bisexual in the crowd. I was the only one honest about it.

After thanking my host two hours later, I walked down the long drive to the valet parking area. Standing there, waiting for her car to be driven up, was one of the most beautiful women I'd ever beheld. Average height, curvaceous figure, china blue eyes, alabaster skin with peachy highlights and flaming red hair, she could have been Deborah Kerr's double at the height of her beauty.

I recognized her as she recognized me.

"Rita Mae, what do you think of these transplanted Yankees?"

"That my great-granddaddy was right to take potshots at them."

She hollered, "You know, I wish a big Rolls-Royce would come on up here and take me home."

At that precise moment, the valet purred up in my Silver Shadow.

"Could I carry you home?"

Her jaw was on her ample bosom. She sputtered a minute, then laughed that southern war whoop laugh we learn at our momma's knee. "Girl, you got an angel on your shoulder or mojo." She accented the -*jo*. She scribbled her number. I scribbled mine. Her all-black 350SL varoomed right up behind my stately mechanical carriage. "Girl, you call me. I wanna ride in your Rolls-Royce and I wanna write a book."

I fell in love with Fannie Flagg at first sight.

59

The Eternal Triangle

HAILING FROM BIRMINGHAM, ALABAMA, FANNIE'S REAL NAME was Patricia Neal. Since that name was taken by one of the best in the business, her aunt suggested she use the name Fannie since it was lucky in show business, i.e. Fanny Brice. Of course, then Patsy embellished it and she became Frances Carlton Flagg.

Her momma still cooed "Patsy," as did the rest of the family. A carbon copy of her flame-haired father, Bill, Fannie learned about the business hanging out with her daddy. A member of IATSE, he was the projectionist at one of the Birmingham theaters. Miz Neal, as she was addressed, doted on her lone offspring. Marion and Bill fought over Fannie or used her in their sniping contests. They were wildly funny even when being just awful. There was a lot I understood about Fannie without being told. Luckily, I had but one funny, though sometimes cruel, parent. Fannie shuttled between two. They also drank. The fuss escalated with the volume of alcohol consumed.

It wasn't that they were overtly cruel to her but that she'd hear Momma's side of the story, then Daddy's. The first time I met Bill Neal he couldn't wait to throw me in the car, drive me to the theater and tell me what a wretched life he had with the "beached whale" (Marion was fat). But when he walked back in the house, where Marion would be holding court in the living room, she'd purr, "Bill, honey darlin', fetch me a cigarette," and he would. "Bill, honey darlin', I need me a cool refreshing libation." He scurried for a drink with tinkling ice cubes. Then Marion turned her charms on Fannie.

"Patsy, precious lamb, climb up into the attic and get out the family albums. I want to show Rita Mae our pictures." Fannie crawled into the stifling, airless attic and obediently fetched the albums.

Marion showed me each photograph, telling me every story, enduring interruptions from Bill as he rendered his version. She was amusing, imperious and in ill health when I met her. But then, how many southern women have used their delicate constitutions to run men ragged? Marion was many steps from death's door.

I adored her, but then I wasn't her daughter. She sent Bill on an errand, a wild-goose chase, so she could tell me her version of the marriage and how every single person who ever laid eyes on her beautiful daughter just knew she'd be a movie star.

Fannie loved and hated her parents. I think that's true for each of us; the balance of the love and hate is what shifts, according to their behavior and our subsequent maturity.

Like Juts, Fannie's parents generated electricity, laughter and an endless stream of commentary on the state of the world. Like Juts and Dad, they worked hard for a living, spurning handouts. To take money from the government even when falling on hard times was a shame no amount of later success could erase. They were southern to the bones. Juts was a Marylander to her bones, which is a restrained variation of the Alabama species. The only people who think they are superior to Marylanders are Virginians and certain species abiding in the Palmetto State, South Carolina. Marion and Bill, relieved of the hard work that snobbery entails, could be purely southern. They never mentioned the Duke of Buckingham or the Queen of England once. Aunt Mimi would have amused them, but then she amused me.

I first visited Mr. and Mrs. Neal after I'd known Fannie for six months.

Fannie did want to write. I worked with her as much as I could while scribbling away for Roger Corman. As with most of us from the South, her view of life was and remains anecdotal. Hysterical as the stories are, anecdotes don't substitute for structure.

She'd say, "Well, I'll tell the stories and you make it work."

"No. You'll never learn that way."

Since Fannie is severely dyslexic, reading her pages nearly blinded me. She earned my respect for not whining about her disability, a genuine hardship for a writer.

We'd meet at her small apartment in Westwood or my house on Outpost. I asked for no money. In fact, I've never asked for money in helping a writer. Literature is a calling, like the priesthood. I'll make money from my work but not from someone struggling to learn. Writing is bloody hard work so you'd better love it.

Fannie, original in her approach to material, truly had talent. I wasn't blinded by love. Actually, I never am when it comes to whether a person has talent or not.

We'd worked together for two months. I knew nothing about her private life. She never mentioned anyone. She owned a house in Montecito but I hadn't seen it.

One evening Arnie Reisman, who worked for WQBH, was in town from Boston and took Fannie and me to dinner. Emboldened by the presence of my friend, I decided to ask her direct questions once he left for the bathroom. But Arnie, enchanted with Fannie, had a cast-iron bladder. Finally I kicked him hard enough to raise a lump on his shin. He excused himself and went to the bathroom.

As he did, Betty White and her husband, Allen Funt, sidled over.

Betty, who has a sharp sense of humor, gives as good as she gets. When Fannie said, "Betty, you have such beautiful skin—and there's so much of it," Betty howled. She and Allen left, and within two minutes a gaggle of street people rushed in, crowding our table and asking for Fannie's autograph. Betty had sent them, making certain the maître d' was in on the joke.

By the time Arnie returned, I was helpless with laughter but I still knew nothing about Fannie other than that she had graduated from Ryder High School, did a funny impersonation of Lady Bird Johnson and now worked on *Hollywood Squares*.

We lingered over dessert. When we'd finished, Arnie rose to collect our coats.

Quickly I said, "Fannie, do you ever go out with women?"

She cocked her head. "Of course, you silly twit."

She didn't say she'd go out with me and I didn't ask but she invited me to her home in Montecito the next weekend.

Baby Jesus liked Fannie. For me, that was a strong recommendation because B.J. loathed humans. This isn't to say she'd leap into Fannie's lap; she wouldn't even leap into mine. But she wouldn't curl her lip when Fannie arrived to work in the library. A few times she sat on her papers, a good sign.

Fannie never made light of my passion for horses or regaled me with stories about the one time she rode a horse. I don't know why people do that but they do. Her friend Brett Somers prowled Santa Anita with her former husband, Jack Klugman, so Fannie had heard horse talk. She herself didn't ride and didn't want to, but she thought they were beautiful animals.

She mentioned there were horses in Montecito. I knew about the polo.

When I drove up to her house, a beautiful white frame house surrounded by large trees, the scent of eucalyptus swept me away. Montecito, serene, secure and spectacular, is rich in eucalyptus trees.

Two crazed Dalmatians bounced out, one black-spotted, one liverspotted, followed by a hollering Fannie.

"You come back here!"

The dogs vaulted onto me, which was fine. That's what dry cleaners are for.

The interior of the house was cozy, unpretentious and impeccably done. A gorgeous sofa in a floral print commanded a sitting room overlooking the pool. It really was a beautiful house and not the least bit garish.

Kate O'Reilly, not her real name, greeted me. She'd been a star in a long-running TV program and had left to take a prominent role in a film. Almost white-blonde, with a heart-shaped face, blue eyes and a great figure, she appeared every inch a woman ready to become a major movie star. She had looks, talent and drive. What she lacked was the ability to kiss ass. Just when her career should have rocketed it began to drop to earth. Approaching forty added to the tension.

Hollywood has never been kind to women who directly command their fates. Mary Pickford, the first international celebrity, directed, starred, produced (she was a fabulous producer) and got away with it because her mother, Charlotte, was the hatchet lady. So Mary maintained that outward femininity so important to the men of film. I don't know why they can't deal with women who are direct. Other men have learned how.

Kate, minus a hatchet lady, couldn't have hidden behind one anyway. She is a fundamentally honest person, a decent one.

Word got about that she was difficult. That was amended to "difficult dyke." It wasn't too long before she languished in her beautiful shared Montecito home wondering what the hell had happened.

Were Kate at the same career fulcrum today, she'd have a fifty-fifty chance of swinging up. In the mid-seventies, she had no chance. Today she's back on television.

Because she didn't marry to play the game, she might as well have announced that she was gay. Other people announced it for her. She kept silent but stiff-armed any attempts to create a bogus heterosexual life. She and Fannie had been together for eight years. The cracks in their relationship widened under the pressure.

Every relationship experiences rock and roll. A straight couple may elicit support from their community. A gay couple toughs it out in silence. Many of Kate and Fannie's friends knew they were lovers, but many didn't. The isolation, under the circumstances, had to have been extremely painful for Kate.

My heart went out to her. After my initial visit, the three of us palled around together. The more I knew Kate, the more I liked her.

Fannie admitted being attracted to me and not just to me but to Kate, which says something about their relationship.

Kate talked it over with me. She knew she was losing Fannie and she was bighearted enough to know if it hadn't been me it would have been someone else. She loved Fannie.

Fannie loved her, too, but Fannie would say, "I can't live with her anymore."

If there had been a way for the three of us to live together, I would have tried it because I grew to respect Kate and to value her for the generous and kind person she is. Like her Irish forebears, she engaged her crisis with good humor and the hope that she'd learn something.

Fannie hated Los Angeles. She'd figured out how to mask her beauty behind comedy. She hid her feelings, second nature to her given her childhood.

Fannie made a good living in television, but the growing sense of emptiness frightened her. It was rotten luck for Kate and Fannie that they reached career crises at the same time. Their relationship probably would have survived otherwise, but each was so exhausted by her individual worries there was little left over for the other. And to make matters worse for Kate, when the roles dry up, so does the money.

A time came when they decided to sell the house, which saddened me. Had I the money, I would have pitched in because that house suited them. It was too beautiful to lose. I wasn't making much, enough to pay my mortgage and groceries but not enough to hoard a stash for moments such as this.

The house sold in the twinkling of an eye. They rented a place in the Beverly Hills flats but the strain wore them down even further.

During this time my house was robbed. The thieves backed up a moving van and cleaned me out of everything except my books (thank God), the huge sofa I'd hauled off the streets of New York, and my dining room table. Everything else was gone: clothing, cutlery, everything. Luckily I had stored a few things in Virginia.

The police were great. My insurance company, however, was not. They argued that because I lived in Hollywood Hills the danger was higher. I got zero. The saving grace in all this was that what few family heirlooms we had remained with Mom. They only got what I'd bought.

Now you might wonder what my neighbors were doing when the van pulled up. This is Los Angeles. People move in and move out almost hourly. It didn't seem strange.

Since whoever robbed me knew my routine, I was pretty sure one of the men who built cabinets in the house must have been in on it. If not him, someone like him. They knew precisely when I would leave and precisely when I would return. And may they experience as much pain as they inflict. That's my wish for anyone like that.

Fannie refused to come to the house. She was sure they'd return to kill me. Since they had everything, I couldn't see why they'd bother to come back.

She shopped with me to buy clothing, a task I hate and she loves. I don't think I've ever looked as good as I did when I was with Fannie. She has a great eye for how something on the rack will look on you. I know how I'll look in Levi's and a white T-shirt and cowboy boots. That's it.

Kate helped out, too. She gave me some sweaters and odds and ends.

Fannie missed Montecito, so we rented a tiny bungalow not far from the ocean. She spent time in Los Angeles with Kate and time back in Montecito with me. I loved the place. It was quiet and I could write. Even better, we had rented it from Virginia Cherrill, who'd played the blind girl in Charlie Chaplin's *City Lights* and had been Cary Grant's first wife. She was Virginia Martini now, having married a World War II ace flying for the Free Polish. That was after she ditched the Earl of Jersey, her second husband. Mrs. Martini must have been in her seventies, but retained her beauty. She wasn't one to yak about her past life, as are so many old people. But if you asked, she would answer.

Since the silents are my favorite period of film history, I bristled with questions. She liked Chaplin but felt he had taken too much on himself. Making films became more of a burden than a joy for him. As for Cary Grant, of him she would say only, "He has the first dollar he ever made." Her stories of England during World War II were poignant and fascinating. She told me many times, "You don't know how lucky you are to be an American." I believed her.

I flourished with the solitude and my occasional chats with Mrs. Martini. Fannie would arrive for weekends and it would become a three-ring circus. Fannie tends to fill up a room.

Then there were her experiments. One time she decided she was spending too much money at the beauty parlor. She'd wax herself. Well, that was tedious and boring, so she thought she'd singe the hair off her legs. However, she dropped the match and I was treated to the spectacle of Fannie, her crotch in flames.

Another time she decided she had to have a Nash Rambler. None could be found. She bought a Pacer, another American Motors vehicle, without a doubt one of the ugliest cars ever built. She loved it. Out went the black-on-black 450 SL.

By now I'd sold the Rolls. I have a knack for knowing what cars and property will appreciate. I figured that a life in the arts is dangerous enough as it is, and I'd better learn how to make money in other places. I leased a car since I didn't want to tie up money right then.

I wanted to rent a Porsche. I love Porsches and think today's 911 Turbo widebody one of the greatest road cars ever manufactured. But Fannie hated the stick shift. I rented a 450 SL, a very good car indeed, and we knew she could drive it.

Kate would visit the Montecito house and roar with laughter. She didn't know how we could stand such a teeny place. My workroom was at one end of the house and Fannie's bedroom/workroom at the other. The cats dashed up and down the hallway between us, sometimes running out to the lemon grove next door.

Paintings by Oliver Messel—he was the famous art designer from the 1930s—hung in the living room. He'd given them to Mrs. Martini. I brought nothing personal to the place, nor had Fannie. Her stuff was in the Los Angeles house.

It was odd, living in a place that held nothing of your own, but I learned that wherever my books and cats are, that's home.

The Dalmatians stayed with Kate, a good thing, since the girls had never bothered to train them. I was up to the task but I hadn't the time because I was working steadily, thank God.

A large Saddlebred stable run by Cynthia Wood and her mother was on Ridge Road not two miles away. I enjoyed watching the horses get worked and I especially loved going over to the polo matches. I considered picking up my old line of work, hot-walking horses, but Fannie thought I was beyond that.

I met Margaret Mallory of Mallory Steamship Lines. Old by then, smart as a whip, she taught me a great deal about art. Her house on Ridge Road had more incredible paintings in it than many museums. She had a John Singer Sargent that almost made me cry when I studied it. He has been underrated until recently, and part of that is because of how he blends beauty with suppressed emotion. That's been out of fashion. People are painting the insides of dead sheep.

What I learned from Margaret was that my favorite area would be sporting art. Figures.

Margaret would give teas on her patio. We'd listen to the ships out in the Pacific and watch the lights on the oil rigs come on as the sun set. She was companionable, lonely and a sparkling conversationalist.

She used to say, "Well, no matter what, I haven't turned into Doris Duke!" Then we'd goad her into telling Doris Duke stories or Betty Hutton stories or Mable Dodge Luhan stories. She knew everybody.

Kate began dating. She was pulling out of her decline and started making plans again. She bought a lovely small house of her own.

The big house had sold at a big profit. I told Fannie if she blew that money I'd strangle her. She put it in a savings account. Fannie is terrible about money; it burns a hole in her pocket.

During this period, Fannie and I were never seen together publicly. She had a holy horror of anyone thinking she was a lesbian. Why in God's name did she fall in love with me?

The only time we were seen together was with Kate or with a few old friends in Montecito and Santa Barbara. The gay ones were lovely but everyone was in the closet. Deep in the closet. I considered buying them oxygen masks.

Since no lesbian in Hollywood would speak to me, Montecito didn't feel any different. No one wanted to be seen with me, except one gay man, Brad, a realtor. He was a joy.

My friends were straight. Which matters little because I don't pick my friends based on race, class, gender or gender preference. If I like you, I like you, and if I don't, I don't. I don't give a fig about your bank account either.

But my persona mattered to everyone else who was gay.

That Fannie felt that way, too, hurt. I said nothing. I'd heard her arguments about how she'd be ruined in Hollywood, and watching Kate get stabbed in the back made the point.

After a while, though, I wondered what I was doing in a business where people jumped at their own shadow. I think of life as a foxhunt. If there's a fence in front of you, go over it. Who cares how you look doing it? If there's snow, go through it. If there's a ravine, lean back and move along. Go.

One bright morning I drove my rented 450 SL, painted metallic bronze with cream pinstripes, to the travel agent. I pulled in next to an XKE in good condition.

A tall, pretty woman came out to the car as I closed the door to mine.

"Nice car, Rita Mae." She recognized me and held out her hand. "Muffin Spencer-Devlin."

We became friends for life. Muffin, a golf pro, was on the road a lot.

Fannie worried about her. Might she be too gay? Aren't all female athletes gay? Etc. Mostly I lunched with Muffin alone when Fannie was in the city during the week. I learned a lot about golf, although I didn't try to play, and I learned a lot about Muffin, who suffers from manic-depression. She battles her illness with a distinct lack of self-pity.

Montecito was jammed with interesting people. I met Robert Mitchum once at a cocktail party and Jane Russell, knitting, happened to sit next to me at a literary gathering in town. Jane Russell has the most extraordinary face. It's more than beautiful: it's lived-in and *real*. Not that the stars would remember me, but what I remember about them was what quiet people they were. If fame had ever turned their heads, they had gotten over it.

Dame Judith Evans lived up the road but I never met her. As she was one of the greatest actresses of her generation, I wished I had.

Fannie still lives in Montecito. She bought the bungalow a few years later.

Much as I loved Montecito, I felt the colors slowly draining from my skin. If I was going to be the lesbian bogeyman, then I might as well be that bogeyman at home, where real stories were, where people talked about something other than "the deal," and where I could hear English, lyrical, majestic, quirky English. I felt as though everyone in southern California talked mush. Not that they weren't smart, far from it, but too few of them had a love of the language.

In Dixie we love the sweep of the sound as well as what we're saying. Of course, many's the time we aren't saying anything, but who cares?

60

The Booby Prize

ONE AFTERNOON AFTER AN ENTIRE DAY OF TAPING *HOLLY-wood Squares,* Fannie hopped into her slugmobile. I'd been shopping at the farmers' market and met her in CBS's parking lot.

"I'll bet you five hundred dollars you won't drive from CBS to the Beverly Wilshire with your shirt and bra off."

"Deal." She shook my hand.

"I'll follow you to make sure you don't cheat."

"This will be the easiest five hundred dollars I've ever made." She beamed as she peeled off her shirt.

She waited until she had passed the guard house on her way out of the parking lot before unhitching her bra. Exposing her full glories to natural light, she drove to Wilshire, turned west and merrily rolled along.

How I stayed on the road I don't know, because I laughed until the tears rolled down my cheeks. What was even funnier was the fact that *no one noticed.* Every person in the opposing lanes was so intent on reaching their destination that they peered ahead—pure tunnel vision. She reached the venerable hotel and turned left, pulling over to the curb across from the cafe in the hotel. She hastily threw on her shirt.

"I want my money now." She rolled down her window.

"Go to the Saks parking lot and I'll write you a check."

We rendezvoused at Saks. I wrote her a check. She promptly spent it.

Saks Fifth Avenue had been the scene of a unique escapade for Baby Jesus. A year and a half before Fannie's excellent adventure, I was staying in a small apartment behind Saks. One warm afternoon I opened the door and Baby Jesus scooted out, a-hellin' toward the store. Flying across the parking lot, she aimed her gray self at the back door, which, being continually opened and closed, was child's play for Miss Jesus. She zipped in like a hardened shopper.

The cosmetics counters at that time faced the back door, as that was the door most in use. The cat considered the merits of perfumes, listened to a few remarks from the exquisitely made-up ladies behind the various counters, then continued on her way.

Men's clothing held little appeal for her. She found the back stairway and marched right up. She settled herself in the leather handbags and small luggage, which then was at the top of the stairs.

By the time I reached Baby, a crowd of shoppers and salespeople had gathered around to admire or admonish her. When she saw me she gave out that wondrous cackle that cats give when prey is in sight. She considered this audience her due.

The best part was that the manager had a sense of humor and issued a Saks card to B. J. Brown. It couldn't really be used but it was fun nonetheless, and Baby Jesus always traveled with her Saks Fifth Avenue credit card, which was a tasteful dark chocolate with white lettering.

Unpredictable, game and ever ready to pop the balloon of a windbag egotist, Fannie reminded me of Mom. Like Mom, she had to be the center of attention, and like Mom, she kept you laughing. Mother wasn't good about money but Fannie was even worse. If I didn't grab her paycheck, she'd spend it before paying the rent, the utilities and the grocery bill that month. But she handed over the money cheerfully. I'd subtract the required amounts and she'd joyously squander the rest. Or maybe she didn't squander it. How can you put a price on fun? She extracted the maximum of pleasure from every penny. Nor was she unwilling to invest, but she needed to see the investment. Stocks and bonds held little allure for her. She was bold enough to buy that house in Montecito with Kate. She wasn't a coward on any level except her own homosexuality and she had plenty of people joining her on that one.

Fannie surprised me by being a good athlete. She doesn't much like sports but she's well coordinated and can learn to do anything. We joined no clubs together. She wanted to keep her public distance. Once Kate took us to her country club at an off time. Country club dues shoot through the roof in California. I don't know how anyone can afford to belong to anything.

Once we played tennis on the Spanish-style grade school's old courts. The late afternoon shadows bisected the worn surface. Fannie ran, giggled and whacked the ball back over the net. When we finished she jumped the net even though I'd won. That's one of my fondest memories of her, the silly, spontaneous line of chatter and her willingness to do something important to me.

When she was at the bungalow we'd walk at sundown. About a half mile down the road, heading toward Carpenteria, sat thirty unspoiled acres filled with golden poppies, the remains of an old played-out grove, and a few eucalyptus trees whose scent floated over the meadows. I'd tell Fannie where the stable should be built, the house sited. What a beautiful piece of land it was. Of course, it's developed now, filled with tastefully expensive houses owned by people who think they're in the country because they own two acres.

California and Florida make an excellent case for environmental control and curbs on development. If I witnessed the destruction of California farmland from the early seventies to today, imagine the sorrow of someone much older who knew paradise, now lost.

Once good soil is built over, it stays built over. The land is lost forever.

Hollywood attracts talent, then destroys it. The endless cycle of actors, writers and directors chewed up and spit out by the system wasn't going to stop with me. Whether it was D. W. Griffith, Orson Welles, Mabel Normand or Rita Hayworth, precious few escape unscathed. Even the ebullient Douglas Fairbanks Sr. sickened of it, walking away toward the end of his life.

Fannie managed to keep her creativity intact by living on the fringes of the system. *Hollywood Squares,* a game show, utilized the tiniest part of her resources, but it paid the bills, leaving her free for other pursuits. Trained as an actor, she believed that was where she'd make her contribution. But Hollywood has trouble with beautiful, comedic women even though film and TV seem to be a women's medium—it's so easy to reproduce "reality" in them. Women fare much better, artistically, in reality than they do in fantasy or thrillers. This is just a hunch, not a real theory. Once comedic actresses dominated film. Then came television in the fifties. Not that television was easy, but the demand for product opened the net wide enough for more women to create more characters. Also, in the beginnings of any industry, it's freer—women had a chance.

Starting with Marie Dressler, a gargantuan talent in figure and expression, the rule has been that a funny woman must be an unattractive woman. Marie started in silents and made the transition to sound, a *rara avis!* Mabel Normand and Mary Pickford were beautiful but they were silent stars. Once talkies arrived, a different type moved forward. Jean Harlow could be funny but she played the dumb blonde; she wasn't intelligently funny. Jean Arthur was. Myrna Loy was in *The Thin Man.* Carole

Lombard was close to divine. If you think about it, you can count the witty, beautiful ones on your fingers.

Fanny could have been one of the witty, intelligent ones, but she came of age when the prevailing film fashion was gruesomely humorless except for television. She was just perfect for a sitcom, but a perfect sitcom never found her.

Like Bea Lillie, she was so original that no one, at that time, was original enough to make something for her.

Heartbreak goes with the territory. Fannie, shrewd and tough, never gave her heart to the business. I learned from her to do likewise. You can hire my brain, my experience, my calm demeanor, and I'll write you a very good piece. If the gods smile on me, I'll write a great piece. But no one in Hollywood will ever buy my heart. If I hadn't learned it from Fannie, and by example from Kate, I would have eventually absorbed the lesson from film history.

I'm starting to believe there's a direct ratio between contempt and talent. The more talent you have, the greater the contempt you are held in. Even the stars big enough to find their own vehicles and get them financed are despised secretly.

In the earliest days of film, the producers at Biograph refused to list the names of the players, fearing that if the public knew them, they'd be forced to pay them bigger salaries. As it was, they paid them little enough. When Mary Pickford and the Gish sisters broke that mold, the business changed forever, but the administration's hatred of the stars hasn't changed. Producers' initial fear of salary demands was prophetic.

The whole point is to get you cheap, use you up and throw you out, then go find another cheap one since there's a steady supply of talent. This applies to any above-the-line talent, which means writers, directors, actors. The writer, always short-sheeted in the money process, is now beginning to have her/his day.

The underlying assumption of this crass misuse of people is that talent is interchangeable. It is not. Sure, there are eleven thousand writers in the Writers Guild of America, but Writer A excels on different territory than Writer B.

Same for actresses. D. W. Griffith found this out when, hoping to put Mary Pickford in her place, he tried to invent a new star, Mae Marsh. He was lucky. Mae made good pictures and the public liked her, but not in the way they worshipped Mary. Woke up Griffith, though.

While contempt is the surface emotion, fear is the underlying one. The money boys need us. If they could act, direct and write, they probably would. Since they can't (even if they won't admit they can't), they are dependent upon those who can. Instead of seeing this as an opportunity to create, the talent is viewed as another mouth to feed. The talent, in return, hates the money men. Since the dynamic is over seventy-five years old, it will take more than Fannie or myself to change it.

And we don't want to be administrators or film revolutionaries. We want to act and write.

Fannie finally knew that age would bring her acting career to a screeching halt. Why not learn another craft before that dreary day?

Writing is close to acting in that both disciplines require one to create character. The Grand Canyon separates them after that, for on one side is a primary art, writing, and on the other side is an interpretive art, acting.

The actor, director, conductor or dancer starts with a piece of work. The writer, composer or painter literally makes something out of nothing, brings temporary order to chaos.

For Fannie to master the discipline needed for this transformation was going to be a genuine leap over the Grand Canyon.

She was willing to put her heart in it. That gave her wings.

Her first novel, which took three drafts, was published as *Coming Attractions*. Wendy Weil, my agent, took her on. Fannie was in business.

Fannie gave me no public credit for the help I had given her. Again, she was frightened of being openly associated with me. And the final rewrite, which she did for her publishers, was strictly hers.

Exhausted by burning the candle at both ends and by the adversarial nature of the industry, I wanted to go home. I figured I could mail my screenplays in, and if Hollywood needed to see my face, I'd endure that long flight to Los Angeles.

More than anything, I didn't want to become an embittered person endlessly reciting stories of how I was screwed in Hollywood. Even Heidi Fleiss got screwed in Hollywood.

The one thing I must protect in this life is my talent. Imagination is exotic; it needs shelter. All the more so since we live in a nonfiction age, duller than dishwater.

I told Fannie I had to go home.

"Where's home?"

"Maryland or Virginia. My people are from those places."

"Well, mine are from Alabama."

"Do you want to go to Alabama?"

"When I'm rich I want to live in Gulf Shores."

Baby Jesus, high in a lemon tree, listened. I was trying to get her down.

An old greenhouse, its glass broken, squatted in the middle of the abandoned grove, and I didn't want Her Highness to run in there. She'd been out for two hours. Even Cazzie and Frip had come in, lured by tuna treats.

Baby Jesus preferred trees. Pecan trees would have pleased her as much as mighty oaks.

"Why don't we look in Virginia first?" I pleaded.

We did. We ran the Virginia realtors, Bill Leach and Chris Georges, ragged. Fannie worried that Virginia was too far north for a sunshine girl, but at least it wasn't Maryland, even farther north and a border state to boot.

Then a simple Federal farmhouse caught our eye. Situated on a scant thirty-four acres, it had a garage and a little gardening shed, and best of all a cow barn that could be converted into a stable. The sheep pens were falling down, though, the fields needed a heavy dose of fertilizer and the fences had long ago rotted away. The house, in decent condition, was large enough for Fannie to have her private quarters and me mine.

On the way back to Los Angeles, we fretted because we weren't sure we had the money. The property cost about $350,000.

Finally, somewhere over Palm Springs, Fannie said, "I'll give you my money. When I need it back you give it back with whatever the place is worth at the time. You're good with money. I know you'll make me money."

She kept her apartment in the Flats but agreed to spend as much time as she could in Virginia.

We sent in the deposit. I don't know who was more scared, Fannie or I. Probably I was because I had to make her some money.

I moved everything to Virginia. Fannie stayed back in L.A.

The first night in that old house I rolled up in blankets just like I used to do in my cold-water flat in New York. Baby Jesus slept next to my head, Cazzie at my feet. Frip had died before we left. She didn't survive a dental operation.

Baby Jesus, who pretended that Frip was a pain in the butt, missed her terribly. But by the time we reached the house framed by huge trees, she was ready for adventure.

The electricity hadn't been turned on. I had no water and no heat. It was early fall and the nights were cool. Despite sending in the required deposits and making numerous cross-country phone calls, this simple procedure proved too much for the power company. I had to go down in person. Had to do it for the phone company, too.

At the end of that week an old car rolled up in the driveway. A petite woman emerged. She marched up to knock on the front door.

"Hi." I stuck my head out the upstairs window. I was trying to put together the bed I'd bought.

"Hey. I'm Betty Burns. Chris Georges said you needed help."

"Help? I need a miracle."

Betty Burns was that miracle. We've worked together ever since. We're growing old together. She cleans, repairs my torn clothes since she knows I rarely shop, and every now and then she brings me food. Betty is a good cook. I don't know what's better, her cabbage or her fried chicken, which is as good as Mom's.

Betty always says to me, "If anyone taped what we talked about, we'd be in big trouble."

True. We talk about everything together: husbands, children, lovers, money, football, the latest scandal. Fortunately, central Virginia abounds in scandals, most of them of a sexual nature. I'm in my element. Started with Jefferson, of course.

With Betty working inside, I spruced up the outside.

By the time Fannie arrived for her first visit it looked as if someone lived there. She wanted a room devoted to ducks. We took the pretty back room overlooking the gardens—the previous owner had been a first-rate gardener—and hung duck curtains, found duck chairs, scrounged for decoys. The room did everything but quack.

The handsome young fellow down the lane, Dannie McLaughlin, built stalls in the cow barn, among other tasks. Danny's a doer, not a talker, but I'd elicit a few tidbits from him. He used to make me laugh because the girls chased after him something awful.

Fannie'd say, "That boy's going to hide up here and some girl'll be showing up with a rifle."

Baby Jesus preferred my workroom, a big room on the south side of the house. It was the prettiest workroom I've had and I miss it.

Fannie's workroom was upstairs. Even she couldn't work in the duck room, but she liked sleeping in there, as the breeze kept the curtains dancing.

Fannie rarely stayed for longer than two weeks but I cherished our time because, more than anything in the world, she made me laugh. Usually I was the sparkplug. How refreshing to be entertained.

The two of us would have been better sisters than lovers. I'm not a romantic person. Fannie needs a great deal of attention. I think she loved me. I know I loved her. I wanted to spend the rest of my life with Fannie.

Her life was somewhere else. She needed the excitement of L.A. and she needed Alabama. The reserve that is so Virginia, friendly but correct, irritated her.

"These people are about as bad as Yankees," she'd grumble.

Then, too, she liked horses but they weren't her passion. I had my stable filled with boarders even before I had my bed put together. I did all the work: mucking, grooming, medications. I loved it. I love physical labor.

"You're wasting your time. Pay someone else to do it."

But I wasn't wasting my time. I get some of my best ideas picking hooves, bush-hogging on the tractor, tying up sweet peas.

I missed Kate. I hoped she'd visit.

Few people visited because Fannie didn't want them to know we lived together. She had some friends in New York whom she didn't mind knowing. When we went to the city, we'd see them, but most of the time she kept people far away.

One crystal clear October morning we walked outside and saw that a banana spider had spun a web as big as a dishtowel between two English boxwoods. Covered with dew, it caught the sun's rising rays and turned from silver to gold to blood red.

Transfixed, we watched until the banana spider popped out from the boxwood. She was a major spider. When bananas get pissed off they sit in the middle of their web and make it sway like a trampoline. I thought she would fly off her web, she was so incensed. We were keeping her prey away, so we left her to catch her breakfast.

As time went by it became more and more obvious that Fannie wasn't happy with me. She loved me but I wasn't what she wanted or needed.

I don't know if she had affairs in Los Angeles. I never asked. It was none of my business. She was good to me and that's what mattered.

She never promised me a lifetime commitment or even one of two months' duration. I had no room to criticize her. Apart from her homophobia, I had nothing to criticize. When she drank, she could be a bad girl. Other than that, Fannie was perfect.

That Christmas she appeared in *Old Acquaintances,* at the Town and Gown Theater in Birmingham, Alabama. The play was about old friends and rivals and it was just right for Fannie. Fannie played the woman who winds up writing the commercial successes, while soap opera star Susan Flannery played the "literary writer." At one point they overdid the fight scene, falling into the orchestra pit. The audience, thinking it was part of the show, applauded wildly. Fannie and Susan, rolling around in the pit, cussed each other a blue streak. When they finally crawled back on the stage the audience was in convulsions. They cracked up, too.

Birmingham, a great city, kept us busy. At Christmas we shopped and visited Tallulah Bankhead's wardrobe, displayed in the basement of the Town and Gown. Tallulah was a childhood heroine of mine.

Fannie drove me out to the Iron Cafe, frequented by the railroad workers. Bill Neal's sister, Iggy, having battled the bottle herself (ran in the
family), helped the railroad drunks dry out. She lived with another
woman. The two women were kind but tough. Fanny always believed her
aunt was a lesbian. As the good woman and her companion had been dead
many years, I had no opportunity to form my own opinion.

We poked, prodded and talked about how to frame the story. Fannie
didn't want to write a lesbian book. What a surprise. But her aunt's story
was a great story. I told her she could soft-pedal it. Just write the women as
she remembered them. I helped her with the structure.

This was the novel that eventually became *Fried Green Tomatoes at the
Whistle Stop Cafe.*

Fannie doesn't need my help anymore. I'm very proud of her.

Riding back to Charlottesville on the train from Birmingham, we flattened our noses, pressing against the cold window, to view Christmas
decorations in tiny towns across Dixie.

I knew I was losing Fannie. Somehow that made every second precious.

No blowup occurred. She just came to Virginia less and less. The following summer, 1978, I met Martina Navratilova and her young girlfriend
in Richmond. Martina had won her first Wimbledon that year, defeating
Chris Evert, and I'd seen her in person when she was fifteen, which I
think was the first time she played in the States. As round as she was tall,
she had tremendous talent even back then.

I was writing *Southern Discomfort,* which has a minor Czech character in
it. Research, important to me, brought me to Martina through a mutual
friend.

I met her for lunch. She was twenty-one, sweet, and wrapped up in her
girlfriend, who was two years younger.

I kept in contact with her after that, usually by letter. I genuinely liked
her.

Her romance unraveled the following January. She began calling constantly. I told Fannie. She wasn't thrilled but she was big enough to recognize she'd consigned me to the shadows.

I planned to meet Martina in Kansas City at a tournament. She was
three weeks on the road, one week off. I drove to National Airport, that
little corridor of hell, and called Fannie in L.A.

To my surprise she begged me not to go, said she'd fly right in. I then
called Martina and made my apologies, saying I owed Fannie a sit-down
talk, which she was now finally willing to have.

Although disappointed, Martina didn't carry on. I turned around and
drove two and a half hours back home in pouring rain.

When Fannie came home she gave me a postcard of two draft horses pulling a plow. On the back she'd written, "Don't break up the team."

She loved me. I know she loved me and I loved her. But we'd gone along for over two years rarely being in the same place at the same time. I would have moved to Alabama, but she didn't want to be a farmer, and for me that's life, real life. I survived the cities. I flourished in the country.

We needed different things even though we needed each other. We hadn't a clue as to how to resolve our dilemma, to know what neuroses we inflicted on each other and to clearly see if we had a future.

Fannie trusted no one, which hurt me. It meant she didn't trust me either. My remoteness hurt her, as did the fact that I communicated through deeds, not words. She used to tell me I loved the cats more than I loved her.

"Close," I'd say.

I thought we might work it out. I wasn't sure. I felt terrible and I knew that she felt terrible. When I got up the next morning there was a note on the refrigerator. She'd left and she asked me to leave her alone. I did but it hurt.

Years later we were sitting in the Jockey Club in New York and Fannie said, "Why didn't you come after me?"

"You told me not to."

"Rita Mae, you don't know anything about women."

I laughed and wondered if that was true or if I just didn't know enough about Fannie.

I kept my promise, though. I made her a little money. When she needed her investment back I sent it to her at the going rate. It wasn't a bloody fortune but it was, as Mom always said, "thankful increase."

As for Fannie, I will love her until the day I die.

Out of the
Frying Pan

MOTHER, IN ONE OF HER RARE NESTING MOODS, VISITED ME. Without Fannie's furniture the farmhouse was bare. I was back to minimalist decorating. Also, carrying the mortgage alone, I worried about buying furniture.

Mom, like so many people of her turn-of-the-century generation, could make something out of nothing. She rummaged around fabric stores. We trolled every Salvation Army shop between Richmond and Charlottesville, to say nothing of the sorriest stores.

Knowing I loved Fannie, she restrained herself from saying, "I told you so." She liked Fannie but had felt my fame or notoriety, take your pick, would pull us apart. Then, too, Fannie wanted to be the center of attention and so did Mother. Now firmly back on center stage, Mom was surprisingly cooperative.

Actually, her cooperative mood expanded over the years as I was able to send more and more money. The high point had come four years before, when I took her to Hawaii for her seventieth birthday. Two islands and one mother. I was exhausted but she was blissful. Before leaving for Oahu, we stayed at the Bel Air in Los Angeles and Mother packed away every ashtray, glass, cup and saucer she could lay her hands on; we were staying in Richard Burton and Elizabeth Taylor's bungalow. I snuck off before we left and paid for it all. The staff of the hotel enjoyed the ruse.

Once in Honolulu she went wild. The flight in sobered us, though. It's horrifying to look down at Pearl Harbor; no amount of time passing can alter the jolt of seeing those ships under the water. Once we recovered from that sight, Mom put the pedal to the medal. After she ransacked Oahu, we forged on to Kauai for relaxation. Her idea of relaxation was rising at dawn, goading me into the car and being chauffeured to every part of the island. I saw enough pineapple farms to consider myself an expert. The one time her strength flagged was when we climbed Waimea Canyon. The altitude made her sick.

Now, as she puttered in the garden, advised me as to how to trim my wisteria and directed me in general, I marveled at her youthful energy. At seventy-four, Mother ran circles around people half her age. She'd endured sickness over the years, always the same trouble—adhesions in her bowel, scar tissue everywhere. Her body produced scar tissue at a bizarre rate. Her heart and everything else were terrific.

If you stared at Mother's face, you would have guessed her age—but only after she stopped talking. Animation made even her face seem young. Her hair, pure silver now, was beautiful. She moved like a young woman, too. Aunt Mimi, by contrast, moved old, but that was due to her back trouble. She had as much energy as Mom. The Buckingham girls had inherited thriving genes.

As we worked we chatted or sang. Mother is the last person in my life who sang with me while we worked. People don't do that anymore. I miss it. Her light voice, quite good, lifted my spirits.

My troubles had just started, although I thank the gods for keeping me ignorant. Had I known what I was about to undergo, I might have turned tail. Instead I chased it.

Mother knew. Not only had she the advantage of age, she had the advantage of knowing me better than I sometimes knew myself. She had been in her thirties *in* the thirties. I was in mine in the seventies and eighties. The thirties are a dangerous decade. You've lived long enough to think you know something.

I inhabited a peculiar territory as the only public lesbian in a nation of 200 million people. Mother sensed this far better than I. It wasn't that other public figures weren't thought to be bisexual or lesbian, for instance Marlene Dietrich, but I said it, no sidestepping or crawfishing. Apart from bringing down abuse on my head, my position forced me into isolation. It's a good thing I'm not a social person or I would have been devastated.

In Los Angeles, people were more than willing to work with me. Why not? I made them money. In Charlottesville, they had no concept of how I made my living. One of the local banks even refused me a credit card because I was a single woman, although I made more money than the bank's president.

Furious, I marched over to another bank. I had to go to three banks before Jane Shield, an officer at Central Fidelity, finally corrected the overt sexism.

I knew that the South was backward in many ways, but I'd been away long enough to be shocked at how backward it had remained.

In 1979, I'd been living in Virginia for two years. Women had been admitted to the University of Virginia, a state-funded school, for only nine years and you could count the black students on your fingers. As for professors from minority groups, don't hold your breath. Business was done by men in sack jackets, rep ties and high-waters (pants that are too short). Many of them were ruddy-faced from bourbon. Hearty, affable and provincial, the "in" male group hadn't a clue as to how destructive they were to other people, including their own wives.

Over time some of them learned, but they taught me the dangers of insularity, of doing business with "your own kind." Your worldview becomes warped. Not that such people aren't often kind, they are, but they really think the rest of the world is like they are. It makes for bad decisions—one of the real reasons Nixon's advisors tripped over their own feet.

When I moved to central Virginia I did two things that were sneaky. First, I never told anyone my bloodlines. This way I dispensed with the blood snobs right off the bat. I lived here six years before I 'fessed up to Buckingham and Venable blood.

The second thing I did was to feign ignorance about horses. My small boarding operation demanded only that I feed, muck stalls and check legs. No one expected me to know much.

My first victim was to have been Dr. Dan Flynn. He came out for a prepurchase vetting of a nasty mare I was boarding, a good-looking but hateful animal. She had vitreous bundles in her eyes, little strands of inflammatory debris that can sometimes cross the field of vision. Unless they shift, they aren't a problem. I waited for him to act in collusion with the seller. Well, Dan Flynn is dead honest. To the bone. He was the first person in Albemarle County to earn my total respect. His wife, a small-animal vet, is equally as principled. Since then Dr. Dan Flynn has become a towering figure in his profession.

Ginny Flynn is still saving little critters.

I found out quickly who was honest, who was conditionally honest and who was a lying sack of shit. Conditional honesty is interesting. This means Miss X will sell you a decent horse because she has to see you frequently. If you'd driven in from North Carolina, she'd have soaked you good.

Once I started taking riding lessons my ruse worked even better because people confused my pathetic efforts with complete ignorance. This is not to say I'm the best groundsperson who ever lived. I'm not. Mom gets that accolade. But I know a bog spavin or a bowed tendon when I see one. Then there are the injuries where the pain is referred just as in a human: your leg hurts but you've really pulled a muscle in your hip. These are harder to figure out.

Mother applauded my tactics. It was exactly what she would have done.

However, the isolation over the years was beginning to tell on me. My small local victories, satisfying though they might be, did not constitute a community.

I needed a community and I was too dumb to know it.

I missed Fannie. I missed Kate, too. Since gay people lived silent, hidden lives, I couldn't even mourn them for fear of exposing them. They were the only family I knew apart from Mom and Aunt Mimi, Julia Ellen and the boys. My success distanced me from some relatives. If they were jealous, they had the good grace not to show it, but as for being confused, of course they were. You can't understand the film business unless you're in the middle of it. Publishing at that time was still a gentleman's business, a bit easier to understand. But my life veered up and off at a wide angle from the rest of them. It made sense, though. I had never belonged to them. You can't tell someone over and over that they don't belong and then expect them to stick around.

Mom sensed she had been part of the problem, not that she was willing to tackle it directly. Her way of trying to make up was to help me now. Thank God she did.

Again she asked if I couldn't marry Jerry. We could lead our lives as we saw fit. She didn't realize Jerry was going through an antiwoman phase that can only be described as faggot bitchery at its worst. The straightness required of him at work was counterbalanced by an exclusively male social and sexual life that bordered on the compulsive. Jerry was sick at heart and couldn't deal with it. Two years older than I, he had hit the glass ceiling. He wasn't going to become a powerful figure at DuPont without a wife and kids. His hatred spilled over everything he did and said. Mostly it spilled over me and his lover, Herb May, a former navy career man.

He used to tell me I was the only woman worth talking to and think I would perceive that as a compliment. Misogyny frightens me because it is rooted in the very inequality that creates the undesirable traits we perceive as belonging to women: slyness, indirectness, emotional blackmail, feigned helplessness. Those traits belong to other pushed-down groups as well, but individual men live with individual women. That's what makes sexism so vicious and personal. You can't mistreat someone without expecting their revenge, and the more oppressed a group of people or an individual, the more malicious and subtle the revenge. Women have been bleeding men drop by drop since B.C. When a man suddenly cries out as an innocent victim, you know one thing: he's dumb. No one is an innocent victim in this dance.

There too, I had Mom and Aunt Mimi as vibrant examples of women wrapping men around their little fingers. They appeared to enjoy the dance of sexism. I didn't.

"You are as sick as you are secret," I told Jerry. He told me to shut up.

What Mother recognized was my vulnerability. I was blind to it. The years of aloneness or being the proverbial backstreet woman had set up a hunger for connection. Since that could not be fulfilled with Fannie, I was about to shoot off in another direction. I'd lived so many years alone that I thought I was made of forged steel. It's easier to live alone, and besides, you learn a great deal. At the same time, we all need other people to push us, to humanize us, to challenge our daily tyrannies. I know that now. I didn't then.

"Do you think you're in love with this girl?" Mother asked one night as I built a fire in the library.

"I don't know her well enough to say that."

"She's young."

"She's traveled all over the world. I think she's a bit more mature than her twenty-two years."

Mother crossed her arms over her chest. Her pose said, "You're full of shit." What she did say was, "Hmm."

"Mom, if I'm going to fall on my face, I might as well fall on my own terms."

The argument reached her.

She piped up, "Now, you know what to do when I die?"

"Mother, I am not doing the death drill. Besides, everything is at your house."

"Practice makes perfect." She got up and pretended we were in her bedroom. "Now here's the bureau. Open the top left drawer. . . ."

Gypsyfoot

MARTINA SHOWERED ATTENTION ON ME, CALLING EIGHT AND ten times a day. Her first present to me was an electric pencil sharpener. She called from Kansas City to ask what I would like. When I told her a pencil trimmer she was surprised. Jewelry, clothing, cars—I don't know what she expected me to request.

I still use the pencil sharpener. She gave me a good one.

She promised not to hide me. She told me she loved me. That sounded glorious although she hadn't spent more than two hours in my company. She was making up for it on the telephone.

The lowest circle in hell is reserved for Alexander Graham Bell. I swallowed my distaste for that most intrusive invention and chatted. Finally, I agreed to meet her in Chicago.

Baby Jesus would sit in my Hunting World duffle. Explaining that she would stay in the care of a good house-sitter did not improve her mood. Even Cazenovia got crabby.

When I touched down in Chicago it was snowing. I've visited this midwestern city many times. Never in the summer. Chicago has the best shops, good theater, good sports while retaining a midwestern solidness that's beguiling.

I arrived at the International Amphitheater as Martina was wrapping up a match. This was late January of 1979. I met her in the locker room afterward. She showered, then burnt the wind getting us back to her hotel.

Exhausted from the bumpy flight, mourning Fannie, wondering what I was doing, I sat down hoping to talk, relax. Martina, convinced that I was the love of her life, was not in the mood for a meeting of the minds. She wanted a meeting of bodies. Not that I was opposed to that, far from it, but I wished we would have talked a bit.

Allow me to digress about sex. I am not motivated by sex. I enjoy it. I can be passionate, even imaginative, but sex for me is on a par with hunger—it's a physical need.

To make sex a metaphor for life, which the arts have done since the 1950s, is foolish, narrow-minded and ultimately boring. If sex were truly a metaphor for life, then the greatest novels would be written by prostitutes, the most marvelous symphonies by call boys.

Sex, especially if allied with love, enhances life. It's the floor of the house you build.

Getting trapped in sex, asking too much of it, is as dangerous as taking drugs. Sex is by definition temporary. Art is eternal. Everything else lies in between.

Gay people are punished for sex. In many states it's a criminal offense. In Virginia a homosexual is considered a felon. It stands to reason that sex will be out of kilter in a gay person's life even more than in a straight person's. The danger of falling into the sex-as-a-metaphor-for-life trap is extreme, and for some poor sods, sex is their life. The shallowness of it borders on both the absurd and the tragic, but then deforming people is absurd and tragic. Such people develop strange ways to survive the daily dose of badgering and occasional outright danger.

Lesbians are beyond sex. Their neurosis dovetails into being women. Some people imagine that lesbians are imitation men. Wrong. They are women to the second power. Love. Everything is about personal love. Sexual attraction has to be love. It can't be an animal attraction. They want to live as magical couples shutting out the world that has so successfully shut them out. No relationship can carry that weight, and many lesbian relationships implode. But once a lesbian matures to the point of realizing she can't escape the world and that her partner isn't Cinderella, she stands a strong chance of building a lifetime relationship, even in the face of unrelenting hostility.

I respect lesbians enormously for this and I hasten to add that I am not one of them on this issue. I am fundamentally a lone wolf.

I wanted a relationship with Fannie but accepted less. The lack of commitment didn't wear me down as much as her homophobia, and again, at the risk of repeating myself, it was homophobia rooted in reality.

I traveled, gave speeches, wrote political articles alone. I live my ordinary, everyday life alone. It suits me.

Martina is a love junkie. Not that I knew that at the time. I wrote off much of her enthusiasm to her youth. She's in her forties now, so youth is no longer a sufficient excuse.

I believed that I was the great love of her life, that she would cherish me and honor me and vice versa. She repeated these protestations until they became a liturgy. There's comfort in the liturgy.

As for sex that first time, I have often been tempted to write on standardized forms where they request your age then sex, "once in Chicago."

Practice makes perfect. We improved.

The world of women's tennis is traveling in purdah. Velocity is confused with achievement. Every week they pack their bags and move on to the next city, serve the next American twist, return the next crosscourt backhand and so on. Then there's all the time spent practicing.

There they are, a handful of athletically gifted kids, shuttling from city to city and seeing only tennis courts. No British Museum. No Louvre. No Metropolitan Museum of Art. Most of them aren't inclined that way, perhaps, but they do occasionally hit the expensive shops where, by virtue of being young, they have no sense of value. The wild spending made my head spin.

Martina's like a raven, she can't resist anything shiny.

She had more gadgets, more junk than I'd ever seen, plus a few very expensive handguns, which I asked her not to keep in the house. She was generous with her stuff and never minded sharing or giving it to friends. It was a good thing, because I didn't want any of it.

But I learned to want her. The ferocity of her passion dazzled me. I was the center of her attention. Everything I said was witty and brilliant. She threw out her entire wardrobe because she wanted to dress the way I did. Although she's taller than I am, 5'8" to my 5'4", my shoulders are broader than hers, so we could wear the same shirts. I tactfully suggested she might enjoy creating her own look, but she ordered tons of the Turnbull and Asser shirts I have made to my pattern. I can't wear off-the-rack shirts because of my shoulders and the size of my biceps. I can't buy boots either. Muscles, today, are in vogue. I wish they had been when I was young. It would have saved me a lot of ridicule.

Everything I did fascinated her.

I learned to love her. She needed me. I felt important and useful. She heaped gifts on me along with physical affection.

She told me the usual things people say to one another but it was either the first time I'd heard them or the first time I'd listened. She said I'd given her the best sex she'd ever had in her life. I was the most exciting human being she'd ever known. I was the most honest person she'd ever known. I was beautiful. (I knew she was lying then, but I liked the way it sounded.) I was the only person she would ever love. We'd be together until death us do part. Etc.

Even when I heard these uplifting sentiments I didn't believe them on an intellectual level, yet I believed them on an emotional level. I was torn, but I loved being loved and I loved her.

As to loving professional women's tennis, never. The duplicity of the Women's Tennis Association at that time was ludicrous. The game exists to make money. That's why it's a professional sport. But to make money for whom? For the players? For the coaches? If you believe that, you still believe in the tooth fairy. Because a few players at the top pull down millions, the public is misguided. Ask how much the middle-ranked players earn. If it's six figures, take out a pad and pencil and figure in hotel costs, food and those expensive airline tickets. They pay their way.

Promoters rake in the chips. Well, they bear a disproportionate part of the risk. As a capitalist, I understand that. And they go to sleep at night knowing that their sport isn't destroying bodies the way boxing or football does, although I hasten to add that Mom made a genuine boxing nut out of me, and Sugar Ray Robinson did the rest. He was the best ever.

The moral turpitude of women's tennis came about in a distressing fashion. It continues to this day. The public face of the sport is that there is a sprinkling of lesbians. However, no one "knows" who they are—everybody just wishes they would go away. Speaking honestly about one's personal life is actively discouraged. Billie Jean King, a woman out of charm's reach, had no trouble 'fessing up to an abortion, but denied being a lesbian until called on the carpet by an irate former lover.

Does the WTA believe that the public is that stupid? They actually think that if the lesbians finally come out of the closet, no one will watch women's tennis. For Christ's sake, the public has always known and watches the game because it's damned good tennis.

That's not the worst of it. The slime award goes to the association for ignoring the abuse within their midst. When a male coach sleeps with an underage girl, this should be called what it is—statutory rape. When the girl is eighteen, no longer jail bait, it's still an issue that might be addressed because the power imbalance is so extreme. And what about two infamous father/coaches who have publicly beaten their daughters at practice sessions over the last two decades? I wasn't the only person to see it. Silence.

I'm not naming names. Let's give the WTA a chance to clean house. If they know that we know, maybe they'll do something. If they do nothing, then I strongly advise those women once abused by their father/coaches to come forward. Force women's tennis to be responsible to the players.

Watching Andrea Jaeger wear out before she was seventeen was painful. Watching Bettina Bunge walk away from the game exhausted was infuriating. Watching Rene Blount battle racism as well as lobs was sickening. She, too, couldn't stand it any longer. Zina Garrison Jackson hung in there longer, but I can guarantee that the black players kept to themselves. Was it self-censorship, or had the unthinking racism become just too damn much?

Martina can't handle conflict. She looked the other way. Everyone around her, from other tennis people to director Milos Forman, a friend because he is a fellow Czech, to her parents, beseeched her to think of nothing but tennis. She did and she didn't.

My purpose in her life was to open the door. Those people whose economic well-being depended on her were terrified. My God, what if she dropped in the rankings? What if the endorsements dried up? They pretended to care about her. The good thing about her agents, IMG, was that they only cared about the money and they were up front about it.

I didn't just open the door for her to see the abuse around her. I opened the door to the world. Did I not love her tennis? Of course I loved her tennis, she was the greatest tennis player in the world, but I loved her more. She could have thrown her rackets down a well. I was making money. If she had invested some of her money, we'd have been fine.

If she wanted to be the best in the world, bestride the game like a colossus, that was fine, too. Only she could make that decision.

As it became clear to the hypocrites in the WTA and the parasites on her own back that she really was in love with me, they struck back.

Hell, it was nothing compared to what the women's movement had dished out.

Billie Jean advised her that having me around wouldn't be good for her career. People would know she was a lesbian. Coming from Billie Jean, a woman Martina had worshipped, this was sad and yet funny.

Martina came back to the hotel one day and asked if I intended to organize women's tennis into a feminist group. God knows what they'd said to her.

I laughed. I couldn't help it. You can't organize children. The last time that was done was in the Children's Crusades in 1212 and virtually all of them died.

Most athletes are by definition apolitical children. They are kept in adolescence an unnaturally long time. I certainly wouldn't have minded if the tennis players had organized for their own self-interest, but since Billie Jean was running the show, forget that. Her interest was their interest.

As I said, Martina can't take pressure. She can on the court. One of the reasons she was such a great player was that the court was her refuge and her excuse. The more her friends attacked me, the closer she drew to me, but she would never face them off. She was afraid of Billie and she was right to be. Martina has no political sense. She can't maneuver, build alliances, create a plan. Why should she? It's not her talent.

Billie Jean and Gladys Helman created professional women's tennis. Billie had enough energy to organize and be the best player of her day. Her drive coupled with Gladys's brains and business acumen carried the day.

Billie could have eaten Martina for lunch.

But on the court, Martina sliced and diced her. Not in the beginning, not when she was still a teenager awed by Billie. Billie's pain—one of many pains, for she's a woman with tremendous inner conflict—is that she will not be remembered as a great player. One of the best of her generation but not one of the all-time greats. But she will always be remembered for what she built.

Martina will be remembered by tennis aficionados as one of the greats, along with Helen Wills Moody, Suzanne Lenglen, Alice Marble, Mo Connolly and Steffi Graf, who may yet tower over all of them.

Luckily, I suffered no illusions about being welcome in women's tennis. Why would that world be different from any other American institution, even though a high percentage of the players and even the administration was gay? As usual, they were more frightened of me than the straight people were.

We were isolated. I noticed right away, but Martina didn't. She was on top of the world, and all that attention distracted her. Her first clue was being nominated for the presidency of the WTA and not getting it. Hurt and angry, she tearfully came back to our hotel room in New York and lashed out at everybody and everything. Fortunately, only I was there to hear it. But she was right. They screwed her not because she was gay, but because she didn't bother to deny it. She didn't say that she was, she didn't say that she wasn't: the closet with the open door. However, given the libel laws of the country, no one could write that she was a lesbian. They could write that I was.

Herculean efforts by IMG and the WTA kept that story off the page in America. Not so when we arrived in London for Wimbledon. Their libel laws are vastly different, and their gutter press makes the *National Enquirer* look like a daily prayer book.

Hounded at every turn, I worried that Martina wouldn't be able to concentrate. I stayed inside at the rented apartment in Belgravia. The reporters camped at the door. When we were short of groceries, I climbed to the roof, went down the fire escape and hurried to a market. No sooner had I turned an aisle in the store than there they were, flashbulbs in hand. I was represented as a lesbian wife.

I sent the garbage that appeared in the tabloids to Mom with the note, "The only time I will be accused of being a wife."

For an American accustomed to thinking the best of England, it's jarring to see the worst of England. Perhaps being jammed so close together there, they must keep a surface politeness, much like the Japanese. Their tabloid press releases the hostility and tension. We released a lot for them.

Later that year in Brighton, hundreds of girls waited outside the building where we were playing matches. They cheered when we emerged, and they apologized for their press. I saw one match at Wimbledon itself, hiding in the locker room, watching on TV. The rest of the time I was literally trapped in the apartment with reporters banging on the door. I guess they paid the super to get into the building.

Martina lost in the semifinal, 4–6, 6–4, 6–2, to Chris Evert, that pretty little girl from my Florida days. I don't know how Martina stood the ordeal. Neither of us complained to the other, though. We made jokes about it.

Of all the strange pressures we endured, sometimes unwittingly, that Wimbledon of 1980 made me proudest of her, all the more so since Billie blamed the ordeal on me: If I weren't in Martina's life, all would be well, none of this would happen. She brought it on herself.

Blaming the victim temporarily soothes people. When a woman is raped, people want to know what she was wearing and what hour it took place and in what part of town. If she wore attractive clothes and it was late at night, then it was her fault. It's a systemic problem but no one wants to look at that. For one thing, it's so big. For another thing, we must each take responsibility for tacitly supporting a system where women get raped, children starve amidst wealth, and a corporate executive can take drugs while street bums get busted.

Martina was the victim then. She, not homophobic attitudes, was responsible for the mess. Get rid of me, they told her, and everything will be okay.

I should have taken the gloves off. I didn't. It was Martina's world and I didn't want to interfere. I was wrong. I should have fought like hell for the woman I loved and for our relationship. I didn't know how badly the furor affected Martina. She can't express discontent directly. She can tell X, hoping X will tell Y, but she herself will give you no direct emotional information.

I thought we were okay. On the surface we were.

We worked well together. She enthusiastically supported my writing and promised that when her career was over, she'd organize my days as I had organized hers. I believe she would have tried, although by the time she retired she'd become jaded. Small wonder.

I could make her laugh. She followed me like a puppy dog, so I felt adored. If I said, "We've got to clean out the damn kitchen," she'd do it. She wanted to be relieved of daily decisions.

In a strange way, Martina wanted me to live her life for her. That added a burden to my writing but she said many times over that her career was short-lived while mine would last until I died.

She tried to read the books I gave her but invariably I'd have to tell her about them. She's not dumb, but she has no intellectual discipline. The time she put into her body I put into my mind.

I was a good enough athlete to hold her interest on that level and she was intelligent enough to keep me from brain death. She has a quick mind, but she's like a magpie—she has bits and pieces of stuff but nothing's pulled together. Alice Marble was like that, too.

My discipline had to grate on her. She subsequently said of our relationship that she was "just" the tennis player whereas I was the writer. I have often been so sorry she felt that way, because I didn't.

But life has taught me it doesn't matter what you felt, it doesn't matter what you meant; if the other person feels differently, that's her reality.

We were both displaced persons. She was stateless at the time, having fled Czechoslovakia. I was an outcast in my own country. Together we made a new country. I give us credit for trying.

63

Bugjuice

BUD COLLINS, VOLUBLE, FIT, FUNNY, MADE EVERY EXPERIENCE richer. His lady, Judy Lacy, guaranteed he'd not be bored. Judy was a beautiful blonde who hit a mean tennis ball. Bud's no slouch either.

Bud and Judy paid no heed to the screeches of women's tennis. They welcomed me with open arms, as did Don and Elaine Candy, two people who ought to have their own sitcom. Don, a fine Australian player of the Lew Hoad generation, sees a tilted world. Elaine, as petite as Don is tall, is as gifted a raconteur as her husband. However, they aren't just verbally funny. They'll do adventurous things, like buy a racehorse. I'm surprised they haven't outfitted a sloop and sailed around the world. They're wild.

Don was Pam Shriver's coach. When Martina was between doubles partners at the end of 1980 she asked me what to do. As I've said, I tried to stay out of her business. Being number one on my high-school and college teams hardly qualified me to dispense advice.

On this occasion, however, I put in my two cents and I'm glad I did. She narrowed the choices down to three: Billie Jean, Candy Reynolds and Pam. Billie's behavior put her out of the running, although Martina wanted me to be the one to say it. I refused, so we both glided over Billie. Candy, a strong player from the Tennessee program coached by my old Tri Delta buddy, Alice Luthy Tym, was a strong candidate and a very nice person. But I kept coming back to Pam. Her reach and buoyant spirit somehow seemed to sync with Martina. After trial and error, playing matches with both, Pam won the nod. Together they won more titles than I can count, including over twenty Grand Slams. Candy Reynolds was gracious about it.

Because of Pam, Don and Elaine and I spent happy hours together.

Pam, eighteen at the time, under pressure to be the next Chris Evert, had the unenviable experience of watching Andrea Jaeger unravel. Tracy Austin, Pam's and Andrea's nemesis, wouldn't last either, but that was due to back problems. Pam, wise beyond her years, said nothing about not becoming the next Chris. She's not a person to make excuses anyway. If Pam didn't attend cotillion, her mother and grandmother worked overtime. She's a person of honor.

High standards of personal conduct kept her out of the fray. She steered clear of both camps with a dexterity that impressed me. I hoped she'd run for public office someday. Pam could be a productive public servant.

Bud, Judy, Don, Elaine and Pam and I never went to dinner or the movies together. Time and everyone's schedules conflicted. But I could sit in the stands with Judy—her running commentary was worth the price of admission—or hide out with Don, who protected me, or giggle at Bud, an engaging man.

Bud has never received credit for what he has done for televised tennis. Let's face it, athletes are rarely good interviews. How many times can you hear "I was hitting the ball well today" before you reach for the No-Doz? Bud invented personalities. He'd study a player, find a distinguishing characteristic and use it. He created color and tension on-screen, and after a few bland replies from the interviewee, he'd interpret and come up with something good. Bud Collins single-handedly made tennis a TV sport.

Many times a player got furious because Bud would say something on camera like "So-and-so gave you the finger" or "So-and-so got in a fistfight in the locker room today. What happened?" But he was right. Ratings picked up.

Bud understood that tennis is entertainment. The players didn't. They want to play tennis, which is natural enough. They're too young to realize that they're competing against films, theater, baseball, soccer, you name it. We, the public, are overwhelmed with choices. Why watch tennis?

Long considered an effete, upper-class game, tennis isn't easily grasped. The scoring system is complicated. Football is complicated, too, but its violence is addictive.

Tennis is physical chess. Your body is not in danger. A show jumper, polo player, boxer or football player is in more danger in ten minutes of contact than a tennis player is in for her entire sporting life. But it is physical, and when two evenly matched people blast away hammer and tongs it's exciting. I love the game and I love what Bud did for it.

NBC shuffled him from anchoring the matches to being the color commentator. They thought an ex-player could anchor the matches. They also realized that no one could do what Bud did, but I liked it best when he was in the booth, living the match. The color stuff has been overdone. They push him too hard to do handsprings for us.

The only equal Bud ever had in the booth was Don Maskell, the extraordinary English commentator who was known as "the voice of Wimbledon"—Bud's opposite in every way save knowledge of the game.

Judy covered tennis for *The Boston Globe*. Once, after she and Bud had a fight, she took his credit cards and maxed them out.

"I'll spend that son of a bitch's money!" she shouted, whipping out the MasterCard as though it were a Smith and Wesson.

What a day. When the fullness of the damage reached Bud, did he hit the ceiling? Hit her? Cry and moan? No. He laughed and laughed.

"Touché," was all he said.

That's a man, girls.

Don Candy is much like Bud in that he too can laugh at himself. Don won my heart because like me he supported his mother until the day she died. Who else he has supported I can only guess, because he has a big heart. He's sensitive to people's suffering. If Elaine didn't keep an eye on Don, he'd give everything away. Even when he blusters, sounding tough, he's the opposite. Elaine isn't hard-hearted but she coaxes him into more "structured" giving.

These people broke the ice surrounding me. I can never repay their kindness.

Virginia Wade extended herself, too. It's harder for a player because of the competition. Virginia brushed that off and on a few occasions Martina and I dined with her. A highly intelligent woman, her mind honed by British university training, her morals shaped by being a vicar's daughter, Virginia was totally out of place in the commercial soup that women's tennis had become. She kept her criticisms to herself, which required restraint because Billie Jean loathed her. Virginia was the only woman on the tour who could successfully challenge Billie's power. Where Billie ruled with a heavy hand because in essence she fears people, Virginia exerted moral authority. Her behavior on the court, in the locker room, and on the streets was literally above reproach.

Like Pam Shriver, she smiled at people and would go out of her way to help when someone needed it. Virginia was the first to alert people that Andrea needed assistance. No one listened, of course.

Pam was too young to lead at that time. Virginia could have. She sidestepped the role. A showdown with Billie Jean might tear apart what was fragile to begin with; women's tennis was so new as a professional sport. Virginia put the good of the game before her ego. Few people know it. She smiled under the yoke of King and Co., then went out and won Wimbledon on its one hundredth anniversary, truly one of the greatest moments in sports.

Another interesting soul, Betty Stove, steered clear of cabals, cliques and "in" groups. I wonder how many stupid jokes Betty has endured because of her height. She's very tall. Luckily she's very Dutch-looking, which means very pretty. The Dutch incline that way.

Quiet, thoughtful, a student of the game, she was consistently underrated because the press kept building up the rivalry between Martina and Chris. The gate was healthy enough. They could have highlighted other players.

The Aussie player Wendy Turnbull could outrun everyone. Chris had the best tennis brain I ever saw, but Wendy came damned close. People say Ellsworth Vines had a remarkable sense of the game, but I was too young to see him play.

Wendy's matches, always exciting, drew fans. People would hang over the railing to watch Turnbull fight until the last second. She never gave up.

These women were wonderful. They built the game with their talent but they couldn't build the administration of the game. They gave what they could.

As for Chris, I could never root against her even when she played Martina. After all, I had held that baby in my arms. I can't claim special closeness to Chris or her family after I left Fort Lauderdale, but I can't forget what the Everts meant to me, as well as to the city itself.

Those close matches between Chris and Martina tortured me. My face got stonier and stonier as the match got closer and closer. I just couldn't cheer when Martina hit a winner, nor could I cheer when Chris threaded the needle with her lethal backhand down the line.

John Lloyd, Chris's husband then (she has always displayed a taste for movie-star-handsome men), would usually be sitting next to me. He was so sweet about it. If "we" won, he'd shake my hand and offer congratulations. He meant it. John Lloyd doesn't have a petty bone in his body. If "we" lost, he'd offer condolences. I was so sorry when that marriage broke up because I respected John, as did everyone. Of course, half the women on the tour had a crush on him, even the gay ones.

Being congratulated for a win embarrassed me. I'd say, "I had nothing to do with it."

John would reply, "You're part of the team."

I didn't feel part of the team. I felt in the way. Not that Martina ever indicated that. She begged me to be with her even through practice sessions. But the reception worried me. Billie Jean, mean-spirited and back-biting, seemed obsessed with promoting a false image of women's tennis: that everyone was a straight all-American pixie.

Poor Martina, she wasn't even all-American and she pulled the unenviable task of battling Chris, the proverbial girl next door. Of course, Chris received more favorable press coverage and better endorsements. Even if Martina had been straight, she would never have enjoyed Chris's popularity. Americans are jingoistic. Olympic sports coverage proves that to a nauseating degree.

This hurt Virginia, Betty and Wendy, too. Later it was to subdue Gabriela Sabatini's commercial possibilities, and she has to be the most beautiful woman ever to pick up a racket—even more beautiful than the young Alice Marble. If she were American instead of Argentinean, she'd be on a par with Michael Jordan in terms of endorsements. The world loves a beautiful woman but Americans only want to celebrate American ones.

I felt I contributed nothing to Martina's tennis, although once I indulged myself and watched Hana Mandlikova practice. Hana has the perfect tennis body for the serve-and-volley game. I told Martina to play her inside since she wasn't handling anything that came into her body.

Martina did and damn well lost the 1980 U.S. Open thanks to my big mouth. Betty Stove, Hana's coach, had obviously worked hard to correct Hana's hands before the match.

What I did was run the house in Virginia, fend off interlopers, keep Martina laughing and write novels. I packed. I unpacked. I packed again. I forced her to make her own phone calls and then I asked her to make mine. I hate the telephone. Grumbling, she'd do it, then we'd laugh about it.

She'd read her contracts. I'd read them, too, but I offered no advice. I knew IMG wanted me out of the picture. I could understand their point of view. They hoped to sell more endorsements without me and that's how they made money. I sometimes felt uneasy about the balance sheets they'd send in, but whenever I suggested she audit IMG, she brushed off the idea.

Bantam has been my publisher for over twenty years. I audit Bantam periodically. It's expensive. I trust them, but machines and people make mistakes. Auditing makes for a healthier relationship and my publisher has never balked even though it's a pain in the ass for them, too. By the way, I love Bantam, having seen it through many incarnations.

To this day, editors will sidle up to me and say things like "Well, you know that Borzoi is a more, uh, more literary house" or "Bantam started out as a paperback house." Snigger. Snigger. "How can they edit a rough draft?" After that comes the promise that I will be better handled at Snot and Snob Publishing Company.

Still, business is business and Martina wasn't vigilant. I suggested turning financial statements over to a conservative, even-tempered Virginia lawyer and an equally conservative accountant if she didn't want to review the statement carefully.

No.

I stayed out of it.

She asked me to stop giving political speeches because she wanted me with her when she traveled. I balked. She pleaded. I finally agreed because I figured I could give them once she was off the road.

At this time, Martina hadn't gone the way of rock stars, dragging with her, like a momma possum, an entourage of motivators, cooks, workout pals, coaches, etc. It was just the two of us and it was a damn sight cheaper and healthier.

If she suffered a moment of the Big Head, I could deflate her as quickly as Mom deflated me. Everyone on top needs that. We couldn't fight, though, because she wouldn't. I'd rather avoid irritations, too, but sooner or later I'll hash it out. You must. She wouldn't.

Storing resentment is a dangerous thing to do. It gets you in the end.

For a brief time her parents lived with her in Dallas, then in a house nearby. When she moved to Virginia they came often and wanted to live with us. I put my foot down, which is what Martina wanted me to do. They were driving her crazy. This way I could be the bad cop. She stayed the good cop.

I liked her mother. Her younger half sister was likable too, but since she was in her teens, I wasn't around her much.

I can't speak about her stepfather, Mirek Navratil, without exhibiting symptoms of Tourette's syndrome.

I will attempt to be brief. He never lost an opportunity to criticize Martina. He never lost an opportunity to tell her he had made her the great tennis player she was because he was there at the beginning. He never lost an opportunity to criticize my country. When he found out Martina was gay he accused me of corrupting her.

May he flourish in the Czech Republic and refrain from visiting the decadent, spiritless, racist USA. He called us worse than that.

That Martina does not share his gene pool has continued to be a source of comfort to me.

What drove Martina around the bend about her parents was their dependency. She almost skipped for joy when they returned to Czechoslovakia. Then she lapsed into guilt.

For a girl raised in godless Communism she could be Catholic, she has so much guilt. She actually was baptized Catholic thanks to her paternal grandmother, Angelika Suberta. I used to kid her that we'd wind up like Mom and Aunt Mimi, fighting the Protestant Reformation between us.

Since she evidenced little interest in organized religion, we were safe.

But we weren't safe from the constant sniping and wearing down, the endless negative information she heard from all sides. It wasn't that she believed it. Martina knows better. But she isn't a person who wants to hear that. She wants sunny days and sunny people. Her work was becoming unpleasant because some of the people were unpleasant.

I loved the one week each month that we'd spend back at the farm. I had to give up the boarding operation, we were away so much, but I'd hop in the car and run over to the Barracks, a big stable, or hang over a fence and talk to horses. The only time I could ride was that one week each month.

Once I took Martina riding with Barbara Malik and Clare Schaeffer, two lively members of Farmington Hunt Club. She enjoyed herself. I allowed myself to hope that maybe someday, far off in the future, she'd come around to my sport.

One of the dumbest things I did was to talk too much about Martina's retirement. I feared she wouldn't plan. I feared the money would be spent, and I'm sure you've gathered by now that poverty has left a deep mark on me. (This doesn't mean that I can't be improvident.) I feared she'd hang on too long, which for an athlete is especially upsetting because the public can't forgive their aging. Athletes are tied to a specific generation's youth and are held there. Younger generations couldn't care less about them, and their own generation doesn't want reminders that they too are getting older.

I worried too damn much and I talked about it because I was miserable. If it hadn't been for Judy, Bud, Don and Elaine, I would have lived in silence.

Not that some of the players didn't talk to me or weren't good to me. They were, as I've said. But they had a job to do. They couldn't sit around and chat with me or read a book I was reading. The players put on blinders much of the time because it was the only way they could compete.

One person who did not put on blinders was John McEnroe. John has an artistic temperament. He soaks up vibes. He always went out of his way to be nice to me when we were at the same tournaments, and once he saved me from missing an airplane.

He'd been raised to treat women as ladies, to be the breadwinner and to protect a woman. You can be the biggest, brawniest woman but John will observe the gentlemanly etiquette. He even paid courtesies to Martina and men rarely did. I adored John for that. After his divorce from Tatum O'Neal he was presented as a sexist bully. Since I wasn't privy to his divorce, how would I know, but it sure doesn't sound like the John I knew. Take magazine reports with a grain of salt.

On the court he'd explode, forget his manners, but it was because he cared so much. In that he was like Virginia Wade. It wasn't enough to win a match, it had to be done beautifully. But Virginia could keep a lid on her emotions. John couldn't. They were both artists trapped in tennis players' bodies.

The most brilliant tennis I ever saw was played by John McEnroe. He'd string points together like pearls.

Lee Jackson, the umpire, was one who warned me not to mention Martina's retirement.

"She won't hear it."

She was right.

I think Martina came to believe I didn't like her tennis partly because of all that retirement talk.

At one point, she suggested I could take a break from my career. She'd pay me a salary.

Of all the things she said and did in our relationship, that one scared me the most. She didn't understand that writing isn't just my work. It's the air I breathe. Every day millions of people inhale and exhale the English language. The atmosphere is saturated with our sounds, our sense, our collective history held in our language. Stop writing? I wrote when I lived in a cold-water flat. I wrote when the money came in and if you, reader, ever leave me, I'll keep on writing.

I deserved her offer, though. I had blabbed on and on about her retirement. Now the shoe was on the other foot. I shut up after that. Yet I know she truly meant the suggestion as a help since I worried about money. It was her way of saying we had enough money.

I'm not sure I could live with someone and not bring in money on my own. This is a comment on my character, not hers.

Visiting Mom tested Martina. She'd never met anyone like my mother. For Mother's part, she'd never met anyone like Martina. They hit it off. What a relief.

Martina's sitting through Aunt Mimi's rendition of "Tiny Bubbles" on the organ, banjo effect to the fore, gave me new respect for the woman. She didn't double over laughing until we crawled into the car.

She learned that all those stories I told about Mom and Aunt Mimi were true. I have few friends left who knew the Buckingham sisters. I'm glad she knew them. She probably never thinks of them, but I'm glad she met them.

Mother and Aunt Mimi didn't have one fight while we were home. And Mother tried not to swear. She buttoned her lip even when she wanted to shout, "Bullshit," and instead said, "Bugjuice."

64

The Cloisters

PART FROM THE METROPOLITAN MUSEUM OF ART, THE CLOIS-
ters at Fort Tryon Park is my favorite American museum. The Middle
Ages feel familiar to me, probably because Medieval Latin is easier to read
than classical Latin, so I've read reams of it.

I took Martina there once. She'd seen more medieval structures than I
had but she enjoyed herself.

I had accomplished a few things that I hope will delight her in her old
age. I pushed her to buy art. I pushed her to express her sense of humor
because she has a good one.

At the New South Wales Tournament in December 1980 in Sydney it
rained and rained. That was when the Australian tournaments were still in
December. Martina and Pam Shriver were to play singles against each
other. I found a deep-sea-diving establishment and sent Phil Rodgers, now
coach of the University of Virginia's women's tennis team, to get scuba
outfits. He brought them back, and Martina and Pam put them on and
went out onto the court to the wild appreciation of the fans.

Little things like that edged her a bit closer, I think, to enjoying where
she was in life and helped create positive press for her. I didn't do enough
of them because I was wrapped up in my own career, and much as Martina
may have wanted to believe a two-career household will work, in that
stratosphere it won't.

I put together a Thanksgiving dinner in Melbourne and invited the
Aussies and players from other countries. Teaching the Aussies how to
cook a Thanksgiving turkey was fun because I can't cook. I simply put
Mom on the phone to the hotel cook, at an ungodly hour for her.

Then I explained why Americans celebrate Thanksgiving, a story they

didn't know. That was the only time during my tour duty that we social-
ized together. No sponsors, no tournament directors, just us.

We'd traveled to so many countries that they blurred, because all you do
is play tennis. Most of the players didn't like Japan. I did. The position of
women rankles but it is an amazing culture. I'd run into bookstores to see
how they sold books and to read books "backward." My favorite haunts
were paper stores since I like the fine texture of the paper, so different than
our own because their ink is different. We rarely could go out but when
we did we moved along.

We caught the bullet train and took a half-day trip to Kyoto, where we
walked up the steps of temples thousands of years old, so old that the
stepping stones were worn like half moons from the millions of worship-
ping feet.

Our return to the States was marred by the death of Judy Lacy. January
1, 1981, started with the announcement being made during halftime of a
bowl game as the NBC commentator extended condolences.

We knew Judy had a brain tumor but we didn't think it was considered
that serious. Martina and I were to meet her and Bud in Sarasota in two
weeks.

Stunned, we stared at the television. Judy had been threatening to write
a book about the tour. Three days before she died we'd called her to firm
up our schedules.

"Hey, help me write my book."

"Yeah, sure."

"Promise you'll write my book."

"You write it. I'm not doing all the work. I'll help."

"Remember."

I remembered.

Several months later I brought this up to Martina. She told me that I
should write it and it didn't matter what people said. It's one of the
complexities of Martina's character that on personal issues, she makes the
right call, then resents it later on. When she moves beyond the personal,
she might originally make the right call, but then the flak flies and she
retreats. She can't take the hostility.

She can also forget what she's said when it's convenient but I think
99.44 percent of us do that occasionally.

Having to make a deadline, I didn't go with her to Amelia Island in
April. It was rare for me not to accompany her.

The day she left, June Arnold, the original publisher of *Rubyfruit Jungle,*
died, a blow to me and other writers.

I was starting to have a funny feeling. I chalked it up to the losses of recent months.

The week before, on April 9th, we'd thrown a hen party at the house, ladies only, although one night we had a big bash and invited lots of men—but no one's husbands. Boy, if that didn't scare the men back home. Every now and then a man needs to know that someone else desires his wife. This was the first big party we'd given together. We even slept in the room over the garage so everyone else would have good beds. As there was no heat in that little room, we piled on the blankets.

Anyway, Martina held up a glass of Cristal and toasted me. She said I made her happy, she'd love me forever. It was the first public acknowledgment of our union.

Everyone cheered.

On April 20, 1981, she slept with someone else, falling instantly in love.

Baby Jesus knew before I did. Baby followed me around, which was hard for her since she was fifteen and slowing down. I don't know what possessed me. On the phone I asked Martina. She admitted it. I give her credit for 'fessing up. I hung up the phone but I didn't hang up on her. Actually, I've only hung up on one person in my whole life and that was because I was overcome.

I had to go to Sacramento to give a speech. From there I flew to Amelia Island. Martina picked me up. She was happy to see me but nervous.

She finished the tournament. We drove down to Mother's because Mother was sick. I was getting hammered.

I cried when I saw Mom.

"Shut up, bawl baby." She pushed me away.

Obviously she was feeling better. Sweetness would have meant she was really sick.

Martina compulsively called her new love as she had once compulsively called me. She made little effort to go to another room. I heard most of their courtship. My many failings were the subject of conversation, the failings she had never mentioned before.

Since I'd been freer in expressing my discontents, she cited those as proof that I didn't love her.

When Martina is done with you she cuts you off in a millisecond. She has no feelings left for you and she can't comprehend that you might harbor feelings for her, although she was still happy to sleep with me. For three weeks she hovered, edging back and forth, but finally she packed her bags and flew to her house in Rancho Mirage in Palm Springs to be with her new love.

Baby Jesus stuck close.

Our two secretaries heard enough from me to bore them to tears. They were superb, nonjudgmental and attentive.

When Martina returned she said she had found the great love of her life and she could only be happy with this woman.

Many people know who this woman is, but since neither she nor Martina admits to their affair, I can't say they had one, although I saw them kissing and holding hands.

When we first moved in together Martina was supposed to get her handguns out of the house. I'm not opposed to guns, but one should know how to use them and they ought not be loaded in the house. You can't live in the country without guns, though. Rabies alone is an important reason to have one.

For whatever reason she had a gun on the bathroom sink the day she was packing for her trip with Madame X. I picked it up and told her to get rid of it.

I often wonder if it was a guilty conscience or if she thought I'd fill her full of holes like Swiss cheese. She hit me. I hit back.

That's not such a big deal. People are passionate and I can put up with hitting a lot better than with lies. Martina is not by nature a violent person and whatever violence is in her she would be more inclined to inflict upon herself.

I'm more inclined to inflict it on the offending party.

She knocked me around and screamed for her gun.

I wouldn't give it to her. She waxed furious, then realized that I had the gun in my hand. She ran down the stairs and hopped in the BMW. I blew out the back window of the BMW.

Rarely have I been that angry. But angry and heartbroken as I was, if I'd wanted to hit her she'd be six feet under. What I wanted was to scare the shit out of her and to make her feel as bad as I did.

What I did was relieve her of moral responsibility for her actions and give her a story she could embellish over the years. Not only has she embellished it, Billie Jean thrives on the story of me as the gun-toting writer. Since Billie Jean was nowhere near the state of Virginia at the time, I find her reports less than trustworthy.

After you're forty you get the face you deserve. In Billie Jean's case she also got the thighs she deserves.

As for Martina, I used to think it was me, that she left me because of my faults. Enough years have passed for me to recognize instead that this was part of her pattern. She heaps abuse on the discarded lover, in most cases returning to make friends with them years later.

It's an immature pattern, but who among us should cast the first stone—or fire the first pistol?

It takes decades to learn how to live with and love another human being, and by the time you learn it you're too old to care.

Finding a new lover renews Martina; that's why she rolls them over cyclically. If she'd consider how she disengages from last year's model, she would hurt people less, including herself.

No matter how she left me, no matter how she tried to publicly humiliate me, she did love me and I loved her. I can't change that, nor would I wish to.

As I've said before, "You can't judge the quality of love by its results."

But I can judge people by their actions, including myself.

I was a damned fool to take out the window of the BMW. Fannie would have stopped the car, tackled me and socked the living bejesus out of me, but then Fannie is from Alabama.

Martina kept running.

I was about to enter that period of my life I think of as my Cloisters, but not before I was dragged through the cesspool by a Martina who needed to beat me, who needed to extract revenge for the petty irritations of the previous three years.

Jesus, had I known I was that irritating I would have gone back to cotillion.

65

M *Is for the Millions of Things She Gave Me*

I MG, EVER VIGILANT, IS SUPPOSED TO BE THE BEST IN THE BUSINESS. On July 31, 1981, they weren't.

Martina and her new trainer, Nancy Lieberman, then twenty-two, gave a press conference in Dallas to declare that Martina had been under my pernicious lesbian spell. Nancy, overflowing with the milk of human kindness—why, she almost mooed—was going to lead Martina back to men. A mistake must have been made, because Martina surely was straight now.

The Washington Post, on August 1, ran a few paragraphs on this subject:

"Tennis star Martina Navratilova is moving back to Dallas, where she will share a town house with Nancy Lieberman of the Dallas Diamonds basketball team.

"Navratilova told *The Dallas Morning News* in yesterday's editions that she is bisexual, but said her relationship with the Women's Basketball League star is strictly platonic."

Nancy Lieberman is quoted in the same article, "I'm not saying it [lesbianism] is wrong, but I want to give her [Navratilova] a fair chance of changing and seeing the other side. I'm not here to force guys on her, but just to help her get out of that environment."

No doubt Nancy heroically applied herself to her task.

However, in giving this press conference, what they did was admit that Martina had been leading a lesbian life. The libel laws no longer held. Had she said nothing, the press could have hinted but not printed.

I woke up that morning to find the lawn liberally sprinkled with stringers from the English and Australian newspapers. Rebecca Brown, my secretary, dashed through a phalanx of photographers to go to the grocery store.

When she returned she said more reporters were walking up the hill.

I called John Lowe, a lawyer who had made his national name representing the Indians after the Battle of Wounded Knee. He lived in Charlottesville at the time.

The lawyer closest to me, Lucius Bracey Jr., excelled at trusts, wills, contracts. This wasn't his bailiwick.

John listened and said, "If you don't give an interview they'll print whatever they like, figuring you don't have the money to pursue a suit through the courts."

Ugly as that statement was, it sounded right. Why do you think the sleaze papers can exist?

Because of its proximity and because I used to know it so well, I chose *The Washington Post*. It wasn't that I thought they'd flatter me, but they would send a writer who would tell the truth as he or she saw it. If they knocked my tits in the sand, I would assume I deserved it.

Since I started out in journalism, I carry a high regard for reporters. It's easy to pick apart a story or find the odd errant fact. I wish more people would try to write a simple report, like covering a flood, to find out how difficult it is to dig out the facts.

Stephanie Mansfield from the *Post* drove down to the house on Flordon Drive. I'd moved out of my old farmhouse because it was an old farmhouse, which to Martina meant poor. Flordon, a stone Norman-style mansion, suited her taste. I liked it enough to live in it, but I would have liked it a lot more on acres and acres. As it was, I sold my farm but held a second mortgage on it. This was later to prove crucial.

Stephanie, young and bright, asked questions. I answered as best I could. The story that ran was a thoughtful piece. It made me think about my situation in a new way. I hadn't placed my experiences in the context of an older wife replaced by a younger wife. Stephanie made that connection.

Martina did say to me as she was leaving, "You're old and I don't want you anymore."

I was thirty-six that April.

John Lowe's advice was blue-chip. Other papers ran Stephanie's article or lifted quotes from it. The reporters left the hill. I granted no more interviews on the subject.

I was grateful to be left alone. Adam Mars-Jones, the wonderful English writer, a student at UVA then, would come and play the piano for me. He read Latin and Greek fluently, displaying a subtle, marvelous mind. He adored Rebecca and spent as much time with her as he could. They were buoyant friends. It wasn't a romantic love but it was a deep one.

Why it's believed that people who physically love a member of their own sex can't love a member of the opposite sex emotionally or physically amazes me.

As for me, I never minded sleeping with a man, I just minded marrying one.

Martina used to say she thought I'd leave her for a man; I wouldn't have. Actually, I would never have left her. I probably would have bitched and moaned about Martina's girlfriend, then gotten over it. Where I come from, mistresses are a fact of life so long as you play by the rules. The first rule is, you don't break up your marriage. The second is that you're discreet. These affairs so often burn themselves out.

Muffin Spencer-Devlin visited from California. Jolly, bright, she acted as though I was utterly fascinating. She deserved an Oscar but she made me feel better.

Charlotte Bunch stopped by. Any time I see Charlotte has to be counted among one of the best times of my life. Juanita Weaver, an old friend from my D.C. days, visited and wouldn't be satisfied until I sat in her lap and cried on her shoulder. I did. I don't know if I felt better, but she did.

Friends filtered in from all over. I hadn't realized I had so many friends.

The biggest surprise was that people on the tennis tour took the trouble to pay their respects. Lee Jackson hoped I would be all right. Virginia Wade called to offer condolences. Bud Collins, being Bud, called often, ready with a joke, ready with sympathy all the while the poor man was in the depths of grief over Judy. She'd been dead but four months. Trish Faulkner, the director of the tour, called. That really surprised me.

Don and Elaine Candy were great. Pam Shriver was kind, too, and that could have gotten her in trouble since she was playing doubles with Martina.

Jerry Pfeiffer decided to come off his antiwoman kick and arrived to spend time with me. We talked a lot about Nixon during his visit, which might seem peculiar since I'd been publicly dumped and branded an evil seducer of young Czech womanhood, but Nixon's trajectory was spellbinding. His resignation in 1974 was burned in our consciousness.

Jerry was hopeful about Reagan. I wasn't. Too many faces from the old regime.

Jerry had come a long way, though. "I used to think the purpose of a corporation was to make a profit. Now I think it's full employment." I almost fell over when he said that.

Martina was telling anyone who would listen that I was Annie Oakley. Jerry thought it was funny.

I said, "It's not funny. We're southern. It's funny to us. Passion expressed through violence doesn't cut it in Cleveland, Ohio. What she's consciously doing is destroying all hope of a political career for me. She knows I want to run for office someday."

Sobered, he stroked his chin. "Run in Virginia."

"Jerry, I'm behind the eight ball. Running at home won't help."

"Would you run as a Democrat or a Republican?"

"Wouldn't you like to know?"

"Cincinnatus is at the plow." He mentioned a famous episode in Roman history, 458 B.C., when the citizens filed out of the city to implore Lucius Quinctius Cincinnatus to put down his plow and save them. The Roman army was about to be destroyed. Cincinnatus defeated the enemy, then returned to his plow once Rome was safe.

This was one of George Washington's favorite stories and one of mine because it involved citizens recognizing a true leader. I also liked it, I guess, because of the Society of Cincinnatus, which was formed by those staff officers serving under Washington. Washington is one of my great heroes.

"Don't hold your breath," I told Jerry.

"What's the first thing you would do if you were president?"

"Taxes were declared unconstitutional in 1913. I'd again declare them unconstitutional. Our nation became great precisely because we didn't tax our citizens."

Jerry said too many people were sucking on the big white titty, our description of the Capitol. I'd never wean them off it.

We batted ideas back and forth. I was my most relaxed with Jerry. He knew me at my best. He knew me at my worst. He loved me anyway.

Martina was making material demands. She wanted to get back everything she'd given me. If she'd let out that steam when she was with me, we both would have done better.

Our financial arrangement had been a simple one. I'd put down the initial payment on the house, she made the quarterly payments. My money paid for maintenance, and so on.

I hired John Lowe. I didn't want to be unfair but I knew I needed time to assess what had happened, why it had happened, and how I had contributed to this pain. Nothing happens in a vacuum. She had wanted me to run her life. Now she wanted to rebel against me. Her behavior carried a whiff of old rebellion, though; it wasn't just about me, but I was the target, a stand-in for people she still couldn't fight.

We made few counterdemands other than that she lower the tenor of the proceedings. Cool off.

If she was blissfully happy with her newfound lover, a woman (although perhaps it was hard to tell), why pound on me? Clearly the heterosexual reclamation project was failing.

The biggest surprise was Mother. She acted like a mother.

She didn't say, "I told you so," although she allowed herself the gray pleasure of saying, "Don't marry a child, have one."

"This feels like a death, doesn't it?"

"A dirty one." Mother offered sympathy and a surprise of her own.

"Your father had an affair in 1933 with a woman named Lola. Everyone said she looked just like me. I caught him and told him, her or me."

She elaborated on this, waxing vituperative even though nearly fifty years had passed. For all her citing the rules of how to tolerate a mistress, she couldn't accept one. I think I could have. We talked about that.

Mother said, "You were good to that girl."

Of all the things my mother ever said to me, that surprised me the most. I hadn't thought about my being good to Martina. I thought about her being good to me because she was. Sure, she avoided making decisions, but everyone around her colluded in keeping her mentally adolescent— except me. I trusted she'd grow up sooner or later, and while she was growing it wouldn't hurt me to grow, either. I hardly had a lock on maturity.

I loved Mother more openly after that. It was the first time I felt that she had met me on an emotional level without making a demand or pushing me to be better and stronger.

Seeing me dragged through the tabloid sludge proved to her, if nothing else, that I'm tough. I had earned her respect through my work and through sending money, but after this I earned her admiration.

I liked having Mother look up to me.

Baby Jesus brought grasshoppers, a chipmunk and one tiny squirrel. At her age these were magnificent triumphs. I pretended to eat them while she purred. She desperately wanted me to be happy.

Me too, but I suffered all the same. I needed to suffer because it was the only way I would learn. We build lives that work, more or less. As we age we must continually dismantle and rebuild, like the pink chambered nautilus. We need a bigger shell. I mean shell, too. A healthy covering is necessary in this world. You've got to know who to let in and who to shut out.

Even Aunt Mimi offered a few prayers on my behalf. She hoped this would bring me to the One True Church. I assured her I'd buy a rosary.

I found out that my friends loved me. No one liked seeing me shredded in the press. No one believed Martina's protestations about how I had lured her into this dreadful lesbian life. Even her friends knew better. God knows what the public thought.

Tove Parker, Dr. and Mrs. Jimmy Turner, Susan Scott and Chic Thompson, neighbors and friends, flew into my life like angels. Suddenly I was part of the varied, exciting social life of Albemarle County. I had never been home long enough to be part of Charlottesville.

I called Fannie. I apologized for not having given us enough time to heal our own relationship, if such a thing was possible. She didn't gloat. If anything, she was sympathetic. I wanted to ask her to come back. Under the circumstances that would have been ludicrous and even shameful. I get dumped and want my old lover back? That's not the way.

Fannie was my great love. If we lived in a society that didn't hate gay people, we might have made it. But we don't.

I love Martina, too, but in a different way. Her dependency lured me into thinking I was important to her. I felt loved for my work, my services. I should be loved for myself. It took this relationship for me to know the difference.

Martina tired of knocking me. She tired of her new love, too. A year later she was calling to tell me what this girl did or didn't do, then she'd quickly hang up when she heard the woman approaching. There wasn't anything I could do about it. She kept saying, "I lost it for her."

By the time she decided to divide up what we owned together in a nonhostile way, the love of her life was out of the picture and she was obsessively calling Judy Nelson. She expected my 100 percent support of their new relationship.

It would have been better for everyone, the principals included, if Martina had not decided that Judy Nelson was yet another one true great love of her life.

Both women were snakebit, but it would take almost eight years for the poison to draw through their systems.

66

Weeping Cross

THERE'S A SOUTHERN EXPRESSION, "I'VE BEEN IN SORROW'S kitchen and licked the pots clean."

I was in Sorrow's kitchen.

I mourned Martina, Fannie, the women's movement, Juliann Young. You name it, I mourned it. The sadness that I'd stored away poured over me. No dragging around with tears in my eyes, though. I kept working.

Work is prayer. I prayed a lot.

Reflection comes hard to me since I exist triumphantly in the present, looking toward the future. I read history constantly, but I don't think about my own history.

I did now.

Being sensate animals, we avoid pain. But being thinking animals, we must conquer pain.

The primary cause of pain, setting aside disease and disaster, is your own self. This is unwelcome knowledge. I knew it intellectually. I had to know it emotionally.

When I went out on the road for my tennis novel, *Sudden Death,* which I will always consider Judy Lacy's book, the press whooped it up about my lesbianism. Big surprise. The literary people paid no attention to the novel since sport cannot be a proper metaphor to carry a novel. Simple reason: In sport you win or lose. Life is complicated, so complicated that you can lose when you win, win when you lose, lose completely yet win your soul.

Since athletes, like insects preserved in amber, live in games, which is adolescence, they cannot represent the journey to the soul. When they're done for, they certainly can.

I wondered what I had done that was so awful. I'd loved a woman. I'd been getting kicked in the teeth for that since age fifteen and I hadn't even loved anyone at that point. This wasn't new information. The media spin was new. I watched with lurid fascination as they boosted their ratings, tittering over the subject. One of the least attractive aspects of our country is our shallow approach to sex and love.

The women's movement had prepared me. I think I interviewed my interviewers more than they interviewed me. I wasn't going to blab on about Martina except to say that she was straight now and that I wished her well. I did.

Book tours are like boot camp but with little sleep and less food. I'd survived a number of campaigns. I'd survive this one. I used it to gather information about how far gay people had come. Oh sure, I was the butt of the joke, but twenty years earlier the issue wouldn't have been discussed at all in public.

This was a left-handed victory.

While I worked on the surface, I worked underneath. I tried to untangle what was me, my distinct character, from the times in which I lived. Where did I start and the twentieth century leave off? Where did I stand firm and Mom and Aunt Mimi fade? I'll never know. If you know these answers about yourself, you're way ahead of me.

I don't know what I would have been like if I'd been born in 1744 in Swabia or 414 B.C. in Athens. My talents would be identical, but what would I have developed and what would lie fallow?

I had to untangle what I could. I paid a heavy price for my honesty. I thought I didn't care, I was above it. I wasn't. The subsequent isolation tainted me with a touch of self-righteousness. By God, I faced down the whole world; I had to be right because I was strong. Not so. The two are not connected.

Fighting for a large principle doesn't necessarily make you a good person. I don't think I would have wanted to dine with Robespierre.

My work was my life. That's not enough. When few people would traffic with me, my work had to be my life. A writer is a small god. Our characters live or die at our prompting—although characters can and do take over. I had withdrawn into my work for obvious reasons, although they weren't obvious to me then. That kid with the big brown eyes heard too many times that she was a stray cat. She worked to earn her place at the table.

Not only did I survive, I triumphed. I owned the goddamn table.

My triumph was my undoing.

I had to open those old wounds, letting out the bad blood. Maybe the doctors from the eighteenth century weren't so far off when they applied leeches.

I remembered what I didn't want to remember: how I'd stared in the mirror, wondering what I had done wrong. Why did my mother leave me? She kept Patty. Why didn't my father find me? He lived less than ten miles away.

The answers are adult answers. Of course I know why. But the pain is the child's pain and I had to feel it. Juts made sure I wouldn't feel it around her. She hated weak things. For her pain was weakness.

Mom was wrong but you take people as you find them. I forgave her. She was too lovable at her best not to forgive her.

The person I couldn't forgive was myself. Why didn't I know everything? Why wasn't I perfect? I was the strongest, the smartest, the best. Everyone told me so. I had track ribbons, tennis trophies and novels on the best-seller lists to prove it.

Victory isn't peace.

Valor isn't self-understanding.

My victories brought me to the point where I could examine my frailties. Had I not written those successful novels, I don't know if I could have taken the time or energy to consider myself. The icon of success would have pulled me away.

The danger in dressing and addressing old wounds is self-indulgence. I fear that like the plague.

The person I thought about at this time was Senator Thomas Eagleton, chosen to be George McGovern's running mate in 1972. The McGovern camp later discovered that Senator Eagleton had once sought help for depression. Eagleton was dumped. McGovern, a man I personally like, having met him three times, sank to his lowest. He hadn't a prayer of winning the presidency anyway. Had he stuck by Eagleton he would have looked less "handled."

That's the trouble today. Public figures don't follow their instincts, they follow opinion polls. Wimps.

Where is Harry S. Truman when we need him?

The reason I thought about Eagleton was that he was punished for seeking health. Had he broken his arm no one would have said a word when a doctor set the bone. His mind hurt him. He went to a doctor. He was crucified.

The fallacy is that to be president or to lead, you can't admit weakness. I now fear the person who doesn't know s/he can be broken. If you don't know where your fault lines lie, that San Andreas of the heart, you will perish.

Certainly, I was afraid to admit weakness.

My struggle isn't darkly glamorous. I didn't take drugs, drink or become wildly promiscuous. I didn't rush into therapy or a rest haven. I worked it out, day by day, puzzling, piecing together, looking inside.

Today people rush to television to display their insides, seeking absolution in publicity. I really think the Catholic Church is missing the boat. A show called *Mea Culpa,* a public confessional, would be the smash of the decade. My mea culpas aren't that melodramatic.

I'm reserved and sometimes withdrawn.

I'd rather be the chief than the Indian.

I have trouble making room for other people's frailties and I have zero tolerance for my own.

I have no self-doubt, even when it might be a prudent response.

I never understood the connection between sex and love until well into my thirties.

The job comes first with me. You can nurse your feelings later.

I am capable of evil just as I am capable of great good.

I like to think of myself as an angel with lice on her wings.

None of the above would earn me a berth on a talk show. Maybe we're glued to those talk shows because a cannibal's confession makes us feel better about our own flaws.

Truly, I loathe admitting I have flaws. People have been pointing them out since my birth, and I don't see why I should waste my time doing it! But there are moments when the ironies of my own life, the ironies of being an American, give me the giggles.

We've got our pants on backward, so to speak. We confuse rigidity with strength. We want people without blemish.

Why are we punishing people for their lives? We punished Thomas Eagleton. We punished Adlai Stevenson because he was divorced. We punished Richard Nixon because he was unlovable.

In Oliver Stone's movie *Nixon,* Henry Kissinger said, "What would he have been had he been loved?"

Nobody's good enough. We raise up actors only to plunge them into the abyss because we're tired of them or because their personal lives disappoint us.

Some people learn from their experiences. Some don't. The ones who learn are the ones who can and should lead.

We want a leader who is faithful to his/her spouse, rarely drinks, doesn't smoke, never smoked marijuana, never smashed up Dad's car, etc., etc.

Who is this person?

The most boring human being you have ever met.

I have made some whopping mistakes. I've written down the ones I know. What don't I know, or what mistakes am I making now? I'll learn from them.

I am not the master of my fate but I am the captain of my soul.

I no longer have any desire to control my life. I simply want to live in divine chaos.

I trust that I will. I have to trust you, too. We aren't going to get anywhere as individuals or as a nation if we don't negotiate our differences with trust.

The dog-eat-dog way of thinking doesn't work. It did for many centuries. It will lead us to mass destruction if we continue it. Hitler should have taught us that. "Us or them" is death. It's "we."

Those are the conclusions I drew from my two years of quiet reflection.

All the issues that I had thought were real, such as black and white, straight and gay, rich and poor, are fragmentations of the key issue. The only issue is life or death.

Are you here to save and nurture this planet or are you here to destroy it?

67

A Cat Can Look
at a King

LOS ANGELES RESTS ON THE PACIFIC OCEAN LIKE A BEACHED GAL-
leon. I enjoy a piratical relationship with the city. I sail in, board the ship,
fight, sail out with booty.

I needed booty, both kinds, I guess.

For whatever reason, Los Angeles is good to me. I knew I had to return
in order to pay my bills. Norman Lear hired me and Rick Mitz to frame
up a two-hour variety special about the First Amendment, later adding
Arthur Seidelman and Richard Alfieri, each of whom has made a place for
himself in the film and television business.

I packed up the car. Baby Jesus was the copilot and Cazenovia, quite a
beauty queen now, was the navigator. We drove across the United States,
taking the southern route, which means we cruised in on Route 10.

Driving across the country gives one plenty of time to reflect. Mostly
what struck me as ironic was that in ditching me, Martina had linked our
names together in the press. We had become a pair like Abbott and Cos-
tello, Fred and Ginger, Frankie and Johnny. The gay community couldn't
get enough of it and at this point the press was giving everybody more
than they needed to know.

I made my way. She made hers. I didn't want to be linked with her in
that fashion and I know she didn't want to be linked with me either. Also,
I have enormous pride. I didn't want her money. I could make my own.
She'd earned her place in the firmament and I'd earned mine.

However, I had sense enough to know that life isn't fair. Exuberant,
dreadful, rollicking, but never fair. While I was getting beaten up, someone else was getting a break. It all evened out.

Much as I would like to regale you with stories about my tour of duty
with Norman Lear, I can't. I rose at five, tried to reach the office by seven

and often didn't return to my small rented house in Studio City until eight or nine or later. Once we started shooting *I Love Liberty,* I lived at the site.

One moment stands out. Norman Lear, king of television at that time, would fire me, then rehire me. He'd heard yes too many times. I said no. Whenever a figure, be it Czar Nicholas II or Norman, becomes muffled in a cocoon of great wealth and obedience, trouble follows.

This hymn to the First Amendment was saccharine and sentimental initially. Norman had been a bombardier in World War II. He had served the United States. My generation only knew a Disunited States. I'd argue for the problems of the country to be included in the program. Back and forth we'd go.

He fired me. I packed. He called and said, "Go home this weekend and write a piece with a black, a Jew, a gay person, a woman, a Hispanic. Did I forget anyone?"

I did the piece. *Bland* doesn't describe it but we had to get it through the censors. Norman, bless him forever, taught me how to combat these guardians of television morality, Broadcast Standards and Practices. Here we were writing a show about the First Amendment, freedom of speech, and we had to pass the censors.

Censors are nothing compared to sponsors, however. Television exists to sell you Preparation H. Anyway, we managed to include this watered-down version of people's discontents and Desi Arnaz Jr., Patty Duke, Rod Steiger, LeVar Burton and others performed the parts.

Mary Tyler Moore performed my piece on Mrs. Stephen Douglas. She shook throughout the rehearsals. She fears a live audience, as do many performers, but when she had to tape before a coliseum filled with people, she transformed that nervousness into character. She *was* Mrs. Stephen Douglas, a fascinating woman because she clearly understood what was at stake during the Lincoln-Douglas debates. Lincoln's credentials for the party's nomination, much less for the presidency itself, were not impressive; her husband's were stronger. Yet she'd seen Abe Lincoln be as slippery as an eel. I'd love to write a complete screenplay about that woman because it would be an incredible way to experience the tensions of the time, still with us despite the War Between the States. As for Mary Todd Lincoln, she would be a foil for Mrs. Douglas. Poor Mrs. Lincoln, she wasn't wrapped too tight.

Kristy McNichol opened the show with my piece about a high-school senior giving her valedictory speech and breaking down in the middle of it.

I didn't get to meet but one of the performers. Writers don't these days, which is a pity. The only actor I was able to meet was Christopher Reeve because he wanted someone in the pit to throw him his lines. Figuring I wouldn't be dazzled by him, and because it was my dialogue after all, Norman assigned me the task.

What woman wouldn't be dazzled by Superman? Today, after his accident, he really is Superman.

I learned to love Norman. He understands the politics of television better than anyone I've ever met. If he'd return to where he was raised, forgo his wealth for a while, he'd find his true inspiration all over again. Creativity knows no age limit.

Bud Yorkin was Norman's partner at the time. A large, powerful man, he sifts through material with a fine-tooth comb. This wasn't Bud's project but he was happy to talk to me or anyone else involved. Once Bud commits to a project, film these days, he becomes totally involved. He's a wonderful producer.

At that time he was married to Peg, a woman passionately committed to righting the wrongs of this world, promoting relevant theater and raising her children.

They were and remain fascinating people.

Peg Yorkin has become a bulwark for the women's movement and a force for women in film, too.

I wished I could have spent more time with such people but time was one thing I didn't have.

Baby Jesus and Cazenovia would attach themselves to me like ticks when I dragged through the door at night. If I could have taken my cats to work I would have, because I have only to chat with a cat and the writing flows. I need animals.

Once the project was finished I moved to San Francisco for six months. I wanted to drink in that city, one of the most beautiful in our country. Armistead Maupin and I wanted to write and produce a gay half-hour show for KGO. Anything but reverent, we knocked out skits such as a gay man and lesbian returning from vacation. This was Armistead's inspiration. The customs official goes through their bags with hilarious results. I wanted to drop a giant prophylactic from a helicopter over Coit Tower in support of Planned Parenthood. Between the two of us we carried on much in the manner of Dorothy Parker and Robert Benchley except that I don't drink.

Armistead, a navy man from North Carolina, suits me to a T. However, KGO blanched before our raucous humor. We made *Saturday Night Live* look tame. Perhaps they had envisioned tepid talks on gay life in San

Francisco; you know, thoughtful pieces addressing the question, Is there a gay culture? Is there gay literature? We wanted to take on the world. We parted ways with KGO, but without rancor.

Armistead, marching on to greater glory, had written the first of his *Tales of the City*. KGO's loss was public TV's gain.

I lived on Jackson Street, right by the Presidio. Each afternoon I could hear the fog banks. Baby Jesus and I would open the windows and watch as the silver mist cast its net over the trees, quickly followed by a dampness that was anything but beautiful.

San Francisco prides itself on its sophistication and artistic largesse. There are moments when that pride turns to self-satisfaction, an insularity close to Boston at its most precious. However, both cities ought to be self-satisfied. They're still on a human scale, still beautiful.

San Francisco seduced me on many levels. Ladies accosted me daily, a not always pleasurable experience but a vaguely flattering one. Jerry Astrove, the second Jerry in my life, became my constant companion. We fueled the gossip mill, since we were inseparable. We pretended to be above all that attention, but we loved it.

No one can make me laugh the way Jerry Astrove can. He is endlessly witty. When *I Love Liberty* was done, he helped me pack and move back east. Donald Alex, strong as an ox, put his back into it, too, as did Deborah Mogelberg, a charming woman who owned two restaurants. Deborah's sense of humor is as caustic as Jerry Astrove's. I adored her.

I belong in the South. My heart is there. My stories are there. The horses are there. We rumbled across the desert, the plains, the Midwest, curling up through Tennessee, rolling into Virginia. Our little caravan crossing America, Lewis and Clark in reverse, kept everyone laughing.

I reclaimed my farmhouse after the buyer went bankrupt, since I held the second mortgage. I had offered him the exact price he paid for the house when he bellied up on the payments. Arrogantly, he thought he could sell it for $500,000, and he spurned my offer. Needless to say, I got back my old farmhouse for a song.

I needed more than a song to fix it. He'd ripped out everything of value, including a stove that had been mortared into the brick. The way the laws work, until bankruptcy proceedings were completed, which usually takes a year, I could not maintain the house. The pipes were broken. The lawn and gardens hadn't been attended to. The small outbuildings had endured the neglect better than the big house. The barn, which was the most important building to me, was fine.

Jerry, Deborah and Donald worked like mules. The guys climbed in the trees, pruned the branches, mended fences. I had to buy all new appliances and the plumbing bill made me gasp. But within one week Firefly Farm twinkled again.

When those three climbed on the plane, I cried. I don't cry in public but I couldn't help it. They busted their asses for me and they wouldn't take a penny.

Baby Jesus, happy to be in her old house, meowed, nosing in this corner and that. She moved slowly. At seventeen and a half, time was running out. She caught a chipmunk. We celebrated.

The next day Baby died at home. Dr. Chuck Wood had her cremated. She sits with me in my workroom in a Thai funerary urn. When I die Baby's going in the ground with my bones, too. I will never be parted from the one creature who suffered poverty, hunger, hostility and the later traumas of success along with me.

When Betty Burns heard I was home and Baby had died, she rushed to the house. She cried, too. Betty, a sensitive, perceptive woman, saw that the repairs had stretched me thin. Cottage cheese and Coca-Cola provided my sustenance.

The following day she and Edward, her lively husband, drove down the driveway with half a dressed lamb. She put it in the freezer and put a pot of her cabbage on the stove.

"You aren't going hungry again."

I said to Betty, once I dried my eyes, that I was grateful. I was. I love Betty and I can't always express how much I do love her. I'm not so hot in that department with anyone.

I felt an odd pang that day and I blurted out, "Betty, Mom's next."

Her face registered both shock and recognition. She said nothing.

68

Easter Sunday

IN 1983 NELLE NUGENT, THE PRODUCER, HIRED ME TO WRITE *Thursdays 'til 9*, an adaptation of a funny book by Jane Trahey that was an insider's look at a big department store. I adored working with Nelle, who has so many Tony awards she needs a room or a new apartment just for them.

I was to fly to New York with the completed first draft on Easter morning. I don't like to work on Easter but as long as I could go to early service or the earliest mass (never telling Mother), I was fine. The rain steadily beat down for two days but the sun shone brilliantly at last on Easter morning.

I drove up Route 20 north, turned onto Proffitt Road and crossed the new state bridge there over the floodplain. Preddy Creek was high, but not near the top of the bridge.

A roar to my right, seemingly out of nowhere, caught my attention. A six-foot wall of water headed straight for me. The spring flash flood had broken and crested, roiling down from the mountains, at that precise moment.

There are a few things to remember in a situation like that. Floor it. Whatever you do, don't stall your motor because it's going to stall soon enough. Put the driver's window down.

I jammed the pedal down. I surged across the bridge. The water hit me full force right on the other side. Had I been *on* the bridge I would have been crushed against an abutment. I was driving my 1981 Mercedes 420 SEL, my pride. The car spun around and nosed down. Not a drop of water seeped in through the engine chamber. The water poured into the window as the nose began to sink. As the car and the water swirled, I crawled out of the driver's side window. Then I struck out for the meadow, which seemed a long way away.

I couldn't swim in a straight line. Dodging logs and other flotsam, I swam at an angle, reaching the grass in what was probably only fifteen minutes but felt like hours because my clothes made me heavy.

The temperature was in the low fifties, and the chill cut through my wet clothes. Shaking, teeth chattering, I headed for home, which was about five miles down the road.

A young man and his wife picked me up in their truck. They were dressed for Sunday service. I didn't want to get them wet so I rode in the back although it upset them. They dropped me at home.

I walked in the house and called Mom, telling her everything.

"I thought you could walk on water," she said.

Then I called Nelle Nugent, who, being a city girl, probably thought I was nuts to live out in the country where such things might happen. She was good about the fact that she wasn't going to get the script that day.

Once I changed clothes and made myself a cup of tea, I thought about Mother's smartass remark. Typical Juts. Even as I sipped, she was surely on the phone with Aunt Mimi, recounting my escapade with Old Man River.

Sadly for Nelle and me, someone in Disney's acquisitions department fumbled the ball on the renewal of the option for *Thursdays 'til 9* and the author asked for more money. I guess she thought since Disney had sunk some bucks into the project they'd jump to renew. They didn't. Disney dumped the whole project, to the dismay of Nelle and me because it really could have been a funny movie and I was fired up for the rewrite. I actually enjoy rewrites.

Jerry and his lover, Herb May, visited me shortly thereafter. Jerry, gaunt and gray, looked older than his father. He hated his job, he hated himself for not leaving. I'd never seen him so wretched and tired.

He went upstairs for a nap.

Herb and I talked and talked for the first time in the fourteen years I'd known him. Herb was hard to talk to because Jerry commanded everyone's attention. When the two of us got together it was a high-level verbal tennis match, and Herb didn't possess the best social skills, a real disaster in Virginia. We always excused him by whispering in a new person's ear, "Raised in Albany."

A nod of recognition would follow.

The joke is, having spent time in Albany, Troy and Saratoga, I know upstate New Yorkers do have manners. Herb just didn't absorb them. But I never miss an opportunity to sideswipe a Yankee.

When Jerry woke we plied him with a bottle of sauvignon blanc.

"We're buying seven acres in Kauai," Herb announced calmly.

Jerry sipped.

"I'll put up half the money," I announced.

"We'll build a bed-and-breakfast for gay people," Herb continued. "If it works, we have room to expand—tennis, a pool, you know. We're leaving Wilmington."

"You'll never leave the South." Jerry sipped some more.

"I'll leave it in February," I said.

"You won't be getting value for your money." He put his wineglass down.

"Yes, I will. Every penny of profit you make you pour back into the mortgage. Once it's halfway paid off then you send me 25 percent of the profit. After it's paid off, send me 50 percent."

"You're a better businessman than that." He smiled.

"Jerry, I'll have a place to go to in the winter and I won't have to worry about running the damn thing. Anyway, what's the point of money if you don't invest it? It's like fertilizer."

"You want me to quit my job."

"I do. You're killing yourself." I could say it. Herb couldn't.

"You work harder than I do."

"I love what I do. You don't. Give them your notice, six months if you need time. Sell out in Wilmington, spring's a good time to sell. Jerry, you're forty. Come on. Hustle your bustle." I quoted Gretchen Summerfield, the city tennis champion from our youth.

"Aren't you still supporting your mother?"

"Yeah, but I can squeeze a nickel until the Indian rides the buffalo. Come on."

He shrugged at Herb. "Why not?"

He didn't do it. He stalled, pushing back his resignation date. I would have strangled the son of a bitch had I known what was in front of him. Better I didn't.

Mother didn't think the bed-and-breakfast was a bad idea, but what did Hawaii have that Florida didn't? I elected not to answer that question.

She enumerated the attractions: polo clubs—more had sprung up; Hialeah, although that holy of holies was on its way down, unfortunately; Gulfstream; and don't forget there are Quarter Horses in Florida. She carried on.

I listened but said that Jerry and Herb thought Hawaii a more alluring spot for vacationers because it was so far away. And it wasn't chockablock with golden oldies, but I couldn't say that to Mom; she was seventy-eight.

I gave up pounding on Jerry.

The summer passed much too quickly, as summers usually do. My trumpet vine, gossip central for hummingbirds, never looked so good. My wisteria bloomed twice, to my delight.

I'd gone hog wild and bought three more horses.

My friends Jimmy and Alice Turner gave me a rough-coated Jack Russell bitch I named Buster. It suited her. I had a black Great Dane named India Ink, and Cazenovia had a kitten buddy, Sneaky Pie, who found me at the ASPCA on St. Francis of Assisi's feast day when I went with a friend to look for her lost cat. I leaned against a cage—they're stacked on top of one another—and this tiny, five-week-old fireball reached through the cage and snagged my hair. Love at first sight.

My house and barn were full of love. My career rolled along. I commuted to L.A. and New York when necessary, but I was able to spend time at the farm. I was in heaven.

The first week of August, I received a call from Aunt Mimi telling me to come home. What I remember is that I'd just met Joan Hamilton and Larry Hodge of Kalarama Farm in Springfield, Kentucky, birthplace of Lincoln. David Goodstein, publisher of *The Advocate,* and his friend, David Russell, introduced me. What sensational horses Joan and Larry had. I couldn't wait to return to Springfield.

Missy Turner, a capable, upbeat young woman, was running my stable. She could handle farm duties while I dashed home.

Aunt Mimi simply said Mom was in the hospital.

By the time I reached the hospital she'd been operated on. The same thing as in the fifties, adhesions.

But she pulled through. I took care of her house. Worked there. Visited her twice a day, and she felt good enough to sit up and run my life for me. Not that it worked. I always did what I wanted to do, but it made her feel better.

"Have I been a good mother?"

That question worried me. Mother wouldn't ask that if she thought she was going to make it. "Mostly, Mom, but you weren't very affectionate."

"Our people aren't that way."

"I know. You loved me as best you could."

"Some people are easier to love than others." She giggled.

"Ah, Mom, I thought I was easy to love."

She grew serious. "Actually, honey, you are. You're one of the sweetest people I've ever known. People don't know how sweet you are."

That made me giggle. She'd never said that before.

She breathed deeply; tubes ran everywhere. "Is the house all right?"

"Mowed the lawn, trimmed the bushes, cleaned every single jalousie. You'll be happy to see it."

"Yeah." She breathed again. "Rita, some day Martina will come back to you. She needs you. No matter what she's done, not just the romance stuff, but in life, help her. She can't help herself." She paused. "Fannie will be fine. She's strong."

I thought this was the oddest thing for Mother to say to me. Also, she hardly ever called me Rita. She used that name to other people but she still called me "Kid" or "Buzzer."

"Mother, what you ask, I will do."

All of a sudden Mom got weepy. "I don't want to leave. I don't want to leave you. You're all alone."

"Momma, I've always been alone. It's okay. It's my natural state."

Mom sobbed and sobbed. I didn't know what to do. I wiped her eyes, gave her a glass of water.

Neither Mother nor I shied from a tough situation, although there's volumes we left unsaid. "Mom, I have my cats, dogs and horses."

"You love your horses. Since you were a little girl. I believe you'd live in a stable and be happy."

"It was good enough for Jesus. It's good enough for me."

"Do you remember when you wanted to see Jesus?"

"Kind of."

"Do you believe in Jesus?"

"Mother, after years of Sunday school, Bible school and catechism, do I have a choice or a chance?" I smiled.

"In your heart, do you believe?"

"Yes, Mother, I believe with all my heart and soul. I just don't talk about it."

"Good."

She relaxed a bit after that.

"Mother."

"Now what?"

"Are you afraid to die?"

"No. I just don't want it to hurt."

She fell asleep. When she woke again she called for the nurse.

I had a cup of tea and came back. She was sitting up in the bed and looked bright again, with a bit of color in her cheeks. "Is my sister, the saint in training, here?"

"No."

"She's like a blowfly."

"Oh, Mom."

"You know that Julia Ellen went crackers. Because of her." Mother relished this story. Although Mother loved her niece, Julia Ellen's problems were proof that being a natural mother didn't make you a good mother. "Took out all of Russell's guns, he has a goddamned arsenal, and fired every single bullet into the ceiling. Whole ceiling fell on her head. Then they took her away. She's better now."

Mother's mind wasn't wandering, but it wasn't moving in a straight line. She scrambled events and time frames, although she always described people accurately.

Now as it happened, Julia Ellen didn't shoot out the whole ceiling. Russell laid all his guns on the table. She was house cleaning and told him to put them away.

He ignored her. She picked up a gun and shot one bullet into the ceiling.

Russell put the guns away.

I hadn't the heart to spoil Mother's version, especially since she had suffered at the hands of her sister over the issue of what constitutes real motherhood, and this was proof that Mom was not alone in raising an imperfect daughter.

Fortunately, Julia Ellen had a good sense of humor about the episode. But she did go through a terrible time when her marriage came apart. She got some help and put herself back together.

"Do you need anything?"

"A new body. I'd like a thirty-year-old model."

"Be hard to find one as pretty as yours at that age."

"You know, Sis always said that Momma told her to take care of me. Momma never said that. Sis made it up, I bet."

"Bet you're right."

"I was the best dancer."

"Still are."

She lapsed into silence.

"Mom, do you have any regrets?"

She smiled at me, "I regret the times I said no, not the times I said yes."

That was the last time I saw my mother alive. She died August 13, 1983.

69

The Death Drill

KNOWING THE DRILL BY HEART, I OPENED HER BUREAU DRAWER, lifted the lid off the glass box, removed the key, pulled the chair to the closet, got the green strongbox, opened it and removed the valuable papers. I called Fairchild Funeral Home, now run by my classmate Ron. I called the pastor at the Lutheran church. I picked out the hymns, arranged the service, ran down to Fairchild's, selected a suitable casket, informed the newspapers. There was no time to sleep between Mother's death and her funeral, which had been arranged so people could fly down for the weekend.

Barbara Bailey, a friend from Seattle, helped enormously. She and Julia Ellen organized food to feed the masses, trimmed the lawn, answered the phone.

Aunt Mimi shuttled between Mom's house and her own. She'd swoop down like a harpy to carry off yet another valuable.

If you've ever seen *Zorba the Greek,* you'll remember the scene in which a woman dies and people swarm in to strip her house bare. In Mother's case, Aunt Mimi performed the work of hordes.

On a few items I put my foot down, but I figured Aunt Mimi's rapaciousness came from her own childhood poverty as well as from a profound misreading of my relationship to Mom. I wasn't Julia's natural daughter, therefore everything belonged to her.

Mother's will passed her property to me, but many items, china, crystal, jewelry, you name it, Aunt Mimi wanted. She wanted Mom's car, too, and I wouldn't stand for that.

As it was, I faced $80,000 worth of hospital and doctor bills. Mom had some insurance but I was going to have to cover the rest, plus the expense of the funeral.

And it was an extravaganza. After all, this was Mother's last social engagement. If her send-off wasn't perfect, she'd haunt me.

Southern biddies like to stroll past flower displays, eye the casket, take note of the funeral home as well as what you wear to the occasion. You may be grieving, but you damn well better look good while you do it.

The church overflowed. The first crisis of the morning was when Aunt Mimi set foot in a Lutheran church. She had tried to con me into arranging the service at the funeral home, which has a room for such things. Never. High church all the way.

This had propelled my aunt into a crisis from which I derived some pleasure despite the circumstances. I had no idea if she would show up. Russell did come.

"I walked you down the aisle when Butch died," he said, "and I'll walk you down the aisle now. The hell with all of them."

Love that man.

He and Julia Ellen behaved impeccably toward each other. Julia Ellen should have cut the cord to her mother when she married Russell.

Mom used to say, "Too much mother in that marriage."

Connie Coyne, my high-school buddy, appeared, as did Pastor Golder, the man who taught me catechism. He'd moved up in the hierarchy of the Lutheran Church, but I was touched that he remembered his original flock. Pastor Golder was a good shepherd.

Mother's casket, closed, reposed before the altar. "I don't want people staring at my old dead body," she'd said.

Metal-flake blue, the casket dazzled. It cost as much as a new Toyota. Mother would have loved it. I'd considered polished walnut and then thought, no, Juts had a wild flair to her. Go for it.

Draped over the casket was a floral covering that incorporated lilies of the valley and orchids in shades of pale yellow to white. You don't want to know how much that cost either.

Then I sent her an enormous horseshoe floral arrangement that took two men to lift it. I failed to inform people as to Mother's track habits. This was between us, and a Kentucky Derby winner would have been happy with it.

Suitably impressed by my handling of the funeral as well as by the fact that you couldn't move for the floral gifts from friends, family and admirers, the southern junta settled in for a cleansing cry.

Dad's favorite hymn, "Beautiful Savior," was on the roster since Mother would have liked it. "Holy, Holy, Holy" was second, and lastly I selected "It Came upon a Midnight Clear," a Christmas carol. Mother loved that carol and I figured each Christmas the song would trigger a memory of the irreverent, irrepressible Juts.

The boys came except for Wade. Eugene and Dorcas came from Pennsylvania, as did Uncle Claude and Aunt Jeun.

Then, lo and behold, on the arm of a subdued Uncle Mearl, Aunt Mimi made her most Catholic entrance, Belgian lace hanky ready.

I had had a stained-glass window installed in the church in memory of Dad years before, and now I made sure that Aunt Mimi had to sit under it. She also had to admire the golden crosier I'd purchased as well as some of the red hymnals.

Mother had her revenge in death. Her sister had to come to our church.

Once the funeral was over we retired to the cemetery. As you know, you sit under an awning with your family. The grave yawns before you, the casket held in place by strong cords.

As the last words were said over Mother's body, the ashes-to-ashes, dust-to-dust hit the casket Toyota, Aunt Mimi emitted a wail.

She'd allowed Juts to be the center of attention long enough. She was going to be the most distraught sister in history. Everyone would be sure to comment on the depths of her anguish.

Everyone but me. She about split my eardrum.

If I heard "my baby sister" one more time, I'd lose it.

Finally, I leaned over, whispering into her right ear, "If you don't shut up, I'm pushing you right in there with your sister. Behave yourself."

She drew herself together for the "freeze," the formidable glare honed by generations of high-tone women. I glared right back.

Uncle Mearl, truly saddened by Mother's death, slipped his arm under his wife's elbow. He rarely asserted himself, but when he did, you'd best pay attention.

She lapsed into a model of grieving restraint.

Then we drove back to the party at the house. We had enough food for an army, which was a good thing because we needed it. I don't know where these people came from or who half of them were, but they had good Juts stories to tell.

I gave each of her dearest friends an elephant. She had collected enough elephants to start a specialty store. I kept the first one she bought, the little iron bank from 1908.

Aunt Mimi seized the beautiful Steuben crystal one as well as the silver Tiffany picture frame.

Mom's little black poodle, B.B., Sunshine's successor, poked his nose everywhere, looking for her. That made everyone boohoo all the more.

This gave Aunt Mimi the opportunity to swoon into a chair. Julia Ellen loudly feared for her angina, and the entire gathering fussed over the shrinking form of Mary (Monzie) Alverta Buckingham Dundore giving a stellar performance.

As Mother used to say about Sis, "She hasn't missed a tragedy in seventy years."

She certainly didn't miss this one.

Barbara Bailey drily commented, "Well, I can see you didn't make anything up in *Six of One* and *Bingo*."

Mother's friends partied until deep into twilight and deep into the grape, too. We finally poured the last one into his car and I sat down for a Coke.

I remembered Mother telling me to jump into her arms when I crouched on the roof.

I remembered her walking me to Violet Hill Elementary the first day of school.

I remembered her destroying my paint set.

The memories rolled in like the Atlantic at high tide: Mother holding down ten bingo cards at the York Fair, determined to win a blanket. Mother tossing off her shoes and wading in the Chesapeake; soft-shell crabs boiling in the pepper pot. Mother joking with a groom at the Shedrow and winking at me to gather more information. Mother and Dad singing in church. Mom dancing better than anyone I've ever seen outside of the movies. Mom calling me "the Pick," "the Ill," "Buzzer" and, on a few saccharine occasions for public consumption, "my Rita."

My favorite memory of Mother involved steeplechasing. She attended the first Montpelier event in 1934, and liked what she saw. When Foxfield started in Charlottesville, she'd fly in for the fall races. She much preferred them to the spring. She'd walk the fence line where the patrons parked. Carrying a bottle of champagne, she'd chat up people, laugh and bet. We all know that betting on horses is illegal in the great state of Virginia, but it's one of those laws everyone smiles about. She'd have a pencil behind her ear, her race card in her hand.

What people saw was this adorable, peppy lady with silver curls who could kill you laughing. What I saw was Pancho Villa without the mustache.

Mother never left Foxfield without at least a thousand dollars in her pocket.

She'd giggle when we drove away. "Never bet against a Buckingham."

"It's a shame the way you take advantage of people, Mom."

"Yep." Then she'd squeal with laughter.

One particular Foxfield when she cleaned the clock of a particularly pompous racehorse owner, she made me laugh so hard I dropped a wheel off the road. A tow truck assisted by pulling us out of the ditch. She had the presence of mind, amidst guffaws, to stick all the money down her bra.

There will never be another Juts.

70

The Amen Corner

DEATH IS A GREATLY OVERRATED EXPERIENCE. I HATED Mother's and I'm not looking forward to my own. Apart from the sorrow there are the bills to be paid.

Nobody dies for free.

I sold my car and most of my jewelry. Seeing my beautiful black and silver car glide down the driveway made me sick. A car for me is more than a means of transport, it's a repository of emotions.

Little B.B. had come home with me. When my back was turned he walked a half mile down to Route 20, still looking for Mother. He found her. Hit by a car, B.B. was buried under the rosebushes.

Martina didn't bother to send condolences when Mom died.

Fannie did, shortly needing my condolences, as she lost both her parents within a year of each other.

My longtime agent, Wendy Weil, lost her mother, father and brother within a year.

Two days after Mother died, an executive from Hill/Mandelker, a film production company, called, saying, "I'm sorry your mother is dead. Think you'll make your deadline?" Phil Mandelker was dead of AIDS by then or that call would never have been made. I finished the teleplay for *The Long Hot Summer* right on time but I never forgot the appalling lack of decency.

Forgetting or remembering became sacred acts after Mother died.

The reconstruction of memory fascinates us. What we remember. What we forget. According to scientists, we literally do reconstruct memory. There isn't a single bank vault in the brain for the past, it's scattered throughout the brain. When you and I recall an event or a person we pull from different areas. Some people may recall a fact more easily than an emotion. For others it would be the reverse.

And an event we know well might be reconstructed with some variation each time it's brought forward.

The delicious dilemma is, can you ever know your own life? Of course you can know events. My memories of Mom, Dad, Aunt Mimi, Virginia, Kenny and Big Mimi illuminate my mind like cave paintings. It's the beginning of my life.

I don't know if an individual's life recapitulates civilization but those early people and memories are my cave paintings.

What I can't know is what my life means to anyone else. I can get the Big Head and carry on about this contribution and that one, but hell, we don't even remember who invented barbed wire in this country and the West couldn't have been tamed without it. We can look up the inventor in a book but we don't know it like we know a Coca-Cola sign. If we can't easily remember *him,* I don't know who will remember me or why.

Then again, will I remember me?

Youth moves out, leaving no forwarding address. No matter how you try, you can't reach that person again or that place.

Even the BVM changes with time. In one century she is the personification of perfect motherhood; in another, she's our intermediary to Christ.

If the Blessed Mother can change, so can I.

But will I change for the better?

A funny thing about America is our attitude toward personal change. We're all for technological advances—at least, most of us are; I'm not sold on it. But when people change, everyone decides something must have been out of kilter before. Maybe that's why some people can't change. They're afraid they'll lose face.

Mother's death fomented major change in my life, internally and externally. I don't know how long it will take me to fully understand those changes.

I sold her pink house.

I started riding with a vengeance.

Those things are easy to catalogue.

What amazed me were the memories flooding over me in the years immediately after her death. Odd bits and pieces of the past, like one winter evening when Mother made me play Parcheesi with Uncle Will, Dad's uncle, while everyone else played poker. Poor Uncle Will by that time had such thick glasses the sides of them were pink. He could barely see the Parcheesi board. He really wanted to play pinochle and I really wanted to play poker.

We played and played, dutifully chatting away. On the surface this is not a dramatic memory. Underneath it is important. We were together enjoying one another's company. I confronted old age with Uncle Will. I learned I could make someone happy by being there, by paying attention. Mother won everyone's money, of course.

Then there was the time Mother and Pastor Golder provided unintended entertainment. Pastor Golder had been trying to lure the congregation into a financial meeting for the better part of 1957. The church was small, the congregation emphatically not wealthy. He finished the service but withheld the benediction. No one could leave.

Then he read out the financial report. Mother, eager to flounce around on the beach, fumed.

The church car was dying a slow death. The local Oldsmobile dealer, a Lutheran, I bet, had given Pastor Golder a very good deal on a new Oldsmobile.

That was too much for Mom. While the rest of the congregation meekly listened, Mother put up her hand.

"Julia Brown."

Mother stood up. She cast her lustrous gray eyes around the congregation, smiling at everyone. "Jesus walked in sandals. I don't see anywhere in the Bible where Jesus drives a new Oldsmobile. So I don't know why you have to have one."

"Oh, Mom!"

I realized I carried ghosts, spirits of the dead. This was less a haunting than a blessing, a repository of memories, a treasure of shared laughter. Big Mimi, Daddy, Ken, Virginia, Jack Young, Mother and Dad Brown, even my hero Citation, pressed against me daily. I could hear their voices, although what I heard was what they'd said in the past. But what they'd said is as true now as it was then.

What I couldn't have was their response to current ideas and events. Or could I? I knew these people, an imperfect knowing, just as I imperfectly know myself, which is a good thing. If I knew myself totally, where would be the surprises? Anyway, I knew them.

I ask, "What would Dad have done?" or "What would Mother say about this?"

I never knew how strong love ties were. Death does not "Us do part." Death takes the body, not the soul. I don't know about karma or life after death or any of that stuff. But I know I can reach that love. If I study the life of someone I didn't know, like Dolley Madison, on some level I can use her experience, her emotions for my life.

Nothing and no one is lost. Dead, yes. Lost, no.

All life is a conversation between those who went before, those alive now and those who will come after. All life is a conversation between life forms, plants and animals.

Life breathes. Life is communication.

I prefer this communication be in English. It's such a robust tongue and I'm spoiled by it.

I can speak cat, hound and horse. I can read Latin, a tatter of Greek. I can understand a little German but I dare not speak it, just as I can understand a smattering of French but am too embarrassed to open my mouth.

But English, that torrent of sound, that cathedral of meaning, that legacy of thousands of years (counting Latin), is all mine.

When I remember Mom and Dad I remember in English. I hear this complex, shaded and ironic language as they spoke it.

Not only did they feed me, clothe me, shelter me and teach me right from wrong (not that I always listened), they gave me my tool, they gave me this tongue. The guttural sound of Anglo-Saxon married to the music of Latin.

I believe language shapes us more than we shape it. I would like to think I would have been a writer no matter when and where I appeared, but to write in English, that's a gift not just from Mom and Dad but from the gods. And to use southern English is piling Pelion on Parnassus: it's perfect.

When Mother died I was both freed and abandoned, as are we all at this profound juncture in our lives. In straining to hear her voice, I heard anew the cadence of comedy. She was nothing if not funny, even when she was dreadful.

That hot, sad August day in 1983 is still with me. It's not that I remain close to her death. I understand death. What I'm trying to understand is whether my passionate love of language, land and animals has relevance for anyone but myself. And I listen for the cadence of her voice, my very first English speaker.

Mother's generation saw more technological change than any generation ever. I doubt future humans will make any leap as big as the turn-of-the-century generation, those born between 1890 and 1910. Mom grew up with horse-and-buggy transport and lived to see a man walk on the moon. She took it in stride, forgive the pun.

I feel closer to her generation than to any other, including my own.

Their resilence, raucous humor and charming civility resonate like an echo of a better time. There are few of this generation left. Many of them survived World War I, plunged into the frenzy of the twenties and then endured the Depression, only to emerge into World War II. They truly were unique.

Mother certainly was. She didn't expect anyone to take care of her, least of all the government. She had a healthy disrespect for government. She didn't pay much attention to economists either. She knew life could be hard but she intended to wrest what joy there was from it. That she did.

When she died I knew I had to hold not just her memory but the memory of her time. I realized that I was like the moon; my shining face was that of my time but the hidden side was Mother's time, Mother's generation. I draw great strength from those people.

Most people present themselves as being on the cutting edge. I'm not. I'm a throwback. I belong to those turn-of-the-century tigers.

Mom, Dad, PopPop Harmon, Reuben and Caroline Brown, Big Mimi and Little Mimi invaded my thoughts constantly. Belle and Beulah, alive again in my dreams, called me to the chase. Which brought me full circle back to Toby, the hound that ran silent.

PopPop, battling the bottle after having battled the Germans, showed me the way. I remembered Mother's respect toward her stepfather. It took me these many years to finally figure it out.

Once PopPop let me accompany him when he released Toby, keeping Belle and Beulah back in the kennel. A big contest was to be held at nine the next morning. We ran after him, the frost crunching underfoot. The hunt was a "drag," which meant the scent was laid out by humans; the hounds wouldn't be finding live foxes. Anyway, the organizers put down the scent at about three in the morning. It was about four when PopPop took Toby out. The frost would hold the scent until contest time.

When we again showed up at nine o'clock, PopPop knew exactly where to cast Belle and Beulah. He won the money and the dog food.

Dishonest? Well, it wasn't sporting, but I was too little to know if this was breaking a rule or not. I never heard anyone talk about a hound running silently except in the most disparaging terms.

What I gathered from this experience was that hounds were all PopPop had left. The trenches had taken their toll, Big Mimi's death had left him hollow, and booze filled up the void. Hounds and hunting by scent kept him alive.

He couldn't hold a job. He had to win these contests at least sometimes. So he figured out a way. Mother respected him for that. He wouldn't take anything she offered other than food or some clothing occasionally. People didn't take handouts then, not even from their own families. The shame was more painful than the poverty.

Mom would say, "You got to make hell with what you have."

PopPop did. So did Mom.

Now it was my turn.

Mother's death brought me right back to my roots. I had been surrounded by imperfect but strong people. No one expected perfection either. Well, Aunt Mimi did, but as Mom always said, "She got radical over there at McSherrystown Academy. Let it fly over your head." Then she'd pass her hand over her head and say, "Blue Angels."

I knew I was imperfect. Plenty of others knew it too, but as PopPop Harmon used to say, "When I can walk on water I'll let you know."

I couldn't walk on water but I could dance.

How like Juts, the best dancer I knew!

Once I passed through the first year without Mom, a time of grief followed by numbness, I was ready to kick up my heels.

Fate had one more dagger to throw. Straight to the heart.

A Long Goodbye

MOTHER'S CERAMIC ELEPHANTS GLARED AT ME FROM THE bathroom wall. One was green, one pink and one yellow, and each colored elephant had a matching baby. They made me laugh.

In a fit of domesticity I decided to take down the old wallpaper in the bathroom. I like paint better than wallpaper but the house, built in the early 1800s, had shifted over the many years, and hairline and not-so-hairline cracks abounded. I had sandpapered and respackled everything in the downstairs but I was losing steam upstairs. Wallpaper covers many sins.

No wonder Hitler got so evil. Paperhanging can make anyone hateful.

Throwing caution to the winds, I called a company in town to hang the damn stuff.

I fretted over the cost but not overlong. Somerset Maugham said, "Life is too short to do the things you can pay other people to do for you." He was right.

Jerry and Herb were visiting. For reasons I can't fathom, some gay men are bathroom queens. When you walk into their bathrooms, tiny crystal chandeliers sparkle overhead, marble washbasins gleam, gold dolphin fixtures beckon—it's quite an event. Jerry and Herb fell into that category.

Jerry quickly dispensed with the wallpaper I had chosen, a restrained vertical stripe, beige on beige. I don't like patterns much. Stripes or the occasional plaid is it and most times I don't even want that.

We spent half the morning ransacking the wallpaper books since the paperhangers would arrive Monday morning.

Herb wanted a pale pink background with velvet reliefs like escutcheons. I gagged. Jerry wanted an expensive grass covering, one of those woven deals just perfect for cockroaches.

They fought. I listened. It didn't matter what they picked because as soon as they got in the car to drive back to Delaware on Sunday night, I'd go back to my chaste vertical stripe and they'd fume the next time they visited.

Jerry would look at me scathingly. "Dykes have no sense of interior decorating."

"Yes, Miss Delaware." I'd taken to calling him Miss Delaware because he couldn't get a spot of dirt on him without having the vapors.

Here we were in the middle of the country, horses in the paddocks—I'd taken in boarders again—cows in the next meadow, enough weeds in the garden to give me fits, and he was in ironed jeans with a crease, Gucci loafers, a maize-colored polo shirt with a turquoise sweater tied around his neck. Oh, the belt was crocodile, of course.

Six feet four inches of muscle honed to perfection in the gym and I couldn't get him to saw a hanging limb off my walnut tree.

As the two of them approached violence over the wallpaper I excused myself to ride a mare I had promised to keep fit for the owner. She was fresh and given to rodeo shows. After ten minutes of her warm-up airs above the ground we settled down to a nice walk on a loose rein. Fortunately, the boys were arguing, for if Jerry had witnessed the spectacle he'd have ranted for an hour about the dangers of equestrian sports, second only to skiing in number of injuries.

An hour later, when I returned to the house, they had settled on a wallpaper I just had to have. The compromise wallpaper was blue with clipper ships on it. This was an improvement. I said I loved it.

Jerry picked up the phone and ordered it. Now I had to make up my mind whether to cancel the order when his back was turned or whether to use it because it wasn't so bad really. I decided to cancel it because Mother's elephants would be overshadowed by the wallpaper.

I sent the boys out to pick up the mail, a long way away, while I frantically called the dealer and returned to my original order. There was no point explaining.

By the time Jerry and Herb returned I was in a better frame of mind. Except now they were hungry, and I can't cook. I'll give you tea, Co'Cola and Virginia peanuts. That's it. They knew this, of course, but now we faced the ordeal of the barbecue.

Two queens in the backyard, cutting each other up over the perfect barbecue sauce, drove me to weed my garden. I did, however, set the table.

I don't have a complete set of china. I've been collecting Tiffany's black-bordered china hand-painted with a small rabbit or whatever around the rim. It's called Black Shoulder. It should be called Highway Robbery. However, it is beautiful. I had only four plates, cups and saucers at the time. Here it is years later and I'm only up to six. That and the Hampton-pattern silver, again six place settings, are the only matched things I've got.

They're too formal for lunch under the walnut tree. I trooped out odds and ends I'd picked up at yard sales, literally a plate here, a cup there. I used linen napkins, red, and I created a country floral centerpiece.

Jerry was actually impressed. "Where did you get the idea for different china patterns for each setting?"

"Necessity."

"I like it."

"All you have to do is hit up the auctions and yard sales."

"He's not going to an auction," Herb grumbled.

"Look who's talking." Jerry pointed his fork at Herb. "The last time you went to an auction you bought a building."

This was in 1984. The years prior to the Tax Reform Act gave all manner of tax breaks and incentives and federal funds for rebuilding inner-city houses. Jerry and Herb had taken advantage of this to buy a lot of houses in the core of Wilmington, Delaware, particularly houses situated around squares. Today those programs have vanished and legislators wonder why core city economies are again stalled out. The people now in government, but most especially the federal government, have no understanding of the profit motive.

Fortunately, Jerry and Herb did. They replumbed, rewired and re-painted old houses. Jerry put up the money, Herb put up the work. It was a good arrangement.

In the thirteen years that they'd been together they'd accomplished a great deal financially. Whether they enjoyed the fruits of their labors I don't know, because Jerry bitched and moaned about everything.

He'd become embittered over the years. While he believed that DuPont was a good company, the pettiness of internal politics depressed him.

"When I started work I tried to do everything right. Over the years, as I rose in the ranks, I figured out who got promoted and who didn't."

"The straight people," I said.

"No, they just had to look straight, but that's not how it works. The guys that get ahead create problems, then solve them. I see this over and over again and I can't believe that upper management doesn't get it."

Jerry was raised to work hard, give his best, put the welfare of the company above the welfare of the individual. It was the way we were all raised, I guess. Frustrated because he couldn't give his best, because he had to play stupid games, he had grown crabby.

No matter how many times I told him to leave DuPont, no matter how many times he agreed to do it, he didn't. Herb had given up.

I watched the boy I had known since I was twelve turn into a shrinking man emotionally. He still worked hard but at forty-one he knew he wasn't going to make vice president, and it wasn't just that he didn't have a wife and kids. In his own way, Jerry was too honest. The irony was that he was completely dishonest about his personal life. He lived the Big Lie.

The widening separation between his professional life and his personal life had become shockingly apparent to me for the first time about eight years before this. Jerry had been assigned to the DuPont plant in Richmond, with many visits to Waynesboro, Virginia, where another DuPont plant was situated. He may have even been plant manager in Richmond—I don't remember his title.

Initially, this big promotion and the subsequent responsibility were thrilling. And the great thing about Jerry from an employer's standpoint, I would think, was that he had started as a chemist—he understood the business from the ground up and he was so motivated that he was studying marketing. He loved the whole thing the way I love literature.

Young, affluent, respected at work, he turned into a rock-and-roll party animal on weekends. He cooked up amyl nitrite in his kitchen, for him an easy thing to do. Then he'd sell bottles of it and people would make poppers, a little mesh-covered firecracker saturated with the chemical. Makes your heart race, and the guys would use it while dancing or having sex. He was making a lot of money with that, about three thousand dollars each month, tax free, maybe even more.

Had I known I would have been so goddamned mad I would have killed him.

The police got wind of it, arrested him and prosecuted. Both he and Herb got off but he had to leave the state of Virginia. DuPont stood by him during this embarrassing episode, probably because he was an outstanding prospect and because everyone is entitled to one whopping mistake. They were kinder than I would have been. I would have fired his ass.

But this compromised him professionally. He wasn't going to make the upper levels of management because his homosexuality was literally tearing his life apart. Had Jerry been heterosexual he might have indulged in drugs, he might have made amyl nitrite, but I doubt it. He needed release. He needed explosions of hedonism to be able to come back to work in a three-piece suit and pretend to be something he wasn't.

Once I got over screaming at him and throwing crockery—I threw some at Herb, too—I settled down. He'd been on the TV news. His case had been in the *Richmond Times-Dispatch*. I knew his career was all but finished. He thought he could overcome the scandal. Herb was smart enough to be supportive but I think Herb knew, too, that for the rest of his days Jerry would watch men far less qualified than himself rise.

He was switched to marketing, traditionally a more free-form department. He worked like a dog to overcome his disgrace. Bright, perceptive, utterly outrageous in humor, he made friends as he always did.

By now I had a name, and association with me wasn't going to help him one bit. He no longer took me to company dinners or even allowed me to visit him at the office—he worked half the week in New York now and half in Wilmington. Not that I was dying to go to company dinners but still, it stung. His crazed weekends continued but without the amyl nitrite. God knows what else he took. He showed up every Monday for work, sober.

We fought a lot. He hated women. He hadn't been that way as a boy but for whatever reason, he'd learned to despise women.

"You don't know how stupid women are," he'd yell at me. "You're surrounded by the bright ones. The average woman doesn't give a shit about her rights. She wants some rich jackass to take care of her. You don't see what I see at work."

He was right, I didn't. But I saw what work was doing to him. The buoyant, butch, athletic guy I'd known had become a real queen after work, a bitchy, hateful queen who cheated on Herb constantly, cheated our friendship and finally cheated himself.

He had learned to hate himself.

When I'd knock at him, tell him to find courage, he'd say, and once with tears, "You're the one with guts."

I never thought I'd hear him talk like that. By the time Mother died he had lionized me in a peculiar way; it sounded as though he admired and loved me but it was also a way to keep me distant. Above is just as distant as below. Besides, I didn't want to be the one woman who was the exception that proved the rule.

Hard emotional work was ahead for him and he ducked out every time. Sex became an obsession, no longer a true pleasure. How Herb tolerated it I don't know, and this isn't to say that Herb was the little woman pining at home. I know he had affairs, too, he told me so, but it wasn't the kind of driven, haunted stuff Jerry was doing: going to the docks at night, etc. Nor was Jerry just into rough trade: anyone, anytime, anywhere. He was sick at heart and he couldn't face what he'd made of his life.

One of the terrible truths of belonging to an outcast group is that it hurts. It always hurts. No matter how beautiful you are, no matter how rich and famous you may become, it still hurts. The pain is systemic. You are judged wanting over irrational criteria: your gender, your race, your age even, and your sexual direction. No human being has control over those things.

Jerry couldn't face the encroaching pain. I faced it early. I hated it then and I hate it now, but it's a fact of my life and I'll be damned if I'm going to throw away this magical life, this earthly delight, just because people will harshly judge me.

The pain takes many forms, but all outcast peoples struggle to be recognized as individuals. The damage of oppression is that it robs you of your individuality. You're just a faggot. Or whatever—fill in the blank. Everything you do is seen through the prism of your gayness or your womanness or your blackness by some people.

That's the deal.

I do not think for one instant that Jerry's pain was as horrible, as wrenching, as devastating as that of parents losing their child to leukemia. But such parents will be, I hope, supported and loved as individuals by the people around them. They will be remembered in prayers and in deeds.

The homosexual suffers alone. He doesn't even suffer among other homosexuals if he doesn't make common cause with them. Sleeping with another man doesn't connect you to him except physically. Jerry wanted nothing to do with gay groups. He was different. He was going to make it. Those gay people were losers, that's why they had revealed themselves. They couldn't call attention to themselves via their accomplishments.

Jerry wasn't the only gay person to feel that way. He wasn't the only one to refuse to examine the dry rot that sets in. Jerry wouldn't be morally responsible and I don't mean about sex. The human animal struggles with sexual rules and always will. He was immoral because he lied. In the long run, it always gets you. It got him good.

Because he was brilliant he could rationalize anything. Why should he sacrifice his career to come out? Well, he sacrificed it anyway, didn't he?

Because he could elude his pain with bouts of madness, if you will, he thought he might win in the end. This is perhaps the cruelest aspect of being a homosexual or a lesbian, the belief that you can escape. You can't escape yourself.

And I don't think straight people are that dumb. After the age of thirty roommates look suspicious.

Who knows who would have comforted Jerry if he had told the truth. Who knows what kind of community he would have been part of.

He turned his back on the Catholic Church, too, which I understand to the marrow of my bones, but there is still holiness amid the ruins—the prejudice, the appalling antiwomanness. There is no perfection in the church, because it has been created by imperfect people, but that doesn't mean there isn't love there.

Helpless, I watched the man I loved destroy himself.

He lied to his family, too, except to his middle brother, Bob, who was also gay.

He had a glib answer for everything he did. In not telling his family, he said he was protecting his father, that the truth would kill him.

I knew Jerry's family. It might have jolted them. It wouldn't have killed them. There was so much love waiting for him there and he brushed it away because he thought he would be rejected.

In the end, Jerry spoke to few of us. I think he was honest with me. He was honest with Herb, although Jerry didn't tell him about his nonstop philandering. He was honest with a good friend from his college days, Lloyd, who was also gay although I don't know if he ever came out.

But in the end all he did was complain.

I guess it was during the wallpaper fight that I realized he was dying. He didn't know it. He was dying inside but I sensed he was also dying physically. He was tired. He said he'd been to the doctor and Herb confirmed that. But detection was spotty in those days. He had AIDS. I felt it.

As the months rolled by, he grew even more tired. He'd have to take naps. Finally he took sick leave from DuPont, which continued to pay his full salary. They paid it to the end.

By now, most of you have seen someone die of this disease. I don't need to chronicle its progress.

But the end was dreadful. Even though I thought I was prepared, it was ghastly.

Because Jerry had AIDS—which he would never admit, by the way—Herb couldn't find a day nurse. Herb stopped working—he ran all the buildings they owned—hired a super to do repairs and nursed Jerry.

The virus attacked Jerry's brain. Lucid moments were few and far between. He'd call me at the strangest hours, the middle of the night, and talk as though we were back at Fort Lauderdale High. It was unnerving.

I was writing *Starting from Scratch* at the time, a writer's manual for which my publisher had no enthusiasm. (Fortunately, the public did.) I'd sit down at the typewriter and my mind would go blank. I couldn't remember what I'd written or what I was supposed to be writing.

Herb took Jerry to Rehoboth Beach, Delaware, where they had a condominium. Jerry loathed Wilmington, another problem he never fixed although he could have lived somewhere else. Herb thought Jer would be happier at Rehoboth, at least when he was capable of knowing where he was.

I'd seen Phil Mandelker, the producer who hired me to write *The Long Hot Summer,* die of AIDS. Funny, energetic, driven, he was a lot like Jerry except he was in a business that allowed more personal latitude, although not nearly as much as the public thinks. If you want to run a major studio in Hollywood, being gay isn't going to help your chances.

I had an idea of what was going to happen but even with Phil's sad example before me I felt crushed each time I saw Jerry. I acted bubbly. Sometimes he recognized me and other times he sat in his wheelchair, face blank.

Rehoboth isn't easy to reach from central Virginia. Either I took the Virginia Beach way, which was more scenic, or I circled Washington on the Beltway and then drove over to the coast. It took five hours no matter how I did it. I was exhausted. Herb was exhausted.

Jerry's parents came up from Florida to help. They were exhausted. I don't know why I was so tired. I didn't have to face 90 percent of what they did.

The last time I saw Jerry he was sitting in his wheelchair staring at the television. He snapped out of his trance and imagined we were playing mixed doubles in the city tournament at Fort Lauderdale. I'd take the backhand court and he'd take the forehand, which threw our opponents because I'm right-handed and Jerry was left-handed. Typically, lefties take the backhand court so they can field the wide shots on their forehand when the opponent goes for the alley. Same on the forehand side. But my backhand was strong, reliable and accurate. Also, we could both cover the middle with our forehands. We were lethal. We urged each other on, praised a good shot, pooh-poohed a bad one, giggled constantly.

"Jerry, if you don't serve aces, this guy will clobber me." I pretended I was at the net.

"Just watch me."

We played a game out in our minds except he thought it was real. He was happy again. Herb laughed.

When I left Jerry had again lapsed into his torpor and Herb was trying to feed him onion soup but he wouldn't eat.

A week later, Saturday, September 14, 1985, Herb called. Jerry was dead. His parents had been with him, as had Herb.

They couldn't get anyone in the county to pick up the body since it was Saturday and, more to the point, he had died of AIDS. No funeral parlor wanted him either.

Herb was frantic and in a towering rage. He had every right to the rage. I told him I'd drive up. Jerry's huge frame had shrunk to less than a hundred pounds. We could wrap him in a heavy plastic sheet and I'd take him home to bury him on the farm. Clearly, we had to do something drastic.

Herb said to hold off. He finally found an undertaker in Wilmington who came to take the body but by the time the man got there rigor was setting in. He couldn't fit Jerry, all bones but long bones, into the box. Herb said he broke Jerry's legs to make him fit.

By the time I reached Wilmington, where the service was to be held, I myself was in a rage. The knowledge of how one contracts AIDS was available but people paid no attention. AIDS affected drug users and queers. "Let 'em die" certainly seemed to be the response of the Reagan administration. I think in the years to come what Reagan will be remembered for is that he had the chance to stop the plague and he chose not to because the "right people" were dying.

In his forty-two years Jerry entertained thousands of people, had hundreds of close acquaintances, and had twenty or twenty-five good friends. He was the belle of the ball, or, as I used to tell him, "the belle of the brawl."

Only two gay friends attended his pathetic funeral. Except for Herb and me, no one was there apart from his older brother, his middle brother, his mother and father, Herb's mother and father and brother, and four couples, people Jerry had worked with.

No other gay person wanted to go to Jerry's funeral because he had died of AIDS. If they were seen there, people would know they were gay. I guess that's what they figured, anyway. Lloyd showed up. He had some balls, for which I was grateful.

In a clear moment, two days before he died, Jerry had asked Herb to have me deliver the eulogy. I did. I still don't know how I got through it. I didn't cry until I mentioned how his parents and Herb had suffered. Herb was sobbing. Mr. and Mrs. Pfeiffer were holding up. Bob, the middle brother, was bent over with grief. God, it was awful.

Three months earlier, Jerry had beseeched me to take his ashes and keep him on my bookshelf. When Herb died Jerry wanted me to mingle their ashes and dump them in Rehoboth, where they'd been happiest. Herb took Jerry's ashes, as he should have.

After the church service the small funeral party gathered at a restaurant where Jerry had been a frequent customer. We sat at the long table swapping stories, laughing at his outrageous antics. Once Jerry had dressed up as a waitress and served one of his friends who had a hot date. Jerry intruded on their conversations, spilled ice-cold tea on his friend's crotch, and finally, as the beleaguered suitor tried to eat dessert, Jerry gave him a pie in the face and revealed himself. That was a performance worthy of Juts.

We laughed and cried and laughed some more. His DuPont coworkers knew about his life even though he hadn't told them. They came because they loved him. If nothing else, DuPont hires good people. The job that killed him inside also provided him with the only true straight friends he had.

I don't know what would have happened to him at DuPont if he had come out. It might have been the straw that broke the camel's back, given his disgrace in Richmond or even without that disgrace.

Herb lost his partner of fourteen years. Sad as he was, he was glad the suffering was over. The end was grim. AIDS leaves one little dignity, especially if it gets in the brain.

Jerry had had an operation to repair a stomach valve. The blood supply wasn't screened then. Even if he contracted the disease in the hospital he no doubt was exposed to it anyway given his sexual exploits. I hated him. I hated him for screwing everything that moved. I hated him for missing my fortieth birthday party, which was the best party I've ever attended. I hated him for how grotesque he looked at the end. I hated him for wearing down Herb and his parents. I hated him for leaving me.

I hated him because I loved him.

I drove home the next day. I remember nothing of the drive. I remember very little of the next year. I scribbled a check to the Walker Whitman Clinic in Washington, D.C. I wrote, always my salvation. I enjoyed the hunt club to which I belonged. I lavished affection on Sneaky Pie and Pewter, her gray sidekick. I spent as much time as I could with the horses. The stable is always where I find my deepest peace.

Finally I forgave him. He didn't mean to hurt us. He surely never meant to die. He was all too human and he couldn't face his fears. Half of him despised being gay and the other half reveled in it, albeit in a childishly rebellious way.

Jerry had promised me since I was twelve that he would take care of me. He didn't. He left me nothing. I asked for his letter sweater but who knows where that wound up. He always said I'd be the beneficiary of one of his insurance policies. I wasn't.

If he had come back from the dead, I would have crowned him with a frying pan. Keep your promises.

Herb was left quite well off and I think Jerry's parents received some money. Those three people earned every penny, but no amount of money can make up for heartache.

Herb bought me a diamond pendant necklace, one small perfect stone. He drove down to give it to me a month after Jerry died. How like Herb, a romantic man. If the shoe had been on the other foot, Jerry would have given me an electric blender.

Herbert May was about to become one of the biggest surprises of my life.

West Side Story

I'D BEGUN RESEARCH FOR MY NOVEL ABOUT DOLLEY MADISON EVEN though the writing itself was years off. While I was roaming around Alderman Library at the University of Virginia and the state library in Richmond, and exploring the path of General Cornwallis's depredations during the Revolutionary War, I thought about a closer war, the War Between the States. I could dimly remember Great-grandpa Huff, who fought in that war. I continued reading Dolley's letters, her husband's papers, her sister's letters, but I jumped full in on researching the war that nearly took us down and is still felt in obvious and subtle ways to this day. I wanted to write a second volume of *High Hearts,* a novel I'd written about the War Between the States.

I'd invite Herb on my forays down the back roads of Virginia, around Richmond, a city I love, back into the Wilderness battleground, Manassas. I crossed and crisscrossed Virginia, trying to visit the sites in the order of battle and during the same time of year that the battles were fought.

Herb would have none of it.

An apartment became available in New York on West Eighty-third Street between Riverside Drive and West End Avenue. I was spending a lot of time in the city due to a television project. A couple in Charlottesville, Clare and Bill Leach, agreed to share it with Herb and me. With four of us splitting the cost it was affordable, and we were never there at the same time. We set up house rules, Bill and Clare moved in odds and ends of furniture and we were in business.

I'd drive up to Washington to catch the Metroliner, and Herb would board at Wilmington, walking the cars until he found me. I looked forward to our monthly visits in New York.

We'd read the newspaper to each other aloud between Wilmington and

New York. I'd get either *The New York Times* or *The Washington Post*. He'd get the Wilmington paper or *The Philadelphia Inquirer*. We'd compare how stories were featured and how they were written.

Herb, curious and critical, had a sharp mind. Since Jerry had talked for both of them, actually for anyone, I knew very little about Herb other than that he had been in the navy.

He enjoyed theater and dance, wasn't that crazy about museums but he'd go to be a good sport. We'd haunt bookstores. Herb could be tight with the buck. In a bookstore I lose all manner of restraint. What fun it was to walk out of Three Lives or Shakespeare and Co. and Herb would have spent more than I did.

Indifferent to food, I usually want an ice-cold Co'Cola and a salad or a hamburger. Well, I'd really like greens and fatback but we were in New York, remember. Herb liked food, though. So I'd tag along to his latest culinary discovery, where I'd order a salad and he'd order salmon poached in parchment with a thin orange dribble on the top. His once trim body ballooned with fifty extra pounds.

I'd get up and hit the gym. I couldn't blast him out of bed. I slept upstairs, he slept downstairs. No amount of pleading or rattling cups and saucers could dislodge him.

Exasperated, I finally said, "Herb, you're fat."

"I know. I'll start my diet today."

He never did. I finally realized that he was overweight because in his eyes that was healthy. Jerry had weighed less than one of my big hounds at the end.

I looked around and saw that many gay men were getting overweight. It was a declaration of not being HIV positive, although you can be fat and still test positive. But the visceral impact is, "Here's a healthy boy."

I finally let it go and he actually dropped a few pounds in gratitude.

I was working on a movie of the week entitled *My Two Loves* about a woman who loves a man and loves a woman. ABC plucked up their courage thanks to Alvin Cooperman, who practically invented long-form when he was a vice president at NBC. An independent producer now, Alvin somehow found me. It was a marriage made in heaven. Alvin doesn't know how to cut a corner, cheat a character or demolish production values. If he's going to do it, it will be done properly. He's got a gift for casting, which was often thwarted by the networks. Alvin thinks of the best actor for the role. The networks want whoever is most popular at the moment even if they can't act their way out of a paper bag—and half of them can't.

Since he was based in New York I needed to be there a lot. Sometimes

I'd call Herb in Wilmington at the last minute and tell him I needed to go over notes with Alvin. He'd hop on the train and our pleasurable odyssey would begin anew.

Jerry had picked a good man to love. This isn't to say Herb wasn't subject to fits of temper. But the anger subsided as quickly as it arrived, except when Jerry would goad him.

We talked about Jerry endlessly, as though our memories would keep him alive, and in a way they did. It was 1986 but enough time had passed that I encouraged Herb to date. He didn't want to. He encouraged me to date, so we were even.

By the summer he felt strong enough to see a few people. He was in an AIDS support group. Men who had lost partners gathered to help one another along. He dated one fellow from the group but wouldn't go to bed with him.

When he came home after the fourth date I heard him walking up the stairs to the apartment. From the way his feet distinctly hit each step I knew he was in a bad mood. By the time he opened the door I was downstairs in my old navy blue bathrobe waiting for him.

"Don't ask."

"Okay, I'll go to bed"—which I did.

Just as I snapped off the lights he called up, "After Jerry, everyone is boring."

I snapped on the light. "Jerry was a domineering asshole. But you're right, he was never boring."

"Yeah."

I snapped off the light. "I'm going to the gym in the morning."

"What do you do after you've had the best?"

I snapped on the light again and leaned over the railing. "Do you want to come on up here for girl talk?"

He climbed up the iron staircase and plopped on the end of my bed. "I never thought I'd be alone."

"You aren't. You have your family and you have me. Alone romantically, yes. Fourteen years is a big chunk of your life."

"I don't know where the fourteen years went."

"Are you gonna cry?"

"No." He laughed at me.

"I'm not either." I handed him the box of Kleenex and we both cried.

Bill and Clare, after a year's lease, gave up their half of the apartment. Herb and I decided it was too expensive for just the two of us, and of course I kick myself in the butt each time I think about it because I wish I still had that apartment, even though I'm at heart an East Side girl, not a West Sider. I learned to like the West Side, especially Riverside Park.

Without the apartment our visits were less structured. He'd drive down to visit me more than I drove to Wilmington, mostly because I had stock to care for, a farm to run and I was between farm managers. He wired overhead lights, stripped furniture, gardened with me. He was heaven. He even took out the garbage before I could get to it.

Herb was HIV positive, too, but everything seemed all right. Then the disease hit him suddenly. He'd suffer bouts of fatigue and night sweats. He stayed in Wilmington more but we'd still visit. He was losing a little weight. He looked really good but he couldn't motivate himself to do anything.

"I need a job. I need to keep my mind active."

"Here's a newspaper." I'd toss him the classifieds.

He'd circle ads. "I'll go back into construction."

"Good idea."

He'd never make the call.

One day stands out in my mind because I was boarding a mare who jumped like a pogo stick. She'd jumped out of her paddock again. She should have been a real-estate appraiser, she covered so much territory. I finally caught her, walking her miles back to the house. As I passed the kitchen I heard the phone ring.

Thinking it was Alvin, I tied the mare to the old walnut in the back and sprinted into the house.

"Rita Mae," the familiar voice said, "I can't get out of bed."

"What?"

"I can't get out of bed." Herb started laughing. "My legs don't want to go."

"Herb, I didn't think you were that sick."

"I'm not sick. My legs are."

He was funny. His mind was perfectly clear, clear enough to complain about his parents, who had moved down to care for him. Yet he insisted he wasn't that sick—he was touched that his folks were there but he wanted to do things for himself.

I asked him if I could come up that weekend. He said he'd come down to me, that he was really fine—he just had no direction in life. He had to snap out of it.

Like a fool I believed him and told him I'd come up in a few weeks.

By then he was dead.

Herb's death certificate, which I have never seen, may say "cause of death, AIDS," but he died of a broken heart.

I used to say anyone who died of a broken heart deserved it. Of course, I was being smart and commenting on drama queens weeping about the smashed-up love of the moment.

Jerry put the gas in Herb's engine. Without him the car finally glided to a stop.

I hope they're together again. And they'd better watch out for Juts.

Rack On

LEST YOU THINK I WILL WALLOW IN LAMENTS FOR THOSE I HAVE lost, let me hasten to remind you of what Mother always said to me: "Worse things have happened to nicer people."

I'd lost Fannie, Martina, Baby Jesus, Mother, Jerry and Herb between 1979 and 1987. Bad as it was, it wasn't the firebombing of Dresden, a V-2 raid on London or the San Francisco earthquake.

If there is an upside to the above war and disaster horrors, it is that they were shared.

If I'd had a grain of sense, I would have sat down hard, but I simply ran faster. Not that I could run away from pain. I knew that. But I felt as though I had to live for everyone I'd lost. Therefore I had to be more successful in the outside world to justify their existence and to justify their faith in me. The books sold well, and Hollyweird kept me busy. These triumphs, large and small, brought no one back. Sometimes in the middle of the night I'd get up, accompanied by Sneaky Pie and Pewter, and sit in the garden. I'd listen to the owls, watch possums and other night animals. I strained for an echo of Mother's voice, Jerry and Herb's laughter.

The echo reverberated inside. The wind carried fragrance and insects. I had to learn to live with my losses.

I was also bored to the point of dementia with being America's leading lesbian. How ironic to be known for something I considered superficial in terms of my character and which, furthermore, was not entirely accurate.

That was another great sadness. I finally had to accept the full damage of being an outsider. Like most Americans, I believed that if you worked hard and stayed reasonably personable, you'd break through these barriers. Not only did I not break through, I was reviled or celebrated for lesbianism, depending on one's point of view.

Past forty, I could no longer believe I would be part of the greater national community or even part of my town. I could no longer believe that if people got to know me they'd see that I was a worthy citizen, not a perfect one but a worthy one.

To further tighten the noose, the country was veering toward the right and not without some justification. The easy money of the Kennedy and Johnson days transformed, in the early 1980s, into a nasty little rollback. No one dared use the word *depression* but farmland plummeted in value and I was a farmer.

Ronald Reagan put together a coalition, in its own way as interesting and powerful as the coalition that FDR created. For Reagan this was a meld of solid, middle-of-the-road Republicans, a smattering of disaffected Democrats and the well-organized, well-funded right wing, including some real wing nuts. But Reagan could hold them together with the force of his personality, with that marvelous Irish charm, which had also helped Jack Kennedy. The Irish do not compel so much as they beguile. Having a strong streak of black Irish in my blood, I think I can say that without being accused of trading in stereotypes.

One of the tenets of this coalition was, we had to return America to its senses. So instead of pot in every chicken it was a chicken in every pot, women back in the kitchen, blacks to the back of the bus, Hispanics in the lettuce patch. Gays should pretend to be straight or conveniently die.

A few silly Republicans were dumb enough to express these sentiments directly. Most spoke in a code that meant the above.

Along with this virulent virus of intolerance came a promotion of business interests and an astonishing understanding of the weakness of the Soviet state. To get the latter you had to swallow the former. I just couldn't do it, much as I believed, like Reagan, that it came down to guns and butter and that the Soviet Union and its satellites were tiring of guns and couldn't pay for them anymore anyway. We drove them into the ground in an arms race that destroyed them economically. It hurt us, too, but we could better absorb it. We are the richest nation on earth. Squandering resources, bad as it is, hasn't destroyed us as it did the Communists. If we keep it up it will though.

The audacity of Reagan's program was interesting to me and, I'm sure, to other political people. The fact that this program involved the bludgeoning and submission of out-groups sickened me.

At this point in our history the Democrats lost their center or maybe their nerve. The energy was with the Republicans, who cleverly tapped into the anger of white men—not all white men but enough white men.

For the first time in America's history the average white man had to contend with those of us rising from the lower orders, as Mother was wont to say. They wimped out. Rather than improve their skills, they pushed us back down again.

The tone of political debate shifted. If you spoke of equal rights, of racial justice, of gender parity, you were accused of special pleading, of being divisive. Every program designed to lift up the downtrodden was raked over the coals. That alone may not be a bad thing. It never hurts to review whether your programs are effective, but the nastiness attending this had nothing to do with effectiveness, it had to do with fear.

Any concept that worked toward the betterment of all was dubbed liberal. That word became a slap in the face. It meant a glut of government spending and interference. It meant unreasonable demands on the community, like the abolition of prayer in schools.

The average white man could no longer assume he'd bump along making enough to pay for a house and two cars and to send his children to college. Note *his* children. Who the hell cared what happened to everybody else's children?

Gloria Steinem once said that women will not truly be equal until an average woman can rise to the same level of incompetence as an average man. Bull's-eye, Gloria.

Many of us who had made gains and were therefore contributing to the tax rolls were stymied. Downsizing, a neutral word, meant women lost their jobs along with men. Usually the women lost their jobs first: last hired, first fired.

You could cut the despair of working people and the "outs" with a knife.

Two things helped the Republicans. One was that my generation was at the peak of its child-rearing years. We still had the kids at home, and our parents were aging, so often we had to care for them too. We couldn't be as politically active as we had been when we were in our twenties.

The second thing that helped them was that we overplayed our hand. We weren't as well organized as we should have been and, convinced of our moral superiority, we let things slide. We'd thought that since we were right, on the side of the future, we'd win. I think an entire generation has now been disabused of this notion.

All this was coming down as I was trying to rise up after my losses.

Did this hurt my work? No. I can write through anything. What it did was slide me away from any task wherein the public could see me. No one wanted the Queer of the Year sitting by their front window. No professorships would be coming my way. Nor would I be on the board of directors for a local bank or a national corporation.

Don't laugh. One of the weaknesses of these boards is that they rarely have members who came up from the people, nor do they have anyone from the arts. You can't succeed in the arts on talent alone anymore (if you ever could). You'd better be a half-decent businessman or surround yourself with people who are.

I had hoped in my middle years to be able to contribute on these different levels—and I wouldn't have minded the compensation, either, since if you're going to do it right, such involvement takes a lot of time.

No government appointments would come my way. I'd served with the Literature Panel for the National Endowment for the Arts during the Carter administration. This isn't to say I understood the inner workings of government but I watched two women who did: Midge Costanza and Donna Shalala. I also closely watched the senator from Kansas, Bob Dole. He knew the Hill. At that time the Republicans used him as the forward or attack man. And always there was Senator Ted Kennedy, who seemed to command a shadow government.

Each of these people was good with other people, one-on-one. They were easy to talk to, often had wit, had fantastic staffs and had clear objectives.

To be pushed aside happens to many people. While Sandra Day O'Connor was the first woman appointed to the Supreme Court, think of the other women, the Democrats, who could have filled that slot. It wasn't their time.

So much of life is happenstance. It makes me laugh when I go to a bookstore and see all those titles about controlling your life. You're lucky if you can control your bladder.

And like those before me who belonged to the party out of power, or to a despised group, I had to readjust.

Bursting with energy and ideas, I couldn't sit around twiddling my thumbs. I accepted never being a part of government with more ease than I accepted not teaching. But in the end, I bowed to fate and asked myself what could I do that was useful above and beyond writing.

Animals. They were the first love of my life, coequal with language. If I couldn't do much for people, I hoped I could do a great deal for my friends without a vote.

Kalarama Farm in Springfield, Kentucky, provided inspiration. Kalarama brought me back "home." I'd met Joan Hamilton and Larry Hodge two weeks before Mother died. David Goodstein, the publisher of

The Advocate, introduced me. These people knew horses. At the top of the Saddlebred game, Joan and Larry also had a keen appreciation for a good Thoroughbred. If it had a leg on each corner, they knew about it.

It's a seven-hour drive from central Virginia to Springfield. I'd put Juts, my Chow puppy, in the car and go. I figured naming the dog after Mother would give Mom a jolt in the Great Beyond. She could rail at my lack of respect. Doggie Juts and I would rumble from Lexington, Virginia, to Lexington, Kentucky. We'd pick up the Bluegrass Parkway and head south to Springfield.

My heart skips a beat each time I pass the grave of Kalarama Rex, one of the great Saddlebred sires. By the time you pass the simple stone you're at the main white barn. Out run Jack Russells, out runs Joan. If Larry's in the office, he runs out, too.

Like so many friendships, this one has deepened over time to the point that I can't imagine my life without Joan and Larry.

I bedevil them with questions because they're at the forefront of knowledge. Kalarama Farm was one of the first farms to experiment with feeds incorporating rice hulls, which supply shine to horses' coats as well as nutrition. Joan studies nutrition, pasture forage, bloodlines. When it comes to breeding, she has a gift, the ability to see what isn't yet there. As for Larry, he has the best hands I have ever seen on a horseman. Jean Beegle, a dear friend of mine, now in her seventies, had great hands like Larry. Part of that is training and part is a gift from God.

I watched how they ran their business, how they cared for their horses. Joan, always up on medical research, would keep me informed as to advances at the Gluck Equine Research Center at the University of Kentucky. She also told me what horses were on the back acres of the big Thoroughbred farms. Many times the best hunter/jumpers come off those back acres.

Even better, Joan and Larry would foxhunt with me. Again, remember that in America we hunt for the chase, not the kill.

One February, Chuck and Jean Beegle, their daughter Lynne and I hauled horses over to Lexington. We threw on two extra horses, one for Joan and one for Larry. We'd called ahead, receiving permission to hunt with Iroquois, a grand hunt founded in 1880. We also thought we'd stay and go out with Woodford Hounds, founded in 1981 by Richard Dole, a keen hunting man, as is his wife. Both hunts have a reputation for burning the wind and we couldn't wait to mount up.

In hunting you cannot wear your colors with another hunt unless the Master gives you permission to do so. Chuck called and received permission. Colors are awarded once a year by the Master. It is the highest honor a person can earn in the field and colors can be earned only in the field. It takes years to win them.

Meg Finney, a member of Iroquois, took upon herself the role of our guide. She was to regret this.

The morning of the hunt the temperature hovered in the high twenties. Skies were overcast. Although it was cold, we figured the day would warm up a tad, and overcast skies usually presage a good hunt because dampness and cool temperatures keep the scent down. When the sun climbs in the sky and the temperature rises, scent burns off.

Excited, we inspected one another's attire to make certain we were perfect. As each one mounted, the person on the ground took a towel and rubbed off whatever specks had gotten onto the other's boots. The last one up dusted off his boots as best he could and off we rode, led by Meg, who is a fine rider, very fluid and easy on a horse. She's also quite a lovely-looking woman and, turned out in proper formal attire, makes men's heads snap around—as they do for Joan, a beauty with big brown eyes, and for Lynne, tiny like her mother, with an infectious smile.

By the time we reached the fixture, the place where the hunters gather, we were limbered up. The first thing I noticed was the horses. What splendid animals, and not one Western color among them: no paints, buckskins, palominos. Every horse was bay, chestnut or seal brown. These were the horses from the back acres of the studs. I hope I remembered to close my mouth. The gathering was impeccably turned out, many wearing the colors of Iroquois, a black collar with robin's egg blue piping, and some had the robin's egg blue vest, too.

Out came the hounds, Cross-bred and English, and that fast, off we went over the undulating green of Kentucky. Our first jump was a stone wall with a log rider over the top. I was riding a big horse called Chester, not pretty but he would jump anything. My Thoroughbred hunter, a smallish, 15.3-hand bay called Jones, was beginning to go blind in one eye so I'd borrowed a horse from Lynne. Jones, by the way, now lives a life of ease. A few more years and he'll be able to vote.

I rubbed the jump and the rail came off. I'd never jumped a true stone wall before. I was amazed at how quickly the rosary came back to me.

Joan, Larry, Chuck, Jean, Lynne and I—off we went at an easy gallop, for the hounds gave tongue. Whatever was in front of us we cleared, sometimes landing on smooth rock on the other side. The hounds sounded glorious. At one point, early in the day, we were in a river bottom looking up at bluffs overhead with the hounds running single file, silhouetted on the bluffs. What a beautiful sight, and the music was good.

Then off we tore, plowing through the river, over more rail fences, paneled fences and the occasional coop.

We clipped along, the wind came up, tears streamed down our faces. The temperature plummeted. I could no longer feel my hands or my toes.

Here I must insert that Virginia foxhunters are not beloved by the rest of America or by Canada. Too often that haughtiness of Virginians, that elegant way of saying nothing yet saying everything, plain pisses people off. We, of course, feel that Virginia is the center of foxhunting in America, and you can hunt the shires of England or you can hunt Virginia.

Naturally, Marylanders take great exception to this, especially Mother's old hunt, Green Spring Valley Hounds.

Iroquois therefore felt a touch of competitiveness toward us. They flat ran our asses off. At one point we had a check, a pause for hounds to again find the scent. The gentlemen of Iroquois offered us libations from their hunting flasks. Libations? That stuff could raise the dead! As I've said, I don't drink, but I will take a nip in the hunt field to ward off the cold. I swallowed a tiny mouthful and was grateful I hadn't imbibed more. My compatriots gulped down large quantities of the stuff as our hosts smiled benevolently. Few people are more hospitable or better storytellers than Kentuckians. All that bourbon has to go to some good purpose.

I looked at Joan as she knocked back a swig, her head to the sky.

Laughing, she handed the flask back to its owner, a tall, good-looking man, saying, "That tastes good."

Right then and there I knew that Joan was made of stronger stuff than I was. Had I swallowed that much of the juice, I'd be dead.

Larry also allowed himself a sip.

No sooner was the cap on the flask then off we boomed at a gallop. We were winding our way at a good speed through low bushes and trees almost stunted, a curious patch of territory. By now it was snowing. You could still see but the flakes seemed as big as pancakes.

Chuck, Jean, Lynne and I somehow had pushed up to the front, and we slowed down to take a fence by a gate. The terrain was narrow, so we had to jump it single file. Usually Iroquois people "take their own line," which means they take the obstacle wherever they please so long as they don't pass the Master.

As we waited, impatient to continue, a lady rode up and shouted, "You've lost one of your people."

Now, in hunting parlance that is a euphemism that can mean "One of your people is dead," "One of your people has hit the ground hard" or even "One of your people has wandered into the back of the beyond and I'll be damned if I'm going to miss a ripping hunt to look for them."

Dutifully the three of us turned our horses back to find either Joan or Larry. Meg wasn't with us either, but since the lady had said "one of your people" we knew it wasn't Meg.

We rode back to find Joan dusting herself off. Feeling the effects of the Kickapoo joy juice, she'd popped off when her horse slipped and twisted out from under her. She must have hit the ground hard because she was a touch nauseated, which can mean a slight concussion.

Gamely she mounted back up. We figured we'd better go back to the stables, but only Meg knew the territory and she said, "You can't get there from here."

By now you couldn't see the hand in front of your face. Occasionally we'd hear the hounds.

Hunched down in our saddles, we picked our way through the countryside, now silent and white. No one thought Joan should jump, but in a few places you had to. She went up and over in good form but her face was as white as the snow.

The temperature was really dropping now. We finally slid over a soft hill about an hour later and there reposed the field. They hailed us. "There are the Virginians."

The field master turned toward home. It was another hour before we finally reached the stables.

Jean got Joan off her horse and into the little stable office that had a cot in it. There was no heat in that room but there were horse blankets, so Jean covered her up as we, fingers stiff from the cold, untacked our horses, rubbed them down, put coolers on them to dry them out and put them in their stalls. Once the animals were dry, we threw on their blankets and fed them hay. The thermometer in the stable read 16°F.

Another hour passed. Jean suggested we take Joan to a hospital just in case. Joan refused and said she needed to rest. Larry, lips blue, bright blue, put her in the car and carried her home, which is about forty-five minutes from Lexington.

I've never been so glad to get in a car in my life. When that heater cranked on, it was heaven. We drove back to our hotel, where Chuck and Jean got into the hot tub. I couldn't do it. It seemed so hot it was painful. I took a shower instead.

That evening we were invited to the clubhouse for dinner. The clubhouse is an old mill with lovely stonework. The downstairs has a long bar and a big fireplace. The upstairs is a big, open room that can be used for various functions. It was filled with long tables, lively conversation and good food.

The weather grew even more hateful and Woodford chose, wisely, not to go out. This gives me an excuse to go back and hunt some more since I really want to go out with Woodford. To this day, when Joan discusses hunting, she says, "I am never drinking that witch's brew again."

Sometimes when I'm faced with a tough decision or a physically unpleasant task I say to myself, "Can't be as bad as Joan's day with Iroquois."

Laughter Beyond the Grave

W HEN THE HEART WEEPS FOR WHAT IT HAS LOST, THE SPIRIT rejoices for what it has found." I can't take credit for that thought. It's a Sufi aphorism.

When losses and heartbreak pile up, my aphorism is, "Dammit to hell." But time and heartache taught me there's great truth in the Sufi aphorism. I learned to be grateful for the time I had with those who had died and even with those who had ditched me.

Many times when someone's mother or a dear friend dies, they are bereft because they've lost a person who loved them, foremost, and some-one to whom they could open their heart. Since I seldom opened my heart to either Mother or Jerry, I didn't search for new sounding boards. I had opened my mind to them, and I missed the free exchange of ideas.

I learned quite young that Mother cared nothing for what I felt. Her focus was on how I behaved, how I achieved, how I looked. In fairness to her, she never cared how anyone felt. For Mother, life was external. If there were any emotions to be displayed they would be her own or Aunt Mimi's. And I learned my lessons well: Nobody wants to know what you're feeling. Concentrate on the other person.

I recognize now that this period in my life was one of my emotional turning points. The fact that I didn't speak of it nor write about it means only that I was figuring it out as best I could. Then, too, I was following my minuet of manners.

Since my writing direction was clear, and my farming was clear, I thought I was doing rather well. I'd go out with people but I wasn't focusing on a deep connection. By the same token, I wasn't focusing just on sex either, and this brought me no end of trouble. In America you either sow your wild oats or make a lifelong commitment. There seems to be little tolerance for a more relaxed attitude about dating people. One is supposed to date with intentions obvious.

I didn't do that. I wasn't looking for a life partner. I was happy to go to the movies, go to a baseball game, or go to bed. This made a lot of people unhappy with me. Not just the woman or occasional man that I would date, but the people surrounding them and the people surrounding me.

I simply did not want to make a commitment I couldn't keep. I was struggling inside to order—strange as that word may sound—my losses. I accepted them, I learned from them, but I had to order them.

I order the socks in my drawer, the books on my shelf, the bridles in the tackroom. It's part of my personality. So I had to order my internal life anew.

While I was coming back to the land of the living, I decided to unpack the big trunk I'd thrown together when Mother died. I took from her house her treadle sewing machine, my ribbons and trophies from sporting events, her accounting books and personal correspondence and one old housecoat because it was so Mom (in her cleaning incarnation). I also packed her jewelry, and I hasten to add we have vastly different taste in jewelry.

I opened the trunk and started reading. It's a good thing Juts was dead because if she'd returned to terra firma I would have brained her.

75

Juts's Secret

ROOTING THROUGH MOTHER'S THINGS, I ENDURED A BOUT OF sadness, getting misty, even missing that wild woman. I held her big bloodstone ring in my hand and thought of the times I beheld her wearing the ring, a Chesterfield between her first and second finger, conversation running along an uncharitable course.

I weakened and called Aunt Mimi, now in her high eighties, sound as a dollar even though she'd been dying since the day she was born and was not one to leave us ignorant of her sufferings. I sniffled a bit about how much I missed my beloved mother. Okay, the beloved part was gilding the lily, but Aunt Mimi liked to hear those things.

"Did I ever tell you about the time we went to lunch from the silk mill?" she said.

Indeed she had, but I pretended that I hadn't heard this tale before. She knew she'd told me many times but the polite thing was to ask. The minute I said no she could trot out the polished story.

"Well, it was 1925 and Juts was working at the Blue Bird Silk Mill. She was palling around with Toot Weigel and Laura Uhlein—it might have been spelled Uhlein but it was pronounced 'E-line' . . . of course, you knew her as Laura Gadd. I was working down on Hanover Square at—" Here there was an interruption because her Pekingese, Chin, wanted attention. "The best puppy in the world. . . . Where was I?"

"You, Mom, Laura and Toot were having lunch at the soda fountain. I think Ev Loss was there, too." I skipped ahead to try to save time.

"Did I get that far?"

"Yes, Chin distracted you."

"Chin is fat."

"Go for longer walks."

"Who has the time?"

I wanted to say, "If you'd stop hanging on the telephone half the day, you'd have a lot of time." She used the phone to keep up with her various grandchildren and great-grandchildren for the express purpose of telling them how to live their lives, down to what kind of toilet paper to use. Instead I said, "Aunt Mimi, you just do too much for other people."

"That's what the Good Book says."

Again I proved that I am a saint. "Yes, ma'am."

"Well, we'd finished lunch and everyone had to go back to work but the day was so pretty I thought I'd walk with Toot and Juts to the railroad tracks and then turn back. I could just make it. We reached the railroad tracks and the ambulance was there, a motorized one. People who could were buying cars and the town had purchased this ambulance. They were putting a dead body, sheet over it, into the back of the ambulance. The sheet was a bloody mess. Naturally, we were curious. You know how my sister was." A pause, waiting for the correct response.

"Curious is a nice way to put it, Aunt Mimi."

"Juts lived in fear that she might miss something. Well, she didn't miss it that day. Anyway, next to the track was a wicker basket and the bottom of that was seeping blood. Everybody knew everybody those days. Toot said to the driver, 'Will, what's going on?'

" 'Guy run over by the train. Took his head off clean as a whistle.'

" 'Who is it?' I asked. After all, if this was a friend, we'd have to go prepare the family. Well, Will didn't know.

"So Toot goes over to the basket, reaches in and pulls up the head by the hair. Not a scratch on the face, mind you, just like normal except no body was attached to it. She looked at the face, then held it out to Juts and me and said, 'Don't know him.'

" 'Me neither.' Toot dropped the head right back in the basket."

"You girls had stomachs of iron."

"In my day you saw everything. Not like now, a little drop of blood and people pass out. Now you know that when my dear Ginny died, we prepared the body."

"Yes, ma'am." I add here that whenever Mother told the tale of the severed head, it varied from her older sister's version but each time either one had recounted the grisly tale details shifted.

"You know I always felt that you were one of the family. I knew you were going to be a big success."

Puh-lease. "Thank you, Aunt Mimi."

"I just could never stand Jack Young."

"Yes, ma'am."

"The Republican Party is bad enough, but you throw him in too and it's ten times worse. I still think Adlai Stevenson should have been elected president and I can't believe that my sister, whom I begged, voted for Eisenhower. Generals don't make good presidents. Look at Ulysses S. Grant."

"George Washington."

She didn't like being contradicted, but she had to consider. "Yes, but he was special. We'll never see a great man like that in uniform again. I mean a man who can command as well as politick."

"I reckon."

"Then, too, President Washington was a Virginian and Virginians make good presidents. Much as I love Maryland and Pennsylvania, Virginians make good presidents."

"Think we'll ever have a president from Florida?"

"Only if you move back."

I laughed. "Thanks."

"Your daddy always said you could do it."

"Can't. I'm gay."

"You know what I think about that? I think you ought to get married in the One True Church and have children. But you told the truth, indeed you did, and you haven't done anything worse than those jackasses on Capitol Hill. I'd vote for you."

By now you could have knocked me over with a feather. "Thank you."

"I won't live to see a woman president but you will."

"You know, Aunt Mimi, I'd like to say I hope so but I don't much care if it's a woman or a man as long as they have guts and brains."

"Short supply. What else do you want to know?"

"When do you want to come visit? I'll send you a ticket."

"I am not getting on an airplane. If God wanted us to fly, he would have given us wings."

"Mother flew." Couldn't resist.

"My sister had no sense. If it was new, she wanted to do it. If she were with us today, she'd have a computer. I heard you can play cards on the computer. Now you know what *that* means."

"Yes, ma'am."

"If she'd ever gone to Las Vegas, they would have thrown her out. She remembered everything. She remembered card hands she played before World War I."

This was true. Mom had an amazing capacity for numbers and cards. It was akin to her mastery of technical stuff. She would have made an excellent chess player except it would have bored her stiff. She needed the speed and color of cards. Then, too, money changing hands enlivened her. Naturally, I did not tell Aunt Mimi that plans were afoot for letting people go to the races via computer.

"I would love to show you my place."

"Thank you, honey, but I'm too old to travel."

This was a flat-out lie. Aunt Mimi thought nothing of getting into her car—her latest was a white Chevy with a green interior, perfectly maintained—and driving all the way to Hanover and York to visit her cronies. She'd zoom right up I-95 not an hour and a half from my place and never stop in.

Aunt Mimi liked me well enough but not well enough to trouble herself to visit. At least Uncle Claude would drop by occasionally. He and Jeun are the only family members to go out of their way. Claude was born in 1915 yet looks ten to fifteen years younger than he is and acts about thirty. He's physically robust, a good athlete, and she's in great shape, too. The difference is that Claude and Jeun are happy people. Aunt Mimi never was happy. If she felt a flash of happiness, she'd have to wreck it because it scared her so much.

As for me, I was always the outsider. After Mom died Aunt Mimi didn't keep up with me. I had to keep up with her. She did send me birthday cards, though, and I was touched by that.

This phone conversation was going to cost as much as my mortgage payment because once she wound up she had to wind down. How anyone can talk that long with so few breaths is remarkable. I heard about her health; that subject was good for fifteen or twenty minutes. I heard about Julia Ellen, Russell, Kenny, Wade, Terry, the assorted wives and children. Then we moved on to the church ladies. Once that was exhausted she allowed as to how she was hungry, thanks for calling, bye.

When I hung up the phone my ear throbbed.

I was hungry, too. Time for tuna with capers. Here's my only recipe. I dump a can of tuna in a bowl, throw in Hellmann's real mayonnaise, some capers cut up fine, two sweet gherkins, sit down and eat it right out of the bowl. I have to share with the cats, of course.

Finished that and back to the trunk, where I pulled out photo albums, finally reaching letters tied in red ribbons. Juts's favorite color was red, red and more red. What a lot of envelopes. The handwriting wasn't Daddy's. He had big, bold, artistic handwriting, very masculine. This was pretty cursive script.

Then I wondered if it was Mom's first husband. The one I was never supposed to tell about but just did.

I untied a red ribbon. These were letters from Juliann Young to Mom covering four decades. Mother always told me she hadn't heard anything from Jule. Another Juts fact.

I read the letters . . . chitchat. But Juliann felt a maternal bond with Mom and I guess Mom reciprocated. I never saw her letters but they would have been peppered with her escapades, the latest Aunt Mimi misery, etc.

There wasn't much about me. That didn't surprise me.

How could I ever get the Big Head? I'd been informed consistently as to my lowly status.

I dug out Mom's address book, a novel in itself, found Juliann's number and called her up.

"Hello, is Juliann there?"

"This is Juliann."

"It's Rita Mae Brown."

She launched right in. She was glad to hear my voice, which actually was quite a bit like her own. I told her I'd found her letters and we talked about her family now, her situation then. She's a very nice woman and a bright one. She told me about a Thoroughbred she used to hunt. We talked a lot about horses and the fact that my half sisters were fine riders, an interesting fact on two levels . . . I didn't know I had half sisters, apart from Patty.

We talked about Mom, Mom and horses.

They were and are the thread weaving throughout our lives. It makes me wonder what's in the genes. It also made me both furious and sad that I hadn't learned to ride as a child. I might have been worth something, but trust the will of the gods. My purpose is not to be a show rider.

"Can you tell me about Gordon?"

"He loved music. We'd go to concerts and symphonies in Baltimore."

"He wouldn't leave his wife?"

"He almost did, but he was Catholic. His sister got hold of him. I don't know really. I want you to know you were born in love. Don't ever think that you weren't. I think of you as the bird that fell out of the nest."

"Actually, winding up with Juts, it was more like falling into the army."

She laughed. We must have talked for forty-five minutes.

Occasionally she writes me a letter or a note. I like her. I think I would have liked Gordon, too, but in my mind he was weak. Then again, I am not a married man with a son and a pregnant mistress. Who knows what one should do? Sometimes I think we would profit by dumping the word *should* from our vocabulary, and yet there are moral imperatives.

Jule was eighteen. She knew little of the world. Gordon was handsome, accomplished and clearly charismatic. She probably believed what he told her. That Gordon violated the sacrament of marriage surely isn't a good thing, but marriage is one of the more difficult goals humans have set for themselves.

I hope he loved her. That's worth something.

You can laugh at me but I take the sacraments very seriously. Baptism, communion, marriage and the service for the dead are holy rites. Do your best by these rites. There is continuity and comfort within them.

"Judge not lest ye be judged."

I have no right to judge my natural father, although I did. I have no right to judge Juliann. The one person I can judge morally is myself. The rest are God's concern.

You might wonder why I didn't hop in the car and drive to see Juliann. She's still alive now, only eighteen years older than I am. I'm fifty-two, so she's seventy. Her birthday's the same day as Jerry's.

It isn't that I wouldn't welcome the sight of her, but I have my pride. I didn't dump her. She dumped me. She has to make the journey. And if she doesn't make it, I'm not angry.

What does she have to gain by knowing me? By seeing Gordon in me? I look somewhat like him, as best I can tell from the few photos of him that I have. It's hard to tell when he aged, because the alcohol destroyed his liver and he blew up like a poisoned dog. At least in the young pictures, there's a marked resemblance.

I would think seeing an echo of the grand passion of your life might be intensely painful.

If nothing else, we could enjoy the horses.

As for me, I wouldn't gain a mother. Juts was my mother and I will be loyal to her until my own death. What I might gain is a friend, a friend who knew all the people I knew but knew them as younger people. That's always fun to hear.

If you're reading this and you, too, have been separated in some fashion from your blood mother or father, you recognize my ambivalence.

If you're reading this and you've been raised by the people who bore you, it may have some interest, especially if you seek to adopt children. One of the greatest gifts any human can give to another human is a home.

People will say, "I used to hope I wasn't related to my mother and father. I used to fantasize that I had another set of parents." You hear this often when people learn you're adopted; it's their way of trying to connect.

But if you are the one who fell or was pushed out of the nest, you must learn to cope with that rupture. When I was tiny I thought it was my fault. When you're little you think the whole damn world revolves around you anyway, and this is just another manifestation of intense childhood narcissism, I guess. You reach adolescence and it's all their fault. You're a pure little daisy in a field of bullshit. After that, whether you mature and draw from experience is up to you. By the time I left college I knew life was a lot more complicated than I realized and that people are complicated as well.

Even the Ten Commandments, which seem so simple, aren't quite so simple. "Honor thy father and thy mother." Why honor them if they've dishonored you?

I've reached a point in my own life where I accept them. I accept Juliann and Gordon and Juts and even Mother Brown (that's hard). I suppose, if the truth be told, I accept Billie Jean King and Nancy Lieberman. If they can't see the good in me, if they can't realize that the tensions were caused by circumstances as well as youth, then they aren't growing.

What happens when you become famous is that people cling to you in bizarre ways. Being the opponent of Henry Kissinger when he played soccer as a child becomes defining. You were important enough to block his attempt on goal. These incidents confirm your sense of self. Think about it: If you blocked Joe Blow's goal, you might remember, but then again you might not. To run afoul of Mr. Kissinger somewhere in your lifetime must make you a big bug.

Perhaps some people are hanging on to a time they were on opposite sides of the fence from me. Get over it!

I've learned I can't change anyone. I can't overcome homophobia. I can't overcome misunderstandings if the other people aren't willing to learn and reach out, too. I can only forgive, hope for the best and keep going.

I decided a long time ago to emulate the best of Juts and Ralph. If there's good in life, I'm going to find it. If there isn't good, then I'll look for a party.

I was about to find both.

Lovestruck

I FIRST SAW ELIZABETH BRYANT AT A FUND-RAISER IN DENVER. THE Museum of Western Art, across from the Brown Palace, was packed with people, and I was speaking for some worthy cause.

In the back of the room stood a tall, slender, smoky-looking woman. She talked to me for a few moments after my speech, then was gone.

On the road again—I must have been on yet another book tour—I called Nancy Severson, an old rugby friend from Denver.

"Nance, I saw the girl of your dreams. Call her up."

"Nah."

"Come on. Just call her up. If I lived in Denver, I'd call her up."

I gave her Beth's number. A couple of months later I called Nancy. Yes, she'd gone to a party at Beth's house but she thought Beth had some running around to do; Beth was in her late twenties.

Time passed. I'd think about Beth occasionally, then forget about her. Muffin Spencer-Devlin was playing in the Dinah Shore tournament that year and she asked me to come on out.

I was working with James Coburn on an adaptation of *The Mists of Avalon,* so I was running back and forth between coasts anyway. I asked Jim if he wanted to go to the tournament. His girlfriend at the time, Lisa Alexander, young and bright, wanted to go, so off we trundled into the desert.

Jim endures a special kind of arthritis; I don't know what you call it. He doesn't complain, doesn't get cross, but I could see him relax more in the desert because the dry heat must have lessened the pain.

We worked on the script the first day, when they held the Pro-Am. He and I sat up that night watching an interview with ex-presidents Carter and Ford that excited us so much we couldn't go to sleep. We talked long into the night about how good people become ground up and ground down by our political process. Freed from the necessities of appealing to special-interest groups, of courting voters, both ex-presidents could speak directly about our problems.

Jim Coburn possesses the sturdy self-reliance and wondrous common sense of Nebraskans. As an actor he can do anything. Typecast young, he played roles that were more alike than different. Now that he's older he is able to create a fabulous body of work. He's doing his best work as an actor right now.

The next day we all arrived at the first tee, ready to follow Muffin. Jim, tall among men, towered over the women. Many recognized him but were far too polite to bother him.

We all started walking as Muffin played. I'd met Dinah Shore in passing a few years earlier. She was warm, great-looking even in old age, and full of energy. She was also a good Tennessee girl, so for me, she was easy to be around. She loved golf the way I love horses. She could play the game, too.

The other thing that was special about her was that she displayed no prejudices. Either she had no prejudices to begin with, or she weeded them out. Here she was, surrounded by thousands of lesbians, and she couldn't have cared less. She took you as an individual.

Jim is the same way. This isn't because they are theater and film people. I know plenty of the same who are shot through with prejudice.

Halfway through the course you reach that point where the tenth hole looks like it's in Abyssinia. We were hungry, tired and thirsty. We bought a few things at a little snack place and hurried back to Muffin, who was hitting off the tee like Superwoman.

By the time we reached the eighteenth hole we were more tired than Muffin. Also, the sun had burned off some of the spectators' diffidence about approaching Jim. The girls were edging closer.

I turned to go up the hill to see if there wasn't some place we could watch Muffin finish and where Jim could have some peace, and I bumped smack into Beth Bryant.

We laughed. Fate?

She flew out to Virginia two weeks later.

Beth had worked her way up in Colorado National Bank. She enjoyed banking. Now, in her early thirties, she had to make a decision about whether to push for upper management, hoping to get there by her late thirties or early forties, or whether to go to law school. A lawyer with a banking background is a pearl of great price.

Beth's long weekend in Virginia introduced her to a cast of characters not often seen in Denver, Ellie Wood Baxter in particular.

Ellie Wood Baxter, one of the best amateur riders of her generation—
she won the Medal Maclay in 1937—is also one of the funniest women
God ever put on earth. She wasn't at all sure about this gay stuff but over
the years she decided I wasn't half bad. Occasionally we'd have lunch.
During hunting season I valiantly tried to keep up with her. Her husband
had died, her son lived in Florida and she liked having younger people
around her.

Ellie Wood especially likes it if you do what she tells you. Younger
people in the South generally do what they are told—or pretend to, anyway.

Well, Ellie Wood decided she'd have Beth and me over to her pool.
This was especially gracious and brave because many of Ellie Wood's
friends wanted gay people to pretend they were straight. The fact that she
invited me over with someone I adored really was Big News. Ellie Wood,
being Ellie Wood, never gave it a second thought. She isn't one to con-
gratulate herself for being open-minded because she doesn't even know
that she is. Kindness covered up by bluster is the way she greets the world.

She'll be horrified when she reads this because everyone will now know
she's a big softie with a heart of gold. She thoroughly enjoys being Miss
Tough-as-Nails.

The day blistered, the pool sparkled. The water felt like heaven. Ellie
Wood brought out iced tea. Popcorn is her favorite food, I think, but it
was too hot for that.

"What do you do?" Ellie Wood was direct since she knew that Beth
was from Colorado. Southerners often assume that nonsoutherners have
no appreciation for subtlety.

Beth explained her involvement with commercial loans, how the business climate had changed from the 1970s and early 1980s. "But I'm hoping
to go to law school."

"Do they have law schools out there?"

Beth, good-natured, replied, "Do they have them here?"

After that, those two got on like a house afire. Ellie Wood jumped in
the pool. She never wades in. She dives or jumps. Her eye was attracted to
the tiles along the inside of the pool. Touches of mold had dared to invade.

She climbed out, disappeared and returned with two square white
cubes. I don't know what they were.

"Rub this on the mold and it will come off." She handed me one and
Beth one.

She repaired to her chaise longue.

Beth and I scrubbed the tiles.

"Is she always like this?" Beth whispered.

"She's on her good behavior."

We giggled.

"What are you two laughing at?" came the imperious question.

"You."

"Me?"

"Yes, you," I replied.

"Why?"

"Heat stroke."

Before I could give Ellie Wood the devil, Shannon Haeffner came in with her two kids. Shannon is married to one of my cousins but I don't know how far removed. If I were to explore fully all my blood relations, this book would resemble one of those genealogies of the kings and queens of England.

Shannon got in the pool and started working on the tiles, too.

We laughed. Shannon has a terrific sense of humor.

After a while Ellie Wood allowed as to how we had worked hard enough. We could take a break.

What a pleasant afternoon, watching the children, chatting with three women who all have lively minds, drinking iced tea. I'm usually on the road or fussing at a broken tractor implement or busting to meet a deadline, so I rarely enjoy leisurely moments like these. It stands out in my memory as a lovely afternoon.

It's my own fault that I don't have more of them.

After Beth returned to Denver I missed her. However, her absence gave me the chance to write good letters and get them in return. I love letters.

I decided that Ellie Wood needed a tweak. One day I bought two pink flamingoes. I knew she was giving a small pool party late that afternoon, one of her soirees. I thought she'd never leave the house that day and she never did. Finally, desperate, I crawled on my stomach through the hayfield in front of her house to the pool in the back. The air conditioner repairman had her busy on the south side of the house, so I hoped I could pull it off. I put the flamingoes, one of which was defecating gumdrops I had threaded on clear fishing line, by the pool.

She had a heck of a time explaining the gumdrops.

Beth and I dated for a year. The more I knew her the more I loved her. She's beautiful from the inside out. I even thought about moving to Denver while she was in law school. But every time I left Virginia to look at houses I was miserable.

I finally figured out that if I moved there, out of my element, I'd make her miserable, too. She's very sensitive and she'd think it was her fault even if it wasn't.

I broke off the relationship. Typical me. I did this with no discussion with Beth since I assumed I knew what was best for her as well as myself. Oh, shades of Juts.

I felt awful. I expect she felt awful, too.

I still don't know if I did the right thing or the wrong thing. Beth graduated from law school, having made the law review. She practices in Denver, enjoys politics even when she doesn't enjoy it, plays golf and is more beautiful than ever.

She always asks me about Ellie Wood so I bring her up to date on Ellie Wood's latest forays, like canoeing the Grand Canyon and going to China.

We've become dear friends, something beyond dear but I don't have the word. It's a love once informed by a physical bond but somehow beyond it. I would do anything for this woman.

The funny thing is, she and Nancy Severson have made a life together. The moral of the story is: trust your instincts.

Angels Keep

ALICE MARBLE STILL PLAYED TENNIS. HER CLASSIC FLAT STROKES remained fluid and powerful. When Alice reentered my life she was in her seventies.

Like Aunt Mimi, her grasp of her own age appeared slippery. Sometimes she'd be seventy, other times seventy-three. I knew better than to be too specific.

Our meeting had been arranged by an official of Procter and Gamble, Jack Wishard. The company was going to sponsor a television series on American women, each show a biography formatted as a movie of the week. I'd been picked to write Alice's story. We met at a fancy restaurant tucked away near the corner of Santa Monica and Wilshire in Beverly Hills.

Of course I remembered her. She didn't remember me, but she did remember coming to the Holiday Park tennis courts and she loved Jimmy Evert. Everybody loved Jimmy.

Alice regaled the assembled with stories of Clark Gable, Carole Lombard, William Randolph Hearst, Joan Crawford and other luminaries of the golden era of talkies. Alice's stories were liberally spiced with innuendo. She was funny. She also had a hollow leg. The girl could drink.

I spent time with her in Palm Desert, where she had a cute little house bought for her by one of her admirers, Will Dupont.

The show was to be about Alice's spy work during the war and how she was nearly killed. She had scars on her back from being shot. The script was good but it was never shot because we couldn't substantiate Alice's recruitment by the OSS (the precursor to the CIA). That's not so strange because Wild Bill Donovan, head of the OSS during World War II, wasn't noted for his filing habits.

By this time I knew that Alice had a million stories, few of them true. But the one about her work for the OSS may well have been fact. Procter and Gamble wouldn't take the chance, which is a pity, because it was a good show and with a star like Cybill Shepherd the ratings would have been great.

The producers, Marcy Gross and Ann Weston, struggled, as did I, to substantiate the facts. As most of the people were dead, we couldn't. I'd worked with Marcy and Ann before, delighting in their company and razor-sharp television instincts.

We were distraught that the show wasn't going to make it, but none more so than Alice.

My riding buddy Dale Leatherman, a newspaperwoman, wanted to write a book. I introduced her to Alice. The wonderful result is called *Courting Danger,* published by St. Martin's Press in 1991.

Alice died December 12, 1990. She gloried in being the center of attention. She was missing her curtain call.

Before she died I would visit her about once a year and I wrote or spoke to her two or three times a month. I loved Alice despite her drinking. I should note here I am not remotely tolerant of alcohol and drug abuse, and if you're loaded, I will excuse myself. I simply can't stand it.

But I could stand it in Alice because I saw in her fragility, vanity and glory. Eroded as her body was by the booze and by her various afflictions, she could still hit a tennis ball with precision and power.

And she knew tennis. I enjoy another sports fan and I especially enjoy learning from someone as great as Alice, who changed the women's game forever. She upped the aggression level with her net play and she introduced glamour. She won the national singles championship four times, 1936, 1938, 1939, 1940, the same years she won doubles or mixed doubles or both at Forest Hills. She won Wimbledon in 1939, also winning doubles and mixed doubles there that year. Alice could play on any surface. She won the national clay court singles and doubles in 1940.

There wasn't much Alice couldn't do except make sense of her life. She reminded me a lot of Martina except, of course, for the drinking. Both had strong performer personalities. Remove the limelight and they wander about.

While Martina may yet find a fulfilling purpose to the second half of her life, it was painfully obvious all Alice could do was relive past glory. But what a glory it was. As beautiful as a movie star in her high days, she attracted male and female alike. She frolicked with them, too.

In me she found new ears, yet someone who also had known her at the end of her career. I hadn't seen her at her peak, but when I did see her, in the early 1960s, she was damned impressive. She still blew me off the court in her seventies.

She'd throw her arms around me and say, "Brownie, if only I could have coached you when you were a kid." Naturally, I felt like a million bucks. Then we'd trot back out there and she'd kill me again. I never short-shotted her. That would have been dirty pool. I stayed in the backcourt, where she'd destroy me with glee.

I think I made Alice feel young again. As she recounted her amours, I'd laugh and that would egg her on.

I felt so sorry for her sometimes, sitting alone in her Palm Desert house. She had golfing buddies but people could only take Alice in short doses, and it was better to see her in the morning before the drinks began.

She gave me a silver cup inscribed in her own handwriting, which says, "Love Forever, Alice Marble." I'm staring at it as I write this. I see it each day I work and it reminds me of how fleeting and cruel fame can be, most especially for an athlete. If you're young, the names Paul Hornung, Billy Cannon, Big Daddy Lipscomb mean nothing unless you are a football historian. To my generation those were the gods, as was Alice a sports goddess to her generation.

Even a starlet has a better chance at a future than a jock. Alice, by refusing to marry Will Dupont, essentially screwed herself. He continued to provide for her but he did eventually marry another tennis player, Margaret Osborne. Margaret supplanted Alice. Alice liked her but was ambivalent even though she approved of the match.

Her best friend was Mary K. Brown, a tennis great from the generation before Alice's, but Mary K. seems to have had a better grip on reality than Alice. When Mary K. Brown died, Alice was up shit creek.

She'd tell me how she loved women as well as men. How she hid it. How she hated herself for hiding it.

I think Alice wanted me to absolve her. It's not in my power to do that for anyone but I would say, "You did what you thought was best. It was a different time."

The last time I saw Alice she was floating in her pool, drink in hand, regaling me with a tale about Spencer Tracy making a pass at her and saying, "Kate and I have an understanding."

No doubt they did. He understood that if Kate found out, he'd better duck. I can't imagine the willful Miss Hepburn putting up with much of that crap.

The dry heat kept Alice's bones moving; she was happy that day, for I was a rapt audience and her mind was happiest back in the 1930s and 1940s.

Maybe, too, in drawing close to Alice I was again in the company of someone of Mother's generation. Both women needed to be stars, although the comparison stops there, for Julia Buckingham was a grounded person. She had a wealth of common sense, and Alice hadn't a hint of it.

As I headed for the door Alice waved and yelled out, "Angels keep." I think of that phrase often. It's a kind of blessing, and I pray that wherever she is now, it's a happier place than her last decades on earth.

Angels keep, Alice.

78

Keep the Horse
Between Your Legs

CHILDHOOD, THE SOURCE OF PRIMARY COLORS, INFUSES OUR daily lives, often without us being aware. You might catch a whiff of a perfume that an elegant lady wore when you were small and a flood of memories washes over you. Or you might hear a song and your internal mercury zooms up the thermometer. Potent sensations, wondrous or dreadful, remind us of that time when the world was new.

Books and horses provoke those sensations for me. And the music of Bizet. When I was tiny Mom used to play Bizet on an ancient phonograph bigger than myself. Bach was for church. Bizet was for the house.

The day I found *Bulfinch's Mythology* at age five in the Martin Memorial Library was the day my life truly began.

Reading, like breathing, is energy, ideas, life. I am a promiscuous reader. Military history, biography, novels, poetry, your grocery list, I don't care. If it's scribbed or in justified type, I'll read it. I love the layout of *Süddeutsche Zeitung* and I buy this newspaper whenever I can find it in the States. My German is verbless, but I love to read the photo captions and the headlines.

Mother, a dedicated nonreader, never minded that I'd snuggle up in a corner and read. It meant I was happily occupied. She never censored my reading, for which I am eternally grateful. Mother figured if something bothered me, I would ask her questions. I'd become immune to violence thanks to Sunday school and vacation Bible school. The Old Testament is one war, murder, mess after another. So *The Red Badge of Courage* wasn't going to put me over the edge.

I had a marked preference for drama. I read the Greek playwrights, Shakespeare, Sheridan, Goldsmith and more before I was ten. I don't know what I understood except that I loved the language. The theater is the supreme test of a language.

In a novel narrative is the connective tissue. Theater lacks that device. Granted, a fine actor can make a weak play much better. Pick up the play and read it first before you see it, if you can. You'll see what I mean. If the structure is sound, then the language will fly up like golden milkweed, little perfect words floating all over the stage, into the audience. One is surrounded by the sound of language in different voices: deep, light, raspy, smooth. Why would anyone take drugs when they can surrender to this intoxication?

When it came to my requests, if they were affordable, Mom and Dad never denied me—except for riding. I asked to go to the local shows, you know, traveling versions of Broadway or junior theater. Mom took me as often as I asked and she also took me to the movies whenever I asked to go, which was a lot.

Sometimes I'd sit there, my eyes closed, listening to the actors' voices. She'd give me an elbow.

I'd scowl. "I'm awake!"

When I told her what I was doing she tried it. Mother was always ready for a new spontaneous experience, which was one of the qualities I most loved about her and a quality I desperately miss in my life at this time because I'm scheduled down to the minute.

I used to do this at the track, too, when horses were breezed. I can hear an irregular gait before I can see it. I still do this and I'm sure people wonder, what is that woman doing there with her eyes closed?

Reading or going to the theater allows me to spend time with the best minds of many generations. I can't think of anything more exciting and I mean that. Sex fades but that moment when Lady Macbeth begins to lose her mind and talks about how all Great Neptune's ocean can't wash the blood from her hand will stay with you forever. Gives me chills.

Horses give me a similar euphoria, but with them I am relieved of language. Strange as that sounds, there are moments when we must set aside our greatest intellectual achievement, language, and return to earlier forms of communication. It's easier to do this with animals than with people. People are prisoners to the word. Horses understand some language but do not feel compelled to repeat it. Neither do cats and dogs, both of whom have good vocabularies. I am more myself with animals than I am with people, which may only mean that I'm a primitive sort.

One of my friends who recognizes this about me is Dale Leatherman. Since she lives in West Virginia, I rarely get to see her, but when I do we

yak forever about books and horses. All the years that I've known Dale she
has mentioned her ex-husband maybe two times. So you know we're
obsessed with books and horses because it's a rare woman who passes up
an opportunity to dissect an ex-husband. (I don't know what pleases
women more: marrying men or divorcing them.)

A woman of exquisite sensitivity and discretion, Dale finds ways to assist
you so you don't know you're being helped. She's far too well bred to give
a direct order. She finds other ways to lead you to water.

In my case she nearly killed me. Dale observed that I was less than my
ebullient self. Not that I moped—my mother's ghost would haunt me:
"Life is a gift. Enjoy it!" But that devilish streak in me was quiet. Apart
from the emotional losses, I was struggling to pay off the last of Mom's
hospital bills plus my own bills, which fluctuate like Elizabeth Taylor's
weight. I'll deny myself for months as I keep my nose to the grindstone,
then I'll rebel, explode and buy a new truck.

Dale was working at *Spur* magazine. I drove up to have lunch in Mid-
dleburg, where the magazine was then located. She regaled me with stories
about horse show mishaps and personalities, I regaled her with the latest
Hollywood silliness afflicting me. I was working on a project that never did
make it to the screen because the producer wasn't powerful enough nor
brave enough to fight the studio. Every time the studio would say change
this or change that, he would. At a recent meeting he had handed me the
screenplay and said—exact words and only words—"Give me more sad."

Dale and I howled.

"Didn't you used to hot-walk ponies at Royal Palm?" she asked once
we had exhausted the topic of Hollywood.

"Yeah, they started the place up when I was in junior high."

"Ever hold a polo mallet in your hand?"

"Hell, no. I wiped down ponies, walked them, then hosed them."

"You ought to play."

"Get a grip. You've got to be rich to play polo."

"Nah. You can play sandlot for about what it costs to play golf, really."

"I didn't think they allowed women to play."

"Well," she drawled, "they aren't exactly welcoming us, but if enough
women learn the game, what are they going to do?"

"Call us all dykes, the usual. Of course, in my case, it's true."

We giggled.

"I dare you to take Rege Ludwig's polo clinic."

"What do you mean, you dare me?"

"I bet you can't last the whole week."

Stung, I replied, "The hell I can't!"

"Five bucks says you can't."

I should have strangled her right there. No, I had to get up at 5:30 A.M., six mornings in a row, to make the 7:00 A.M. clinic presided over by Rege Ludwig, who bellowed, "Get in your two-point!"

The first time I rode in the ring—the University of Virginia Polo Club wouldn't let us on the grass field—I felt like I was at Forty-second Street and Seventh Avenue and all the stoplights had failed. Jesus H. Christ on a raft.

The polo seat is different from the hunt seat. Polo requires a behind-the-motion seat, which means you're more upright, your legs a bit more forward. While you're not as behind the horse's motion as you are with the saddle seat, you're not as forward as with the hunt seat.

I struggled but I hung in there. By Thursday morning I hurt all over but I wasn't quite so dazed during scrimmages. I was, however, feeling the first hint of the flu. By Saturday, the final scrimmage and playoff, I felt rotten. I went out and played, but I didn't do squat. Still, I survived. Dale sent me the five dollars, which I still have.

Rege Ludwig has coached the winning team of the U.S. Open polo tournament twice and he'll probably win it more times in the future. He possesses an eye that can break down your movement. It's biomechanics. He tries to make your particular movement at, say, the forehand the most efficient motion you can produce. That sounds simple but it isn't. An average teacher teaches the basics. A gifted teacher applies the basics to your body and mind. Some people need the carrot, some the stick.

One thing I learned: I was awful. I could hit some, but my riding was inept and that's putting it nicely.

I tried to join the Charlottesville Polo Club, but they turned me away. There were no women in the club and they didn't want to be bothered with a beginner. There was nowhere else to go and I wanted to learn. Dale was wise—polo brought back my childhood in some ways, and I was picking up steam.

I called up a bunch of women who rode, and eleven people showed up on June 23, 1988, at an old arena on Garth Road. (It has since been demolished.) The next thing I knew, more women began to show up for weekly scrimmages. Nobody much knew what they were doing, but people like Lynne Beegle, Donna Eicher, Diana Robb and Joyce Fendley could ride, and soon other women came along who could ride, too.

Dr. Herbert Jones lent me three ponies, tack and saddles. Frank Kimball would come over and drill me on my near side forehand shot, a shot I love. He has such a beautiful near side, and he was determined to pass it on to me. Donna's husband, Jack, was a tremendous help, too, when he wasn't covering his eyes and laughing at us.

I played polo in the summer of 1988 for a thousand dollars. People spend more on their beer bill than I spent on polo.

Polo isn't spiritual like foxhunting. It's intense, even obsessive. If your mind wanders, you can wind up in traction. Because it's so intense you feel mentally refreshed. The cares of the day or even the decade disappear.

That's how I came to found the first all-women's polo club in the United States, Piedmont Women's Polo Club. They're still going strong. I rarely get to play with them these days since I've moved over to the next county to tree-farm and grow hay.

I envy the generation of girls in school now. They will have the athletic opportunities denied my generation. Sports are such a good way to meet people, learn to handle stress and discharge the tension from your everyday life. If it hadn't been for polo and foxhunting, there would be dead producers in Hollywood.

Nineteen eighty-eight was a watershed year. I found my childhood sport anew. I found my land in Nelson County, 430 acres no one else wanted. Soil tests told me the soil was good so I grabbed it. It may be one of the smartest things I ever did.

I wasn't doing much romantically but enough to rile the local homophobes. How dare I date in front of them? I don't mean hold hands or display affection, I mean go out with some local ladies, date. Heaven forfend.

In my twenties I would have attacked them back. I really can't do that anymore because that would dignify their ignorance. And as is always the case with such stuff, I wasn't doing half as much as they thought I was.

Not that I told anyone. I hate to disappoint even my critics.

What a year. The Writers Guild went on strike, which meant I could take no Hollywood jobs. At first I paid little attention because I'd been through these strikes before and I do support the Guild. Absolute support.

But the strike dragged on. Months. It was finally settled in August after five months.

A bold tributary to my income was drying up and I had just committed to buying raw land. I still had to pay rent, too. The horses, thank God, didn't cost much since I had boarders, which covered most of my costs.

Watching your bank account slip away is a sickening experience but not a life-threatening one. I fear poverty but I know I can live through it. Yes, it's easier to survive it when you're young than when you're old, but God never gives you anything you can't handle. You must have faith.

I had faith. It was money I needed.

Help came from a small, hairy angel.

79

Sneaky Pie to the Rescue

Oh, the toils of literature. In Sneaky Pie's case, littera-ture.

By now you have gathered that I'm half cat myself. Good thing, as it allows me free converse with other cats, dogs, hounds and horses.

One blistering August day, I was bending over my black Italian desk, an odd creation that I love, writing checks. *Serious* literature. I had enough money to last six more weeks. At this point my books were not yet earning royalties, which they are now, thank you, Jesus. Of course, I never know what those royalties will be. Two dollars? Two hundred? Two thousand? It's always a financial adventure.

Sneaky Pie enjoyed working alongside me. If I sat down, so did she. I keep Baby Jesus's bones by my desk and often Sneaky would sit respect-fully by the Thai funerary urn. Juts was plopped under the desk. That dog and cat loved each other, engaging in mutual grooming, playing with little jacks balls, chasing each other in the yard.

Distress transmits. Juts rose, putting her head on my knee. Sneaky patted my cheek with her paw, as she would do when she wanted breakfast. Thinking she wanted catnip, I crunched some on the desk. She ignored it, but Pewter, the gray cannonball, hurtled into the workroom. Far be it for her to miss a treat. I gave Juts a Milk-Bone, which I keep in a jar by my desk. She held it in her jaws, not eating it.

I looked at these two loving pairs of eyes and thought, "Flush or broke, I've always got love."

Pie could type. She'd hit the keys of the typewriter. Once a friend visited me with one of those electronic musical keyboards and the cat went wild. It sounded as good as some of what is recorded these days.

She pounded away on the typewriter, stopping to bite the page. As I had a page in there filled with what I thought was deathless prose I was not initially pleased with her performance. That's all I needed, another damn critic.

I looked at the page, then at the cat as my huge tricolor Corgi, Bandit, strolled into the room. Sneaky leaped off the desk onto Bandit's back. Bandit raced around the house, Juts in pursuit. Sneaky lived to torment the Corgi, who loved it. She'd hang under Bandit's belly, too, for a stride or two. Belly laughs, literally.

Thus was our collaboration, the Mrs. Murphy series, born. (Originally I called it the Kitty Crime series, but Bantam changed it to the Mrs. Murphy Mysteries.) Sneaky wanted to write mysteries. Being a novelist, I felt grand and airy about genre fiction even if it does rake in the coins. Genre fiction is a story, plot-driven, with a specific format. Think of it as a sonnet. The beauty of it is that you have a structure. That also robs it of the ability to go beyond that structure.

Sneaky Pie, having no such worries, eagerly mapped out her first mystery, *Wish You Were Here*. I cringed that it would be too cute. She might be cute. I am not. To my surprise it really wasn't. Her work is warm—I mean, it's not gruesome except in spots—but it isn't adorable.

Bantam was not enthusiastic. They only published the book as a sop to me and with little in the way of promotion.

Still, I was grateful for the small advance Sneaky brought into the coffers. It carried us through until the strike ended.

The mystery took off. She wrote another one. Each one she writes, I think, is better, although I admonish her to pay more attention to the human characters. We fight over this. I also resent being called her secretary, which I have heard her say to other animals.

A major star in Germany, she receives over two hundred letters a week from fans overall. I now address her as Frau Pie.

Even Pewter gets fan mail because of her supporting role in the mysteries, as does Tee Tucker (Bandit).

The first book tour that Bantam sent me on for Sneaky Pie was for *Murder at Monticello,* the third in the series. Although Sneaky had done a few local signings—especially distinguishing herself at the Book Stack in Staunton one Christmas by rearranging and befouling the window display—we hadn't gone on the road.

Wisely, I left her home. I had no desire to pay for whatever damages she would incur in bookstores and hotel rooms. Once Sneaky's patience evaporates, the claws come out.

Her fans are different from my fans. I was surprised and delighted to meet them. Around 80 percent of my fans are female and young, although I'm lucky enough to grow apace with my generation, so there's a good middle-aged contingent there.

Sneaky's fans are hard-core mystery readers, often a bit older, and maybe 60 percent of them are female, 40 percent male. They tend to be logical people, people who solve puzzles, people often quite involved in community affairs.

Many of my fans are still too young to be invested in a community. They are finding their way in the world. By the time they're in their middle thirties and upward then they, too, are people very active in politics and charity work. I count special-interest politics as charity work, because people work long and hard for causes, never receiving a penny.

My readers are fascinating people. Many of them are horse people. I should add here that horse people fall into two groups: the highly literate and the illiterate. Cooky McClung, a delightful writer focusing on the equine world, has two books out, *Horse People Are Different* and *Horse People Are Still Different*. Boy, did she hit the nail on the head.

But I learn much more from my readers, I believe, than they learn from me. I especially gravitate toward military men and women and one day was lucky enough to have Colonel Joseph Mitchell find me. Now deceased, this combat veteran of World War II was a provocative military historian. He opened his world and his mind to me. I don't think I can ever repay the debt. Here was a resource person who'd been there when the artillery fire was thick as mosquitoes. Many of his books are now out of print. If you can find them through book searchers, grab them.

Thanks to Joe, I could be directed to any expert for any war. This proved priceless during the research for *Dolley,* which was set during the War of 1812.

Joe and his wife, Vivienne, even liked Sneaky Pie. She liked them, too.

Another married couple, big Sneaky fans, made her a small barn with all the creatures from her books in it. She plays with this daily.

I am amazed at the outpouring of love she inspires.

My own fan letters, a far more modest fifty a week, usually contain criticisms. The occasional neo-Christian will take me to task. The occasional radical lesbian will excoriate me for not being gay enough. The politically minded send spirited letters. The horse people aren't so argumentative. Every now and then I will receive a letter from a literary person and enjoy a chat on style, not necessarily mine, but, say, Nabokov's.

Sometimes a letter will arrive from someone who says I saved his or her life. Thank you, but I didn't. You saved your life. I just reminded you that life is worth living even when one is suffering.

Remember your Seneca: Scorn pain. Either it will go away or you will.

The great thing about Sneaky's success was that her efforts allowed me to take a hard look at my involvement in the film and television business. Many of my contacts and biggest supporters had died young of AIDS. People were coming to power a generation too early. That hurt me but it hurts the business too! There is no substitute for experience, regardless of brilliance.

I understand why Douglas Fairbanks Sr. left the film business he helped to create. It wasn't fun anymore. After *The Thief of Baghdad* he grew more and more disenchanted.

Hardly at Fairbanks's level, I think I know how he felt. Since those early days when everyone was young and the industry itself young, the business's arteries have hardened. By the time I entered the lists, in the seventies, profit was the only motive. I never had to endure the heartbreak of those early people who wanted to really create a film that soared. But when I came into the business, three generations were working in it. Now there are only two.

By the end of the eighties, the early nineties, the studios, committed to the megahit, seldom wanted anything but formula stories. Foreign grosses often determine whether a film was profitable, so we want audiences everywhere to go to our movies. Everyone understands special effects. Well, that's what we've got.

Can I write that kind of movie? Of course. I can write anything for the camera. It may be immodest to say that, but I can. Do I want to write a disaster movie or a testosterone saga? If it would let me pay off the mortgage, I suppose I'd write one, but if I had to make a diet of it, I wouldn't do it. That's not why I'm on earth. I want to write about real people in real situations and I prefer the comic tradition.

Being part of the Directing Workshop for Women at the American Film Institute helped me immeasurably. Directing is exciting. I love the idea of being able to manipulate and control the image but I am also smart enough to know I'm not going to be hired to direct. My chances are the same as hitting the state lottery, and gender, once the overriding issue, is now augmented by age. I'm middle-aged. Everyone is supposed to be thirty-one and hot. Well, I'm fifty-two and hot. But the institute taught me to look at work with a director's eye, which sharpened my ability to create more visual impact consistent with emotional impact.

Anytime you can stretch yourself, add to your craft, do it!

Besides, everything is cyclical. I may yet get my chance to put something on the screen that is deeply telling and outrageously comic.

If it weren't for Sneaky, I might not have stepped back and examined film and TV.

I had to find another way, and the financial rewards were lower but the emotional rewards were higher. Sneaky Pie really did come to the rescue.

80

A-list

IN HOLLYWOOD THERE'S AN A-LIST AND A B-LIST FOR WORK, FOR parties, for just about everything. A producer might want Brad Pitt for a movie but know the chances of getting him are slim. So she or he will have an entire list of other possible actors.

It's that way for writers, for directors, cameramen, everything.

Someone like John Alonzo, who worked on *Chinatown* and *Close Encounters of the Third Kind,* is on everyone's A-list of cameramen. A kid fresh out of the American Film Institute, New York University, or the University of Southern California, all fine programs, isn't on any list.

It's a hopped-up version of the tracking system in high school.

For television I had been on the A-list except at CBS. (For whatever reason I've never had much luck with CBS. Maybe it's because it's so hard to park there. The running joke used to be, "CBS, the network that dares you to do business with them.") My work continued to stand me in good stead, although my contacts were dying in terrifying numbers.

Thanks to Sneaky, however, I could and did back away. I don't know if that will be temporary or permanent. I can't dissemble about my distress over the business right now. It's so bad that in most sitcoms, with a few marvelous exceptions, when someone wants to speak a line that's supposed to be funny, they shout it. That kills wit right there. Wit is always quiet and sly. These days every emotion is signified and underlined three times. I don't know how the actors stand it, and film isn't much better. The independent films are better, God bless them, but the studios are out of it.

I hope the 1997 Oscars woke them up. Talk about egg on your face. The independents walked away with everything.

Even if the studios are committed to profit and profit only, the question has to become, how much profit? Why can't the studios go back to the old system and make the blockbuster as well as a few modestly budgeted movies that are about real people?

A studio executive has a responsibility to the shareholders. Actually, if I am hired to work on a picture, I feel I have a responsibility as well. People are risking their money on "my" project. I want a good return. Again, how much profit? If I can take a $15 million film and when all the costs are toted up deliver a $10 million net profit to the studio, I have done my job and so has everyone else on the project.

Budgets are so bloated, people are forgetting how to be creative. Often, having to find a less expensive way to accomplish a result brings out creativity. Just shoving more money at a director is lazy and is also financially irresponsible to those same shareholders.

As for the salaries of the heads of the studios, they're bigger than the gross national product of Peru—or so it seems. If they can deliver, I suppose they're worth it, but I wonder what kind of signal it sends throughout the business. There is a point when people, in and out of the business, recoil in disgust.

I've been fortunate, though, to work with some good, good people. I count Alvin Cooperman at the top of the list. He's blue-chip. Norman Lear taught me a lot. We'd fight and make up and I think, on looking back, that the sparks made us both more creative. He knows story, he knows production and action, but above all, Norman knows network politics. Watching him schmooze with an executive ought to be part of a university course.

An actor who helped me as a writer was Jason Robards. He goes to the text. When we shot a new adaptation of *The Long Hot Summer* he'd sit down at a picnic table with me and he'd meticulously examine the text.

"I hate Faulkner," he'd grumble. "Can't understand a word of it."

"This isn't really Faulkner," I'd parry.

"It's based on his short stories."

"This is to Faulkner as military music is to music."

Then he'd laugh that rolling, Irish laugh of his and he'd set to work.

But then, Jason Robards is of the theater. He is classically trained. He's also one of the greatest actors of his generation. What a body of work he has created.

The Long Hot Summer let me watch good actors and great actors develop their characters. Dennis Turner, who rewrote part two (no, I didn't mind a bit—he did a good job), wasn't called on the set. I was. We worked our asses off.

Don Johnson had to carry the show, even though he was thrown against Jason Robards, Ava Gardner and the extraordinary Judith Ivey. Everyone wrote off Cybill Shepherd, thinking she was there for beauty. She fooled them.

As it turned out, Don Johnson did carry the show. He had a lot more inside him than the network thought he did—and there was more than one executive waiting for him to fail, since he was a pain (in their estimation) on *Miami Vice*. If he was a pain, get him better scripts. If actors are really working and growing, they don't have time to bitch and moan.

Stars bitch and moan. Actors act.

Cybill blossomed during this shoot. She was scared to death initially. I liked her immediately. She's southern, after all. But as she opened up her character I grew to respect her.

Romances? No. I had a crush on the assistant director but he paid me no mind at all.

Mother gave me a harsh piece of advice when I was young. It's crude but I pass it along because it's the God's honest truth: "Don't shit where you eat."

I have never and will never sleep with anyone I work with on any project. After the project, hey, fair and clear. I never did, though, because we're all gypsies and we're moving on to the next project.

This might be a steamier read if I could pretend I've had wild sex with stars or they're my nearest and dearest friends. But it's not true. I'm a farm girl. I take the money and put up fencing or buy more land. I hardly qualify as an interesting person by Hollywood standards. I'm not on the party A-list and wouldn't be able to attend if I were.

The strangest episode I observed involved Roseanne and Tom Arnold, who were married at the time. They hired me to adapt *Graced Land* by Laura Kalpakian. It's a well-written book, peeling away welfare fraud to reveal the fraudulent emotional life of the main character. In the wrong hands this would be plowing through mud. She wrote a light, funny novel and made it work.

Roseanne was perfect for the lead. A lot of my friends regaled me with horror stories from the set of her TV show. I did as I usually do: I listened and kept my own counsel.

I met Roseanne and Tom in their trailer on the back lot. We hit it off. She had a good grasp of her character and he understood his character, too.

Tom can't sit still, so as Roseanne and I discussed the story he was like a kangaroo. He'd jump up. He'd sit down. He'd jump up. He'd go outside. A very masculine fellow. I understood why she was attracted to him.

The first thing I noticed about Roseanne is that she trusts no one. She trusted me to get her a good script but I doubt she would ever trust me as a person. Her experiences in this world have left her wary. She wants to trust people but something pulls her back.

I'm not sure she trusted Tom but she loved him. She's a passionate woman who needs male attention. He doted on her when I was with them.

Each time we discussed the script, I was impressed with Roseanne's understanding of the subtext of the story. The politics of the piece touched her. I was crazy about working with her. She made it easy. Her staff also was very good. And the network executive, Phillipe Perebinossoff, gave me the best set of notes I have ever gotten from a network executive. (Usually network notes are pretty poor. The execs may understand structure but not character. No one understands pace, I swear.)

The other great thing about Phillipe is that he wouldn't give in to Roseanne. She needed a strong hand. She was acting in her first movie of the week, her husband wanted to codirect (the network nixed that), he was costarring opposite her and she was starring in the hottest show on television. It was too much and, while Phillipe was sensitive to her desire to control everything, he wasn't going to let her overload.

Living in Virginia, I missed out on the daily politics of the show. Halfway through the second draft Phillipe was pulled off and a new executive put in charge. I never met her. I can't say anything about her, good or ill.

But I sure can tell you what happened to the show. ABC hired Bill Bixby to direct. He was a good director but he wasn't right for this piece.

The opening scene sets the lead. The heroine's husband left her five years ago for a younger woman. Joyce, the lead character, is obsessed with Elvis Presley. She's a con artist and, to add to the irony, her ex-husband occasionally comes back and sleeps with her. He's cheating with his wife, as it were. It's too delicious.

Bill Bixby called me up. "What's going on in this scene?"

I explained.

"Does he fuck her?" His exact words. Obviously, Bill wasn't southern.

"Uh, yes, he does."

"She can't fuck him. The audience will lose sympathy for her right away."

How wrong he was. That opening scene established what was good about Joyce, and what was delusional and deceitful. She still loved him and she made good on it in bed. Ninety-nine women out of a hundred, seeing that, will feel sympathy for Joyce and fear that he'll hurt her all over again. The hundredth woman will write an irate letter to ABC declaring we've all gone to hell in a handbasket. The candyasses tend to listen to the hundredth all too often.

Why Roseanne allowed that to happen I don't know. I wasn't on the set. Either she was tired of fighting or they convinced her this was the better way. The opening scene was changed. Joyce didn't sleep with her ex-husband.

Why would anyone involved with *The Woman Who Loved Elvis* (ABC changed the name) undermine its star that way? Did the network, sick of dealing with her, decide to get even? That would be colossally stupid. Was Tom so worried about his role that Roseanne put her energies into him and forgot to protect her own character?

When the show was aired it did quite well and Tom gave a good performance; it was his springboard. Roseanne gave a credible performance but not the one she intended to give. Her character's teeth were pulled. No fangs. The supporting cast was quite good. I was beside myself when I watched the rush cut, however. No fool, I didn't call Roseanne or the network. Done is done.

I will always believe she was betrayed. Roseanne has a peculiar acting range. Her stage work is that of a stand-up comedienne. That means she's going to have problems with her timing in films because film requires a vastly different timing than a live audience. She won't have a problem understanding character and she will flourish with good people around her. I don't know if she wants a cinematic career or a long-form television career. Her series has been phenomenally successful. But if she wants to grow as an actor, she can. There's a lot inside.

Actors, like horses, have different speeds, different abilities, different temperaments.

I love them. I love working with them. I've seen some of the best onstage. Helen Hayes, Maggie Smith, Janet Susman in London, Glenda Jackson in London, Colin Blakely (I miss him), Linda Lavin, Jason Robards, James Earl Jones, Vanessa Redgrave, Derek Jacobi and Timothy Piggott-Smith are the ones who spring immediately to mind.

I prefer watching actors on the stage. I get a much better sense of their abilities. In film a great director, a great editor can save an actor's ass. On the stage they live or die alone.

The greatest piece of television acting I ever saw was Dame Peggy Ashcroft's Barbie Batchelor in *The Jewel in the Crown*. Nothing prepares you for the scope of her performance. Get her old films on video and watch her give performance after performance of splendor.

A favorite piece of film acting that most of you might toss off as too light is Sir Alec Guinness in *Captain's Paradise*. How funny, believable and subtle.

I could go on and on about actors. I feel for them because they're badly treated until they get to the top and then they can still be badly treated because producers and directors prey on their insecurities.

Cherish them. They give all they can give and are dependent on others for the work. I can walk away and say, "The hell with you," and write another novel. An actor has to wait for the script and the call. Therein lies their conundrum.

Oh, the bravest actor I ever saw was Richard Chamberlain. When he walked away from *Dr. Kildare* to learn his craft on the stage in London, he was much derided in the press. But he was right. The best place for an actor to learn is on the stage. When he came back he performed the title role in *Richard II* and he was good. Richard II can so easily be played as a tragic fool or a swishy queen. Chamberlain got him just right. Richard II never truly understood power. He was enchanted with the image.

As I was wrapping up with *The Woman Who Loved Elvis* a female walked into my life who was more bullying, uncooperative and self-absorbed than any star. Peggy Sue was a holy horror.

81

Between a Rock and
a Hard Place

HALF PERCHERON, HALF HEINZ 57, PEGGY SUE WAS FOUR YEARS old in 1991. The only reason anyone put up with her was that she was very talented. She can jump the moon but you've got to keep squeezing or you'll take the jump and she won't.

Gordon Reistrup worked with me then and with Peggy Sue, too. I've been fortunate in my assistants over the years, most of them leaving me for greener pastures. Rebecca Brown is now a published author. Claudia Garthwaite bought her own small publishing company, then sold it later at a nice profit. Gordon worked for me for five years, leaving to devote himself full-time to a magazine he started the last year he worked for me.

But Gordon was a twofer. He could bang away on the computer, edit and ride extremely well. To him fell the unenviable task of civilizing Peggy.

To him also fell the unenviable but often funny task of coping with Judy Nelson.

Over the years I'd see Martina about once a year. Both of us were on the road a great deal, rarely in the same town at the same time. If we were, I'd make an effort to see her and Judy Nelson, her partner.

The first time I met Judy, in 1984, I was taken aback. How often do you meet a woman whose hair can be ruined by a ceiling fan? Loud, flashy and extremely controlling, she seemed to be everything Martina ever wanted in a woman. She'd organize the day, pack the suitcases, intrude into every aspect of Martina's life and look good doing it. Martina was blissfully happy in the beginning. I sure as shooting wasn't going to say a word.

I'd seen the lovers before me and enough of the lovers after me to shut up. I'd do the same for any friend. When the fairy dust is in their eyes, why spoil it for someone?

As Dad used to say, "Marry in haste. Repent in leisure." Life will teach us soon enough.

Ambitious with no appreciable talent, Judy's talent was her Maid of Cotton looks. She tried to make room for love but vanity got there first.

Martina didn't seem to notice because she was freed from the nattering daily chores that drive us all crazy. She could play tennis—and play, period. In exchange she heaped mountains of jewelry on Judy, shared houses in Texas and Colorado and bought hers and hers Porsches.

A few snags created drama. Judy's ex-husband, Dr. Ed Nelson, for one. He didn't want their two sons living in a lesbian household. Judy's parents, Frances and Sargent Hill, took care of the boys, who were then in grade school. As the years passed, Ed softened somewhat. A new wife certainly brightened his picture. Then, too, the boys were doing fine. Not once did they try on dresses or whatever it is straight people fear will happen to children in gay homes. (The statistics bear out that nothing happens. Kids are kids. Anyone who thinks they can truly control their children has a screw loose.)

All this cost money. Martina's money.

But once a routine was established she was happy.

Martina is a woman who has to be in love, and therein lies the problem. "Look before you leap" is not part of her operating procedure.

But who among us hasn't made that mistake once or twice? Good judgment comes from experience and experience comes from bad judgment.

As the years rolled on, Judy's iron grip tightened. Not only did she love Martina, she actively loved her every second. There was no escape from the magnitude of her devotion, nor from the constant stream of orders and demands.

That Martina happily submitted to this obsessive and controlling relationship is a measure of how desperately she didn't want to be responsible. Let Judy do it.

And Judy did.

The two women made a video that defined the disposition of material goods in the event of one partner's death. Simply put, it was a visual will. Not so simply put, it was a testimony to the seriousness of their commitment. This proved extremely troublesome later.

Judy knew Martina's history well enough to be worried. She kept on good terms with Martina's exes, even agreeing to enter promotional or business relationships with a few. They never could get their hands out of Martina's pockets. Judy, rightly so, made sure they took only so much.

That Martina would allow this kind of hanging on unnerved me. She started traveling with a retinue of coaches, cooks, gofers and God knows who else. They may have made her feel important and they may have provided some services sometimes, but the scale of the operation was really unnecessary. It all looked like money down the drain to this farmer.

Added to that was the compulsive spending of Judy and Martina, too, although I think Martina could have had some sense knocked into her on that issue if anyone had cared to staunch the hemorrhage of funds. She usually blames the other person for the spending sprees.

To be fair, poverty has marked me. I'm far from a miser and I can make foolish purchases, too. But their spending bordered on the neurotic. Of course, one of the few times a woman has naked power is when she purchases.

Judy needs to be the center of attention as much as Martina does but Martina had a great gift. She deserved the attention so long as she kept it in perspective.

I sometimes wish that Martina could have knocked around more. She lived in a state of protracted adolescence without the hard knocks of adolescence. She'd played tennis throughout her young years, her career controlled by the Communist state of Czechoslovakia. She missed that leveling experience of American high school and she missed the concept of citizenship in a democratic country. It wasn't that Martina hadn't had an eventful life, but up to the point of the split with Judy it was a life shielded from emotional development. It's nearly impossible for athletes to grow emotionally at the same pace as their generation.

For the seven and a half years that they were together, 1984 to 1991, Martina wouldn't contribute to any gay causes nor work for them. She hadn't the time. Occasionally I'd ask for help for the Lambda Legal Defense Fund or for someone fighting to keep her kids. I even asked her to give to the Gay Games, which I thought for certain would be up her alley. She never would, saying it would jeopardize Judy's custody of her sons. Well, paper bags of cash are often given to political candidates' campaign people. I suggested she could do the same to help people in desperate trouble. Few outcast groups are as despised or as vulnerable as gay people. Other people will band together to protect themselves. Gay people often avoid it for fear of being associated with other gays.

I don't think she would have been exposed. I don't think the boys would have been jeopardized.

Martina would argue with me. "Why should I be the sacrificial lamb?"

As that very sacrificial lamb, I was not moved by this line of reasoning. But a friend is a friend and you take your friends as you find them. I wasn't going to change her. Sure, I was disappointed that she couldn't identify with people who were struggling but money and fame came so early, maybe she will never be able to do that. I don't know.

I couldn't even get those two to give money to PEN International when Vaclav Havel was imprisoned. Writers the world over worked tirelessly to get that remarkable man out of jail.

Maybe Judy didn't want the money to go for anything but new shoes, vacations, a snakeskin interior for the Porsche or to pacify a few exes and hangers-on loyal to Judy. Again, I don't know. And I hasten to add that I wasn't suggesting they fork over a hundred thousand dollars. Ten thousand would have been quite nice, but I would have been proud if they'd even written a check for a thousand.

Each time I saw Martina I saw less of her. More and more, Judy dominated. It wasn't that I didn't like Judy—I was neutral about her. It was just that I loved Martina. If Judy made her happy, then I'd accept the way things were going.

Also, Martina gets furious if you criticize her on any count whatsoever. She can dish it out but she can't take it. Why fight when I saw her so infrequently?

God knows I can still fight with Fannie if either of us has a mind to—but Fannie is independent and strong.

Then, too, it's difficult for most people to accept criticism from a former lover. Martina never bothered to criticize me to my face so I didn't have to cope with the immediate experience.

When the bloom was off the Judy rose, Martina followed her pattern: She tossed her over for another woman. Part of the bonding process is that the new lover can then bear the slings and arrows directed at Martina from the traded-in model.

This time Martina ducked more than slings and arrows or smashed-up windows in the BMW. That stuff was nothing. Even the sly bids for money from the exes were nothing to this.

Judy sued.

Worse, she had the damned video.

Judy wanted seven million dollars for her services. This sum was half of what Martina earned while they were together, including real estate purchases and other investments. Whether Judy's lawyers actually pinpointed this sum in the pretrial hearing, I don't know. Judy declared she had helped earn the fabulous sums and she wanted half. She'd kept track of Martina's earnings by reading the various financial statements. This is not to suggest her computations were correct. There's no way to check that.

As this unraveled in the beginning of 1991, both began calling me. Gordon Reistrup would pick up the call, march into my office and say "Victim number one" or "Victim number two."

God, he was funny.

Judy sobbed and carried on high.

Martina, glad to be rid of her, shed not a tear. But she waxed furious on the subject of the lawsuit. Also, her latest love was religious-minded and quite nervous about being gay, and Martina wondered if I knew any books that could help.

"A little late for that now," I wanted to say, but I didn't. I suggested a few books and perhaps a chat with the young woman's pastor. You'd be surprised at how understanding many pastors are. After all, we're all God's children, and as far as I know, no pastor has the right to judge his flock.

I sympathized with Martina. Judy wanted half of all she'd earned while they'd been together. Her argument was that of any wife of any successful man. The argument had worked with Dr. Ed Nelson. But Martina wasn't Ed Nelson.

The reality is there are no culturally agreed-upon guidelines for same-sex relationships. Heterosexual relationships have canon law and state law. Personally, I oppose the state's being in anyone's bedroom. I've heard all the arguments about tax breaks and so on for straight couples but I believe the state's abiding interest in marriage has a dark side, that it was originally meant to stop miscegenation (the old word for mixing the races). If you had to show up at court for a license, they had you.

If you make a life with another human being, if you verbally promise to love, honor and protect, with or without the blessing of your pastor, it seems to me some fiscal responsibility is in order.

Martina and Judy indulged in not one but two marriage ceremonies. If the word *marriage* offends you, use *holy union.*

If Martina had made a reasonable offer (at that time any offer was unreasonable to her), Judy would have accepted. By opposing Judy, by declaring her a gold digger, Martina gave Judy exactly what Judy has always craved for herself: publicity.

Judy knew her woman and she played her like a harp.

Martina picked the wrong time to fight back. She has no political sense, but then, does Bill Clinton have a great serve?

Judy's suit made sense to most women in America, straight or gay, who have been dismissed by their partner.

Meanwhile, the newspapers and the TV shows churned out copy. Judy appeared at each interview impeccably dressed, spending hours on her turnout and wearing some of that expensive jewelry Martina had showered upon her.

Martina grew more and more truculent. Her new love grew more and more anxious. She didn't want to be dragged through the wringer. She thought she'd lose her job and she did. I don't think she was called on the carpet and fired for being a lesbian. People are too clever for that.

Martina would pay her way, sure. But her new love had before her very eyes the example of another woman whose way had been paid.

Anguish in Aspen was setting in.

In May of 1991 Judy decided I was the one person who could settle this dispute. She also decided that I understood her suffering. Of course, I suffered when Martina left me, telling me at the age of thirty-six that I was too old. But I learned a great deal from that experience. Nor did I want money for my pains. What I wanted was wisdom and what I gained was heightened compassion for people. We are such foolish creatures, but we're all we've got.

Martina's lawyers slapped Judy in the face with various low offers. I think the highest was $225,000. No way would Judy walk away for such a small amount—big to you and me, maybe, but peanuts to her. She'd lived high on the hog and she wanted the chitlins.

So far as I was able, I kept counseling both, trying to lower the hostility level on one end and the flood of tears on the other.

I thought I could get them through this. I did, finally, help settle the mess by getting them to sit down and talk, but not before a high price was paid—by me.

82

Silly Girls

WHILE THE MARTINA VS. JUDY BOUT WAS IN PROGRESS, AUNT Mimi relished our regular conversations. The glorious thing about Aunt Mimi, on cruise control in her nineties, was that I didn't have to be around her, so I'd write letters, and I would call once a week.

Still vying for sainthood, she reported the family events but without Mother's sting. Then, too, she was reporting on her grandchildren and great-grandchildren. If they were related to her, they had to be oh so good. I was the only one who was imperfect. Therefore she loved talking to me. It gave her the opportunity to swing incense, light candles and pray for my soul. It also gave her the opportunity to traipse down Memory Lane. Actually, it was more like riding in a panzer. Aunt Mimi's memories were always purposeful and instructive.

"Those silly girls." A long pause would follow, and her voice would drop into the "important" register. "Can't you talk sense to them?"

"You try it, then tell me how easy it is."

A slight hesitation while the sass set in. "Are either of them members of the Church?"

"No."

"Well—any church?"

"I think Judy was raised a Baptist, and Martina was raised a Communist."

"No hope, then. Baptists can't read, you know."

"Aunt Mimi, of course they can."

"Kin to the snake handlers. A Communist and a Baptist." She clucked.

"Martina was raised a Communist but she isn't a believer. In fact, she was baptized a Catholic."

"Ah." Her tone lightened.

"Never confirmed."

Her hopes were dashed again. "She could take her catechism now."

"If she could figure out how to read while skiing, maybe so. Aunt Mimi, I don't think a religious solution is at hand."

"If those two girls get into court, the fur will fly."

"Yes, Ma'am."

"You're supposed to be their friend. You keep them out of court."

"Like I said, Aunt Mimi, I'm trying."

"You're persuasive when you want to be." She thought a long time. " 'Course, you'll solve the problem and then they'll both be mad at you. That's the way these things happen."

"I don't care."

"That's what used to happen to me, you know. Julia Ellen and Russell would fight. I'd make the peace, then they'd be mad at me."

"They were mad at you because you meddled nonstop in that marriage."

"I did not. You sound just like Juts. She was always taking Julia Ellen's part and I can tell you what: I didn't like it."

"Maybe so, but I bet you'd like her back."

A sniffle carried over the line. "My little sister . . . when Momma died she said, 'Mary, take care of Juts.' "

There she went again. First of all, Big Mimi rarely called her Mary. Second, Big Mimi knew better than to entrust Juts to her older sister's care. Those two would kill each other.

However, Aunt Mimi had told this story so many times over so many decades that you couldn't cross her on it. It was part of her loving, responsible, honorable big-sister image, which in reality translated to: The Tyrant.

"You were a good older sister, Aunt Mimi," I lied.

"I tried. I tried." Her voice trailed off, filling with emotion as she again reran all her sufferings.

Twenty minutes later she switched back to the subject at hand: "Can't you get those two girls to shut up?"

"No."

"I don't care what they say to one another. Keep them away from the press. Looks bad for you people. Know what I mean, Reetsie?"

There was no point in explaining to her that Judy wallowed in the attention, and, if the truth be told, Martina doesn't mind seeing her name in print either. She assumed, and this struck me as odd, that people would automatically believe anything she said. If she and Judy were crossing swords, she believed the people were with her.

The real world doesn't work that way. You can be God's chosen on earth and people will disbelieve you, torment you and finally nail you.

"That Texas girl gives more information than society requires." Aunt Mimi sniffed. "Those people are that way."

"Not all of them. But this one is."

"Are you writing any more books?"

"Yes, ma'am. All the time."

"Don't you dare put me in another book, Rita Mae. Do you hear me?"

"Yes, ma'am."

Of course, if I didn't put her in a book she'd skin me alive.

By the time I hung up the phone with The Only Living Saint on This Sinful Earth my ear ached.

The Sisters of Perpetual Pleasure, which is how I thought of Martina and Judy, were wearing me out.

A stiff upper lip holds no appeal for Judy. If she wasn't calling me, she was calling anyone who'd listen.

Martina's calls were sporadic. She really is a Sister of Perpetual Pleasure. Why deal with a problem if you can pay someone else to do it for you? No matter how she'd try, though, this problem would boomerang back.

In total frustration, Judy flew out to spend a few days with me. She invited herself but on reflection I thought it was a good idea. If nothing else, I'd get a clear sense of how much money she wanted and how far she would go to get it. My brighter hope was that I might calm her down a bit.

Judy boohooed a lot but I threw her on a horse and her mood improved. The dogwoods bloomed, the redbud covered the mountains, the robins had come home. She began to feel better.

Gordon was attentive. Judy craves attention from young men. Her mood improved even more.

She promised me not to attack Martina during Wimbledon, the last week of June and the first week of July. She broke that promise.

I figured out that a house, a car and a lump sum somewhere around a million dollars would do the trick. Small details might change but Judy would drop the suit. At first I thought a monthly stipend might work, so that Martina wouldn't have to come up with a lump sum. But the more I thought about it the wiser a lump sum seemed to me. It would prevent Judy from trying to renegotiate down the line as she blew through the money. Also, signing that monthly check, assuming Martina still signed her own checks, would upset Martina.

Before Judy left she said how close she felt to me.

I was getting nervous. She tried to kiss me and I walked away. "I can't do that because I don't feel that way and because I'm trying to settle this mess. I can't be more on one side than the other."

After Judy flew back to Aspen, I called Martina and tactfully suggested she get out while the getting was good. Give her the house in Aspen. Give her whichever one car she asks for and a lump sum of a million dollars.

Martina hit the roof. She couldn't see that paying now was going to save a hell of a lot of money later. I listened again to how she had employed Judy's brother, father, brother-in-law and how she paid for the boys, etc., etc. She did, too. But none of us could understand why she did it in the first place. Why become chintzy now? Pay her off. Get her off your back. Be furious but get over it. You play, you pay.

I got nowhere. Judy pressed on.

The compelling reason for me to work so hard to keep this out of court and off the public record was what it would do to other gay people. We'd worked so hard for our gains. All we needed was a messy, sleazy sex scandal.

Straight people can dive into sex scandals every day. Rob Lowe endured one. The men mentioned in *You'll Never Make Love in This Town Again* certainly had their faces rubbed in it. But their misdeeds and cavorting aren't going to be used against other straight men. Straight women emerge a bit more damaged, but still, Sydney Biddle Barrows's call girl ring isn't held against other straight women. Oppression works in such a way that it holds every person responsible for the acts of any wrongdoer of the oppressed group.

The stakes were high in this galimony suit.

They were about to get even higher.

The great state of Colorado passed Amendment 2 as Nelson vs. Navratilova dragged on. This was the amendment that declared gay people deserve no special protection under the law and rescinded all such statutes on the books. Read "It's open season on queers."

Martina said she was outraged and would move out of Colorado, but she didn't.

Judy suddenly cast herself as a gay heroine. She was going to fight Amendment 2 as well. And she did. She hammered away each time she had a public appearance or interview and she made it a point to drop by groups organizing against the amendment.

The longer I struggled with this lawsuit the more I perceived Judy's stamina. She's a bulldozer. There's not an ounce of subtlety in her, but she doesn't give up. She can see only what benefits her, but in this instance what benefited her also benefited other people. She's clear about her self-interest, which fuels her drive.

Martina doesn't understand politics on any level. It disgusts her. She doesn't mind receiving applause for showing up at some gay-related function if the mood strikes her, but fundamentally she is apolitical. The heat and battle of politics frighten her.

Many athletes are apolitical. The time they spend perfecting isolated body movements, mastering strategy and game plans, leaves time for little else. Also, there's no reason for them to be political. Joe Louis, great as he was, wasn't political even though he struck one of the great blows for people of color when he knocked out James Braddock in 1937.

While those two carried on, I now had a new problem on my hands. Judy was getting amorous. Luckily, Aspen is a long way away. If she could snare me it would be backhand revenge against Martina. I didn't think Martina cared one way or the other, but there was something collusive about it. Everything Judy said or did at this time was aimed at Martina. Because of that, I didn't take her overtures seriously. I did notice, however, that if I listened and said supportive (not romantic) things, I was able to lower the outraged tenor of the proceedings.

Meanwhile the lawyers for both parties were raking in the coins. Judy's money was running out. Martina's legal team, on a huge retainer, was playing starve the wife. You see it every day in divorces. It's a nasty ploy but effective.

They misjudged Judy. Their tactics only made her angrier and more determined on financial revenge. They probably made the mistake most people make about Judy: They assume she's a pretty airhead. She's quite bright where her self-interest is concerned. She appears to have no interest in literature, drama, serious music or the outside world, but about her own world she knows what she wants and she'll hang in there to get it.

Martina, also, completely misjudged her. She thought she could walk away without reprisal. Okay, maybe she'd have to cough up a few items, but she never thought Judy would bring out the big guns.

Bad as all this was, I hoped it was a wake-up call for Martina. People aren't cars. You can't trade them in without emotional repercussions.

Unfortunately, Martina forced my hand, not Judy's. Her lawyers argued in the pretrial hearing that Martina and Judy had had a contract for sex. It amounted to prostitution and therefore was against public policy. According to this argument Judy was entitled to nothing.

Martina avowed that she hadn't understood what she was doing when she made the video "will." The video was shown on television. Boy, Aunt Mimi was on the phone after that. She was aghast.

"Martina seemed happy as a lark. What's she mean, she was lured into that?" was just one of the things Aunt Mimi had to say.

As for not reading contracts, another of Martina's claims, she's signed so many in her career that these protestations rang hollow.

I could brush aside the contract argument and the video lament. I couldn't blame her. Making the video was so stupid, I wouldn't want to claim being in full possession of my faculties either.

What I couldn't brush aside was the viciousness of her lawyer's arguments, arguments that could inflict colossal damage on every gay person in the United States.

Martina's justification was that this was what her lawyers had told her to do. The client directs the lawyer, not vice versa.

The moral issue was that Martina was willing to jeopardize all of us. For what? For a small fraction of what she has earned over the years. For the egotistical pleasure of beating a woman she loathed in court—and who knows if she would or she wouldn't?

Would Judy have been awarded seven million dollars? No. Even if she had won—and her case was much more straightforward than Martina's— the judgment would have probably been reduced.

Martina's lawyers created a scenario of the tennis great living in reduced circumstances on her Aspen estate. They deplored the fact that she lived over the stable. I've seen the stable. Most of us would be happy to live in the quarters above it. Men's lawyers do this all the time in divorces. They counsel the soon-to-be ex-husband to sell off the Mercedes and the condo at the beach and create a diminished income tax return if possible.

But Martina had made upwards of thirty million dollars off the sweat of her brow and this doesn't count endorsements and investments. With continued prudent investments, she could have recovered whatever she settled on Judy in less than five years.

No doubt when the bills spilled over the grotesque retainer Martina paid, she told herself that those lawyers were working in her behalf. She took no responsibility for their tactics, which besmirched her honor, even as it potentially devastated the rest of us.

Had this case come to trial, had Martina's lawyers carried the day in Texas, where the trial was to be held, it would have been cited in any legal action involving gay people in similar or even dissimilar circumstances. It would have been stretched to cover many contingencies. To a legal mind, precedent is extremely compelling.

It's not such a big step from the argument that a contract for sex is against public policy to unnatural acts being against the public good to gay apartheid. After all, Martina's home state, Colorado, was showing the way.

Martina was arming our most dangerous enemies.

The tatty truth was that Martina banked on the issue fading away, that gays who understood the viciousness of her lawyers' arguments would overlook it if she showed up at the Gay March or the Gay Games. Some of these organizers actually invited her. Talk about sending mixed messages to the rest of us.

This crisis plunged me into soul's torment. I hadn't wrestled with logic, emotion and spirit like this since the early days of the feminist movement. I was torn in two. Emotionally I felt much closer to Martina than to Judy, even though this pretrial hearing made me question why I cared about a person who could do something like that. Intellectually, I knew Judy's case was about the worth of women's work. Fundamentally it wasn't about a relationship between women but about the worth of the supporting part- ner's contribution. In our society that person is usually the wife. This was and remains a critical issue in a culture that discounts support work. We remain task-oriented. Whoever accomplishes the task is the important person. Emotionally, I felt antipathy for Judy. I believed she was a gold digger and I guess I always had believed that. Spiritually, I struggled be- cause I had to put the fates of thousands or even millions of people I don't know before two that I did know—and know well.

I recalled shooting out the window of the BMW with the .38. I had wanted to scare Martina. I hadn't wanted to hurt her physically, though I wanted to upset her as much as she upset me. But I blow up and then it's over. Judy wanted to go to war.

How wrong I was to indulge in a violent act. The more I considered their battle, the more I had to review my own actions. I was wrong. You can't make people love you. You can't hold them back. And you can't hit back. I had learned that. Judy's entire being was on the line with this lawsuit. She wanted to inflict permanent damage . . . as much for ego gratification as for money.

I understood that I loved Martina more than Judy had ever loved her. I also understood that that didn't matter. Getting beyond my ego wasn't the issue. It was getting beyond their egos, and neither one could do it. Granted, it would be tough to do for any two people in such a sorry situation.

Judy was wrong emotionally but right politically. That preyed on my mind.

Many was the night I'd slide out of bed, put on my coat and walk the pastures trying to find the way and trying to understand what makes peo- ple so hateful who were once so loving. It's not rational. Animals don't behave as badly as we do.

One night the moon was half full, the stars sparkled white, blue and even a kind of red. Peggy Sue, in a rare moment of interest in my person, walked over for a hug. Juts, at my heels, happily greeted Peggy, who stretched down for a hello. Bandit raced around in circles, very busy doing nothing. Sneaky Pie sat on the fence post. She didn't like Peggy much, so she wasn't going to touch noses. On the other hand, that cat lived in cold fear that she'd miss something, so she followed me. The dew glistened in the silvery half-light. A whipporwill called, as did an owl, a big owl. I knew what I had to do.

"Let my people go," Moses said to Pharaoh.

"Let my people go," says I.

Haven't we suffered enough to make straight people feel superior? Haven't we carried straight people's sexual sins on our backs like the scapegoats the ancient Hebrews drove into the desert? Haven't we fought wars, bought freedom for all with our blood? Haven't we tilled the soil and built our cities? Haven't we wept when straight people's mothers have died and rejoiced when their children were born? Haven't we been at their sides throughout the centuries and today?

Many of them have mocked us when they didn't know us. When they knew us by the few who had the courage to come out, many were confused. Some straight people hate us. Most don't care. A few understand.

The only people who are queer are the people who don't love anybody.

Let my people go.

I had to oppose Martina. If it came to a public trial I would have to support Judy.

Wuss Patrol

THE GIRLS, AS AUNT MIMI CALLED THEM, SETTLED OUT OF COURT shortly before they were to go to trial, thus sparing me the agony I had feared. Given the media feeding frenzy surrounding such events, they behaved prudently at last.

I don't know the details of the settlement. One of the points of the settlement is that only the parties involved, their lawyers and their accountants know the deal. I was glad I had helped to achieve this settlement but I was even more glad that they both realized no one could do this but themselves.

By this time Judy had decided she was in love with me. I knew she wasn't but she thought she was. Tired and not a little heartsick because I missed Beth through the years, I began to enjoy the attention entirely too much.

I flew out to Aspen, a rough ride that gave me a migraine. The two of them were dividing up the contents of the house there, a situation ripe for a mess.

Martina knew I would never cheat her on money or worldly goods and I wouldn't let Judy cheat her. They actually divided things up fine. I was proud of both of them. Settling their legal dispute seemed to clear the air enough for them to get the job done.

As is usual with Martina, her anger toward me came out publicly later. She was quoted as saying, "Those two deserve each other," plus a few other jibes.

Judy thought my understanding the legal issue meant I believed she was right. I didn't. That she helped Martina when they were together is indisputable. But how much?

Then Judy wrote a book about her life and begged me to write an introduction. I did. She didn't much like the finished product but the publisher wanted my name on the book. I most emphatically didn't take her part but tried to explain the emotional situation clearly.

Spending time with Judy was a lot like spending time with Aunt Mimi. Both like to give orders. Notes littered the interior of automobiles, the doors of refrigerators, desktops and bathroom mirrors. When I visited the house in Aspen I observed this organizing tactic, which works so long as you remember where you stuck your notes.

Trained to be a trophy wife, Judy carried out the daily tasks with ruthless efficiency. Not that she did the work, mind you. She'd cook and she'd clean a bit, but mostly she'd find someone else to do the work and you'd pay them. The house in Aspen was well run but I began to understand why Martina's staff had ballooned to such ridiculous proportions.

Judy has an unconscious motto: I can't always do it the hard way but I can try. If there is any way to complicate a situation or add another person to it, she will.

Martina handled these complications by withdrawing and by enjoying the occasional flirtation. Then, too, Martina's profession rewarded her for keeping a false exterior. It became habit. She started being false at home. Even if she had been inclined to stop the Judy juggernaut, I don't think she could have, because Martina won't fight openly. If you want Judy to hear your point of view, don't whisper. Shout. Judy has tunnel vision. If she wants to play golf and there's a bear on the links, she'll ignore the bear until it's too late. She only sees her goals.

Martina only sees her pleasures but over time she will listen to new and different ideas. She's struggling to become who she can be for the rest of her life, and it isn't easy. There are few curses worse than money and fame at a young age. If nothing else, Alice Marble taught me that and so did Alexis Smith, who possessed the extraordinary wisdom not to buy into it.

Judy's like a steamroller. I am not a person who makes emotional decisions quickly. In fact, I make few decisions quickly, although I can if I must. I like to think things through if there's time. If not, I go with my instincts.

I can be decisive in literary terms and with horses or animals, but with a decision like whether to try a new seed crop or find some more bottom land, I plan.

Judy had moved in before I knew it. One day I walked back in the house after a road tour and the whole damn house had been rearranged with lots of gaudy crap in it. I nearly passed out. It's a good thing Mother wasn't alive or I would have flown her up here for a mighty move moment. Nobody could move furniture, in, out or around better than Juts.

Exhausted, I said on my way to the bedroom, "Get this crap out of here."

She did, too.

I'd turn around and there'd be a brand-new John Deere tractor in the shed. She wouldn't wait to find a good used one. It had to be brand-new. Judy doesn't even know how to drive a tractor.

She bought trucks, she bought whatever she wanted without really examining it. And that went for horses, too.

Most times I'll vet a horse, including X rays, which are expensive, but money up front can save you a lot of money later. If she liked the way the horse looked, she'd buy it. I put my foot down and insisted on vetting, but a lot of times I wasn't around when the siren song to spend money overtook her.

I should never have let her in my house in the first place. I knew better. Her revenge against Martina hadn't cooled completely and she needed to get on a more positive track for everyone's health. No matter what Martina had done, she deserved a grand finale year. The one good thing about letting Judy on the farm was that I kept her busy.

And she'd ride faithfully each day, which was important to me.

She'd come down to the stable in her jeans and boots. Her hair would be pulled back and tucked under a cowboy hat (the pretty kind, not the working kind), her earrings in place, her lipstick freshly applied. She looked so uncountry, but this is her life—her appearance.

It doesn't matter how much you tart yourself up; if you're fifty-two, you're fifty-two. You might look like a great fifty-two, but why try to look young? Let the young have it. We had our shot.

She paid for her face-lift with her MasterCard. That nearly sent me into the hospital myself from laughing so hard. Of course, I made the big mistake of telling Aunt Mimi, who then began to check the credit limit on her credit cards. After I told her she was too old for a face-lift, she didn't speak to me for a few weeks.

Well, time marched on and I wondered exactly how I had landed in this soup. I am not a passive person but I can have passive moments, especially if I'm internally exhausted. My guard was down. I think the damn settlement between Judy and Martina took more out of me than it took out of them, because I truly understood the political consequences. And I had to shut up. If anyone else who understood the consequences had tipped off the media, the Far Right might have exerted pressure to bring the suit to trial. They would have done this by sending a shill to woo Martina, not physically but intellectually, someone to heighten her anger.

Besides, I don't mind having someone fall all over me. I prefer it to be a trifle less mushy, but show me the woman who doesn't like being told she's special and I'll show you a dead woman.

I was seduced and I liked it. Judy has a great sense of humor, and that's the first way to my heart. The second is horses, cats and dogs. She wouldn't listen to my suggestions about riding and caring for her horses but she was out there every day. She gave it her all. Impressed me.

There was little doubt in my mind that Judy didn't love me. She needed me. She didn't love me. Truth be told, I think I needed her, too. Without her struggle I couldn't have healed my old wounds from the tennis days. I'd not taken the time to reexamine those experiences. As they were so fresh for Judy, they called up my memories.

We shared riding together. Judy hops on the horse's back and expects all will be well. I told her not to override her horses. She didn't listen. She bowed Fayez's tendons. Fayez, a good horse, deserved better than that. I turned him out for a year. Now he gives trail rides at a neighboring farm.

I could have decked her for bowing that horse.

Judy blew through her settlement money like a wind through Kansas. Poof, it was gone. I have never seen anyone spend money like that woman. It scared me.

She wanted me to join her in an Argentinian investment, a factoring scheme. I think the technical term for such a thing is a Ponzi scheme. The investors take your money, promising a rate of return over a period of time, like a step deal. You invest $500,000. Twelve months later you receive $250,000. Every six months or one year thereafter you get $100,000 or some designated sum, which is the interest on your principal. Some interest. At any time the investors can return the full principal to you, but as long as they have your money they must guarantee this high rate of return.

I remember standing in front of the tack shop in Camden, South Carolina, saying, "You go right ahead. I'll watch." I'm too dumb to play the stock market. All I understand is good land. How could I track investments in Argentina?

She finally backed off. And I did buy a young horse from the guys in Buenos Aires, a Criollo called Toma. He's a dream.

Anyway, she lost that entire investment, and the rest she spent on stuff. But some of that stuff, like a shedrow barn, improved my farm.

Fair is fair. I pay her back monthly for her improvements.

I pity Judy. What does a woman who has made it on her looks do when she's older? How do you learn the job skills the rest of us learned in our twenties and thirties?

When Judy left me she didn't leave in a huff. There wasn't enough emotion in the relationship to get upset about it.

And then, too, I had been a rock when she needed one. She bears me some residual gratitude. I'm grateful to her for allowing me to learn I can't be in a relationship where ethics differ, nor can I abide being controlled.

As for Martina, she has never once thanked me for helping to keep her out of court, for going the extra mile.

If she'd sat down alone with Judy in the beginning and just let Judy vent and wail, she'd have saved herself a whole lot of money. A couple of weeks of discomfort, some guilt, some anger, some sadness, and Martina could have spared herself a shabby episode.

Few incidents in my middle age have troubled me as much as this one or reminded me how much I care about what happens to my people.

Nobody cares about gay people. Black folks don't want their queers. White people can't stand theirs. Rich people send theirs to psychiatrists. Poor people kick theirs out on the street. Nobody wants us.

I want us.

We've got to stand up for one another.

The funny thing is that I don't feel especially gay. I never did. But hateful people force me to examine why they are hateful. Who gives them the right to judge? Who gives them the right to ostracize, fire, belittle or even kill?

The differing forms of oppression—sexism, racism, religious persecution or hating homosexuals—are the same meat but different gravy. Sadly, many people in these disparate groups don't understand how much they have in common with one another. It's like a reverse snob game: Who is the most oppressed? Hey, who cares?

Pain is pain. Get off your ass and fight back. Do you really believe if you don't make common cause with me, the Man will give you a bigger crumb off his table?

I don't want to spend my life focusing on what is least interesting about me. And I'm not even a good lesbian. I'm much more bisexual, but if you want to step on my neck and call me a dyke, don't be surprised if I sink my fangs into your ankle. I'm smart enough to know that the reality of who I am is not as important as what people perceive me to be. My reality is important to me. The public me is why I must fight.

You can't let people treat you like garbage. If you do, they'll think you are.

As much as our enemies hate being challenged, it makes them respect you even as they hate you.

No one respects a wuss.

The Judy vs. Martina lawsuit was supremely foolish. It wasn't a wise choice of battleground. But once they were locked in combat, we had more to lose politically by not solving the problem than by solving it.

That time could certainly have been put to better use.

Herein lies the secret of successful politics: Don't fight defensive battles. A good offense is a good defense. If you're defensive, you're always on your enemy's ground or fighting to your enemy's game plan. You can't win that way, you can only limit damage.

I wasn't winning anything.

I was relieved when Judy left. The invasion of the pine beetles eating away at my crop coincided with her outrageous spending.

I wondered if I would have to sell the farm. I was relying on my pine crop to retire some debt. The trees were falling down before my very eyes.

I was beginning to think that no good deed goes unpunished. Self-pity isn't part of my emotional makeup but I was feeling a touch of it.

My redbud clover seed burned up in a small drought. Thirty-five hundred dollars' worth of seed, fried. There went the next hay crop. (I'm a big believer in soil tests, overseeding and fertilizing.) Everywhere I looked I saw losses.

And Aunt Mimi was failing.

I shook myself out of this pity party.

Citation kept running. So would I.

84

The Death of Dragon Lady

ER MIND CLEAR AS A BELL, AUNT MIMI'S BODY BEGAN TO FAIL. Her old back problems felt worse and she couldn't get around the way she used to, which upset her.

To Julia Ellen had fallen the task of caring for her mother, a mother who loathed taking orders. She'd growl at Julia Ellen, yell at her sometimes. Julia Ellen had her own problems to contend with; after all, she wasn't getting any younger, either, and she can't take a lot of stress.

I'd write my aunt or call. She'd brighten and tell stories, and at the end she even forgot to lash me with her rosary beads.

She shocked me when she said, "The Church is wrong about divorce. My Julia Ellen would be better off today if she could have divorced Russell years ago."

"Aunt Mimi?" I wasn't sure I was speaking to my real aunt.

"Oh, yes. I sits and thinks and sometimes I just sits." She laughed, quoting her own mother. "I think the Church is wrong and I was wrong."

"You did what you thought was right at the time."

"Who is going to take care of Julia Ellen when I'm gone? He's spent all her money."

I interrupted, "He's good at heart, Aunt Mimi."

"I know he is. I like him but I don't like him as my daughter's husband. I never should have let her marry him in the first place. I wanted her to marry—"

"Aunt Mimi, she hated that rich guy." I stepped in before she could go on a tear about the "chosen" son-in-law.

"She'd be well off today."

"She'd be miserable."

"She's miserable now."

"She's miserable because she sees you in pain and she can't do much. Basically, Julia Ellen would be a happy person if everybody would leave her alone."

Oh, there was an icy silence on the other end of that line. "You're turning into my sister!"

"Were you ever bored around Juts?"

"No."

"Neither was I."

"Well—you've got a point there." She paused a moment. "Rita, I won't live much longer. I've lived a long time as it is. You won't forget me when I'm gone, will you?"

"Aunt Mimi, I could never forget you, and I promise to light candles for you in church, in your church."

"Really?"

"I promise. You held me during that blizzard, you fed me. You helped Dad drive the car. I'll have a mass said for you and I will light candles for you until the day I die."

A moment passed—and not a tearful one, I might add. "Do you do that for Juts?"

"No. I say prayers for her but not in the Catholic church."

"Oh—I can't wait to tell her!" She laughed.

Aunt Mimi died in her sleep on May 20, 1993, at home. Odd that she slipped away on Dolley Madison's birthday. Two women, both of them guides, if you will. The one gone since 1849 but leaving behind a legacy of deep moral conviction and tremendous courage. The other despotic, rigid and trying to be something she wasn't, a saint. Underneath all that baloney, Aunt Mimi was as gay (old use of the word) as Juts. The raucous humor, the love of dancing and parties, the desire to shine . . . it was all there, but she'd worked so hard to cover it up.

The few times I saw Aunt Mimi let 'er rip, like at the butchers' picnic or at the York Fair, she was as much fun as Mom.

They were all gone now. Mom. Dad. Aunt Mimi. Bucky. Mother and Daddy Brown. My beloved PopPop. Virginia. Even Earl, whom I could never stand, but still, he was gone, too.

I realized that liking or not liking someone was irrelevant. It was the time in history that you shared. A time binds you to another person just as passions bind you to the dead. I am bound to foxhunters I have never met, to Aristophanes, to Dolley Madison, by our mutual passions and concerns. But the people of the flesh, the ones I heard, smelled and watched, the giants of my childhood, they're gone.

This time comes to each of us and each of us must light a candle.

I supposed in Aunt Mimi's case I should light a blowtorch.

I miss the old dragon.

And I miss those times, those primary colors of early memories, the 1940s and the 1950s. I miss the cars and trucks with the big rolling fenders. I miss the tinny music swinging out of the radio and Mom dancing as she worked, singing along in her lovely soprano. I miss seeing Dad lift a three-hundred-pound side of beef as though it were no heavier than a cinder-block. I miss Bucky, paint-splattered, putting me on his shoulder and telling me what a wonderful little girl I was. I miss Mickey and always shall.

Was it the time? Or were the people kinder then? Perhaps if I were a child now, people would be equally kind, as they should be to small ones. I don't know.

But my memories are that it was a unique time. We'd won a terrible war. Life could begin again. We could build cars for pleasure instead of tanks for killing. We could thank God for our deliverance. People were happier then, I think. And I think, too, they had more respect for horses and animals because they were closer to them. We still had a good-sized population of people who lived on farms. Now the percentage is so small that the city people and suburban people will eventually destroy us with legislation and taxes. When I was little you could make a living as a small farmer. It's almost impossible now. In some ways, I feel that loss as keenly as the loss of the people.

Aunt Mimi left a legacy. It may not be what she intended, but then, does life ever turn out as you intend it to? No. Aunt Mimi and Juts will live as long as people want to laugh at the foibles, pettiness, battles and love that exist in families, in small towns.

Aunt Mimi and Mom gave me my material. They dug a well that can never run dry. If I had a hundred years, I couldn't run out of stories.

I've kept my promise to Aunt Mimi. I light a candle for her each time I visit St. Patrick's Cathedral in New York. If I happen by a Catholic church when I'm on the road and have a few moments, I light a candle and say a prayer of thanks. There's a nice church in Staunton, Virginia—St. Francis. I'll have to go there from time to time for her.

There's a lovely old Episcopal church in Greenwood, up the road from me on Route 250. Sometimes I go there for Mother. There's not a Lutheran church nearby, and I'm as happy in an Episcopal church as in a Lutheran one anyway. Truly, Mom wouldn't care so long as it's not a Catholic church.

I think I'll say a prayer for Aunt Mimi in Emmanuel Episcopal Church and light a candle for Mom at St. Francis. Wonder what will happen. Just because they're dead I see no reason not to torment them.

But then again, they aren't truly dead, are they?

As long as you love someone, the best part of them lives.

85

Let There Be Light

THE UNDERGIRDING OF EVERY NOVEL IS STRUCTURE. I BUILD THEM as I would build a house. The two-foot-thick basement walls are not visible to the eye, but they are necessary.

Over the years I've worked at structure and I've learned to love it. At first I resisted. Being southern, I loved the anecdote, the chat of characters. I still do, but the actual building of a novel has become a deep joy for me.

It's no surprise I like building, period. Whether it's a run-in shed, a stable, a house, I love creating spaces. Gardening is born of this same impulse, and there I feel close to Mother.

We have a good team at the farm and it took years to assemble it. You kiss a lot of toads before you find the prince. Calvin Lewis, Robert Steppe and John Morris are the princes.

The hunt staff, most of them friends and volunteers, enliven the days: Herbie Jones, Jim Craig, Sara Taylor, Amy Burke, John Gray, Eleanor Hartwell and Cindy Chandler. Cindy gardens like she rides: perfect form.

Sometimes Robert Lyn Kee Chow joins us in the summers. He brings along his green horses and he brings us along, too.

And always, there's Betty Burns.

Good people make for a good life.

If you wrote the story of my life, you could probably structure it better than I can. It's extremely difficult to reach the critical distance necessary to shape your own life with language. The closer I get to the present the more difficult it becomes. I lose my sense of proportion, a sense that comes quite easily when I regard 1954. Perhaps this nearsightedness occurs to everyone attempting the brazen task of setting down their life as they lived it, especially as lived from within.

The constants in my life have been cats, dogs, horses, the arts and my friends. I have often said that friendship is love made bearable.

The older I get the more I realize that I am absorbing my friends' experiences. I'm not only living my life, I am living their lives. I am stretching my mind that much further to grasp their brilliant thoughts.

My friends are all smarter than I am. That may be the smartest thing about me: I surround myself with people who are above me and then I try to catch up.

I'll never catch up. I know that, but trying is almost as good as getting there. Process is as much fun as product. The journey is in many ways more luminous than the destination.

What would my life be without my friends? Nothing. I've often wondered what I would do if given the chance to be frozen before I die and to be revived whenever scientists can restore our health and perhaps a bit of our youth. Would it be worth it? I don't think so, because that silken web of love, those glistening filaments that connect us to one another, would be sundered. Life is not worth living without those connections.

Evil is born in loneliness and despair. One of the cruelest punishments for a human being is to be separated from other human beings—or to be told s/he is a lesser human being. How can people learn to bind themselves to others if they're being pushed away?

I kept coming back. I was lucky. Some people took the chance on being my friend, just as Juts and Ralph took the chance on adopting me those many years ago.

Love is an act of faith.

I never thought I would have a partner in life. Being the one Out There lesbian for those many years certainly squelched my chances for a life with a man or a woman. The man would be badgered daily by his friends— "Hey, Hank, think she's sneaking off?"—and the woman would hear nonstop homophobia dressed up as concern.

I had resigned myself to a series of idle affairettes and I was even losing interest in them. And then Hunter Hughes, an old acquaintance, who deserves his own sitcom because he's funny, perverse, rebellious, oversexed—well, you get the picture—Hunter sent me a smartypants note about how I should come down off the mountain and he'd spring for a free golf lesson at Farmington Country Club. The lady golf pro signed it also. Naturally I was curious.

What was Mr. Wonderful up to?

The golf pro trotted me out to the driving range and dumped the balls on the ground. Now, I don't know how to play golf, but if there's a stick and a ball, I'll figure it out. So I started hitting these golf balls. Half of them soared high up in the air, straight and true and way out there. The other half soared up in the air and turned right, like little UFOs making ninety-degree turns.

The next time I took a lesson we pitched and chipped. If I couldn't drop the shot into the cup, I was furious. I hated pitching and chipping. In fact, I got so mad because I couldn't sink the ball that I stayed out there for two hours, which made the golf pro laugh.

I, however, was not laughing. Golf is an expensive way to make yourself miserable.

Once she explained to me that the object was to get close to the cup, not make a hole-in-one, and that I was doing pretty well, I felt somewhat better but not completely.

The next week we played nine holes. I liked that a lot.

The week after that we had lunch. That was four years ago.

I love her for many reasons, but best of all she makes me laugh.

Elizabeth Putnam Sinsel, Betsy, has bequeathed to me her entire family, and there are a lot of Sinsels, Lehmans and Valiants, funny, funny people. There are also nieces and nephews by the bushelful, all of them under seven.

Betsy descends from General Israel Putnam, hero of the Revolutionary War. What a pity Aunt Mimi is gone, because she could inflict the genealogy game on Betsy.

The cats, dogs and hounds love Betsy, too. She's not much for horses but she'll ride sometimes, and one of my horses, Tommy Sundae, loves Betsy. He's a sweet Quarter Horse, young, and he lets her do whatever she wants to do.

Those horses are my structure. I love to rise before the sun, drink my tea, walk out and listen to them or call them over.

GROWING UP WITH FOXHUNTING, I'D ALWAYS LOVED IT AND WAS PROUD to hunt with Farmington Hunt Club in Charlottesville. Over the years I've hunted behind many packs and have learned just when I think I know something, the fox shows me I don't know beans.

I always wanted my own pack of hounds. It's a foxhunter's dream. At the end of the eighties I made a concerted effort to study those packs hunting today in America. Mrs. William Moss, M.F.H. of Moore County Hounds in Southern Pines, North Carolina, answered my questions over the years. She always had the time to invite me over for tea and patiently listened to me.

The closer I got to striking out on my own, the more I realized what a gigantic task I was taking on: opening land, landowner relations, building a pack from scratch, finding good hunt staff and praying I could show good sport—in Virginia yet! Since Virginia considers herself the center of fox-hunting, I had not much room for error. Thank God, Dr. Herbert Jones, the dean of foxhunters in these parts, threw his hat in the ring with me. He's been my rock, my sounding board, my hero.

I'd learned a fair amount by watching Mrs. Paul Summers, Jr., M.F.H. of Farmington. She's a great hunting master and knows more about blood-lines, not just on paper but how it all turns out, than many people who call attention to themselves. Jill, by nature reserved, lets her pack speak for her, and speak they do. They are well matched—good voice and perfect for her countryside. She breeds crossbreds and American hounds. When I lit out on my own she gave me twelve hounds, an act of faith that forced me to give my best. I couldn't fail my own master.

My other angel was Lynn Lloyd, M.F.H. of Red Rock Hounds in Reno, Nevada. Lynn will go down as one of the great masters of my generation, just as Ginny Moss is a giant of her generation and Jill an outstanding master of the succeeding generation.

Without these three women I'd still be out there with a pooper-scooper. Jack Eicher, former huntsman at Farmington, now hunt staff with Keswick, also pitched in.

I learned how many friends I have, and this overwhelmed me. It's painfully difficult for me to ask for help, but I had to ask. There's no way you can foxhunt without people's help.

By guess and by God, I got us going. A field of riders materialized October 22, 1994, in front of John and Rhonda Holland's estate, Oak Ridge, in Arrington, Virginia. Off we went.

We're still running.

Foxhunting, for me, is so spiritual that I find it hard to write about it. I only know you can't be out there and not be amazed at God's creation, how we all fit together on this great big planet and how fragile the balance is.

If nothing else, foxhunting has made me determined to preserve as much as I can for future generations, not just of humans but of foxes, mice, horses, hounds, eagles—all of us.

Someday I will write about this way of life and I will try to convey what it means, a sport thousands of years old. I wrote about it a bit in my novel *Riding Shotgun,* but I'd like to go further. In the meantime, I thank every single person who helped me, most especially Lt. Col. Dennis Foster at the Master of Foxhounds Association of America and Ben Hardaway and Mrs.

John B. Hannum, who have taken us to the next level of hound breeding. Their work will be taken up by all of us of the next generation, with Mr. and Mrs. Martin Wood III leading the way.

The characters who hunt, those hardy souls out there on horseback, delight my days. Wimps don't foxhunt, so I am in my element. I have only to look around me and see people ready to get up and get over.

I hope you have something in your life which thrills you as much as this thrills me. Life is too short not to be this happy.

During hunting season we push off early. Hunting season is usually from Labor Day to mid–March. The hardest work is not during the season but in the off season. We have to bring along the green horses as we turn out the ones who have hunted all fall and winter. We walk out the hounds, work and play with the young ones and clear trails.

Sometimes I can walk out on a regular schedule and sometimes I can't. It depends on my deadlines, but I love working with young animals, hounds, horses, cats. The minute I get my pages done for the day I'm out of the house like a shot. Being outside is heaven. I'd rather pick cotton than work in an office, even though those bolls make your fingers bleed.

Picking cotton reminds me of the current flap about the battle flag of the Confederacy. I was talking to my buddy Bill Sloan, a North Carolinian, and he said, "When you lose a civil war, you're lucky to keep your women, much less the flag."

Funny and on target!

I think the last time I laughed that hard was after Lorena Bobbit removed her husband's dangling participle. I was talking on the phone to Larry Hodge in Kentucky around that time.

"Larry, come on over here and hunt with me."

"I'm afraid to come to Virginia. You women are dangerous."

Better dangerous than boring. Although Lorena took it a little too far. If every woman did that, we'd really be bored.

But I confess I don't understand hating men. I don't understand hating anybody.

Big Mimi once said, "People are like snowflakes. No two of them are alike."

I live by that. Once you start lumping people into groups, you rob them of their individuality. It's easier to kill them if they're blacks or gays or Germans or Muslims. But if instead of groups you are looking at individuals from those groups, William Raspberry or Ellen DeGeneres or Steffi Graf or Salman Rushdie, then those categories fade away. You're faced with a complicated human being, like you in some ways and not like you in others. The fun is finding one another out.

What are we so afraid of?

Other people?

Ourselves?

On September 6, 1996, the horses were nibbling down on the lower pastures, the floodplain of the North Branch of the Rockfish River. When possible I like to buy bottomland because it's cheap—no one can build on it—and because the alluvial deposits enrich the soil. By the same token, you can lose acres of pasture in a storm as it's washed down the Rockfish into the James River.

Hurricane Fran was heading northwest but no one knew where she would hit. The skies darkened and a stiff breeze aired out the day. Still, things seemed fine and the weather station couldn't be certain if Fran would head straight up the coast, drift inland or slam inland on a northwest course, much as Camille had done in 1969 and Hazel in 1954.

Since power goes out in storms, small or large, we'd taken the precaution of cleaning out the oil lamps, putting new batteries in the flashlights and filling jugs with water.

Light rain turned to steady rain, which turned to lashing rain.

By midnight Betsy and I knew Fran was coming straight for us no matter what the weatherman said. We hopped in the truck to drive the mile and a half down to the lower acres. The road by the first river pasture was still dry but the river was over the banks. The wind blotted out sound but would sporadically stop, producing eerie silence.

Realizing we had to get the horses out of the lower pastures, I sent Betsy back for buckets of grain. I turned off my flashlight and sat on the snake fence, made from railroad ties given to me by John Holland, a generous gift indeed.

I'd tried to catch Kaiser Bill, a sensible, sweet horse, but I hadn't been able to get a lead shank on him. He was running around like a chicken with his head cut off. Most of the other horses ran around with him. It occurred to me that I might be badly hurt, but those are the chances you take in the country. Crazed or not, my horses had to be saved.

I was sending up a prayer of thanks that the two steers, Pooter and Pumpkin, were already on high ground. Pooter, enormous and friendly, tosses his head around playfully. I'd have been hooked with his horns.

As I sat on the fence, the wind stopped. I heard snufflings and scufflings. My eyes had adjusted to the dark and I saw walking through the lowlands deer, bobcat, even a bear, walking toward the high ground, which was not a quarter of a mile away. No wonder Kaiser Bill was acting like a lunatic. Horses are frightened of bears.

The animals proceeded in an orderly fashion, predator and prey, united by a common enemy, the hurricane. They noticed me but betrayed no fear of a human nor much interest. They probably wondered why I didn't join them.

Betsy had more trouble getting back, as the waters were rising rapidly. We lured Bill in with the grain and the others settled down. We had eight horses to fetch from those pastures, but the pitch-blackness was occasionally illuminated by lightning.

We also had well over a mile to walk them up to the barn. About all we could do was pray. A flaming chestnut, a baby still, Lil' Red (also called Brady) was the first one to come over to me. He lowered his head for the halter. I rubbed his ears and told him it was going to be a scary walk.

Of all the horses there, he was the youngest; he should have been the most frightened. He trusted me with all his heart. The others came up and we slipped halters on them. Kaiser Bill loves Betsy, so he behaved for her. She had four horses, I had four horses. My ancient Barbour coat kept my body dry.

The winds picked up. Trees creaked, branches were torn off. We couldn't hold the horses and carry flashlights. We stuck the flashlights in our pockets and began the long walk back.

We'd fall off the lowest part of the road, pick ourselves up and start again. At no time did any horse pull away when one of us fell. No one reared or screamed in fear. Brady led the way. I had him on my right, with Trumpetta. In my left hand I had my best broodmare, Cool Morning Star, and another Throughbred mare, Sydney.

Betsy had Kaiser Bill, Carvelle, Willie and Boy Scout.

Pitch-blackness enveloped us. I noticed tiny yellow and green sparkles on either side of the road.

Betsy noticed them, too.

We stopped, I handed her my fistful of lead ropes, and on my hands and knees I got down to examine the little lights. Trapped by the rain and the winds, there were thousands upon thousands of fireflies nestling down in the long grasses.

Those lightning bugs lit our way to the barn. We made the horses comfortable, having to rearrange the other horses in their stalls. Some grumbling was heard but everyone cooperated. I told them to think of the overcrowding as a slumber party.

Then, following the fireflies, we walked the long way back to the truck. The hardest part, the lowest stretch, had no fireflies, and the water was now up to our ankles.

With great good luck we got the truck turned around and through the rising water. Everyone was safe: horses, hounds, cattle, cats and house dogs.

By the morning the waters were twenty-one feet over flood stage. I had no road. Betsy and I trudged over the hill, avoiding the floodwaters, to see if the bridge had held. We couldn't even see the bridge. The water was roaring over it with whitecaps as big as an ocean's. The noise was deafening.

By some miracle everyone still had power. That went out in the middle of the day on September 7.

As the waters receded I walked my fence lines. I'd lost everything by the river, of course. Luckily, I'd had the sense to put up strands of high-tensile-strength wire there instead of board because I'd seen the river go over the banks before, though never anything like this.

My little bridge over the creek feeding into the Rockfish was in tatters. A four-foot chunk was gouged out of the road and the plank fencing was smashed to bits. The sides of the bridge had been eaten away. The huge culverts were jammed with debris. But with a day of tractor work with the front-end loader we could fill the hole and repair the bridge enough to get trucks over it. A bulldozer and backhoe would have to do the rest, though it might be months before we got to that, there was so much damage.

As we walked along we marveled that not one of our animals was lost, our neighbors were in good shape, no cars or trucks had been swept down the river. The state bridge held although the road surface looked like a moonscape. Two big power company poles leaned precariously, but still, we'd made it.

In the days it took the water to recede we found pieces of the old steel bridge that had originally been destroyed by Camille. It linked the east side of the Rockfish with the west side, to a small road going out to Route 151. This bridge, buried under the debris from that hurricane, which changed Nelson County forever, had been ripped from its grave, girders twisted like pretzels and thrown all over my riverbanks.

We also found one dead cow, which with difficulty we dislodged to bury.

Every single foxhunting trail at every single fixture was crisscrossed with big trees. Every single bridge and fording place had been destroyed. As this was the beginning of cubbing season, we were wiped out. Sadly, too, some of our grouse, other ground birds and foxes had been killed. Actually, it was amazing that as many lived as did, but they stayed up on the mountain ridges.

For six weeks we worked every day but Sundays to clear the trails to be ready for formal hunting. As it was, we could only open the major ones. It will take us years, really, to get back into shape.

Hurricane or not, I still met my deadlines.

This storm vividly haunts me, probably because it is close in memory and because I'll be paying for it for a long time. The government offered no relief on private roads or bridges, and insurance companies don't cover them. We may receive a small sum to help put back the fences. There was no tax relief either, just as there had been no tax relief on the pine beetle damage.

All those taxes we pay and not a penny to help us when we needed it. The money was sure there for Chrysler when they needed it. Farmers just don't count.

Despite this I continue to farm. It's in my blood. Raised on a farm, I dreamed always of making enough money to buy my own. It can be a life of physical and financial hardship, but it is also a life of spiritual joy.

Every day I see miracles. Right now my new-plowed pastures are greening up. I'm trying a timothy grass on them. I'm excited about finding out if I've chosen a seed that will give me a good yield per acre.

This morning the Canada geese squawked and hollered down at the pond. Their buddies half an acre over on the Rockfish River babble also. Geese are noisy birds. I want to build a house in the middle of the pond for the geese and ducks but I haven't quite figured out how to do it yet.

It's spring. The dogwoods, pink and white, cover the mountainsides. The redbud is still blooming. The horses are shedding out. Indigo buntings, airborne sapphires, zip in and out along with the swallowtails in the barn and more bluebirds and goldfinches than I have ever seen in my life.

The azaleas are just opening. The tulips are fading. The mountain laurel hasn't bloomed yet. The apple blossoms are turning to green. The pears have bloomed. The crabapples are in good color and some cherry trees are still luscious pink.

The bumblebees are back, along with the carpenter bees, which are such pests, but I never kill them. They fascinate me as I find their small piles of sawdust.

The snapping turtle, the small one, about a foot in diameter, showed up last week. That means the gigunda, really a whopper, can't be too far off. I steer clear.

Haven't seen one box turtle yet or one terrapin.

The skinks aren't out yet either, nor has the wisteria bloomed. The skunks are traveling, though . . . I see them everywhere.

I've got two pastures left to clear, uprooting those stubborn tree trunks, discing, grading, then seeding. That's going to take a couple of years since I have to scrape the roads and put down more gravel, thanks to Fran.

I know the next seven novels I want to write. Sneaky Pie has rough plot outlines for her next ten. I mean, she's already blocked out the plots. I don't know how she does it.

We're hoping for thankful increase, as my grandmother used to say, on the farm and with the novels.

I pray that I can remain strong and clear in my mind so that I can continue to work. I love to work. Idle hands do the devil's work. I used to hear that when I'd plop down in the hammock. Mother would flip over the hammock and hand me hedge clippers. I guess that's how I learned to love work.

People in their middle years tell you how young they are. I'm not young. I'm fifty-two years old and I wouldn't trade one year off. Oh, I wouldn't mind looking younger but I'm not obsessed about it. The years are my wealth.

Mother used to say, "All the sweetness is in the bottom of the cup."

I figure I'm at the halfway mark. I want to write a good novel when I'm a hundred. Aeschylus wrote plays well into his nineties, fine plays. If he can do it, I can try.

The other thing is that I have no fear. I remember the lines from *For Scirnis:* "Fearlessness is better than a faint heart for any man who puts his nose out of doors. The length of my life and the day of my death were fated long ago."

And if the storms should come again and I can't see the hand in front of my face, I'll follow the fireflies.